WITHDRAWN

WORKING PEOPLE OF HOLYOKE

CLASS AND CULTURE
A series edited by
Milton Cantor and Bruce Laurie

WORKING PEOPLE OF HOLYOKE

Class and Ethnicity in a
Massachusetts Mill Town,
1850–1960

WILLIAM F. HARTFORD

RUTGERS UNIVERSITY PRESS
New Brunswick and London

Chapter Eight has been previously published in *Labor in Massachusetts*, edited by Kenneth Fones-Wolf and Martin Kaufman (Westfield, MA: Institute for Massachusetts Studies/ Westfield State College, 1990).

Library of Congress Cataloging-in-Publication Data
Hartford, William F., 1949–
    Working people of Holyoke : class and ethnicity in a Massachusetts
mill town, 1850–1960 / William F. Hartford.
        p.   cm. — (Class and culture)
    Includes bibliographical references.
    ISBN 0-8135-1576-9
    1. Ethnicity—Massachusetts—Holyoke.   2. Working class—
Massachusetts—Holyoke—History.   3. Irish Americans—
Massachusetts—Holyoke—History.   4. French-Canadians—
Massachusetts—Holyoke—History.   5. Social classes—Massachusetts—
Holyoke—History.   6. Holyoke (Mass.)—Social conditions.
7. Holyoke (Mass.)—History.   I. Title.   II. Series.
F74.H73H37 1990
305.8′9162074426—dc20   90-30666
                                                                          CIP

British Cataloging-in-Publication information available

Copyright © 1990 by William F. Hartford
All Rights Reserved
Manufactured in the United States of America

For My Mother and Father

CONTENTS

LIST OF TABLES

ACKNOWLEDGMENTS

THIS STUDY could not have been completed without the aid of numerous individuals. Any acknowledgment of these debts must begin with an expression of gratitude to the many librarians and archivists who helped ease the burdens of research. I especially wish to thank those at the Holyoke Public Library; Connecticut Valley Historical Museum, Springfield Public Library; the Lyman Mills Collection, Baker Library of the Harvard Business School; American International College, Oral History Collection; and Archives and Manuscripts, the University of Massachusetts at Amherst. At the last-named institution, Kenneth Fones-Wolf was particularly helpful. During the course of my revisions, he not only acquired several manuscript collections that proved vital to the work, but was also a regular source of stimulating conversation.

Over the years, I have received valuable assistance from a number of people in the city of Holyoke. William Dwight, Jr., kindly granted me access to back issues of the *Holyoke Mirror* and *Holyoke Transcript*; Raymond Beaudry and George Fitzgerald provided an assortment of useful documents, in addition to sharing their broad knowledge of local labor and industry with me; and as a consultant to the Shifting Gears Project, a public history program on the changing meaning of work in twentieth-century Holyoke sponsored by the Massachusetts Foundation for the Humanities and Public Policy, I had the immense good fortune to be able to work with Christine Howard Bailey. A word of thanks is also due another onetime Holyoker whom I never met, the late Constance McLaughlin Green. Being able to draw upon her study of the city made my task immeasurably easier.

Comments and criticism from a variety of people have made this a much better book than it otherwise would have been. At Rutgers University Press, Marlie Wasserman provided sound editorial advice, and Raymond McGill copyedited the manuscript with great care and

precision. In their reading of the study, Dan Clawson and Thomas Dublin offered a number of instructive observations. So did Milton Cantor, whose admonitions to stop procrastinating were often needed and always appreciated. Apart from a collective debt that I owe the history faculty at the University of Massachusetts for my training as a historian, three members deserve particular mention. My course of study may have come to an early end had it not been for the guidance of Gerald McFarland. His patient criticism did much to expand my then primitive notions of what historical investigation was all about. As a graduate student, I also had the opportunity to teach under Stephen Nissenbaum in a "New Approaches" course that he had helped pioneer. By introducing me to new historical concepts in a unique pedagogical setting, he provided an experience that contributed substantially to my development as a historian. My greatest debt is to Bruce Laurie. This study began as a dissertation under his direction. He has since then read numerous drafts of the work, each time providing a list of suggestions on how it might be further improved. The main thrust of many of these comments was that I had a better story to tell than I was telling. Whatever success I have finally achieved in relating that story is due in no small measure to Bruce's counsel.

Lastly, I must thank my parents, Francis and Julia Hartford. Their contribution began more than forty years ago and continues to this day. This work could not have been started, much less completed, without their support.

WORKING PEOPLE
OF HOLYOKE

INTRODUCTION

IN THE MID-1840S an awful famine devastated large regions of southern Ireland, spreading death and misery among an already impoverished people and forcing a massive emigration. One area where they sought to begin anew was Holyoke, Massachusetts, then a rural backwater just entering the early stages of industrialization. Local elites valued the newcomers' labor, but otherwise had little use for them. Too preoccupied with matters of simple survival, the Irish seemed scarcely to notice and set about establishing an ethnic enclave in which they struggled to preserve their religion, customs, and identity as sons and daughters of Ireland. Tradition and the harshness of day-to-day existence dictated that the saloon and church would dominate this early community: in one immigrants found a brief respite from life's crushing burdens, while in the other they laid claims to a heavenly reward that a neo-feudal religion promised those who submitted to poverty and deprivation in this world. But these conditions would not persist indefinitely, and two generations later the immigrants' grandchildren would lead a vigorous labor movement that subordinated ethnocultural concerns to class interests.

This is the story of that transformation. It is also an effort to move beyond the ethnic determinism-assimilation perspective that Oscar Handlin introduced in his seminal work on the Boston Irish and that continues to dominate the historiography of Irish America. As Robert Sean Willentz has noted in a review of *Boston's Immigrants*, Handlin tended to subordinate "social distinctions among the Irish to his idealized notions of their community 'group consciousness' " and to equate assimilation with the attainment of middle-class status and norms of conduct. "By stressing the unquestionably important bonds of ethnic solidarity," Willentz adds, "Handlin skirts the equally important tensions within the Irish community." In one respect these criticisms are not entirely fair. The tensions of which Willentz speaks were

1

only barely discernible by 1880, the year in which Handlin's study concludes. But his broader points are well taken. The present work stems from a conviction that, as Willentz suggests, historians of Irish America would do well to "explore how Irish ethnicity shaped an identifiably Irish-American working-class outlook, and then see how these developments were challenged, engulfed, and muted by the kind of inter-class 'group consciousness' that Handlin outlines."[1]

I must hasten to add that I am not the first historian to undertake such a venture. There are broad conceptual similarities between my study and the recent work of David Emmons on the Irish miners of Butte, Montana. Each makes extensive use of John Bodnar's concept of the enclave, and each focuses on the interplay between class and ethnicity. Yet, Holyoke was not Butte and the lives of Holyoke workers differed in important ways from those of Butte's miners. Unlike Holyoke, where an Irish middle class exercised limited economic power, Butte was a one-industry town in which Irish capitalists and mine managers controlled access to many of the best jobs. Equally important, the population of Butte contained a much larger proportion of first-generation Irish immigrants than Holyoke throughout the late nineteenth and early twentieth centuries. As a result, ethnic concerns tended to overshadow class interests and defuse class tensions for a longer time in Butte than was the case among Holyoke's Irish. In all these matters, I believe that Holyoke was more typical of the Irish experience in America, though this assertion is in no sense intended to diminish Emmons's achievement. I have benefited greatly from reading his work and feel that our two studies can be viewed as variant treatments of a common set of themes.[2]

To give an identity to the Irish trade unionists who are the main protagonists of this study, I have adopted the concept of respectability that Robert Q. Gray and Geoffrey Crossick put to such good use in their work on British labor aristocrats. This borrowing is not based on any precise parallels between the lives of Holyoke trade unionists and the skilled Scottish and English workers examined by these historians. Instead, the concept is used because the term respectability so well captures how the Holyokers saw themselves and what they were all about: their efforts to set themselves apart from local saloonists, their struggles to preserve an independent voice in community affairs, their actions to promote worker education, and as an extension of all this, an abiding concern with their reproduction as a reputable social group.[3]

In relating their story, I have chosen to focus on three facets of class relations. One is the relationship between capital and labor. Although Holyoke was the scene of numerous strikes, these contests lacked the bloodshed and violence that marked so many industrial conflicts of the era. This relative civility owed much to the behavior of local millowners. Like their counterparts elsewhere in industrializing America, Holyoke manufacturers tried to maximize the amount of surplus value that they could squeeze from wage earners. In so doing, though, they generally avoided the thuggery that often formed an integral part of employer tactics in other locales. My early chapters thus examine bourgeois Holyoke and the social relations of production in the city's two main industries, paper and textiles. Their purpose is to delineate the worldview of Holyoke capitalists and show how they sought to protect and further their interests in the community as well as the workplace.

Relations between workers and an immigrant middle class were another important determinant of class development. As part of a community in which they labored alongside petty entrepreneurs to forward their aims as producers, Catholics, and Irish Americans, wage earners for many years exhibited an enclave consciousness that celebrated ethnic accomplishments and disavowed class struggle. All this began to change during the late nineteenth century when increased class differentiation within Irish Holyoke combined with altered productive relations in the broader society to erode the social bases of the enclave. Workers adapted to these events by creating a class-conscious labor movement and forging a culture of Catholic trade-unionist respectability based on the family-wage ideal. Despite mounting tensions, worker—middle-class relations did not break down altogether. In the vital area of politics, for example, Irish trade unionists remained dependent on middle-class representation. But they did change. Henceforth, such cooperation would depend more on a reconciliation of antagonistic class interests than the assertion of shared ethnocultural concerns. These developments constitute the main focus of chapters 3 to 6.

Chapter 6 also looks at a third dimension of class relations: the ways in which Irish trade unionists interacted with other groups of workers. After World War I, Holyoke's Central Labor Union briefly considered forming an independent labor party. One reason it did not was that no social base existed from which to launch such an initiative. Unlike Irish trade unionists, French Canadian factory operatives

were still living out an enclave experience in which ethnocultural cares dwarfed workplace concerns. Occupational differences further separated the two groups. Confined largely to low-wage jobs in local textile mills, many French Canadians were unable to meet the economic standards of the family-wage ideal. These sociocultural dissimilarities would continue to divide Holyoke workers into the 1930s. Chapter 7 extends and deepens the examination of these and other matters by viewing them against the backdrop of labor's relations with the Catholic church.

Holyoke textile operatives were finally organized during the late 1930s. But this did not signal the beginning of a new era of worker prosperity. As in other New England factory towns of the period, mill closings annulled the benefits of unionization and spread insecurity among an aging work force. Deindustrialization also hastened the demise of Holyoke's French Canadian enclave, as workers' children were increasingly forced to look elsewhere for the good life promised by Henry Luce and other exponents of the American Century. The response of unions and wage earners to these events is described in the last chapter.

Before beginning, I should note that in at least one respect the present study is less complete than I would have liked. Although Polish immigrants became an increasingly important part of the industrial work force after 1900, the historical record proved too scanty to permit an extended examination of their activities. This is in part explained by the fact that they lived across the bridge from Chicopee, one of the great regional centers of Polish migration and culture. Close proximity to the vigourous institutional and cultural life of Polish Chicopee doubtlessly enriched their lives, but it also diminished their visibility in local sources.

1

YANKEE HOLYOKE

IN THE LATE eighteenth century a traveler journeying north of Springfield along the Connecticut River would have soon come to the beautiful Hadley Falls, where the swiftly moving waters of the great river plummeted nearly 60 feet. Aside the falls on the western bank of the river lay a tiny farming village called Ireland Parish because John Riley, a Protestant Irishman, had first settled the area a century earlier. Here rich lands yielded ample crops of hay, corn, rye, potatoes, and oats as the Connecticut's annual overflow regularly replenished the mineral content of its broad meadows. It provided largely a subsistence economy: Local farmers produced enough to meet their basic needs and a small surplus, which they marketed at Northampton and Springfield, the region's principal trade centers.[1]

The first attempt to develop the area came in 1792 when a group of Northampton and Springfield merchants formed the Proprietors of the Locks and Canals on the Connecticut River, a corporation whose major purpose was to facilitate the movement of goods upriver from Springfield. In 1795, the proprietors completed construction of a canal around the falls at South Hadley and during the next decade undertook similar ventures at Turners Falls and Bellows Falls, Vermont, thus allowing a threefold increase in the amount of merchandise shipped above Hadley Falls between 1795 and 1820. Although the proprietors did much to stimulate commerce, they showed little interest in developing the vast industrial potential of the Hadley Falls. Before mid-century, Ireland Parish's major enterprise was a small cotton mill, which employed fewer than seventy operatives and in 1845 produced goods valued at a modest $60,000. Indeed, local residents viewed the falls more as a source of salmon and shad than

waterpower. When the fish began to run each spring as many as 1500 horses could be seen aside the falls as farmers came from throughout the region to exchange news and supplement a meat, grain, and vegetable diet.[2]

All this began to change during the 1840s, a decade that saw a dramatic expansion of the New England railroad network. Where in 1840 even the Southern states eclipsed the region's 512 miles of track, by 1850 the length of New England roads had increased fivefold and not only exceeded that of the South, but was only slightly less than that of the Middle Atlantic states; relative to its size, New England had more railroad mileage than any region of the country. In 1839, the Western Railroad reached the Connecticut River at Springfield. A few years later, the merger of the Springfield and Northampton Railroad Company with the Greenfield and Northampton resulted in the formation of the Connecticut River Railroad, which in 1846 bridged the Connecticut at Willimansett and ran a line through Ireland Parish. Besides its cotton mill, Ireland at that time contained a grist mill, planing mill, two physicians, a shoemaker, tailor, wheelwright, painter, blacksmith, one school, two churches, and a "tavern of modest appearance, but of wide fame." As its residents would soon realize, though, the arrival of the railroad signaled the beginning of a new era for the sleepy agricultural village.[3]

A group of eastern capitalists, collectively known as the Boston Associates, held a controlling interest in the Connecticut River Railroad. "Merchant princes" of Boston, the associates comprised a group of families bound together by marriage and financial interest who by the mid 1840s had already erected industrial towns at Lowell, Chicopee, and Lawrence in Massachusetts, and at Manchester, Dover, and Nashua, New Hampshire. At mid-century they controlled 40 percent of Boston banking capital, 39 percent of Massachusetts insurance capital, and 30 percent of the state's railroad mileage. Because of its interests at Chicopee, the group had long been aware of the tremendous industrial potential offered by the Hadley Falls. That a dam had not already been built at the location "would be inexplicable," a study later commissioned by the group observed, "were it not obvious that the extraordinary magnitude of the enterprise required, in a corresponding degree, more than ordinary forethought, skill, and capital for its accomplishment." In 1847, the associates decided that they possessed those prerequisites and obtained an act of corporation under the name of the Hadley Falls

Company "for the purpose of constructing and maintaining a dam across the Connecticut River."[4]

As their local agent, the associates chose George Ewing, an official of the Fairbanks Scale Company who had for years been urging investors to develop the area. Ewing's first task was to buy all land adjoining the dam site. With one exception, Ewing quickly made the necessary purchases. The exception was Sam Ely, a local farmer who owned a critically placed piece of property close to the falls. Declaring that he would not sell to the "cotton lords" of the Hadley company "if they covered the entire field with gold dollars," Ely further remarked that "he was damned if he wanted to see the corporations control everything." None of Ely's neighbors apparently shared his aversion to the new order and he soon found himself alone. Just as local farmers welcomed the coming of the railroad because it promised lower transportation costs, they readily acceded to the generous offers of the Hadley Falls Company. Although Ely lashed out at surrounding farmers for leaving him isolated, he too sold out.[5]

The company next began construction of the dam. Upon its completion in November 1848, crowds of people lined the Connecticut River to witness the grand opening, and as the last gates closed a roar of approval rose from the interested onlookers. But complications soon developed. At noon a company official telegraphed Boston that "the dam is leaking badly." A further report an hour later evinced growing panic: "We cannot stop the leaking." The last message to Boston that afternoon simply read, "Dam gone to hell by way of Willimansett." The structure's collapse did not dim the enthusiasm of the watching crowd. "Well, some of that property was mine," one local farmer reportedly remarked, "but it was worth all the money I put into it to see it go." Meanwhile, one thoughtful observer sent off a telegram to Springfield, warning that there was a "big freshet coming."[6]

A second dam, which proved more durable, was finished the following October. In March 1850, the locale also obtained a new political status when Ireland Parish became the Town of Holyoke. Now that the area had a growing Irish population, the company did not wish to advertise the fact and, as Constance Green observed, "hoped that the Puritan label would lend the place dignity." Whatever dignity a town charter and new name gave Holyoke it was not enough to insure its continued growth. Much to the disappointment of the Hadley company's directors no major manufacturing concern chose to locate at Holyoke during the early 1850s. Moreover, before 1852, depressed

market conditions prevented its textile mills from operating at full capacity, and an 1854 treasurer's report showed that the company owed more than $1 million with little revenue coming in. In order to raise additional capital, the directors divided the company into two separate corporations: the waterpower and real-estate operations retained the name of the parent concern, while its textile mills became the Lyman Company. Yet despite extensive publicity measures, the prosperity promised by the promoters of the "New City" remained elusive.[7]

Conditions had not improved appreciably three years later. The Parsons Paper Company, which began manufacturing in 1855, built a second mill and in 1857 the Holyoke Paper Company and a small iron-wire factory opened for business. But they were the only three mills established at Holyoke during these years, and in the fall of 1857 a financial panic brought a sharp curtailment of production at the Lyman Mills and hobbled operations at other local businesses as well. By the following spring the Lyman Company had returned to full production, but the Hadley Falls Company was not so fortunate. Although short-lived, the panic of 1857 proved sufficient to send the corporation under. In January 1859, the company's property was sold at public auction: investors received $1.32 on each hundred-dollar share.[8]

In commenting on the company's failure, one of its directors, Alfred Smith of Hartford, wrote that "I trusted quite too much to my notion that so many Boston gentlemen would never invest so large an amount of money, without knowing what was to be done with the property, nor without backing up their investment with money to put the property to *some* profitable use." Smith fixed the blame for the corporation's dismal performance on its policy of absentee control: "The management of large stock capitals, at Boston, is not in accord with principles on which private *business* operations are managed." Such an arrangement, he contended, prevented "that strict attention to details or to economy, which I deem indispensable." Because Smith believed that under responsible management a power project at Holyoke could yet prosper, he purchased the defunct concern's property at auction and organized the Holyoke Water Power Company. Buttressed largely by local capital, derived from the proceeds of commerce, land sales, and small industrial ventures, Holyoke's industrial development began in earnest during the following decade.[9]

The Civil War years were a major turning point. During the period, government contracts, high tariffs, and soaring prices insured the

success of several newly constructed textile plants. The war boom also stimulated expansion of the town's fledgling paper industry. And as these enterprises prospered, a host of small tool and machine shops grew up around the mills to meet their needs. By 1870, Holyoke was no longer the agricultural backwater it had been two decades earlier. Population had increased from 3,245 to 10,733 and it was well on its way to becoming the "Paper City." Eleven paper mills employed more than 1,000 workers who produced tissue, book, collar, and the fine white writing paper that would make the city famous. A decade later the population had more than doubled to 21,915 and local industries had grown briskly. Nearly 1,900 workers now labored in its paper mills and another 4,000 produced cottons, woolens, thread, and silk. With a few notable exceptions, the mills were locally owned and managed by entrepreneurs who could be seen daily on the shop floor as well as in the front office. The business careers and social outlook of these men are the main focus of the remainder of this chapter.[10]

LIKE OTHERS of their class in post–Civil War America, Holyoke manufacturers subscribed to a free-labor ideology that proclaimed a mutuality of interests among classes, revered economic expansion, and celebrated the promise of social mobility. The basic precepts of this ideology were simple: Individual labor was the source of all wealth, and hard work and self-improvement would bring material success to anyone willing to expend the necessary effort. Few Holyokers who had acquired a comfortable portion of this world's possessions questioned these maxims. Editorials in local newspapers declared that all early industrialists had begun at some manual occupation and that one could emulate their success through a comparable application of industry, foresight, and self-discipline; only the lazy and spendthrift had anything to fear in this land of boundless opportunity. At an 1871 meeting of the local debating society, both judge and audience affirmed that "individual success is due more to talent than circumstances," after a one-sided debate in which "local illustrations were freely cited." An examination of the careers of Holyoke's leading millowners reveals that there was some basis for such self-congratulation.[11]

One indication that not all local manufacturers had moved effortlessly from the paternal mansion to the family mill was the degree of

geographical mobility that characterized so many of their early careers. Of the thirty-three men for whom sufficiently detailed career information is available, only six had grown up in the area and started out in family-owned enterprises. Another thirteen had, with varying degrees of success, entered the labor market elsewhere before embarking upon profitable careers in Holyoke. The early work lives of the remaining fourteen exhibited a great deal more variety. For example, Timothy Merrick began work in a Connecticut cotton mill at age ten before apprenticing as a shoemaker. In 1847, when he was twenty-four, he entered the employ of the Willington Thread Company and thirteen years later established a bleaching and thread company in partnership with his father-in-law at Mansfield, Connecticut. In 1868, Merrick moved to Holyoke and formed the Merrick Thread Company.[12]

The sparse educational background of many manufacturers also suggests the degree to which individual effort outweighed family sponsorship as a factor in their success. Of the twenty-seven men for whom pertinent data is available, only two attended college. An additional twelve went to high school, though only a few remained to complete their course of studies. The remaining thirteen advanced no further than the district school.

In place of an extended formal education, nearly half of the manufacturers undertook managerial or craft apprenticeships. Rather than receiving close instruction in the mysteries of a specific craft, the typical managerial apprentice spent his indenture moving from department to department within a factory. In a paper mill, he might begin in the beater or engine room, learning how the stock was prepared. Later, he would tend one of the massive fourdrinier paper machines and move on to the finishing department. In the course of his training, the apprentice became intimately familiar with the vagaries of production. He also learned who the key figures were in the process: Machine tenders and beater engineers could halt production and were not easily replaced; the women in the rag and finishing departments were vastly more dispensable.[13]

Holyoke manufacturers insisted that successful apprentices needed "pluck" and "grit," in addition to "brains, mechanical aptitude, ambition, acute observation [and] executive ability." Expressed at the turn of the century, these observations were not simply the self-approving pieties of men who had undergone such training during their youth. In Holyoke mills managerial apprenticeships required four years of hard

labor and were intended to test both the character and technical competence of trainees.[14]

Holyoke manufacturers who received craft training went through a comparable regimen of character development. During the years that these men served their apprenticeships, the traditional master-apprentice relationship was undergoing important changes, as increasingly fewer apprentices lived with their masters' families. In this new and more formalized relationship apprentices simply exchanged their labor for training, and masters no longer assumed responsibility for the moral development of apprentices. Yet, problems of labor control led master artisans in many locales to establish organizations that would function as surrogates for the vanishing family-based mode of craft training. In neighboring Springfield, the Hampden Mechanics' Association was one such organization.[15]

Comprised of the city's artisans and manufacturers, the association was formed in 1824 to promote good relations among Springfield employers. On one level, it sought to regulate the local labor market: Members agreed not to hire apprentices who prematurely left the employ of a fellow member; and at the end of their training period apprentices were awarded a document from the association certifying that they had successfully completed their course of instruction. Association members were also expected to monitor the behavior of their charges, and the especially dutiful apprentice received a medal that declared he had "entirely abstained from the use of ardent spirits, or the intemperate use of any intoxicating liquors, during his apprenticeship, and [had] otherwise conducted himself in an honest, obedient, and orderly manner."[16]

At a school that the association sponsored, the principal subjects included bookkeeping, simple arithmetic, writing, and other skills that apprentices would need to secure and maintain an independent existence as petty producers in a marketplace society. The association also opened its library to the city's apprentices and urged members to provide "friendly counsel" on the most appropriate texts. An 1834 report reinforced this recommendation with an arresting commercial metaphor: The library's books "like the Bills of a bank in order to do good, must be put in circulation and no one need feel a *pressure* for want of *this* currency as the Cashier has no wish to keep his funds in deposit, but discounts liberally to every applicant." Not all apprentices absorbed these lessons or observed the many strictures imposed by an organization like the Hampden Mechanics' Association; the

very need of such an association is in itself evidence of that. Even fewer qualified for a temperance medal. But those who did could use the award to establish a reputation as good credit risks. They were, in short, just the kind of people who would go on to become manufacturers in developing industrial centers like Holyoke.

Before drawing any conclusions about the degree to which our manufacturers were self-made men, we need also to look at their ethnic and family background. All but six were native-born sons of native-born parents, and the immigrants in the group were from either England or Scotland. Of the native born, at least ten came from families that traced their origins to seventeenth-century New England; most of the remaining families had settled in the region before the Revolution. The manufacturers' ethnic background did not in itself aid them in their rise to entrepreneurial success. It did, however, insure that they would not be subjected to the discrimination that so many non-British immigrants faced during these years.[17]

Also, the fathers of our manufacturers, while seldom men of great wealth, were nevertheless people of some substance within their communities. Of the twenty-seven fathers for whom such information is obtainable, seven were merchants and nine were either manufacturers, small businessmen, or factory managers. Another six were farmers, a number of whom owned extensive acreage or were characterized as "successful" in biographical reviews. Even fathers with less prestigious occupations—tavern keeper, shipping porter, tanner, and harness maker—followed respectable vocations.

Finally, family aid and connections were a factor in the success of a number of the manufacturers, particularly in the crucial early stages of their careers. Not everyone had access to a managerial apprenticeship. A well-placed relative or family friend often sponsored and supervised the young trainee. John and James Ramage served their apprenticeships as papermakers at a Scottish mill with which their father was "connected," and D. P. Crocker's father guided him through a similar program. A propitious marriage helped some of these men: C. H. Heywood married the niece of Jones Davis, agent of the Lyman Mills; Timothy Merrick married the daughter of Origen Hall, the nation's first thread manufacturer; and E. C. Taft married the daughter of Joseph Parsons, Holyoke's first paper manufacturer. Filial ties also helped, as in the case of the four Newton brothers. Their father was a successful Bernardston lumber dealer who insured that each of his sons received an extended formal education. Added to this

support was the mutual aid that the brothers gave each other. A careful division of labor characterized their many business ventures. Daniel and James handled financial matters, while John and Moses supervised their numerous construction projects.

What can we conclude about the careers of these manufacturers? If they are compared with the typical mid-century Irish or French Canadian immigrant, the advantages of family and social background loom large. Their ethnic background alone assured them easier access to capital. For our purposes it is more important that they believed individual effort was the key to success and denied that a propitious set of circumstances in any way explained their own material advancement. Equally important, their adoption of the free-labor ideology was not simply a hypocritical gesture designed to justify their wealth and status. For many of them, the ideology offered a plausible explanation of their own experience.

LOCATED IMMEDIATELY beneath the millowners in Holyoke's social hierarchy was a middle class of professionals, merchants, contractors, realtors, and petty manufacturers. Although less prosperous, members of the Yankee middle class mixed freely with the manufacturing elite in their associational life. They lived in the same neighborhoods, belonged to the same clubs, attended the same churches, and joined together on Election Day to vote for the Republican party. The inclusive and indiscriminate manner in which the two groups appeared in the listings of an 1889 Bluebook provides additional evidence of the close ties between them. Furthermore, both groups shared a belief in the free-labor ideology that left an indelible imprint upon Holyoke's institutional life during the late nineteenth century.[18]

Some sense of the nature of this influence can be gleaned from the proceedings of the lyceum and debating society, which before 1880 served as a popular winter retreat for the city's upper and middle classes. At its meetings, Holyoke's established citizens presented and refined their views on the major issues of the day. The level of discourse, with some embarrassing exceptions, was generally high, indicating that participants took their duties seriously. The audience followed the proceedings closely and, with the judge, rendered its verdict at the conclusion of a debate. To the degree that a coherent worldview emerged from these debates, it embodied the primitive

labor theory of value contained in the free-labor ideology. At an 1871 debate, the audience refused to affirm the proposition "that capital is more powerful than labor," even though the judge decided the question in the affirmative. The character of the debate was one reason for the audience's decision. "With one or two exceptions," the *Transcript* reported, "the question was discussed as if it read, *Resolved*, 'that gold is more powerful than labor.' " But beyond that these people would not accept any argument implying that factors other than individual effort accounted for their own success. At the same time, they unquestioningly supported the principle of private property. At an 1873 debate, the house unanimously rejected the proposition "that communism as a system of property holding is correct in theory and efficient in practice." While the speakers in the affirmative cited the example of the Shakers and noted that the "Golden Rule calls for a more equal division of the good things of life," the audience found the argument of the negative vastly more compelling: "Such a division would be a death blow to energy and ambitions, . . . would be fatal to intelligence, and transform men into a set of drones."[19]

Class relations also elicited the attention of the lyceum and debating society. At an 1871 debate on whether labor reform in politics should be encouraged, Henry A. Chase, son of a prosperous lumber dealer, asserted, "Not a man in this place who stands at the head of his business inherited his money. Everyone was born poor and worked himself upward by his own exertions. Equalization of property is the grand hobby of the labor reform party." Henry C. Ewing, son of one of the town's founding fathers, reinforced Chase's argument with the declaration that "If labor reformers should equalize property there would be some . . . who would not work." He then asked, "What would labor do without capital?" No one answered, but James Ramage, then a paper-mill superintendent who would later establish his own company, insisted that capital also had duties: "If a corporation cannot afford to pay its workmen, to support them without getting in debt, it had better take Greeley's advice and 'go West.' " Workers did not receive their fair share, he further declared, and it would be far better to have the legislature correct this abuse than to have the workers take the matter into their own hands through trade unions and strikes. The *Transcript* did not record the audience's verdict on the debate, but a year later the house unanimously voted down a resolution to give the legislature authority to regulate the hours of labor. In 1872, even the self-serving ameliorism of James

Ramage proved unacceptable. In later years, however, other manufacturers would demonstrate that they shared the sophisticated approach to labor relations suggested in Ramage's declarations.[20]

The city's Protestant churches were also important centers of associational life for the Holyoke elite. Although one local manufacturer
was heard to quip that his sole religious and temporal belief was that
"life is too short for a man to smoke poor cigars," the majority of his
peers took their religious duties more seriously. In their churches,
entrepreneurs received further confirmation that the world they were
creating was just, and in periods of crisis ministers provided their
congregations with moral support and a comforting analysis of
events. The Reverend J.L.B. Trask ascribed the depression of 1873 to
the unscrupulous manipulations of a few gamblers and speculators,
as he assured his affluent auditors that "confidence and action will
cure all," so long as one did not lose faith.[21]

God and the businessman seemed often to occupy coterminous
spheres. This became nowhere more evident than at an 1884 fellowship
meeting of the area's Congregational churches, where clergy and laity
discussed the question, "From the temporal side, is the maintenance of
the Christian church worth its cost?" Responding to a related question,
"By what evidences must Christians vindicate the Church's value?" a
South Hadley Falls minister noted that the churches supplemented the
schools' secular education by teaching morality and concluded that
"what is done for the church is one of the best investments a community can make for the right going forward of its interests." No one
disagreed. Nor did they challenge Moses Newton, a Holyoke manufacturer, when he declared that "the church paid in a business way as well
as spiritually." In support of this contention, Newton asserted that "by
resting and attending church on the seventh day people can accom-
plish more on the other six days." Furthermore, he added, "the church
(indirectly) fosters interests which create demands, out of which comes
the necessity of manufactures, be it of wool, silk, or paper."[22]

In addition to reassuring Holyoke's established classes of their rectitude, the city's churches also reminded them of their duties. Ministers
periodically cautioned against the sin of display, while the Reverend
Trask told his congregation that "it is the business of man to recognize
evil and reform it." By a wide margin, the most recognized evil in
Holyoke was drunkenness. The city's first temperance society was
formed in 1857 and in ensuing decades concerned citizens established a
host of similar organizations, hoping to extinguish what they saw as

the community's one besetting sin. As elsewhere, women dominated the Holyoke temperance movement, attacking liquor dealers in the name of home protection. For many of these reformers, intemperance was not simply an evil in itself, but the root of all evil: a diseased growth that ultimately produced a harvest of crime and poverty. From time to time, local temperance lodges achieved some success. In the 1870s, numerous reformed drunkards told the Sunday Evening Temperance Meeting of past sins and current prosperity: Stories of the "guilt, shame, and degradation of drunkenness," vast earnings "squandered in dissipation," and "the delightful consciousness of manhood that comes to one who truly reforms" inspired the wavering tippler; they also reinforced the reformers' conviction that intemperance directly engendered broader social ills, and that by taking the pledge individuals could place themselves on the road to material comfort as well as moral regeneration.[23]

Not all of the city's temperance societies could match the achievements of the Sunday Evening Temperance Meeting. More typical was the experience of the Reform Club and Temperance Union. In 1877, when its supplies ran out, most of the group's converts left with them, one man boasting that the reformers "didn't make much out of him. He had his 'nip' every day all the while." Some Holyoke clergymen maintained that upper-class indifference was one reason that temperance forces did not attain greater success locally. "If all our citizens in the upper walks of life would take the pledge," said the Reverend R.J. Adams of Second Baptist Church, "many a poor drunkard, seeing the respectability of the blue-ribbon company, would be encouraged to take shelter in the only asylum which offers him safety." The men who would constitute this "blue-ribbon company" failed to respond. After an 1873 debate, a committee of five decided, by a three to two margin, that prohibition laws did not furnish the best means of checking intemperance. Those supporting the majority position argued that only the sale of hard liquor should be restricted, as "men will have some stimulant." This common-sense approach was based on experience. An 1868 experiment with prohibition had failed abysmally, resulting only in increased corruption, ill feeling, and, some insisted, greater drunkenness.[24]

Probably the best summary of the many factors conditioning one's reaction to the temperance issue in Holyoke appeared during the course of an 1881 debate between "Peasant" and the Reverend William S. Heywood, a prominent local prohibitionist. Claiming to be a

former prohibitionist himself, "Peasant" exposed the many tensions engendered by the issue in a merciless attack on Heywood:

I read an article in which the Napoleon of the prohibition army wandered about among the dismantled guns and other wreck of war, surveyed the field of his defeat, and laid some of the things it revealed, to heart. As Waterloo was more than Wellington against Bonaparte so was the Waterloo of the prohibitionists more than license against prohibition. . . . It was tolerance against intolerance. It was the lessons of experience against zealous bigotry.

The claim of this Napoleonic prohibitionist that God is on the side of prohibition has no weight with thinking men. It was the claim of Cotton Mather when he persecuted and hung women as witches.

The prohibitory law was a "farce." Hotel proprietors knew in advance of the raids by state constables; . . . gold watches were presented to officials by liquor dealers; . . . and it was almost impossible to obtain a conviction before a jury.

Again,—the prohibitory law allowed the rich man to buy imported liquors in "the original packages" so that Mr. Bullion could purchase cases of imported brandy and champagne and Mr. Shinplaster could look on and see Mr. Bullion allowed by law to indulge in stimulants to his heart's content while he, Mr. S., was prohibited by the same law from even having a smell of "the critter."

In closing, "Peasant" acknowledged the imperfections of the current license law and scored city officials for lax enforcement. But, he added, the law had diminished whiskey consumption in favor of ale and beer, and forced "intemperate men to aid in supporting the paupers in the city."[25]

Among Holyoke's established classes many people found "Peasant"'s argument more compelling than Heywood's rejoinder that a city without a prohibitory law was one in which "the elements of barbarism held sway." They did not like intemperance; it made a mockery of the moral-pecuniary code that governed their lives. But they liked even less impractical experiments that only exacerbated existing problems. "Peasant"'s thrust at the element of class discrimination in the temperance issue also struck a responsive chord. By 1880, the chasm between classes had become uncomfortably wide and no one gratuitously sought to expand it.[26]

The local public-school system provided another prop to the prevailing ethos of the dominant classes. Elite Holyoke's approach to

public education comprised a mixture of social control and social duty, informed by the self-reliant values of the free-labor ideology. Early school reports declared that the maintenance of a republican form of government required that the "masses" be educated; that those who did not attend good schools would find their learning in "schools of vice"; and that it was thus "cheaper to support *good schools than poor farms, penitentiaries, jails, and prisons.*" The same reports enjoined teachers to stress self-reliance as the only sure means to success. The town's industrial development made good schools even more necessary. The 1863 report observed that the increased division of labor caused by industrialization tended "to dwarf, if not crush out the power of the mind, to defeat all breadth of culture, to beget little men, the subjects of mere caprice in the social and civic actions, neither fit to govern, or to be governed, upon the basis of our free institutions." This did not mean that industrial development should be slowed. The abundant editorial praise local newspapers accorded modern machine production indicated that any such proposal would have been considered fatuous, if not dangerous. Instead, the 1863 report continued, the degenerative effects of the division of labor must be countered by the *"liberalizing influences of an efficient, early education. . . .* Then though the hum of spindles and machinery be heard on every side, we know, that *manhood* will not be swallowed up in the exacting, cramping routine of daily life." The school would, in short, protect society from industrialization's more baneful effects by instilling in working-class youths those values and skills that factory work tended to obliterate. At the same time, schools offered an avenue out of the mill that the established classes had a duty to keep open for the city's workers. "We must remember," Mayor William Whiting said of public schools in his 1878 inaugural address, "that the capital gained here is the only reliance of many a poor boy and girl, and that accordingly, a great responsibility rests upon us."[27]

In that same year, one of the town's founding fathers, George C. Ewing, also reminded Holyoke citizens of that responsibility. Noting that many families would sink into pauperism without their children's earnings, Ewing proposed a law that would use state funds to pay such families the amount that their children would have earned while attending school. The suggested reform elicited little support and was soon forgotten. But in this and his other activities Ewing demonstrated that the dominant ethic included a reform dimension. Ewing himself was an inveterate activist who managed to combine

the roles of businessman, lay preacher, prohibitionist, and labor reformer within a coherent worldview. Whether attacking intemperance, calling for school reform, or endorsing shorter hours to facilitate worker self-improvement, his manifold efforts were all of a piece and reflected an unqualified belief in the free-labor ideology:

> It is important that young men should be impressed with the fact [he said at an 1871 debate] that there is no royal road to wealth and influence. Your success in life will not depend upon your capital, but upon your own individual effort. Let a knowledge of this truth put a restraint upon all immoral tendencies and prompt you to habits of activity and industry.[28]

At the apex of Holyoke's public-school system stood the high school. The first high school was established in 1852, and although the town meeting did not regularize its operation for another decade, local residents had high expectations of the school's students. After a disappointing annual examination in 1864, superintendent Buckland complained that "there was not that independence of thought and power of expression, which is expected in those who are soon to be men and women. The public have a right to demand that the recipients of such advantages shall ever display a spirit of eager and thorough research, of vigorous and self-reliant thought and mature and critical study." Four years earlier the school committee had appointed Buckland principal of the high school after his predecessor had resigned under fire for having given his students the questions prior to the annual examination. The incident revealed the town authorities' special concern for high-school students. Since the high school primarily served their own children, Holyoke's middle and upper classes demanded that its students be given rigorous preparation for the larger world they would soon be entering. It was especially necessary that they internalize the moral-pecuniary values contained in the free-labor ideology. A review of some published high-school essays and orations shows that they did just that.[29]

In many cases the titles of these essays and orations alone indicated the values inculcated by home and school. Efforts entitled "Labor and its Rewards," "Self-Denial," "Success through Toil," and "Self-Reliance" did little to veil their prescriptive import. The necessity of hard, unremitting, and self-disciplined labor was a recurrent theme. In her essay, "The Race Is Not to the Swift," Carrie Averill observed that "moral, patient industry often accomplishes more than

the most brilliant tastes," while in "Perseverance," Alice Flanders declared that one would invariably find that persevering men were "more competent, reliable, and devoted to the interest of their employees than any other class." Edward Whiting gave speculators a justly deserved flaying in an oration that asked his auditors to judge, "Which is preferable, the life of the unscrupulous speculator, or the life spent in honest toil and devotion to the cause of right and justice?" No one had to poll the audience for their response to that question. Production also triumphed over finance in Matilda Hardy's essay "Borrowing." This "disagreeable habit" was so prevalent, she wrote, because it "is so much easier to borrow than to make or purchase." The successful entrepreneur would do well to eschew the bank, she concluded, as "men are often ruined before they are well aware of the fact, simply by unnecessary indulgence in this habit."[30]

By the mid-seventies, the competitive and individualistic aspects of the prevailing ethos dominated the lives of high-school students, locking them into an increasingly rigid meritocracy. In 1875, monthly ratings of the top ten high-school students began to appear in the *Transcript*. At the close of the school year, the paper also published a numerical ranking of the graduating class. Not all educators approved of the trend. "We should doubt the sanity of a clergyman who estimated the state of religion in his parish as .83 or .97," remarked superintendent L. H. Marvel. "Is it not as great a fallacy," he then asked, "for a teacher to submit the statement of education in his school in accordance with any such arbitrary standard?" Others apparently felt that it was not, for the practice continued. A decade later, when an anonymous writer complained to the *Transcript* that "I have stood low marking as long as I can," the editor unsympathetically replied that "if the writer would spend the time in study that is wasted writing anonymous letters . . . he or she might perhaps have better marks."[31]

Yet, the manner in which the dominant ethic influenced Holyoke's institutional life did not secure the nodding approval of everyone. In his 1881 high-school valedictory address, Walter A. Tuttle presented a damning critique of the city's school system. "The popular idea of education," Tuttle began, "supposes it to be a proposition for money-making." In the schools, he continued, "children are taught that money making is the chief aim of their existence, . . . and to so wide an extent do these ideas prevail that studies are examined as to their practical nature before they are admitted to our high school course.

Teachers are frequently called upon to explain the relation of certain studies to business life and if they do not have that use, parents protest against the so-called waste of time." Tuttle conceded that the practical side of education was necessary, but only to provide that material development that frees individuals for "loftier thought." In concluding, he urged that greater attention be given to moral education and criticized a recent proposal for the elimination of free high schools, remarking that a "city is frequently without a respectable government because of the selfish spirit of its business men."[32]

Walter Tuttle's indictment of the Holyoke school system exposed the harsh, utilitarian underside of the free-labor ideology and revealed the extent to which the schools had become a caricature of the broader society. As William Whiting had stated a few years earlier, education was capital. The new marking system provided a means of measuring just how much of this capital a student had amassed. Also, grade competition presumably maximized production by impelling the ambitious student to work harder and exercise an ever greater measure of self-discipline in accumulating that capital. By applying the dominant ethic to schooling, Holyoke's elite hoped to create a system that would produce individuals who were not only hard working, sober, and thrifty, but also acquisitive and intensely competitive. Walter Tuttle's oration eloquently described the effort; it also provided evidence that the project was less than a complete success and that competition was not an imperative spur to achievement. In Yankee Holyoke during these years, Tuttle was not the only critic to question the unbridled individualism sanctioned by the dominant ethic. By the 1880s, other complaints could also be heard from the city's native-born craft and industrial artisans.

THE RISE OF factory production in nineteenth-century America shattered a number of traditional crafts. By mid-century in such industries as paper, textiles, and shoes, most workers had become factory operatives, engaged in routinized, if sometimes still complex, productive tasks. But the rise of the factory system did not destroy all crafts at the same time; nor did it make factory operatives of everyone pursuing the trades that it did transform. Many craftsmen avoided the factory for decades. The ambitious and the fortunate established themselves as petty producers, and others worked in small shops alongside these

independent proprietors. Independent production marked the pinnacle of ambition for most Yankee artisans, providing them the autonomy they cherished above all else. At mid-century in a young and growing town like Holyoke, there existed ample opportunity for those possessing the requisite skills and access to capital.[33]

In 1850, besides one small cotton mill, Holyoke contained nineteen craft-based shops that each employed less than six workers. Brickmakers, shoemakers, harness makers, blacksmiths, coppersmiths, and others conducted small, independent enterprises. As more mills were built in subsequent years, a host of small supporting businesses grew up around them. Some did not remain small for long. Thomas Kelt arrived at Holyoke in 1859 and established a foundry and machine shop that soon employed thirty workers. Before coming to Holyoke, Kelt had worked for thirteen years at the Whitin Machine Shop, where he had acquired a reputation as a gifted craftsman based on his skill in turning a wide range of castings.[34]

Whatever their ambitions, not all Yankee artisans found their position agreeable. In 1850, one group formed a local chapter of the New England Industrial League and sought a ten-hour day, in order to have additional time for education and self-improvement. But the Holyoke chapter soon folded. The extensive geographical mobility of the period, coupled with the wide range of opportunity available in a growing town like Holyoke, precluded the careful nurture such a movement then demanded. Moreover, a number of local institutions bridged the gap between Yankee artisans and their employers.[35]

One was the fire company. Unlike those in some antebellum cities where fire companies served as an extension of saloon culture, Holyoke companies were models of respectability. The resolutions of Engine Company No. 1 stated that anyone appearing intoxicated in uniform would have his uniform taken from him; and only a member "well known by the community as a good, respectable citizen and not addicted to intoxication" could parade with the company. One Sunday in 1863 the Mechanics Engine Company attended the Baptist church in a body and announced afterwards that it intended to continue the practice. The companies also operated as social centers. The Holyoke Engine Company staged an annual ball, while other companies invited artisan-firemen from neighboring communities to their dances. In 1861, the Mechanics Company formed a baseball team and bested a local Irish squad in its first encounter, 31–15.[36]

Yankee artisans also found relaxation in the rituals of the Masonic

order. Like the social affairs of the fire companies, the Masons provided a means of staying in touch with artisans in surrounding communities. Nearly twenty-five members of a local lodge, the *Transcript* reported in 1863, "made a friendly call upon their brother craftsmen in Chicopee." Organizations like the Masons and Odd Fellows also did much to defuse the social tensions that accompanied industrial development. Many local lodges had a cross-class membership and promoted an ideal of brotherhood that was based on the moral-pecuniary values of the dominant ethic. Through their membership in fraternal orders, Yankee artisans joined local elites in affirming that this was a land of equal opportunity in which the temperate, thrifty, and industrious would receive their just rewards. As Brian Greenberg has written of Odd Fellowship in Albany, the social relationships formed in such organizations "symbolized the free labor principle of an inherent mutuality of interests between capital and labor."[37]

The most important event in the lives of this generation of Yankee artisans was the Civil War. Of the first thirty-six volunteers at Holyoke, twenty-four were artisans or skilled factory operatives. Many others subsequently went, and those who did not gave their unqualified support to the Union cause. When R. P. Crafts, a local Democrat, refused to allow the establishment of a recruiting office at the Hook and Ladder Company's room at the Exchange Building, the company voted to vacate the premises. Another expression of the Yankee artisan's commitment came from Thomas Kelt, the machinist who had established a foundry at Holyoke. Upon a brief return visit to Holyoke from Newark, where he had moved in 1863, Kelt reported finding some Newarkers a little "copperish," particularly the "blue noses;" but he was trying his best to "instill into their veins some of the good old Massachusetts loyalty." Regarding the war's impact on this generation of workers, Alan Dawley and Paul Faler have written that the "mythology that came from the Civil War tended to persuade workers that their power and destiny were inextricably linked to the military heroes, civilian leaders, and existing frame of government that won the war. It was not necessary for bourgeois ideologists to go about preaching a 'false' consciousness to working people who had risked their lives to bring down the slave power." There is no evidence that Holyoke's artisans constituted an exception to this generalization. For more than a decade after the war's end there was no revival of the feeble strains of prewar labor protest.[38]

In the decades following the Civil War, petty entrepreneurship

remained a viable alternative for some artisans. The 1880 manufacturing census showed fifty-seven establishments employing ten workers or less. In these shops, machinists, blacksmiths, coppersmiths, tailors, printers, and others practiced their crafts free from the grinding routine of the factory. On the whole, such establishments exhibited a remarkable degree of stability. A decade later, thirty remained in operation, a few having grown considerably in the interim: The Perkins Machine Shop now employed twenty men rather than five, while the work force at Watson Ely's lumber company had expanded from ten to forty. Another eleven businesses survived at least four years before going under. As late as the 1880s, then, the Yankee artisan who hoped to establish his own business was not living in a fool's paradise. The material basis for such aspirations still existed.[39]

Economic growth thus sustained hopes of independent production. Yet corollary developments transformed the community in ways that some Yankee artisans found hard to accept. The growing concentration of capital meant that proportionately fewer artisans now operated their own shops. Also, by the late seventies, the power rental arrangements of the Holyoke Water Power Company clearly favored large mills, making it even more difficult for aspiring petty entrepreneurs. In an 1879 letter to the *Transcript* criticizing local boosterism, ARTISAN gave vent to the growing discontent of Yankee craftsmen. "The indiscriminate 'hollering' for everybody to 'come to Holyoke' without regard to their character or reputation is stupid," he wrote. The city already has "enough of tramps, enough of loafers, enough of swindlers, but not enough of honest men, laborers, artisans, skilled workers, sound business establishments, etc." The complaint contained an apt summary of the forces then impinging on the artisan's world: immigrants who had not internalized the moral-pecuniary values of the dominant ethic; speculators who did not engage in productive labor; and, one suspects, the whole process of industrial growth that in the end threatened the artisan's very existence.[40]

In response to these growing threats to their current fortunes and future prospects, Yankee artisans began to look beyond the fellowship offered in fraternal orders like the Masons and to band together in associations designed to protect their material interests. At Holyoke during the postwar years, one such organization was the Sovereigns of Industry. The first Massachusetts chapter of the Sovereigns was formed in 1874 at Springfield. A group of Holyoke cooperators, formerly organized as the Holyoke Cooperative Association, estab-

lished a local council shortly afterwards. Acting in concert with the Patrons of Husbandry, the Sovereigns made bulk purchases of commodities, which they sold at a small markup designed to cover operating expenses. The organization's stated purpose was to "establish a better system of economical exchanges, and to promote on a basis of equity and liberty, mutual fellowship and cooperative action among the producers and consumers of wealth throughout the world."[41]

A secret society, steeped in ritual, the Sovereigns admitted "any person engaged in industrial pursuits, not under sixteen years of age, of good character, and having no interest in conflict with the purposes of the order." The vagueness of this standard—which seemed to accept all but lawyers, politicians, liquor dealers, and some merchants—reflected the organization's attitude toward class relations. Pitting itself against the "personal and class pursuit of selfish interests," the Sovereigns sought to abolish the "monopolized privileges" of the "aristocratic classes." At the same time, the group denounced any form of class struggle. Looking out upon a world of producers and nonproducers, the Sovereigns defined and judged others in terms of their functional roles rather than their class interests. In this regard, organizations like the Sovereigns remained firmly rooted in the free-labor ideology and were as much a demonstration of its flexibility as a challenge to its adequacy.[42]

Through their later activities as members of the Knights of Labor and the Trades and Labor Assembly, a number of Yankee artisans would participate in the formation of the Holyoke labor movement. For the most part, however, they played a subordinate role in these developments. As bearers of an ideology that viewed social mobility as a civic duty and as members of an ethnic group for whom such opportunities were particularly available, Yankee artisans were by the 1880s a small and declining segment of the local working class. In the increasingly militant and vitally important building trades, for example, less than 20 percent of skilled construction workers in 1880 were native-born craftsmen. This figure rises to 26 percent if immigrants from England and British Canada are added to the group, but this is still a far cry from a period two decades earlier when nearly three of every four building tradesmen hailed from Massachusetts and other northeastern states. Often torn between conflicting class and cultural loyalties, those Yankee artisans who did enter the labor movement tended to do so with mixed allegiances.[43]

As they sorted all this out, the choices facing Yankee artisans were

not made any easier by the character of Holyoke's elite. In local factories, many manufacturers had craft backgrounds and could often be found on the shop floor of their mills, where they mixed easily with their most skilled workers. The flexibility of the free-labor ideology also softened class tensions. Although the dominant ethic of the city's upper and middle classes contained a number of harsh features, it did not preclude reform altogether. There were always some people who realized that life existed below High Street. George Ewing was one who, using his own reformist interpretation of the free-labor ideology, sought to bridge the growing gulf between the established and working classes. He was ultimately unsuccessful, but the effort is still noteworthy. For if his prescriptions were generally ignored, his implicit warnings of impending class conflict were not. Likewise, James Ramage's declarations did not bring higher wages or shorter hours, but they did reflect a certain sophistication among some manufacturers that would mitigate the intensity of later struggles between capital and labor. Finally, admonitions to moderate display were not the idle preachings of a conscience-stricken clergy. Compared with their workers, Holyoke manufacturers did live lavishly. But they also viewed conspicuous consumption as a vice that heightened class tensions. These observations are important because class development does not occur in a vacuum—not in Holyoke, nor anywhere else.

2

SOCIAL RELATIONS OF PRODUCTION: TEXTILES AND PAPER

IN 1856, when the Lyman Mills installed a new bell, the *Holyoke Mirror* observed, "We could but think how much more pleasant, to be summoned to work by the musical sounds of such a bell, than by the harsh, discordant twang of the one to which we have listened a few weeks past." The statement revealed both the paper's boosterism and its assumption that it spoke for all elements of the community. But the bell did not call the *Mirror*'s editor to work each morning. For those whom it did summon, the throbbing resonance of the Lyman Mills's bell and others like it sounded considerably less mellifluous, speaking not of wealth and progress, but of long hours, low wages, and dependency. This chapter looks at the work lives of these operatives and their counterparts in Holyoke paper mills.[1]

In 1880, the more than 3,600 textile workers who entered Holyoke's mills each morning comprised about half of the local work force. Six of every ten of these workers were women. Through their sweat and toil they provided the ballast of the local economy, enriched their employers, and helped to clothe the nation. Ten hours a day, six days a week, they performed the many operations necessary to transform raw cotton, wool, and silk into finished cloth. Because their productive activity formed so large a part of their own lives, it would be worth our while to follow them into the mills for a day and to observe them at their work.[2]

In a typical cotton mill, the process of cloth production began in the picker room, where several powerfully built young men weighed incoming bales of cotton. After weighing the bales, the picker hands opened them and mixed the cotton from several bales to form a bing.

This operation homogenized the raw cotton before the hands fed it into the picker, which filtered out any dirt that had escaped the gin. The picker hands then took the fleece and put it through the blower, producing a long, smooth sheet or lap, ready to be wound on wooden drums and delivered to the carding engine. Although most Holyoke picker rooms were clean and well ventilated, this was hot and dirty work, as the operation of the picker filled the air with flying dust.[3]

At the carding room, the card tender took the tangled mass of cotton that emerged from the picker room and ran it through the carding engine, which straightened out individual fibers so that they lay roughly parallel with one another. Afterwards, male card strippers cleaned the fibers and other residual materials from the teeth of the card cylinders. The most skilled and highly paid carding-room worker was the card grinder, who kept the cylinder sharpened and adjusted the machine so that the teeth were set apart at a proper distance for the grade of cotton being carded. The most important nineteenth-century innovation affecting this department was the development of a revolving flat card. Widely adopted after the mid-eighties, its steel construction permitted more accurate adjustment. Employment of the revolving flat card also reduced the labor cost of carding, because it required less skill to operate and increased machine productivity.[4]

Not yet ready for spinning, the loosely twisted rope of carded cotton then demanded further twisting and drawing. After 1860, twisting was performed on fly frames, which were longer than the speeders that they replaced and required twisters to tend a greater number of spindles. During the seventies, the application of electricity to the fly frame's stop-motion forced operatives to watch over an even larger number of frames. After twisting, the cotton went to a drawing frame, and then to a roving frame, which produced a filament that was wound on bobbins and delivered to the spinner. Postwar improvements in the drawing frame's stop-motion also increased the number of frames that these operatives had to tend.[5]

The dominant figure in the spinning department was the mule spinner. Assisted by piecers and doffers, who repaired breaks in the roving and removed full bobbins of spun yarn, the highly skilled mule spinner manipulated the mule's spindles, which were mounted on a moving carriage, so that the roving was simultaneously drawn and twisted, thus producing a particularly fine and even yarn. In the postwar years, the mule spinners' penchant for strikes and trade unionism led many manufacturers to replace their mules with ring

spindles, a much less complex frame. The ring spinner's principal task was to piece together breaks in the roving, a job that could be done by women and children, who were paid about half of what mule spinners had received. Postwar improvements in the ring frame's design permitted manufacturers to increase its speed from 5,500 revolutions per minute in 1865 to 7,500 revolutions a decade later; in subsequent years speeds reached 10,000 revolutions per minute.[6]

Similar developments occurred in woolen spinning. After 1870, manufacturers installed self-operating frames in place of hand-operated jack spindles. In the process, semiskilled operatives replaced highly skilled jack spinners, reducing the labor cost of spinning by half. In 1881, when a dozen jack spinners at Holyoke's Beebe and Webber Woolen Mill struck because they were put on piece work, the owners immediately replaced them, stating that they "were intending to discharge them for cheaper help."[7]

The spun yarn was wound onto bobbins or cops. The cops of mule-spun yarn went straight to the weaving room, but spoolers transferred the warp yarn from small bobbins onto larger spools and took the latter to the dressing room. Before the Civil War, dressers wound the warp yarn onto a yardwide beam, after which dressing frames sized the yarns with a starch and tallow solution and a blower dried them. The dresser then rewound them onto another beam and, using a steel hook, drew the sized yarns individually by hand through the loom reed and harness. During the postwar years, many mills divided this complex operation between warpers who wound the yarn onto beams and slasher tenders who sized the warps. The installation of slashers allowed one man and a boy to do the work formerly performed by seven or eight workers.[8]

Weaving was the last step in cloth production. In weave rooms, a largely female work force tended looms that wove the various yarns together according to a specified pattern. Because weavers comprised as much as half or more of the work force in many textile mills, the operation formed a significant part of the labor cost of manufacturing, particularly in fine mills where weavers had to be especially careful. Manufacturers thus evinced a lively interest in technical innovations that promised to reduce the labor cost of weaving. Between 1860 and 1880, increased loom speeds led to a 20 percent rise in output per machine. Although weaving was a more skilled operation than most phases of spinning, later improvements made the task sufficiently routinized that manufacturers could reduce

supervisory staff and assign more looms to each weaver. By 1890, most weavers operated six looms, where a decade earlier they had tended four; some weavers would later be given as many as eight or ten looms. Again, the critical innovation was an improved stop-motion, which automatically brought the loom to a halt when a thread broke or a shuttle slipped out of place.[9]

Holyoke's other major industry was paper. In 1880, nearly 1,900 workers, comprising about 25 percent of the local work force, found employment in paper mills, where they produced book, collar, and fine white writing paper. Although the history of paper production leads back into antiquity, the labor process changed little prior to the mid-eighteenth century, when the Dutch developed the first beater engine. Until the introduction of the fourdrinier paper machine in the 1820s, however, paper making remained largely a hand process. At the traditional one-vat mill, the work force consisted of four men and a boy, who began work early each morning, stopping for breakfast and a grog before noon. The work day lasted nine hours, and early in the afternoon when the small force had completed its daily task of twenty posts, the workers departed for the village tavern. The vat-man was the key figure in hand production. With large hands reddened by frequent dipping into warm water and pulp and shoulders rounded from long days bending over the vat, the preindustrial papermaker stood out among his fellow workers. But his appearance did not detract from his prestige, for all respected the skill and strength necessary to produce a sheet of paper by holding the mold with its fiber and water at a carefully balanced level.[10]

All this changed during the second quarter of the nineteenth century with the introduction of the fourdrinier paper machine. The fourdrinier met the need for a means of hastening the transformation of pulp into paper created by the development of the beater engine, which had substantially increased pulp production. By mid-century the vat man and one-vat mill had become symbols of a passing era. Meanwhile, improved transportation facilities extended the market and manufacturers constructed ever larger establishments, often concentrated in certain favorable locales. In the postwar years Holyoke became one of these centers. Its tremendous waterpower and ample supply of chemically pure wash water made it an ideal site for the production of the better grades of paper. In 1880, Holyoke's seventeen paper mills had an average workforce of 140 employees.[11]

In fine-writing-paper mills, the production process began in the rag

department. After stockmen removed a delivery of rags from the bales in which it had been shipped, women rag sorters differentiated them according to quality of fabric, removed any buttons or hooks, and loosened seams and hems. Because some suppliers wet their goods in order to increase the weight, sorters often took a few handfuls of rags, weighed, dried, and then reweighed them to insure that the company had not been defrauded. In performing her job, the rag sorter had to exercise judgment and skill to prevent the mixing of better quality rags, which she set aside for writing paper, with fabrics of an inferior composition. Rag sorting was dirty and dangerous work, as the rags were often filthy and sometimes carried infectious diseases. Health officials invariably began their investigations of smallpox epidemics in the rag departments of local mills; the dirty, congested atmosphere of these rooms made respiratory disorders another occupational hazard.[12]

The sorted rags went to the rag cutters, who reduced them to fragments sufficiently small that they would float in the rag engine without becoming entangled in the roller, but not so minute that an excess of fiber would be lost during the willowing and dusting operation. Rag cutters also removed any impurities that rag sorters had missed. Prior to 1880, women performed this task by hand, but the subsequent introduction of the Coburn rag-cutting machine largely replaced the female hand cutter. This was the first in a series of innovations that significantly reduced the proportion of women in the paper work force. At Holyoke, the Whiting Paper Company claimed that with the Coburn rag cutter thirty-five operatives could do the work formerly performed by more than one hundred women. Where women constituted 62 percent of Holyoke paper workers in 1880, three-and-a-half decades later they formed slightly less than one-third of the statewide total. Yet hand cutters did not disappear altogether. Because cutting machines sometimes missed unpicked seams and failed to eliminate all impurities, mills producing fine writing paper often maintained a number of hand cutters in their employ.[13]

At some mills, male operatives put the rags through a machine called the willow, which loosened their texture. In other mills, a combination willow and duster removed dust from the rags as well as loosening them. Following this operation, workmen known as "rotary fillers" placed the rags in large, revolving wrought-iron boilers that eliminated any greasy substances and dissolved the starch size in cotton fabrics. Boiler operators had to be careful that the tank was not

set at too high a pressure, otherwise the dirt and coloring materials would be fixed on the rags rather than dissolved.[14]

From the rotary boiler the stock passed to the washing and breaking engine. Constructed on the same principles as a beating engine, with a rotary cylinder washer, beater roll, and knife-studded bedplate, this engine reduced the rags to tiny fragments, while a constantly flowing stream of water carried away the separated dirt. When the stock was adequately "broken" and the water flow appeared clear, washer engineers added a bleach solution and continued agitating the stock until the pulp was thoroughly saturated with bleach. They then ran the engine's contents through an auxiliary pipe into large brick vaults called drainers, where the bleaching liquor slowly seeped away through the chamber's perforated tiles. In performing his job, the washerman had to insure that he did not break the rags so thoroughly that an excess of fiber was lost.[15]

Workmen next placed the massed cakes of pulp, now called "half-stuff," in boxes and transported them to the beating engine, where the engineer's helpers slowly filled the beater until the mass became so thick that it barely moved. Engineers first eliminated any lingering traces of chlorine from the pulp by adding a neutralizing agent to the half-stuff. If they did not adequately neutralize the bleach, it could later render the size ineffective and corrode the strainer plates and wire gauze of the paper machine. European authorities considered beating the most important operation in paper production, because the paper's strength depended on the length and quality of the fiber that emerged from beater engines. As one French expert explained:

Upon the management of the beating engine the character of the paper produced largely depends. What is wanted is not a mincing or grinding of the fibre, but a drawing out or separation of the fibres one from another. . . . Long, fine fibres can only be obtained by keeping the roll slightly up off the bed-plate, and giving it time to do the work. Sharp actions between the roll and the bed-plate will, no doubt, make speedy work of the fibre, but the result will be short particles of fibre only, which will not interlace and make a strong felt. . . . Practice and careful observation can alone make a good beater-man, and for the finer classes of paper none but careful, experienced men should men should be entrusted with management of the beating engine.[16]

In addition to supervising the reduction of the half-stuff, beater engineers loaded, sized, and colored the pulp. The first operation

involved adding sulphite of lime to the stock. This made for the production of a stronger and smoother paper by closing the paper's pores
and rendering it nonabsorbent. To size the loaded stock, beatermen
applied a resin soap solution to the pulp, followed by an alum mixture, which set the resin free in the form of tiny particles that would
later, during the drying process, cement together fibers and alumina,
making the paper nonabsorbent and improving its whiteness. In com-
pleting this operation, beater engineers needed to make sure that the
resin was thoroughly dissolved, or it would subsequently form clear,
transparent spots in the finished paper. Lastly, beatermen added a
small quantity of blue and pink coloring to the pulp so that it would
not acquire a yellow tinge when converted to paper. Throughout the
nineteenth century, the development of these and other chemical addi-
tives made the work of beater engineers increasingly more complex.[17]

By opening a valve at the bottom of the engine, beatermen sent the
pulp through a pipe to the "stuff-chests"—large, cylindrical vessels,
twelve feet in diameter and six feet deep, usually located in the basement. The stock was then pumped into a supply box, which furnished a uniform measure of pulp to the sand tables, where it was
rinsed with water. The diluted pulp passed through a number of
bronze-plated strainers with narrow slits into a vat. There horizontal
agitators mixed the pulp and water and transferred it to the wire cloth
of the fourdrinier. As the pulp and water proceeded along the paper
machine, the water fell through the fine wire cloth, leaving only the
white pulp, which a series of rollers pressed into consistency. Drying
cylinders and cast-iron, steam-heated smoothing rolls then flattened
the paper before it passed through the final drying cylinders.[18]

During the course of these operations, which occurred at speeds
greater than any description of them could suggest, machine tenders
had a number of important tasks to perform. They regulated the
paper's thickness by coordinating the supply of pulp with the speed
at which the machine was running. They also provided for the
smooth transference of the paper from the couch roll to the felt of the
final drying cylinders by adjusting a series of levers that governed the
pressure of the upper couch roll upon the lower roll. The observations
of a visitor to an early Holyoke mill amply illustrated the vital role
machine tenders played in paper production:

In the movements of this wonderful machine, with its almost infinitude of
parts, the least degree of success requires well-nigh a hair-breadth accuracy

33

in the adjustment of every feature. Should a wheel, required to be exactly ten feet in circumference, happen to fall short or overrun by the distance of half an inch, or should the drier-felt, for example, move an inch in an hour faster than the wet-felt, the continual breaking and tearing of the paper-belt would soon prove the necessity of re-arrangement. Frequently small bits of thin leather are fastened upon the periphery of a wheel, or a piece of paper or a rag is wound around a roller, to correct a seemingly imperceptible deficiency of the kind. In reply to some remark of mine, in reference to this great exactness required, the operator philosophically observed, "We can't do anything unless all parts of the machine *draw together*."

In most fine-writing mills, loftmen next transferred the paper from the machine to upper story "drying lofts," where it was hung on poles to dry.[19]

In a final series of operations, workers finished, cut, and inspected the paper. Like rag rooms, finishing departments contained a predominantly female work force that manufacturers sought to reduce through the installation of labor-saving machinery. In 1876, a Whiting Paper Company workman invented an automatic self-feeder, which, when applied to a calender machine, allowed one woman to watch several calenders. In the same year a local mill experimented with a folding and cutting machine that, it was claimed, did the work of five women. These innovations did not totally eliminate the need for experienced female paper workers. Calender operation still required skill and judgment, and paper sorters, who performed an important quality-control function in fine-writing mills, were largely unaffected by the introduction of new machinery. Nor was the skilled work force in the engine and machine rooms entirely immune to technical innovation. The development of larger machines, running at increased speeds, affected workers in both departments. Yet the differential impact of these innovations is worth noting: Where new machinery eliminated rag- and finishing-department positions, the employment of larger and faster paper machines made the tender's job more difficult and provided the rationale for a shorter-hours movement among machine and engine room workers.[20]

ALTHOUGH the organization of the work process was a major determinant of the social relations of production in Holyoke mills, their place in the work force was not the only criterion wage earners used to

define themselves within local industries. Ethnicity was also important. Between 1865 and 1890, Holyoke regularly had a higher percentage of foreign born in its total population than any other city in the
state; only Fall River occasionally eclipsed it. On its streets and in its
factories, men and women from Ireland, Great Britain, Canada, and
Germany lived and toiled together. In leaving the lands of their birth,
they took with them distinctive cultures that they did not willingly
surrender here. Once in Holyoke, each ethnic group staked out its
own territory and attempted to preserve its cultural heritage, while
adapting to the strange ways of a new homeland.[21]

Before 1880, the Irish comprised the largest immigrant group in
Holyoke. In Ireland during the early nineteenth century, persistently
deteriorating conditions reached a fateful climax in the mid-forties,
when the potato rot triggered an horrific famine. Arriving shortly
before mid-century, the first Irish to appear in Holyoke came from the
famine ravaged southwestern counties and quickly took jobs as laborers on construction of the dam; they also dug the canals of the Hadley
Falls Company and helped build the city's first mills. Some later entered the mills in hopes of establishing a more stable existence than
the life of a casual laborer permitted. Many women and children also
filed into factories in order to do their part to support often precarious
family economies. Mere survival thus became the first goal of the
town's earliest Irish settlers. But amid much death they did survive
and amid an even greater degree of transiency they stayed in Holyoke. As early as 1855, the Irish constituted more than one-third of
the town's population.

The second largest immigrant group in Holyoke was the French
Canadians. Between 1784 and 1844, the population of French Canada
increased more than 400 percent, without a commensurate expansion
of available agricultural lands. This in itself placed tremendous pressure on those who wished to maintain the family farm as the basic
unit of production. But there were other problems as well. A reluctance to adopt modern farm techniques led, after 1824, to declining
harvests, and during the 1830s and 1840s a severe agricultural depression struck the region. At the same time, the area's underdeveloped
industrial sector offered little in the way of alternative employment.
Survival ultimately compelled movement, and in the last four decades
of the nineteenth century more than 300,000 French Canadians left for
New England.[22]

Throughout the latter part of the nineteenth century, the city's two

major industries constituted separate, if overlapping, labor markets for the Irish and French Canadians. In 1880, the Irish formed 38 percent of the paper work force. By contrast, barely more than one in ten paper workers were French Canadians. In textiles, on the other hand, French Canadians comprised 43 percent of the work force, while only 17 percent of textile workers were Irish. French Canadian predominance in textiles was not simply numerical. By 1900, it extended to all departments and skill levels within local mills (see table 2.1). Irish textile workers initially resisted French Canadian incursions, sometimes with violence. But the greater access of Irish workers to jobs in the local paper industry mitigated, without eliminating, tensions between the two groups. The higher wages paid at paper mills doubtlessly drew at least as many Irish out of the textile work force as the French Canadian influx forced out (see table 2.2).[23]

Great Britain and Germany furnished smaller, but important, additions to the Holyoke working class. In 1880, 5 percent of the populace hailed from England and Scotland. Most worked in cotton, woolen, and paper mills. Possessing much the same cultural heritage as native born workers, they mixed freely together. Their relations with the city's other ethnic groups, while not amicable, lacked the enmity that separated Irish and French Canadians. Frequently more skilled than Irish workers, French Canadian immigrants did not pose as grave a threat to their livelihood as they did to that of Irish wage earners. Holyoke's German community was even smaller than that from Great Britain, in 1880 comprising little more than 2 percent of the total population. Most worked at the Germania Woolen Mills in South Holyoke, where they established a culturally distinct neighborhood that set them apart from the city's other ethnic groups.[24]

THROUGH the eighties class harmony was the principal characteristic of social relations within Holyoke's two main industries. A mixture of paternalism, ethnic conflict, and craft exclusiveness diffused any sustained movement toward united class action. At times workers exhibited a greater readiness to attack each other than to confront the bosses. Yet amid this quiescence there existed ample cause for dissent. Why these hardships did not spark greater resistance is the main focus of the remainder of this chapter. For these early inhibitions persisted in attenuated form and remained a deterrent to class development.

Any investigation of the social relations of production must include some mention of what day-to-day operations looked like from the top. In textiles, the treasurer stood at the apex of a mill's operating hierarchy. Besides overseeing all financial matters, his main duties included buying cotton and, together with the selling agent, determining the specifications of cloth output. Although treasurers often intervened in daily mill operations, the agent or superintendent had primary responsibility for production. Each day this official attended to a host of production-related concerns. The 1873 notebook of one local agent contained formulas for determining horsepower, the weight of goods, and the amount of power required to drive various types of spindles, looms, and cards in addition to price lists for different weaving cuts. The notebook also contained model forms for affidavits and invoices, as agents inspected incoming cotton shipments and frequently sought appointment as justice of the peace so that they could sign claims against poor cotton.[25]

Despite the overlap in their activities, treasurers and superintendents viewed the industry from much different perspectives. Where treasurers saw it as part of a broader system of political economy, superintendents believed that the technical side of production was "the life and the success of manufacturing." This difference of outlook was evident in the trade associations that each group established. The principal organization of the region's agents and superintendents was the New England Cotton Manufacturers Association, founded in 1865 by Jones S. Davis, then agent at the Lyman Mills. The organization functioned chiefly as a clearinghouse through which these officials exchanged information on the latest technological developments. Although treasurers were allowed to join after 1867, they were never really at home in the organization. In fact, the only attempt to change the association's focus came in the nineties when a group of treasurers unsuccessfully sought to add political and economic questions to its agenda. Thus, dissatisfied with the New England Cotton Manufacturers Association, the treasurers in 1880 formed their own organization, Boston's Arkwright Club. The club's initial purpose was to lobby against labor legislation in the General Court, but it soon expanded its concerns. With declining demand and falling prices during the crisis of the eighties, the club attempted to enforce a production-curtailment program. It never took hold, but the treasurers did manage to effect a number of short-term, price-fixing agreements at the club's monthly luncheons. Before the nineties, treasurers found these unstable ac-

TABLE 2.1   Textile and Paper Work Force, 1900

Industry	Irish		French Canadian	
TEXTILES				
carding	M	F	M	F
picker	2	2	4	3
carder	26	39	33	32
speeder	1	4	1	4
twister	6	29	8	33
drawer	1	16	1	4
	36	81	47	74
SPINNING	M	F	M	F
	36	77	153	205
DRESSING	M	F	M	F
winder	7	190	3	85
spooler	8	64	21	183
warper	3	11	2	32
beamer	17	1	1	0
reeler	1	17	2	3
	36	283	29	303
WEAVING	M	F	M	F
	45	152	298	326
FINISHING	M	F	M	F
dyer	53	0	5	0
packer	1	11	3	3
	54	11	8	3
SKILLED	M	F	M	F
loom fixer	13	0	33	0
mule spinner	6	0	32	0
dresser	18	3	6	0
	37	3	71	0

TABLE 2.1   Textile and Paper Work Force, 1900 *(continued)*

Industry	*Irish*		*French Canadian*	
PAPER				
PREPARATORY	M	F	M	F
rag cutter, duster, and sorter	27	476	5	15
washer	8	0	2	0
sizer	4	0	0	0
	37	476	7	15
SKILLED	M	F	M	F
beater engineer	35	0	3	0
machine tender	56	0	8	0
papermaker	132	0	26	0
millwright	3	0	37	0
	226	0	37	0
FINISHING	M	F	M	F
finisher	70	105	30	9
calenderer	57	66	8	7
loftman	19	0	7	0
plater	2	31	1	4
cutter	19	74	14	9
ruler	14	12	2	2
counter	4	39	3	10
others	15	7	9	1
	200	334	74	42

Note: Data for the tables are from the manuscript population schedules of the 1900 census and include native-born workers of foreign parentage. In some enumeration districts, census takers recorded only the industry in which a person worked, rather than the specific job that he or she performed. These workers are not included in the tables.

cords more than satisfactory, as most believed the industry's problems were only a temporary condition.[26]

One reason why the crises of the seventies and eighties did not rattle the basic confidence of textile manufacturers can be found in their cost-of-manufacturing reports. This monthly statement served as the prism through which treasurers and superintendents viewed the work force. It recorded the labor cost per pound and per yard of the

39

TABLE 2.2 Textile and Paper Wages, 1870–1876

Position	1870	1874	1876
LYMAN MILLS (COTTON)			
Overseer	3.50	3.50	3.50
Second hand	2.25	2.00	2.00
Picker	1.25	1.00	.90
Card stripper	1.25	1.00	.90
Grinder	1.63	1.42	1.17
Doffer	.47	.40	.28
Spooler	.72	.65	.50
Spinning section-hand	1.69	1.70	1.50
Weaver (female)	1.25	1.21	1.02
Spinner	1.05	1.01	.83
Common laborer	1.33	1.28	1.25
WHITING PAPER COMPANY			
Foreman	3.25	5.00	5.00
Overseer in rag room	2.50	2.00	
Rag sorter	1.00	1.16	1.00
Rag engineer	3.00	3.00	2.75
Rag engineer's helper	1.50	1.75	1.50
Machine tender	3.00	3.00	2.75
Back tender	1.67	1.75	1.50
Boss finisher	4.00	4.00	4.00
Finisher's helper	1.87	2.00	2.25
Loftman	2.00	2.00	1.85
Calenderer (female)	1.00	1.00	1.00
Folder (female)	1.75	1.35	1.75
Laborer	1.50	1.75	1.50
CROCKER PAPER COMPANY			
Foreman	3.50	3.50	3.50
Overseer in rag room	2.50	2.50	2.00
Rag sorter	1.25	1.25	1.00
Bleacher	1.75	1.75	1.50
Assistant bleacher	1.50	1.50	1.40
Rag engineer	2.75	2.75	2.25
Rag engineer's helper	1.50	1.50	1.25
Machine tender	3.25	3.00	2.75
Back tender	1.75	1.75	1.40

TABLE 2.2   Textile and Paper Wages, 1870–1876 *(continued)*

Position	1870	1874	1876
Boss finisher	3.00	3.00	2.50
Cutter (females)	1.25	1.25	.90
Folder	1.25	1.25	.90
Millwright	2.00	2.75	2.25
Laborer	1.50	1.50	1.40

Note: The wage schedules are taken from *Tenth Census of the United States, 1880: Statistics of Wages in Manufacturing Industries,* Vol. 20, 274, 348. All wages listed are daily wages.

four major departments (carding, spinning, dressing, and weaving) and permitted a comparison between the total labor cost and total cost of production. In the two decades following 1870, technical innovations that increased work loads and machine speeds combined with a steady downward pressure on wages to reduce labor costs in all departments. In making reductions, manufacturers tried to undercut worker discontent by acting in concert. Although superintendents were sometimes reluctant to exchange accurate wage data with rival concerns, treasurers usually took a broader view of the matter. This, coupled with the fact that cutbacks in production often accompanied wage slashes, explains why workers at a given mill did not more actively resist the cuts: they had nowhere else to turn. It does not tell us, however, why deteriorating work conditions failed to produce a city or statewide organization of textile workers. For this, we must probe more deeply into the nature of social relations within Holyoke's textile mills.[27]

In textiles, paternalism was a major feature of local labor policy. Before coming to Holyoke in 1874, William Skinner had controlled a mill village that bore his name; here paternalism was the principal motif of his approach to labor relations. During the seventies the Germania Mills and Farr Alpaca Company both instituted primitive employee-welfare programs. But it was the seemingly remote Lyman Mills and its ill-fated predecessor, the Hadley Falls Company, that perhaps best appreciated the benefits of mill paternalism. At the latter company, agent Stephen Holman maintained a regular correspondence with a number of people in England and Scotland who served him as labor recruiters. They included not only individuals employed in banks, travel agencies, and the like, but also a network of former employees. The latter assured Holman that the women whom they

recommended were both competent and of good character. In 1857, Jane Wallace wrote from Glasgow that she had recruited fifteen weavers, whom she "knew to be good girls and good weavers of fine cloth." Holman's reputation for paternalism was such that one Scottish woman wrote to ask whether he knew anything about her daughter, who had not communicated with her in more than a year.[28]

When the Lyman Mills found its Scottish operatives to be insufficiently docile, agent Jones Davis began to look elsewhere. During the late 1850s, he hired Nicholas Proulx as a labor recruiter to direct the growing stream of French Canadian emigration towards Holyoke. In addition to seeking out the most docile labor force available, Davis consciously attempted to assume a paternalistic presence in his workers' lives. Though a non-Catholic, he sometimes attended mass and contributed generously to the Catholic church, urging his workers to do likewise. At annual Christmas parties, he personally distributed gifts to workers' children and reminded them that "you must not forget your duties to each other, to your parents, or, above all else, your duty to your savior."[29]

The key figure in the day-to-day functioning of textile paternalism was the overseer. He hired workers, gave them their orders, and often ruled on their petitions for better working conditions, job transfers, and individual pay increases. Holyoke textile workers well understood the decisive role that overseers played in their work lives. Local newspapers contained frequent notices of operatives presenting gifts to foremen and overseers. Although the practice was most prevalent at the absentee-controlled cotton mills, it occurred at one time or another at most of the city's textile establishments. Occasionally overseers reciprocated. In 1873, weavers at the Hampden Mills gave departing overseer Milo Chamberlain a watch chain. Three years later, Chamberlain, then an overseer at a Rockville, Connecticut, cotton factory, obtained work at the latter mill for many of the same, now unemployed, weavers. After 1880, the practice of giving presents to overseers declined. A work-wise and less submissive second industrial generation found such acts degrading, particularly in the face of speedups and wage reductions. Before the eighties, however, mill paternalism operated with real success in diffusing discontent among the first industrial generation of Irish and French Canadian workers. Nor did the policy entirely collapse after that date, as the large wave of French Canadians who entered the mills in the late seventies were often as submissive as their more seasoned predecessors had once been. Also, by their mere

presence, this later group provided another reason for the general quiescence of textile workers during the period.[30]

For mill paternalism was only one factor accounting for the dearth of resistance among textile workers. Ethnic conflict was another. The post-1860 influx of French Canadians provided a ready pool of surplus labor and heightened ethnic tensions within the city. The massive migration of the late seventies appeared particularly threatening to textile operatives. Stories that some French Canadians had offered to work for twenty-five cents a day, coupled with the French Canadian practice of sending their children into the mills at the earliest possible age, both frightened and infuriated textile workers. In an 1879 letter to the *Transcript*, ONE OF THE WORKINGMEN wrote that "men not mechanics, going to some of the mills for work . . . are told [by management] that they can hire all of the French they want on their own terms." Many French Canadians, the writer added, "will work for 50 cents per day." Although the migration affected all wage earners, the letter indicates why the Irish felt especially threatened: they were the workers least likely to possess the skills of a "mechanic." In responding to the threat, the Irish often relied more on hard muscle than cool reason, as fights begun in textile mills carried over into the city's streets.[31]

Craft exclusiveness afforded a final reason for the absence of organization among textile operatives. This was especially true in weaving departments, where loom fixers assumed the key role in production. Their duties entailed cutting off the cloth and replacing the beam in warps that had run out, repairing broken looms, and periodically checking looms in their sections to insure that the cloth was weaving properly. They were the most skilled and indispensable workers in these departments and they knew it. Indeed, loom fixers hardly considered themselves ordinary workers. An 1899 pamphlet of the National Loom-Fixers Association listed a number of do's and don't's to guide them at their work. Heading a column of the latter was the injunction: "Don't explain to a weaver or anyone who is not a member of the union the reason why you did so and so to a loom to make it run." A desire to safeguard craft secrets was not the only matter dividing loom fixers and weavers. The pamphlet also recommended that loom fixers maintain a social distance between themselves and weavers: "Be pleasant and courteous to the help, patient and forebearing, and do your duty like men. . . . Don't be partial to one or more weavers but serve all alike, without regard to sect, creed, or

nationality." Lastly, loom fixers should not hesitate to perform the punitive role to which their superior skills presumably entitled them: "Don't hold an argument with the weaver over any part of your work, but do your duty and if they fail to do theirs report the case to the second hand or overseer." Given these attitudes on the part of loom fixers, it is scarcely remarkable that no broad-based organization of textile workers occurred. This particular manifestation of craft exclusiveness is all the more significant in that weavers comprised a major portion of the textile work force and were especially subject to manufacturers' efforts to reduce wages and intensify the work pace. At Holyoke during the seventies, they offered the most active resistance to early wage cuts. In 1874, however, such resistance as they could muster proved to be too little, too early.[32]

In failing to mount any sustained resistance to the manufacturers' attack on wages and working conditions, Holyoke textile workers were not alone. Significantly, the only city in which such a counteroffensive occurred was Fall River, where a veteran force of English operatives adamantly opposed capital's impositions. Elsewhere, employer paternalism and ethnic divisiveness obscured the meaning of capital's assault and undercut organized resistance. As undiminished competition among producers led to further impositions, textile workers would periodically combat employer efforts to stabilize the industry on their backs. But with the exception of the highly skilled mule spinners and loom fixers, Holyoke's textile work force would remain unorganized until the 1930s.[33]

AS IN TEXTILES, class harmony was the principal characteristic of social relations within the Holyoke paper industry. But here too industrial peace rested upon an uncertain economic foundation. Although paper prices soared during the war years, bringing unprecedented profits, the next few decades saw a precipitate decline, as many new mills entered the field and manufacturers installed ever larger and faster paper machines in their establishments. The better grades of paper in which Holyoke mills specialized were particularly affected. Between 1865 and 1880, the price of superfine writing paper plummeted 58 percent and machine-finished book paper dropped 53 percent. In response to this situation, manufacturers in 1873 formed the Writing Paper Makers' Association, which often met at Spring-

field and was controlled by area manufacturers. In 1878, the organization was superseded by the broader based American Paper Makers' Association.[34]

From the outset the problems of declining prices and overproduction absorbed the attention of association members. They initially proposed a number of production-curtailment agreements, but these were not always successful. As a *Paper World* correspondent noted after speaking with some of the association's most prominent members at the 1880 meeting, such conversation brought "to light everywhere, sometimes in the most unexpected quarters, a decided tendency to exert a large share of individual independence." Not surprisingly, though curtailment agreements continued to be made, manufacturers began to search elsewhere for a solution to their woes.[35]

The most popular new panacea was the export trade. Senator Warner Miller of New York told the 1881 meeting that "south of us are the great non-manufacturing countries . . . [and] their trade should be ours and our government should see to developing it at once." In 1883, the association's export committee called upon the government to establish foreign depots, while individual members later recommended strengthening the navy and called for government subsidization of steam transport. But the campaign was no more successful than the various curtailment programs. Although paper exports rose steadily during the seventies, they peaked in 1881 at $1,048,976; a decade later they stood at only $1,226,686 and that figure comfortably eclipsed those of any of the intervening years. The association's 1884 meeting concluded that cooperative efforts to boost exports had failed and recommended the pursuit of individual initiatives.[36]

As successive production-curtailment programs proved inadequate and hopes for increased exports failed to materialize, manufacturers protected profit margins in the only other way they knew how: by slashing wages, first during the mid-seventies and again in 1884. The latter reduction brought a heated reaction from local paper workers, who asked what had happened to the increased profits created by the introduction of the Coburn rag cutter and other labor-saving devices. The manufacturers' declaration that a wage reduction was preferable to half-production because the latter would decrease pay even further and place workers in "the undesirable state of being idle one-half of the time" met with a cold response. PAPER MAKER felt that he spoke for most his fellow workers when he stated that he "would prefer to work four days for six dollars, [rather] than six days for the same

amount." Yet, the manufacturers refused to rescind the reduction and little more was heard of the matter. That 1884 was a depression year partially explains worker reluctance to resist the cut more actively. Equally important was the fact that divisions within the work force inhibited any concerted response to a general wage reduction.[37]

Although craft exclusiveness formed the basic line of demarcation separating beater engineers and machine tenders from semiskilled rag- and finishing-department workers, differences in wages, hours, and relations with the owners reinforced the division. Rag- and finishing-department workers put in a sixty-hour week at wages that ranged from 30 to 60 percent of what engineers and tenders received. With the exception of a partially successful 1882 loftmen's strike, job actions for higher wages led to the summary dismissal of the strikers. This was in stark contrast to the cautious, even sympathetic manner in which manufacturers responded to the grievances of skilled workers. An 1888 speech before the American Paper Makers' Association by Warner Miller, a U.S. senator and paper manufacturer from New York, highlighted the difference. "It is the almost universal rule of the paper industry," Miller stated, "that proprietors prefer that their skilled men should be owners of their homes. This is the key to the situation. In the concern that I am connected with we almost require the skilled married men at least, to own their homes." Where necessary, Miller continued, manufacturers furnished down payments that would subsequently be repaid in monthly installments. There is no evidence that Holyoke millowners followed this practice, but the statement does reflect the careful attention they gave their skilled workers on other matters.[38]

The major grievance of beater engineers and machine tenders concerned the long hours they had to work. Because it took from two to five hours to prepare stock for production once it became cold, paper manufacturers kept their machinery in continuous operation, twenty-four hours a day, six days a week, and required engineers and tenders to work twelve-hour daily "tours," which they reasoned was not very tiresome as the workers had only to watch the machinery. The tour workers felt otherwise. In 1884, a group of beater engineers and machine tenders organized Eagle Lodge and began a movement for shorter hours that drew on a broadly conceived social and economic rationale. By closing the mills from six P.M. Saturday to seven A.M. Monday, an 1886 petition contended, tour workers would be able to spend the Sabbath with their families in a proper manner. "If instead

of sending missionaries to Africa," one worker declared, "they were sent to the manufacturers of Holyoke, this matter of a little leisure for the men who work hard might be helped." The tour workers also maintained that the introduction of larger engines that were more difficult to manipulate, and the employment of a broader variety of stock required the almost uninterrupted attention of beater engineers during a given tour; and in machine rooms, the installation of larger and faster paper machines, producing a more diverse range of papers, had appreciably increased the physical and mental strain on machine tenders. Lastly, they argued, shorter hours would reduce production and raise prices.[39]

The initial response of many manufacturers differed considerably from the manner in which they treated the wage demands of semi-skilled workers. Orrick Greenleaf stated that the petition had his sympathy, "for he [had been] a working man himself once." "The paper industry has been singularly fortunate in its freedom from labor troubles," another manufacturer declared, "Let us keep it so. In our mills the help have always been loyal to us, and we mean to keep them loyal. It is truer economy for us to keep our help loyal than to make petty savings in wages and working hours and make our men dissatisfied." William Whiting congratulated the tour workers on the "firm yet orderly and respectable way in which the matter of short hours has been agitated. There was a laudable lack of that braggadocio which is so common in connection with such movements." The language used by these manufacturers—"firm yet orderly" manner and references to having once been a "working man"—is important. Judith McGaw has observed that a bond of "shared masculinity" acted to defuse workplace tensions and deter collective action in many nineteenth-century paper mills. It was only now that beater engineers and machine tenders were beginning to discover the limitations of such bonds. For with the exception of William Whiting and James H. Newton, few manufacturers reduced hours before August 1887, when the tour workers threatened to affiliate with the Knights of Labor; and within a short while thereafter most had returned to a seventy-two-hour week.[40]

The failure of the shorter-hours movement marked a turning point in labor-capital relations within the paper industry. Where most tour workers had previously believed that the indispensability of their skills and a shared ethic of manliness insured fair treatment from employers, they now recognized that industrial justice required some

measure of struggle. As one paper worker declared during the midst
of the 1887 petition campaign:

> Tour workers can have their wrongs reduced by becoming organized and
> raising a gigantic fund; we then and not until then can compel manufactur-
> ers to give us our rights. They at present take advantage of our unorga-
> nized condition, and while we remain so we may expect injustice meted
> out to us[;] . . . organized we are an irresistble power.

By the 1890s, organization was an accomplished fact and the only
remaining question was what shape it would take in future years: To
be specific, could machine tenders and beater engineers rise above a
deeply inbred sense of craft exclusiveness and include less skilled
workers within their ranks? As we shall see, they could. But in so
doing, a conviction that their craft knowledge set them apart from
other wage earners remained an integral feature of tour-worker consciousness. And if shared notions of gender no longer provided a
common bond with owners, these workers still embraced a masculine
ethos that would complicate their relations with women operatives in
other departments.[41]

In closing, it should be noted that the world of the Holyoke working class embraced more than the workplace. Outside local mills, the
family, church, benevolent society, saloon, and other institutions enriched working-class life, providing a host of experiences that shaped
the kind of person one became. Within such institutions workers
defined themselves and created a number of distinct cultural worlds.
The next chapter examines these developments within Holyoke's
Irish enclave.

3

IRISH HOLYOKE

THE IRISH immigrants who built the Holyoke dam, dug the city's canals, and later worked in local mills knew they had little in common with those who purchased their labor. In their efforts to understand their new environment, comparisons between Yankee capitalists and British landlords must have sprung readily to mind. Indeed, a willful refusal to recognize reality would have been necessary to avoid making such comparisons, and these were people with few illusions. As veterans of the Great Famine, the mere fact of their survival indicated a remarkable capacity to comprehend and engage reality. Yet, despite their awareness of the vast gulf that separated them from bourgeois Holyoke, it would be inaccurate to view these workers as a class-conscious proletariat. In a very profound sense, they were Catholics and sons and daughters of Ireland as well as workers. In their world-view, class interest conjoined with ethnic pride and religious commitment to form what can best be described as an enclave consciousness: a consciousness that, as John Bodnar has written, stemmed from "a common experience that fostered community—rather than class-based behavior." This chapter examines the formation and evolution of that community-based consciousness in Holyoke's Irish enclave.[1]

In January 1848, Irish laborers working on the Holyoke dam laid down their hods and walked off the job to protest a five-cent reduction in their already meager daily wage. As the threat of violence loomed, local authorities summoned a militia company from Northampton to break the strike. Tensions remained high, however, until a Springfield priest appeared and counseled the laborers to return to work. For both chronological and thematic reasons, it is a fitting incident with which to begin our examination of Irish Holyoke.

Catholic priests played a vital role in the development of the city's Irish enclave.[2]

According to recent research, many mid-century Irish immigrants had not been to mass or taken the sacraments for years and only became closely affiliated with the Catholic church after arriving in this country. It is not possible now to determine the spiritual state of Holyoke's first Irish immigrants, but if a significant number had drifted away from their religion, the city's first Catholic pastor, Father Jeremiah O'Callaghan, was just the priest to reclaim them. After nearly a quarter of a century at Burlington, Vermont, O'Callaghan came to Holyoke in 1854 and established St. Jerome's parish. Born in county Cork in 1780, he spoke fluent Gaelic and often delivered sermons and heard confessions in that language. An unpretentious man, Father O'Callaghan mixed freely with his parishioners and, despite the financial needs of a struggling young parish, he adamantly refused to charge pew rents or employ other means of extracting from his congregation more than it would willingly contribute. He also posed as a feisty and articulate defender of the church and, by extension, the entire Irish community.[3]

In the winter of 1857, Father O'Callaghan attacked the practice of bible reading in the public schools. In response, a *Mirror* editorial set the tone of the subsequent debate by characterizing O'Callaghan's criticisms as a "foolish and pitiable spurt of Catholic bigotry." A further claim by the local Presbyterian minister that Catholic priests exploited the poor and used the confessional for proposes of extortion placed the exchange on an entirely new level and allowed O'Callaghan the necessary topical breadth for the full employment of his forensic powers. "The cap he has prepared for me," O'Callaghan retorted, "fits his own head." "For if report be true," he explained, "pew selling with all its abominations—regard for the rich, contempt for the poor, *respect of persons*, are practiced without disguise in his meeting house; and he would not accept his office, nor even open his lips, before the society had guaranteed him a fat salary." Where Catholic priests attended the sick and administered the sacraments, Protestant ministers apparently had no greater duties than to lounge around all week reading newspapers and concocting "foul and filthy slanders." Now fully warmed to his subject, O'Callaghan added that Protestantism's shortcomings extended beyond its contempt for the poor and the craven behavior of its clergy. The true measure of its moral vacuity could be found in its endorsement of usury, a matter of no

small concern to O'Callaghan, who reportedly refused absolution to money lenders and had once been suspended from his clerical office for his outspoken views on the subject. In concluding, he observed that the "laboring classes" were fast becoming the "slaves and serfs of rag money makers" and called for the formation of a popular movement that would "concentrate upon one issue—NO BANKS."[4]

Father Jeremiah O'Callaghan was one of those maverick priests who have forever been the bane of a conservative Catholic hierarchy. His social critique clearly drew upon the antibank ferment of the Jacksonian era, but had equally deep roots in Irish anti-landlordism. Addressing a congregation that had only recently escaped the oppression of British landowners, his manifest piety, concern for the poor, and attacks on privilege engendered intense loyalty among his parishioners. When an 1860 *Mirror* article erroneously reported that he had returned to Ireland, a member of his congregation notified the paper that as much as some "*higher* church dignitaries" desired his departure, he was still in Holyoke: "true to duty—true to his convictions of right—true to the poor and unfortunate and true to his God." O'Callaghan passed away a few months later, but even in death he remained a source of contention. JUSTITIAE corrected the *Mirror*'s report that the bishop of Boston had attended O'Callaghan's funeral: "The Bishop is a man who takes more pleasure in visiting the living than the dead; and the better persons live the more he is inclined to call upon them." JUSTITIAE also complained that Father O'Callaghan's successor had not honored his last wish: "that his bones find a resting place in that church which he erected, and presented *free* to his people, but which alas! is *free* no longer."[5]

O'Callaghan's successors belonged to a generation of Catholic clergymen aptly called "brick and mortar priests," who often evinced as great a concern with temporal matters as the priest's traditional duties of visiting the sick and hearing confessions. Neither pew rents, nor money lenders ever elicited their scorn. This complicates any assessment of Father O'Callaghan's impact on Holyoke's Irish Catholics. Their later attraction to greenbackism may have been influenced by his social teachings. Nearly two decades after his death, Irish America's most outspoken greenbacker, Patrick Ford, reminded a local correspondent to the *Irish World* that he had promised to send Ford a copy of "that book [on usury] written by Father Jerry O'Callaghan." More important than any of his specific prescriptions, though, was O'Callaghan's rejection of Catholicism's static, neo-feudal view of

society as a place where the church mediated between the benevolent rich and the hard-working poor, teaching each its rights and duties: the poor that this was a world of wearisome toil, where poverty and suffering were all part of God's design, before which one could only submit with resignation; and the rich that they held their wealth in trust, and were enjoined by God to expend it in a socially beneficial manner. His forthright encouragement of social change made it difficult for any of his successors to counsel social resignation without evoking the contempt of their parishioners.[6]

O'Callaghan's most prominent successor was Father Patrick J. Harkins, who served as pastor at St. Jerome's nearly half a century until his death in 1910. A "brick and mortar" priest of the first order, Harkins had no sooner arrived at St. Jerome's than he began efforts to place Holyoke Catholicism, and with it the city's Irish enclave, on a solid institutional basis. At the same time, he became the foremost proponent of a culture of respectability within the enclave. Avoiding Father O'Callaghan's confrontational approach to the larger society, Harkins located his adversaries among his fellow countrymen: in the world of saloon culture and a lingering Irish sectionalism that manifested itself in faction fights pitting "Kerrymen" against "Corkonians." As late as 1900, he could be heard denouncing local comedians who parodied the Irishman as a "coarse, drinking, fighting buffoon," thus perpetuating stereotypes that Harkins spent much of his life trying to eradicate. Yet, despite the actions of Harkins and others, saloon culture would remain an integral part of Irish Holyoke. And to obtain a full understanding of the culture of enclave respectability, we need first to take a closer look at the world of local saloonists.[7]

SALOON CULTURE emerged as a separate working-class culture during the course of the industrial revolution. In the preindustrial world, work and leisure were inextricably mixed. Periods of conviviality, during which masters often joined their workmen in a few bowls of rum or some equally heady brew, punctuated each day's work. Workers regularly observed "St. Monday," beginning a weekend's revelry on Saturday afternoon and not commencing work again until Monday afternoon. Election Day and fire and militia musters were holidays marked by gambling, drinking, and quite often a few fights.[8]

The spread of industrial production changed all this. The capitalists who spearheaded the industrial revolution demanded a more disciplined work force. Apprentices now received temperance medals rather than lessons in how to drink. Schools and evangelical churches inculcated a new industrial morality that stressed hard work, temperance, and self-discipline. Intensified competition forced an increasing proportion of employers to require such behavior of their workers. Those that did not risked falling into the growing army of wage labor. Yet not all workers conformed to the new industrial morality. Some persisted in following the more casual life-styles of the previous era. As capitalist production first divided traditional crafts and then obliterated them altogether through the development of machinery, these men often refused to enter the new factories and sought casual labor in the interstices of the emergent industrial economy. At mid-century in Holyoke, those immigrants who had only recently left the preindustrial southwestern counties of Ireland comprised the group most resistant to the new industrial morality.

The laborers who built the dam and dug canals formed the backbone of saloon culture within the early Irish community. But as the initial wave of construction abated, many of those who did not move on sought work at the city's mills, where they encountered the new industrial morality. Beginning at 4:40 A.M., a succession of bells punctuated the work day, telling workers when to get up, when to eat, and when they could return home in the evening. Not all mill operatives immediately internalized the new morality. In 1881, one South Holyoke mill discharged eight workers when they failed to appear the day following payday. But it was not among factory operatives that saloon culture flourished. The dangers alone of such work made clearheadedness imperative. Rather, the culture's most dedicated supporters tended to be those who continued a more casual occupational existence. As late as 1897, the *Transcript* complained of laborers who chose to work irregularly for the city at two dollars a day rather than enter the mills where they could obtain an assured weekly wage of between $7.50 and $10. These men simply would not accept the disciplined routine of factory work. They remained a small but regular part of the working class, and their lives revolved around the saloon.[9]

The dominant faction within the Democratic party also centered its activities on the saloon. Characterized by the *Transcript* as "rumsellers who never did an honest day's work," but sought the votes of local

workingmen, these politicians assiduously courted the laborers. During the closing decades of the nineteenth century, the wage scale of municipal laborers became one of the most heated issues in local politics. Democratic aldermen regularly fixed the scale above the local market rate for that grade of labor, a policy that enraged local capitalists, who saw it as a violation of one of life's verities: To ignore the dictates of the market, they argued, invited catastrophe. But the practice continued and in return for this aid, laborers became the shock troops of the Democratic machine. They yelled the loudest at party rallies and on Election Day worked to get out the vote. As a supplement to this more routine work, they occasionally showered stones and mudballs on a Republican parade.[10]

Successive waves of young, unmarried workers joined laborers as the mainstays of saloon culture. Although no one was fated to enter this cultural world, the city's truants passed through a fitting apprenticeship. Holyoke school authorities considered truancy a major problem. In some cases, parents abetted truant children. One woman boasted that her children had not attended school in two years and that no one could make them go. Yet, by the mid-seventies when this statement was reported, such declarations represented a minority opinion. Only a few months later the *Transcript* insisted that "all classes of parents" actively assisted the truant officer, "even those who at first were strongly opposed to him." The truants themselves were seldom as accommodating. In one 1877 incident, a group of boys stationed a safe distance behind the official could be heard "reviling him with insulting words." A decade later, after the courts had decided that a truant officer could not arrest a boy without first obtaining a warrant, a group of eighty-five "incorrigible and defiant truants" regularly assailed officials investigating their neighborhood with "derisive and defiant talk."[11]

School authorities offered a number of explanations for the prevalence of truancy: child labor, parental neglect, and the group life of the youths themselves. The 1890 school committee blamed the "older boys, fifteen and sixteen years old, that neither work nor attend school, 'only the school of idleness and vice,' [and who] entice the younger ones away and encourage them to play truant and commit depradations upon property, or else train them to a life of idleness." In its indictment the report reflected a growing late nineteenth-century concern with the activities of youth gangs. In 1900, the Holyoke Sunday correspondent of the *Springfield Republican*

observed that gangs had recently become more organized, establishing their own clubhouses. "The roaming of 'de gang' haphazard about the streets was bad enough," he wrote, "but the selecting of a rendezvouz where matters could be deliberately planned, was a step in advance of the haphazard method of mischief." The observation revealed more than middle-class fears. Gang membership constituted an important part of growing up for many working class youths.[12]

By the 1880s, if not earlier, gangs had become an established fixture in the lives of young people from the city's lower wards. In that decade, they exhibited a clear ethnic basis, as rival groups of Irish and French Canadians regularly beat each other senseless. At times gangs seemed to recognize that their activities stemmed from a culture of their own making, and they did not lightly accept or tolerate outside interference. In 1889, when three newspapermen attempted to stop a rock-throwing battle between rival gangs of Irish and French Canadians, "they no sooner interfered than they were made the object of the vengeance of both sides."[13]

Moving from the streets, poolrooms, and back-alley clubhouses of the city, gangs later reconstituted themselves within saloons. In the process, they acquired new pursuits. Drinking was the most obvious of these, and one's capacity for drink became a further test of the young worker's manhood. In 1883, one saloon staged a competition to determine which of its regulars could consume the most within the shortest amount of time. As a prize, the young man who won the contest received a leather medal with a star in the center, surrounded by the words, "For the biggest drunk in Holyoke." At these events, saloon regulars laughed at themselves and the shocked reaction of the dominant culture.[14]

In embracing drink as a new activity, gangs did not forsake their former pursuits. Gambling and fighting were also integral parts of saloon culture. Here exotic competitions like cock fighting supplemented more customary games of chance. With the rise of organized boxing matches, one could vicariously indulge in a favorite pastime, while making a bet on the side. Local boxers like John Scully, whose great dream in life was to go "bare knuckles to a finish, for a purse of $25 or $50 a side" with a South Hadley Falls slugger named Hickey, could find ready support in the city's saloons. Some did not confine their martial enthusiasm to witnessing staged contests.[15]

Saloon culture contained a host of colorful, if not very pleasant,

characters like "Shack Nasty" Jim Sullivan. One day at the circus Jim knocked down three men and chased any number of women around, until one of the circus employees stopped him—"with a blow from a sledge-hammer of a fist." The Irish did not have a monopoly on such desperadoes. Fred Barney, "the fighting Frenchman," almost killed Eugene Sullivan in one saloon brawl. Barney received four months in the county jail for the assault, but it did not deter him from nearly chewing off the ear of one of his countrymen in a subsequent encounter.[16]

Within the world of saloon culture, work-related tensions erupted into open violence. In one incident, a local contractor hired a group of French Canadian strikebreakers to replace thirty Irish laborers seeking a pay increase. Before the French Canadians could begin work, however, the Irish laborers, who had awaited their arrival in ambush, assaulted them with a barrage of rocks. At the city's mills, numerous disputes between Irish and French Canadians were later settled in the streets. And where the Irish had once attempted to protect their neighborhoods from the arbitrary intrusions of Yankee policemen, French Canadians later sought similar self-protection against a predominantly Irish police force. One evening in 1890, Officer Ryan manhandled a disorderly French Canadian youth who had dilatorily responded to Ryan's order that he go home. The young man's friends, who had initially departed, soon returned with reinforcements and attacked Ryan. But before they could disable him, another Irish policeman happened upon the scene and together with Ryan clubbed the crowd into submission.[17]

Although primarily a man's world, some women also made their mark in saloon culture. Catherine Moran managed a small drinking establishment on the Patch and actively participated in the brawls that took place there, on one occasion splitting a policeman's nose with a teapot. In 1879, a visiting fourteen-year-old girl from Westfield, who obviously did not know Catherine Moran, refused to move when Moran ordered her from the steps of a tenement where she had been sitting. Incensed by the girl's temerity, Moran threw her into the street and then beat her "black and blue" with a broomstick. Occasionally an unseasoned youth failed to recognize that not all Holyoke women closely observed the prescribed rules of female decorum. On a Sunday evening in 1882, one such young man recklessly thrust himself against all the young women who passed him on the sidewalk. To his regret, he tried it once too often. The last woman whom

he insulted that evening struck him with a solid blow "straight from the shoulder," dropping him where he stood.[18]

For all its rowdiness, saloon culture held a certain appeal for many workers, if only as a brief escape from life's burdens and worries. But the escape could be no more than brief. Otherwise, the culture's activities conflicted too sharply with other responsibilities, the main one being the duty workers had to their families. Many of those who remained habituated to saloon culture became a reproach to their class. Frequent newspaper articles about wife beating, desertion, and nonsupport reflected more than the middle-class biases and fears of their authors; they also spoke of a serious problem that plagued working-class life and was as much a source of fear to the majority of workers who sought some form of respectability as it was to the middle-class journalists who reported it and the women and children who were its victims. One could always jest about the other excesses of saloon culture, but when it impinged upon family life, it became subject to attack from the whole community—workers as well as middle-class reformers. In the end, the young worker who wished to establish a family of his own had to leave the saloon and the old gang behind. Even where workers did not totally sever these connections—and many did not—the break was real nevertheless. Henceforth, the emotional focus of their lives lay elsewhere.

In its own negative way, saloon culture represented the purest and most enduring expression of enclave consciousness. Nowhere else in Holyoke did ethnicity mean so much for so long. For much the same reason, however, saloon culture would contribute little to class development among local workers. Arguably, its partisans did possess an incipient sense of class consciousness that made them resistant to upper- and middle-class intrusions into their world. But this consciousness remained stillborn. It was a consciousness that was acutely aware of the differences, but obtuse to the commonalities between it and other groups; the road to class cohesion was not paved with the stones and brickbats of intra-class ethnic violence. As the unquestioning foot soldiers of a Democratic machine more interested in the self-aggrandizement of its leaders than ameliorating the abysmal social conditions of working-class life, the culture's adherents contributed even less in the political sphere. Finally, in its threat to the family, saloon culture threatened the very existence of the working class. It was this last perception that drove many workers to seek some cultural alternative upon which to base their lives. And it was to these

workers that Father Harkins appealed in his efforts to forge a culture of enclave respectability.[19]

THE CULTURE of enclave respectability did not emerge full-blown at a specific point in time, but evolved over a period of years. Although famine immigrants did not as a rule come from the most depressed and dependent rungs of Irish society, they were, as Kerby Miller observed, "generally poorer, less skilled, and more in need of charity than their predecessors." Compared with earlier immigrants, they were more likely to embrace a tradition-bound worldview that devalued individual initiative and encouraged a passive acceptance of existing conditions. Not surprisingly, the world of saloon culture, with its intense parochialism and contempt for industrial morality, had a strong appeal to these people. Yet, as Miller further notes, for many it was not enough. Growing "desires for greater security or stature also necessitated some participation in either specifically ethnic or Irish-dominated *national* institutions."[20]

One was the Catholic church. At Holyoke, priests played an indispensable role in the creation of the culture of enclave respectability. Formative steps involved placing the enclave on a firm institutional foundation, and during the first decade alone of his long pastorate Father Harkins amply demonstrated why many referred to him as "the builder": In 1867, he secured land for a cemetery; the following year he built a convent and school; and he later acquired land for a school and church at South Hadley Falls and Holyoke's Sacred Heart Parish. With each building campaign, Harkins compiled and published a "Roll of Honor," listing those who contributed and the amount each gave to the subscription fund. Despite its coercive features, which some duly resented, the "Roll of Honor" served to bind the Irish community together in activities that functioned as important statements of group respectability. As Father Stephen Byrne observed in his immigrant guidebook, the appearance of good churches bespoke "a thrifty and prosperous Catholic people"; wretched church structures, on the other hand, indicated "a people given up to drunkenness and other degrading vices."[21]

The connection between church building and group respectability was drawn even more forcefully by John Maguire, an Irish M.P. and nationalist, whose *Irish in America* combined description and prescrip-

tion in a work that was both a guidebook for new immigrants and a celebratory account of Irish social progress in North America. "To the stranger entering the harbor [at Prince Edward's Island]," Maguire remarked in a typical observation, "the most striking object is a well-built church, with lofty spires surmounted by a gilded cross." Later conversation with one of the islanders revealed that the church's parishioners fully shared Maguire's appreciation of the structure:

> Peter gloried in the site, at once beautiful and commanding—in the solid, well-made bricks, and the manner in which they were laid—in the buttresses, which he patted with a caressing hand, as if he were encouraging them to do their duty faithfully; but, above all, in the steeple, which could be seen far and wide.

One indicator of the importance Irish enclavists attached to church structures was the local correspondence section of the *Irish World*, which was regularly filled with news of recently constructed churches, schools, rectories, and social halls. In 1871, as the residence of Springfield's newly appointed bishop neared completion, a local correspondent declared it "a magnificent structure [that] cannot fail to promote the interest" of Catholicism in the new diocese. And when Holyoke's St. Jerome's Temperance Society dedicated its social hall a few years later, *Irish World* readers learned that the ceremony included addresses by Mayor Parsons and other local notables.[22]

Of his many building projects, Father Harkins greatest interest was in school construction. Schools would not only introduce Catholic youths to the mysteries of their faith, but also inculcate respectable forms of behavior. Harkins saw such institutions as one of his most potent weapons in what became a lifelong personal war against saloon culture. By 1880, parochial school students constituted 35 percent of Holyoke's total school population, a figure that rose to 40 percent a decade later.[23]

The primary mission of parochial schools was to introduce children to Catholic doctrine. Instruction in the workings of the sacramental system was especially important, as it not only formed the core of church practice and justified the priest's role, but also served as a means of social discipline. The keystone in the arch of sacramental discipline was the practice of confession. What must be understood about the sacrament of penance is that it was not, at least so far as the church was concerned, a mere shame mechanism, allowing penitents

through a few moments mortification to externalize their sins so that they could cheerfully sin again. Public-school textbooks sometimes portrayed the sacrament in that manner:

> As for old Phelim Maghee, he was of no particular religion. When Phelim had laid up a good stock of sins, he now and then went over to Killarney, of a Sabbath morning, and got relaaf by confissing them out o' the way, as he used to express it, and sealed his soul up with a wafer, and returned quite invigorated for the perpetration of new offenses.

The passage presents more than just another reason for Catholic antipathy to public education. It also touches upon a deep concern of Catholic educators. Because confession could easily degenerate into a routinized device for sin disposal, the church emphasized that the remission of sins had to be accompanied by a conviction, on the part of penitents, that they would not sin again. If confession was to function as an effective disciplinary agent, Catholics had to be made to feel uneasy with sin and to understand that absolution required a continual searching of one's soul, an ongoing interior battle with the forces of evil; and that penance, as a Springfield priest declared in an 1882 sermon, necessitated submission to "the divine demand for a contrition of the mind and heart in cooperation with active corporal effort." To inculcate Catholic youths with this understanding demanded careful catechistical work by dedicated teachers.[24]

It is not easy to assess the actual impact of Catholic schooling. On one occasion Father Harkins maintained that parochial school students were clearly more obedient than their public school counterparts. But his regular denunciations of youth excesses and active support of a 1900 curfew law suggest that even he sometimes had his doubts. In large part, the parochial school's influence on youth behavior depended on the degree to which it elicited submission to the sacramental system. For obvious reasons any conclusions on this matter must be conjectural. Some youths responded to Catholic sacramentalism with cynicism and unhesitatingly rejected the church's admonitions when they conflicted with the pursuit of life's pleasures. The confessional held no terrors for these youths; it was simply irrelevant to their lives. Others deeply internalized the church's teachings and for the sake of a spotless soul sublimated worldly temptation through a disciplined regimen of work, study, and the like. The majority probably fell somewhere in between.[25]

The broader social implications of Catholic sacramentalism were equally variegated. On one hand, its frank recognition of human imperfectibility reinforced the peasant pessimism that was part of the cultural baggage of many famine immigrants. In so doing, it addressed some of the most deeply felt emotional needs of nineteenth-century Irish Americans: by offering hope and assurance to people whose lives were often too short; and by providing psychic stability in a chaotic world too often disrupted by the arbitrary shifts of an unregulated marketplace. Yet sacramentalism could also be a source of the assertive pride that distinguished enclave respectability from more tradition-bound forms of Irish culture. As the *Irish World*'s Patrick Ford in his characteristically contentious fashion explained:

> Protestants call Catholics slaves for revealing their sins to a man. What would they have us do? Imitate *their* example—cover up our sins and sing only our praises in men's ears? They don't seem to consider that a man is never a more cowardly slave then when he commits a sin and is *afraid* to acknowledge it. Catholics are not slaves. . . . There are tens of thousands who bend the knee to a priest—a weak man subject to the same passions and temptations as themselves—who would brave the lordliest despot on his throne, and shout defiance to his myrmidons![26]

Introducing youths to Catholic teachings and practices was not the only function of parochial schools. According to Catholic educators, they were also necessary to prevent social disorder and preserve the immigrant family. In 1866, the Second Plenary Council of Baltimore voiced one of the most frequently heard criticisms of public education when it warned parents of the dangers of giving their children an education that would leave them discontented with their social position. In parochial school classrooms, school readers also urged children to be satisfied with their station in life, reinforcing the message with numerous stories about the saintly resignation of the church's early martyrs. In part, these injunctions issued from a fear of social disorder. By encouraging the poor to rise out of their class, said one Catholic spokesman, the public school made "the young discontented, ashamed of their parents, and eager for show and display." Such an education, this writer continued, was "adapted to children of the middle and wealthy classes and is in no respect a suitable preparation for a life of toil." Public-school ridicule of Catholicism, others contended, further undermined the family. Any questioning of their

religion led children to lose respect for their parents and often resulted in antisocial acts, as the child's moral development depended more on the parents' character than any schooling the youth might receive.[27]

It is easy to dismiss these declarations as self-serving cant, intended to promote institutional consolidation. But they should not be ignored altogether, without recognizing that most Catholic parents were immigrants and without considering the attitude of public-school authorities toward these parents. A number of educators maintained that immigrant parents were unfit to raise their children, at least not without the aid of public schools. "With the old not much can be done," said one mid-century contributor to the *Massachusetts Teacher*, "but with the children, the great remedy is EDUCATION." In Holyoke at mid-century, school authorities regularly assigned blame for classroom disturbances to a "want of proper and salutary home restraints and discipline." An 1867 *Transcript* editorial declared that corporal punishment could not be abolished until there was "less laxity in family discipline." Within classrooms, teachers sometimes humiliated immigrant parents. In 1888, one parent wrote to the *Transcript* that a local teacher "had the ill-breeding" to expose before the whole school his misspelling of a word in a note he had written for his child. The same teacher also sent children to the school basement "because their breath smelled of onion and cabbage."[28]

Of equal significance, the construction of Catholic schools was an important expression of that group pride that lay at the heart of enclave respectability. In 1874, when attendance at Holyoke's parochial schools passed the 1,000 mark, a local correspondent informed *Irish World* readers of the accomplishment, observing that it "must be encouraging to Catholics everywhere else, when from any one locality comes word of the great progress of Catholic education." It is against this background, as well as the church's needs, that its statements concerning education must be judged. For it was within this context that immigrant parents made decisions about the respective merits of public and parochial schools.[29]

There is also reason to question whether priests like Father Harkins stressed, or even acknowledged, hierarchical declarations urging Catholics to be content with their social station. As institution builders, many such priests assumed an entrepreneurial cast of mind and recognized that prosperous parishioners facilitated their own work. Guidebooks by both clerical and lay authors further encouraged immigrants to make the most of available opportunities. The recom-

mended route to advancement, however, did not run from school-room to office. Father Stephen Byrne counseled immigrants to obtain at least a primary education, but warned that clerkships were almost invariably filled by "special acquaintances of the men in business." It would therefore be "false policy," he added, for a newcomer "to count much upon the accidental throwing up of 'situations,' when, if he has ordinary health, he can get good wages at almost any kind of manual labor." John Maguire underscored the point by denouncing that "pestilent Irish gentility" who sought wealth without work, and by paying tribute to the dignity of labor. "In America there is no disgrace in labour," Maguire declared. "It was labour that made America what she is; it is labour that will make her what she is destined to be—the mightiest power of the earth."[30]

Catholic mobility literature also contained a number of cautionary notes. "Eagerness to become suddenly rich is a sin," Father Byrne stated, "and generally it cannot be done except at the expense of our own honesty and our neighbor's property." More significant were the frequent warnings admonishing Catholics not to let their material endeavors compromise their religious commitments. In a study of nineteenth-century Catholic literature, Paul Messbarger found that, with the exception of mixed marriages, writers consistently depicted worldly ambition as the greatest threat to one's faith. The Catholic Alger, Messbarger observed, had to "practice all the virtues of the traditional rags-to-riches candidate—patience, humility, sobriety, loyalty, temperance, honesty, and instinctive good timing—plus a special steadfastness against the rewards of apostasy." Such strictures were essential to preserve the very notion of the enclave and reflected a perspective that subordinated personal advancement to community values and defined success in group rather than individual terms.[31]

Moreover, the main end of Catholic mobility was not so much riches as independence. Guidebook writers unanimously agreed that immigrants could obtain this desideratum by avoiding large cities—which were invariably described as centers of pestilence and intemperance—and returning to the land. But relatively few immigrants did and further counsel on the matter showed subtle, yet significant, shifts during the latter half of the nineteenth century. Writing at mid-century, Father John O'Hanlon emphasized the importance of self-employment, noting "what a difference is produced in this respect between the independent bearing, comfortable position, and respectable standing of the man who commands his own services and perhaps those of others, and

the man who obeys the orders of an employer, and depends upon
precarious chances of employment." By the 1870s, however, prospects
for self-employment had dimmed considerably, and Father Stephen
Byrne placed greater emphasis on homeowning as a basis for independence. Mechanics and laborers "who have a prospect of making independent homes" in Ireland, Byrne advised, should not emigrate; and
"those who cannot acquire *homes of their own* in one part of the United
States by honest industry, frugality, and sobriety, ought to go where
they can."[32]

Immigrant workers intent on following Father Byrne's counsel
were not well advised to come to Holyoke. Throughout much of the
nineteenth century it remained a city of tenements and apartments.
Yet, given the significance that proponents of enclave respectability
attached to home life and the differences in skill level, income, and
life-styles among Irish workers, the question of comparative living
conditions within the Irish community demands some attention; for it
involves the important matter of just which workers fully participated
in the developing cultural world of enclave respectability. A useful
source for such a query is the 1875 investigation of wages and expenditures conducted by the Massachusetts Bureau of Labor Statistics. The
study found that where metalworkers and building craftsmen relied
on the earnings of children under fifteen for less than one percent of
family income, this source provided 24 percent of the family budget of
unskilled mill operatives. At the same time, the latter spent only half
the amount that building tradesmen and metalworkers paid for housing. In a mill town like Holyoke this determined whether one lived in
a relatively spacious and clean apartment or in one of the local tenements described in the 1875 MBSL report:

> The sanitary arrangements are very imperfect, and in many cases, there is
> no provision made for carrying the slops from the sinks, but they are
> allowed to run wherever they can make their way. Portions of yards are
> covered with filth and green slime, and, within twenty feet, people are
> living in basements of houses three feet below the level of the yard. One
> large block, four stories high, and basement, has eighteen tenements, with
> ninety rooms, occupied by nearly two hundred people; and yet there are
> only two three-foot doorways on the front, and none on the back, with an
> alley-way in back of only six feet in width.[33]

Within homes, skilled workers were much more likely to have
carpeting on the floor, and it was only in their residences that one

64

could find that ultimate symbol of working-class respectability, a piano. They also spent more on clothing and owned sewing machines so that it could be kept in a suitable state of repair. These distinctions did not prevent unskilled mill operatives from participating in the world of enclave respectability, where ethnicity, religion, and behavior were more important than occupational status; in this respect, the culture contained an admirable potential for inclusiveness. There was, however, a tendency among enclave respectables to identify personal character with material circumstances. Father Byrne declared that thrift was nearly as important as employment itself, adding that everyone "must remember in his lifetime numbers, even of laborers, who, if they had been *moderately* saving, might have been independent." The existence of such attitudes suggests that mill operatives at the bottom of the skill hierarchy may have been viewed as second-class citizens in this sociocultural world, to the degree that they participated at all.[34]

In addition to thrift, temperance was an equally important component of enclave respectability. After describing Father Matthew, the popular Irish temperance reformer, as the "greatest benefactor of his race" in modern times, Father Byrne observed that "millions now living, if not in opulence, at least in independent circumstances and enjoying the comfort of peaceful homes, are indebted to him for all they possess." Similar sentiments were expressed by John Maguire, who declared drink "the most serious obstacle to the advancement of the Irish race in America." Those able to bypass the rumshop, Maguire added, would be "amply rewarded in [their] safety and independence; an enlightened interest in public affairs becomes the freeman; drudgery and inevitable debasement are only worthy of the willing slave."[35]

To diffuse these values, proponents of enclave respectability recommended the formation of self-help groups. The first of these at Holyoke was the Catholic Mutual Benevolent Society. Founded in 1857, it provided sick members three dollars a week, unless the illness was "induced by intemperance or other immorality." Its most prominent successor was the St. Jerome's Temperance Society, established in 1869 by Father Harkins as another instrument in his war upon saloon culture. Within a year the organization had 500 members, 150 of whom belonged to the juvenile branch. The early formation of a debating society and reading room indicated that self-improvement was also a major concern. In terms of class, the society had a mixed membership.

Builders, grocers, foremen, and professionals joined with paper-makers, textile workers, machinists, and building craftsmen to take the pledge and engage in the group's various activities.[36]

Although the middle class dominated the leadership ranks of the St. Jerome's Temperance Society during its early years, by the eighties equal numbers of working-class members could be found among the group's officers. Within the society, there was initially little social distance between its working-class supporters and an emergent middle class. As children of the famine, most shared the same background and experience. For example, Maurice Lynch, an up-and-coming contractor and the organization's vice president, was born in county Kerry in 1837 and came to the United States a decade later when the potato rot devastated the region. As a boy, he sold apples at the Lyman Mills's gate and later apprenticed as a brickmaker. After operating a grocery store for a short while, he formed a successful contracting business in partnership with his brothers. Although he had little formal schooling, Lynch placed a high valuation on learning and saw that each of his children received an extensive education. A veritable model of self-improvement, Lynch was the walking embodiment of enclave respectability.[37]

A final component of the culture was Irish nationalism. Long after they had departed their native land, Irish Americans remained preoccupied with the liberation of Ireland from British oppression. During the first four-and-a-half decades of the nineteenth century, a series of campaigns to obtain full political equality created a sense of national identity among broad segments of the Irish populace. The famine deepened and transformed these convictions. There were not only painful recollections of those who perished. There were also deep feelings of shame that more had not been done to avert the catastrophe, particularly among those who fled to America. As a famine veteran in Jim Tully's *Shanty Irish* (1928) remarked: "They died like whipped curs a-whinnin' under the lash—whimpering from the ditches and bogs. Holy Mary—Mither of God—pray for us starvin' sinners now and at the hour of our horrible death—Amen." These bitter memories of peasant passivity enraged survivors. And in 1869, Holyoke Fenians gave vent to these passions by joining in an ill-fated invasion of Canada.[38]

Revenge was only one of the motive forces behind Irish nationalism. By the 1880s, if not earlier, these primal yearnings had been joined to a broader culture of respectability. But this was not, as some

historians have asserted, a narrow middle-class respectability. It is true that middle-class leaders assumed prominent roles in nationalist organizations, and some doubtlessly exploited nationalist sentiments for their own personal gain. Nevertheless, such characterizations obscure the emphasis on group uplift that informed Land League activities in many locales during the early eighties. Holyoke was a case in point. Through picnics, parades, indignation meetings, and torchlight processions, the league both advanced the cause of a free Ireland and served as an important center of social activity. At its meetings, supporters sang traditional Irish ballads and listened to members recite essays on current events and English, Irish, and American history and literature. The recitations, A CONSTANT NATIONALIST declared, indicated the stress on self-improvement that permeated the organization and "set men thinking, reading, writing, and speaking." Taken together, the foregoing were hallmarks of an enclave rather than a strictly middle-class respectability.[39]

By 1880, Father Harkins could take great personal satisfaction in much that he saw during his daily walks about the city. Various churches, schools, and social clubs all testified to his impact on local development. Yet there was still much that would have troubled him. The partisans of a raucous and hard-drinking saloon culture continued to defy his counsel. More important, the culture of enclave respectability that he had done so much to foster had evolved in ways that he had not anticipated. For in 1880, Father Harkins was in the fifth year of a frequently bitter and acrimonious struggle with the members of one of his most prized creations, the St. Jerome's Temperance Society. An examination of that struggle sheds light on important aspects of the inner dynamics of the culture of enclave respectability.

IN 1875, Father Harkins assigned the brickwork on a new Holyoke church to a local Yankee contractor rather than the Lynch brothers because, he remarked, their earlier efforts had been "unworkmanlike." To protect his reputation, Maurice Lynch felt compelled to disclose the details of a recent rift between Harkins and the members of the St. Jerome's Temperance Society. The previous November the society had leased its lower hall to a group of Liberal Christians. Although Bishop O'Leary subsequently sanctioned the arrangement, Father Harkins continued to withhold his approval. He also launched a

series of personal attacks on leading members of the society. As Lynch explained, Harkins was an agreeable man if one submitted to his opinions, but those who dared disagree with him were soon "marked out for slaughter." The Lynch incident was only one skirmish in a struggle that lasted another six years. In 1877, when the society asked Harkins to resume his position as spiritual director, he demanded that he be given full control and that the members again take the pledge before him. They refused, calling the conditions "an infringement upon their self respect and their rights as a society." A few years later the organization further clarified its position: "The priest is to be respected and obeyed in all that pertains to the church, [but] when it comes to outside matters, [laymen] have a right to do as they think best; and when the priest comes into their society he is but one of them, although from courtesy they call him spiritual director."[40]

Ironically, the dispute was in one sense a tribute to Harkins's efforts to forge a culture of respectability among local Irish Americans. Given the culture's emphasis on self-improvement, it was inevitable that enclave respectables would develop an independent cast of mind. It was similarly ironic that the clash centered on lay relations with groups outside the enclave. Few people had done more to create links with the broader community than Harkins had through his various fund-raising activities. These were important developments that explain how the conflict began, but we need to look beyond them to understand why it lasted six years. For the struggle ultimately involved much more than the society's leasing policies. There is strong evidence that conflicting approaches to Irish nationalism were also an issue.

In the late 1870s, radical Irish nationalists centered their activities around the Skirmishing Fund. Controlled by the Clan na Gael, the fund was intended to subsidize guerrilla warfare against the British Empire. Despite clerical opposition, Irish enclavists in numerous communities established Skirmishing Clubs and solicited contributions for the fund, which were then sent to the *Irish World*. Local contributors not only included the city's leading saloonkeepers, but prominent members of the St. Jerome's Temperance Society as well: people like Maurice Lynch, policemen Jeremiah J. Callanan and M. D. Fenton, clothing-store proprietor Edward O'Connor, and P. J. Moore, who was then developing a reputation as the city's most articulate labor spokesman. In addition to these individual contributions, the proceeds from a play conducted by the society's gymnastic club were also donated to the fund.[41]

The mere fact of such support from some of his most distinguished parishioners could hardly have pleased Father Harkins. Even more alarming were the sentiments expressed by local contributors. In a letter to the *Irish World*, P. J. Moore and M. D. Fenton declared that, unlike "Irishmen of the milk and water type," Holyoke Skirmishers fully endorsed "any punishment you may inflict on the government of England, whether it be with bullets, dynamite, or infernal machine [bomb]." Another communication stated that local nationalists were "ready at all times to shoulder a gun or a pike" and in June 1878, Jeremiah J. Callanan, a veteran of the previous decade's Fenian expedition to Canada, began organizing an Irish military club.[42]

Although Holyoke's Irish nationalists disbanded local Skirmishing Clubs before they could again take to the field, the tensions engendered by their activities resurfaced a few years later during the Land League agitation of the early eighties. Initially the league had two branches at Holyoke. The Parnell League, headed by Father Harkins, supported the parliamentary aims of Charles Stewart Parnell: the formation of a peasant resident proprietary that would allow Irish tillers to purchase the land that they farmed and the establishment of home rule under conditions similar to those that had existed between 1782 and 1800. Former Skirmishers organized a competing branch, the Michael Davitt League, which stressed the need for land redistribution. In 1881, the two organizations united under the banner of the Davitt League, but not before Father Harkins had engaged the Davitt leaders, many of whom also belonged to the St. Jerome's Temperance Society, in yet another dispute. The stated reason for the conflict was Harkins's opposition to the activities of the women's branch of the Davitt League. Characteristically, he took to the pulpit to declare his conviction that "women ought to do their part through the men" and to denounce those women who had joined the organization. When LAND LEAGUER issued a public rejoinder, asking "Why are women condemned in certain parishes for joining the movement and streams of vituperation and ridicule heaped on their devoted heads, while in other parishes they are lauded to the skies?" Harkins temporarily withdrew from league activities, tacitly acknowledging defeat.[43]

It is likely that Father Harkins also objected to the more pronounced radicalism of the Davitt League, which endorsed the writings of Henry George and maintained close relations with the *Irish World*'s Patrick Ford, who sought to join league efforts with "the war of the great army of the disinherited of all lands, for their Heaven-willed

possessions." During the late nineteenth century, Ford's majestic figure cast a broad shadow over Irish America. No one better articulated
its current claims and future hopes. As the voice of Irish enclaves from
Lowell, Massachusetts, to Butte, Montana, Ford was no stranger to
Holyoke nationalists. In an 1878 note to local readers, he expressed
surprise that alderman John Wright's name was not on a recently
submitted list of Skirmishing Fund contributors: "I slept at his house
one night, and he talked as if he were a Skirmisher." There was also
the memory of Father Jeremiah O'Callaghan. "Holyoke was always
good," Ford commented on another occasion. "It is up there amongst
you Father O'Callaghan is buried, and his patriotic spirit ought to
infuse life into you." In that Ford's relations with church authorities in
many ways paralleled those of Holyoke's enclave respectables, his
views merit further examination.[44]

During the early 1870s, Catholicism had few more ardent advocates than Patrick Ford. Not only did he urge readers to safeguard
their faith, Ford also defended the temporal powers of the Pope,
claiming on several occasions that throughout history no institution
had matched papal efforts to uphold "popular rights"—an extraordinary reading of history that probably would have seemed as surprising to Pius IX as it does to modern readers. Although Ford's devotion
to Catholicism never dimmed, his other activities—as collection agent
for the Skirmishing Fund, supporter of greenbackism, and exponent
of the land theories of Henry George—brought him into increasing
conflict with church authorities. By 1880, at least one diocese had
placed the *Irish World* under ban and several bishops had denounced
its teachings.[45]

It was not in Ford's nature to suffer criticism silently. Whether
defending papal ultramontanism or espousing land redistribution,
Ford spoke in forceful, often provocative tones. Indeed, it sometimes
seemed that he was constitutionally incapable of moderate expression. Thus when Bishop Gilmour of Cleveland stated during the
course of an attack on the *Irish World* that social inequities were inevitable, Ford declared the bishop "an iron-hearted political economist . . .
in the service of the monopolists." And when Archbishop McCabe of
Dublin condemned Irish land agitation because it was creating a division between priests and people, Ford observed: "If the union of
priests and people is to be purchased on the condition that the former
are to be political bosses, it is better for both people and priests that
no such union should exist."[46]

Yet, contrary to the assertions of his conservative critics, Ford was no more a revolutionary socialist than the Holyoke Land League was the "first class socialistic movement" that local socialists claimed it to be. Like Holyoke Land Leaguers, Ford's approach to class relations was deeply rooted in an enclave consciousness. Perhaps the fullest expression of his views on the matter appeared in an editorial, "A Few Words to Workingmen," that Ford wrote shortly after the great railroad strike of 1877. "In a broad sense," Ford began, "we are all workingmen."

> Employers and employees are in the same boat. There may be differences between them; these differences can and should be settled by arbitration; but despite these differences we are all in the labor movement; our interests are identical; and the foundation of the workingman's party, if now contracted, should be expanded sufficiently to take in all who are willing to fight under labor's banner.

Ford thus cautioned workers to avoid demagogues who "rise up and scream out: 'More pay and less work!' 'All employers are rogues and tyrants.' "[47]

In an effort to develop a theory of value for this view of class relations, Ford fused employers and employees together in a construct called labor-power capital that was responsible for the creation of wealth. Pitted against these productive classes were the plundering bondholders, bankers, and monopolists of money-power capital. Ford then compared the two groups:

> Labor-Power Capital *adds* to the positive wealth of the human family; Money-Power Capital simply *subtracts*. It adds nothing. This stolen wealth, of course, is taken from labor—all wealth being realized labor; and that which is subtracted is taken from the toiling many and concentrated in the hands of the scheming few. These few are the lords and masters of the civilized nations of the earth; and all the inhabitants of those civilized nations—the captains of industry as well as the wage-earning classes—are the bond slaves of those lords and masters.

To remedy this state of affairs, Ford urged workers to avoid strikes and organize politically. The road to a just society began in the nation's polling places and workers could find adequate solutions to their problems through political action: "in Free Lands for the People, in Honest Money, and in an Industrial System which will develop the resources of the nation under protection of Government."[48]

For a church that reflexively equated grass-roots ideological innovation with heresy, there were, to be sure, disturbing elements in Ford's
critique of capitalism. His call for the nationalization of mines and
demand that government "be recognized as the landlord of the nation" alarmed even the most liberal bishops. Yet there were also striking parallels between Ford's views and contemporary developments
in Catholic social thought. During the closing decades of the nineteenth century, a number of Catholic authorities began to reassess the
church's traditional social outlook. The widespread labor unrest that
began during the late seventies made pious admonitions to submit
meekly to God's will seem absurdly anachronistic. By the 1880s, some
Catholic spokesmen had begun to appraise labor in a new light. The
working class has finally come to recognize its power, wrote one
contributor to the *American Catholic Quarterly Review*:

> the power and the force that lies in numbers. It has sore grievances; . . .
> intelligence and energy at its head. The intelligence may be used as false
> light; the energy may be misdirected. But there they are and stand, living
> forces in the world, never more to be expelled.

Besides voicing a new awareness on the church's part, the passage
reveals another concern: Who would lead the growing labor movement? Deeply worried about the spread of socialism, but recognizing
the need for reform, Catholic leaders wanted social change without
class struggle. Their statements on labor leadership, strikes, and government intervention in the economy indicated the manner in which
they sought to deal with the dilemma.[49]

On the question of labor leadership, Catholic spokesmen counseled the selection of conservative men who would avoid violence
and do nothing that would threaten private property. Father John
Talbot Smith, a frequent contributor to the *Catholic World* on labor
matters, asked workers to look outside the ranks of labor and to seek
"the advice of all good men in the community." The same desire to
avoid class struggle informed Catholic declarations on strike policy.
Some Catholic commentators advised that strikes be abandoned altogether. Others declared that restrictions should be placed on their
conduct, one priest stating that strikes were permissible so long as the
strikers did not "prevent men working at lower wages than they
themselves are willing to accept." The most popular approach con-
doned strikes, but urged the prompt submission of grievances to

arbitration, where a presumably neutral panel would settle the dispute. The popularity of arbitration among Catholic leaders reflected the persistence of traditional notions about the dynamics of class relations. Where the church had once mediated between the benevolent rich and hard-working poor, it now encouraged surrogates to assume a similar role in dealing with capital and labor. One of these was the arbitration panel; another was the government.[50]

Once workers found sober, conservative men to lead them and developed efficient organizations, Father Smith advised, they should "practice strict obedience to their leaders, then frame laws which will root out abuses, and bring them to the legislatures." Besides its potential role in quelling class conflict, the church looked to government for legislation to protect working-class families. Catholic spokespersons supported tenement-house reform and laws to abolish child labor. The church's concern here was in no sense gratuitous, as mothers assumed a role of paramount importance in the Catholic scheme of social and moral order. "In no faith but the Catholic," wrote AN AMERICAN WOMAN in the *Catholic World*, "is the mother taught to believe . . . that she will be held responsible for the eternal welfare of her children, that they must be saved with her or she must perish with them." The church thus urged women to stay at home and heartily supported social reforms that facilitated their remaining there.[51]

When these developments in Catholic social thought are compared with Ford's views on class relations, the similarities are evident: both opposed strikes, urged class cooperation, championed arbitration, and endorsed political action. This is not to suggest that Ford played an essentially co-optative role. As he knew and stated, even a proximate realization of his vision of the good society would have required a fundamental restructuring of the economic system. Rather, it is to delineate the intellectual and social forces that shaped his approach to social change: on one hand, a tradition of social thought that condemned class struggle; on the other, a sociocultural world in which workers and petty entrepreneurs labored side by side to advance their claims as producers, Catholics, and Irish Americans. In this latter regard, Ford's social views both reflected and shaped those of his readers in the nation's Irish enclaves. And within these communities, Catholic social teachings had as great an influence on the enclave consciousness of Irish workers as they did on Ford's approach to social change. Thus, when members of the St. Jerome's Temperance Society stated that "the priest is to be respected and observed in all

that pertains to the church," they announced their submission to clerical guidance on a broad range of matters—political as well as doctrinal.

To return to Holyoke, the dispute between Father Harkins and the St. Jerome's Temperance Society finally reached a head in 1881 when Harkins's regular pulpit denunciations of the society prompted an equally vituperative public response. "When a priest prostitutes his sacred office, and desecrates the altar of God by using language suitable to the region of Billingsgate, why is he surprised that men use their pens to rebuke the scandalous and unseemly exhibition?" asked CATHOLIC in a letter to the *Transcript*. "Is it for this," CATHOLIC further queried, "that he is paid so liberally, supported so sumptuously, and housed so grandly by the poor Catholics who can ill-afford the numerous and heavy contributions laid on them?" The conflict abated soon after, and while Father Harkins would remain a formidable force among local Catholics for another thirty years, the struggle illustrates another important dimension of church-laity relations. To resolve it, Harkins had been forced to give ground on several issues that he deemed significant: lay relations with the broader community and the political emphases of local nationalist activity. And what happened in Holyoke was occurring on a broader scale elsewhere. It can be seen, for example, in hierarchical efforts to prevent a papal condemnation of the Knights of Labor. There is a danger, Cardinal Gibbons wrote at the time, "of losing the love of the children of the Church, and of pushing them into an attitude of resistance against their Mother. The world presents no more beautiful spectacle than that of their filial devotion and obedience; but it is well to recognize that, in our age and in our country, obedience cannot be blind." What Gibbons understood, and we should as well, is that while the church did set real parameters on the political development of Catholic workers, these boundaries were constantly shifting. Outside the fevered imaginations of anti-Catholic zealots, the church was rarely ever the authoritarian monolith of episcopal dreams and nativist nightmares.[52]

In sum, the culture of enclave respectability had much in common with the free-labor ideology of Yankee Holyoke. Both eschewed class struggle and proclaimed a mutuality of interests among a loosely defined community of producers. Such ideological convergence doubtlessly explains why the great labor struggles of the 1870s and 1880s had little direct effect on the city. Yet, there were equally important differences between the two worldviews, particularly as they con-

cerned working people. Herbert Gutman has written that "A central tension exists within all modern dependent groups between individualist (utilitarian) and collective (mutualist) ways of dealing with and sometimes overcoming historically specific patterns of dependence and inequality." The tension that Gutman describes not only existed within groups, but also constituted a significant area of difference among them. Compared with the culture of enclave respectability, the free-labor ideology placed much heavier stress on individualist behavior. Indeed, stripped of its appeal to social mobility, the ideology was at best a flaccid justification of the status quo. What is important to note is that, in places like Gilded Age Holyoke, opportunities for social advancement were much greater for native-born workers than Irish wage earners. Thus, while their belief in the free-labor ideology did not prevent Yankee artisans from adopting collective forms of action, it is not surprising that they posed no serious challenge to its individualist emphases.[53]

The culture of enclave respectability also had its individualist features. As noted earlier, it is difficult to square hierarchical injunctions to accept one's station in life uncomplainingly with the entrepreneurial mind-set of brick and mortar priests like Patrick J. Harkins. Nor was such counsel likely to appeal to people who believed so strongly in self-improvement. At the same time, however, the culture's guarded approach to social mobility, coupled with its tendency to subordinate individual to group interests, clearly set it apart from the dominant ethic of Yankee Holyoke. Yet this greater emphasis on group interests did not eliminate the tension between individualist and collective ways of dealing with enclave problems. And as this tension worked itself out, it would result in the social fragmentation of the enclave and formation of a class-based labor movement. These developments form the main focus of the next two chapters

4

ENCLAVE POLITICS
AND WORKER ORGANIZATION,
1873–1893

THE DEPRESSION of the 1870s did not strike with the devastating force of later crises; however, business failures, wage reductions, and unemployment created a sense of unease among all groups in the community. The great railroad strike of 1877 had a particularly jarring impact on local sensibilities, prompting the *Transcript*'s editor to recall an earlier era when farmers' wives and daughters produced their own cloth, shoemakers and tailors conducted their trades with the aid of a few journeymen and apprentices, and farm laborers could look forward to owning farms of their own. Those days were irretrievably gone, he observed, and the great danger now was "that we shall have a permanent operative class." A new structure of class relations was emerging, and if the recent strike demonstrated anything, it was that capital could not rely on force alone to meet labor's demands. Perhaps, he concluded, the laws dealing with taxation, education, the "proceeds of labor," and the "distribution of property" needed revision. Although no subsequent *Transcript* editorial would evince such skepticism, the questions it raised would not go away. This chapter looks at the ways in which the enclave consciousness of Holyoke's Irish workers shaped their response to these matters.[1]

Most of Holyoke's principal mills survived the depression of the seventies. Battered, but still solvent, local manufacturers could even take some satisfaction in the belief that the one major enterprise to go under, the Boston-owned Hampden Mills, offered further evidence that absentee-controlled firms could not prosper at Holyoke. The

demise of a host of small shops and mercantile establishments was an entirely different matter. During the first months of 1877, an unparalleled series of bankruptcies darkened numerous storefronts in the central business district, as creditors scrambled to salvage what they could from broken concerns. In March, when the Second Congregational Church announced a 20 percent reduction on pew rents, matters appeared ominous indeed. But the church's sale proved better than anticipated, and in time a number of bankrupt enterprises secured new lines of credit and resumed business. A moment of crisis had passed.[2]

The crisis for Holyoke workers began four years earlier and continued unabated into 1878. On any given day at the city's fruit and vegetable stands, wrote the *Transcript*'s editor during the summer of 1873, one could see "a drove of poverty stricken children, often girls, clad only in one or two ragged and dirty garments, down on their hands and knees in the gutters, greedily picking out of the mud and dirt and eating the bits of spoiled and decaying fruit which have been thrown out as worthless." Not all working-class families suffered such privation, but the wage reductions of that winter coupled with intermittent periods of unemployment during the next four years placed serious pressure on the family economies of even the best-paid workers.[3]

By mid-decade Holyoke workers had begun to organize and demand increased expenditures on public-works projects from municipal authorities. The initial response was chilling. In his 1876 inaugural address, Republican mayor W.B.C. Pearsons articulated a public-works philosophy that drew on some of the most hidebound features of the dominant ethic:

> Some insist that we should provide work for the poor, *make a place*, where poor people can have a chance to earn a few dollars. I trust that we shall do nothing of the kind. Better would it be for us to provide them a living, than engage in an enterprise that was not of benefit to the people; better still would it be, if those out of employment could get places upon the lands that lie spread all over this great country, waiting for the husbandman.

Rather than dampening the petitioners' enthusiasm, the rebuff only sharpened their political awareness. At a September 1876 meeting of the unemployed, Dennis Glavin urged his auditors "to follow the petition into the council room, and 'spot' every man who voted

against it, and to remember him." That winter, Holyoke had a new Democratic mayor, and in February the City Council voted $15,000 for a sewer project. Few additional expenditures followed, as Mayor Crafts proved nearly as penurious as his Republican predecessor, but Holyoke workers had a fleeting glimpse of what their united effort could accomplish.[4]

That winter also saw the formation of a German-speaking chapter of the Workingmen's Party of the United States (WPUS), and in March, following a series of addresses by P. J. McGuire, a New York City carpenter then working as a party organizer, fifty native-born, British, and Irish workers established an English-speaking branch; by October the two groups had more than two hundred members. Committed to the abolition of the wage system and creation of a classless society, the WPUS sought to develop a viable socialist movement through the formation of trade unions. The party's platform called for an eight-hour day, child-labor legislation, and employer-liability laws and included a demand that all industrial enterprises "be placed under the control of the Government as fast as practicable and operated by free cooperative trade unions for the good of the whole people." Party leaders especially stressed the importance of the eight-hour day. The issue, wrote P. J. McDonnell, editor of the *Labor Standard*, was not only a popular recruiting tool, but made workers aware that "the very system of wage labor is wrong because it compels the workers to perform more or less work which is not compensated."[5]

At Holyoke, greenbackism was more popular among Irish workers, who followed Ben Butler in attributing the depression to the misguided and self-serving hard-money policy of "coupon clippers." As the state's leading greenbacker, Butler enhanced the doctrine's appeal for Irish Americans by linking it to Irish nationalism. On the stump, Butler was a master of political invective and Irish voters applauded his vitriolic denunciations of Great Britain no less lustily than they did his attacks on "monopoly and aristocracy." Throughout the period, Butler consistently outpolled his competitors in Holyoke's Irish wards.[6]

The greenbackers' approach to class relations was also more congenial to Irish enclavists than that of the WPUS. Greenbackers believed renewed prosperity required only the reignition of latent productive forces among a vaguely defined strata called the industrial or producing classes. Local party leaders included petty entrepreneurs like the Irish contractor Maurice Lynch, who at one time or another had

doubtlessly experienced difficulty obtaining the capital needed to fund a proposed building project. By contrast, the WPUS saw overproduction as the main problem and looked to wage earners alone for salvation. The *Labor Standard* thus found greenbackism inadequate and complained that financial reformers paid no attention to the hours question. The greenbackers' goal—to stimulate production—was praiseworthy, one contributor remarked, but "without some such break-water as an eight hour day . . . a tidal wave of production will sweep over the land and swamp every aspiration of the laborer and citizen for a broader and fuller life." These differences can easily be overstated. At a Butler rally in Fall River, the general's supporters carried placards reading NINE HOURS AND NO SURRENDER as well as WHO SHALL RULE US, MONEY OR THE PEOPLE; and the *Irish World*'s Patrick Ford called for an eight-hour day as well as an end to interest on money. At the same time, however, Ford was well aware of the class dynamics of greenbackism. "This new movement is, indeed, primarily in the interests of the laboring classes," he observed in an 1878 editorial, "but in battling for their rights it meditates no assault on the rights of any other class."[7]

In the end, neither movement had a lasting impact on Holyoke workers. Local interest in greenbackism had all but disappeared by the early eighties, while the WPUS expired even earlier. With the general return of prosperity in 1878, party membership declined and the organization faded from the local scene. Within four years, however, a successor group, the Socialist Labor Party (SLP), had formed a Holyoke chapter. Locally, Germans dominated the SLP and during the first years of its existence the party was confined to German Holyoke. Although it subscribed to the doctrine of class struggle, the SLP explicitly repudiated violence and sought to work amicably with other labor groups. By 1885, it had begun to perform on a larger stage. As the economic crisis of the eighties deepened, interest in trade unions revived and the party played a major role in the formation of the Trades and Labor Assembly, where it championed a broad reform program that included demands for a government-issued currency as well as the eight-hour day and the right of legal incorporation for all labor organizations.[8]

Despite the SLP's role in establishing the Trades and Labor Assembly, it played a subordinate part within the body. The assembly's most prominent spokesman and a leading figure in the Knights of Labor was P. J. Moore, an aspiring lawyer and familiar figure in Irish

Holyoke. He believed that there was no fundamental difference between capital and labor, but that competition forced employers to reduce wages. His approach to class relations mirrored that of the Knights' state leadership. A. A. Carlton, head of District Assembly 30, though sometimes forced to support strikes, never tired of decrying such actions: "Judging from some of the reports in the *Journal* [*of United Labor*]," he wrote, "many Districts as well as locals imagine that to strike is our highest aim and to win a strike the greatest victory that could be achieved. Instruction seems to be badly needed." When local Knights did support job actions, they proceeded with caution. During an 1886 strike by German weavers at the Skinner Silk Mill, Moore took steps to secure a boycott of the company's products. But he did so only after arbitration efforts by C. H. Litchman had failed and more than a month after the SLP had taken similar action. This desire to avoid confrontation in turn elicited the support and applause of regional Catholic spokesmen. Worcester's Irish Catholic weekly, *The Messenger*, regularly carried notices of Knights activities and counseled workers to adopt the organization's position on strikes: "They are an important element of the workingman's ammunition in industrial warfare, but like gunpowder, unless handled carefully, are likely to do more damage to workingmen themselves than to those against whom they are fighting." In the *Irish World*, Patrick Ford expressed similar sentiments in editorials applauding the moderation of the Knights' strike and boycott policy.[9]

Rather than direct economic action, District Master Workman Carlton urged the formation of cooperatives and political activity to obtain legislation favorable to workers. At Holyoke the Knights undertook few cooperative projects, but the Trades and Labor Assembly did support the order's legislative program. More a pressure group than a political party, the assembly instructed workers to support the party and candidates most committed to labor's cause. Its principal legislative aim was an arbitration law that would force capital to the bargaining table without having to engage in protracted conflict. Desiring social change without class struggle, the assembly reflected the attitudes on class relations of the enclave respectables who dominated the organization.[10]

The assembly's local platform indicated its cultural orientation. At an 1885 meeting, it demanded reform of the city's poor-relief system and called for the establishment of a city hospital and farm. At the latter institution, the dependent poor could engage in productive

labor that would restore their sense of dignity and allow them to resume an autonomous social existence. Other demands included the construction of a public bathhouse, elimination of library fees, and school reform. Workers showed particular concern about primary education. In protesting the school committee's policy of placing the least experienced teachers in overcrowded elementary schools, one assembly spokesman articulated the organization's assessment of public education:

> The Trades and Labor Assembly . . . don't care much about the high school. The greatest influence can be had on the little children. Instead of crowded rooms for little children we want more room, and the best teachers. . . . The high school needs only the poorest kind of teachers. [There] the examination is the chief thing. Instead of that it is made a buncombe.

These disparaging comments are explained in part by the fact that few workers' children could yet look forward to a high-school education. But the critique cannot be fully understood unless viewed against the backdrop of the self-help philosophy that lay at the core of enclave respectability. Throughout the eighties numerous groups of Holyoke workers established reading rooms, debating clubs, and literary associations. At these institutions, they extended their education through an interchange of ideas, unencumbered by high school "buncombe." Beyond providing fundamental cognitive skills, the public schools were superfluous to this world.[11]

In sum, the SLP, Knights of Labor, and Trades and Labor Assembly institutionally represented the Holyoke working class during the decade in which it first emerged as an organized force. Their collective membership, however, comprised only a fragment of the local work force. German workers from a broad range of occupations joined all three groups, but only the more skilled Irish workers participated and French Canadians were virtually absent. Moreover, popular acceptance of enclave principles inhibited any autonomous expression of class interest. Indeed, these workers sometimes seemed more self-conscious than class conscious. When George Ewing, a local businessman interested in labor reform, told an off-color tale at a meeting of the Trades and Labor Assembly, WORKINGMAN scolded him for reciting stories in the lower wards that he would not repeat among his neighbors: "It doesn't help our cause to have citizens get the impression we like that sort of thing." All this takes on added significance when we

CHAPTER FOUR

recall that the assembly sought political expression through the two major parties, where an immigrant middle class mediated its demands.[12]

IN AUGUST 1887, when the tour workers at the Whiting Mills were
informed that their hours had been reduced, before they even returned home a group of them walked up to High Street to share the
good news with Jeremiah Callanan at his grocery store. "There was
no reason that they should hasten to Mr. Callanan's store," observed
the perceptive Sunday correspondent of the *Springfield Republican*,
"except that he would rejoice with them in their victory and be sure to
enlighten them out of the abundance of his political experience as to
the effects of this move." How many times this scene was repeated at
Callanan's store or others like it is impossible to determine, but the
political significance of people like Callanan can scarcely be overstated. They functioned as a link between worker respectables and
the two major parties, just as a corps of saloonkeepers connected the
Democratic machine with saloon culture. Born in county Cork in 1841,
Jeremiah Callanan arrived in the United States while an infant and
grew up on an Agawam farm, where he learned the trades of cigar-
maker and carpenter. After serving with the Union army in the Civil
War, he worked as a carpenter and put in a few years on the Holyoke
police force before entering the grocery business.[13]

Callanan was an ardent Irish nationalist, who had accompanied
local Fenians on their invasion of Canada. He was also a leading
figure in the St. Jerome's Temperance Society, an affiliation of no small
significance in that enclave respectables took a dim view of saloon
politics. More important, the society provided the impetus for early
Irish initiatives in local politics. During the formative years of the late
seventies, it functioned as a "school of oratory" for aspiring politicians
and orchestrated several naturalization drives to increase the number
of Irish voters. Although the society fielded a string of middle-class
candidates, working-class members felt confident that they would be
fully represented. As one wrote, responding to criticism of increased
Irish political activity, the Irish would reclaim in the political arena
part of what they had lost at the city's factories:

The Patch in Holyoke is in every sense a better location than Quality
Avenue, and if the honest industry of the people had received its just

reward, the houses on the Patch would have equalled those on Quality Avenue. . . .

You say we rule or ruin, and own no mills. The St. Jerome society is my evidence to the contrary, and in addition you could not run your mills, except we did the work from which you realize your profits. . . . And in conclusion let me say we have not ruled Holyoke, but in the future we shall endeavor to do so.[14]

By 1880, the increasing assertiveness of Irish enclavists had caused a split in the Democratic party. Led by Jonathan Allen and the ubiquitous P. J. Moore, the Irish faction established the Andrew Jackson Club "for the purpose of self-improvement in a literary as well as a political sense." Allen was a contentious and feisty lawyer who sometimes "accompanied an argument with a blow as the most fitting answer to insolent ignorance." An active Irish nationalist, who had spent five months in a British prison, he was a popular figure in the city's Irish community. In 1880, Irish enclavists secured the mayoral nomination for James J. O'Connor, a Harvard-educated doctor who as city physician had demonstrated an acute awareness of the manifold health hazards in the lower wards and urged their amelioration. He was narrowly beaten in the ensuing election.[15]

The other faction, led by veteran party warhorse Roswell P. Crafts, formed the Thomas Jefferson Club. Dedicated to the proposition that the "best government is that which governs least," the club declared itself opposed to "class legislation, special privilege, and monopoly under the Federal and state governments, and to intrigue, incapacity, and extravagance in municipal affairs." An unstable coalition of old ward healers like Crafts and proto-Mugwumps interested in putting the "best men" in office, the group was held together by a commitment to reduced government and a mutual detestation of the Irish. In 1880, they watched from the sidelines as the party's nominee, Dr. O'Connor, went down to defeat. The following year Crafts obtained the mayoral nomination and won in an election so close that it required a recount.[16]

An incident that summer, involving the Irish political leader Jonathan Allen, illustrated the degree of bitterness that had arisen between the two factions. In one of his lesser actions after assuming office, Crafts decreed a curfew law that prohibited anyone from remaining at Hampden Park after 10 P.M. Allen decided to test both the law and the mayor by refusing to leave the park at the appointed

hour. As if to publicize his defiance, Allen struck the police officer who ordered him to leave, an act that prompted the latter to reciprocate with a few blows. Seeing that a crowd had now gathered, Allen remarked to the arresting officer that he would "pay dearly for his night's work." In response, the officer struck him again, as many in the crowd cried "shame." Allen subsequently received a small fine, but two days later Crafts rescinded the curfew. The incident was a fitting prelude to the 1882 Democratic caucus.[17]

The 1882 Democratic caucus was one of the most raucous in the city's history. The mayoral contest pitted the Irish faction's James E. Delaney against the incumbent mayor, Roswell P. Crafts. Delaney's supporters initially attempted to make Jeremiah Callanan permanent chairman without consulting the Crafts group. When this maneuver failed, they stacked a seven-man committee with Delaney stalwarts and Callanan assumed the chair. Maintaining some semblance of order was another matter altogether. Throughout the day, amid a bedlam of noise, Callanan could be heard shouting "Sit down, you crank" and other expressions that reflected his exasperation. When, during the course of an endorsement speech, one Crafts supporter rhetorically asked, "Why do I support Mr. Crafts?" a shrill voice from the audience instantaneously responded, "Cos ye don't know noting, d—n ye." The balloting finally took place and Delaney won by a decisive margin. Afterwards, however, two Crafts men reported finding 300 of their candidate's ballots stuffed in a toilet located in a room adjoining the one in which the count had occurred, and various men could be overheard explaining how they had managed to vote two or three times. In the election, Crafts again won, running as an independent.[18]

The following year the Democratic faction finally defeated Roswell Crafts, who had secured the Republican nomination, and placed James Delaney in the mayor's chair. They did it, though, with strong support from an unexpected quarter. In the closing days of the campaign, some of the city's leading manufacturers and merchants publicly endorsed Delaney. Telegraphing his support from Washington, Congressman Whiting stated his conviction that Delaney's administration would be "economical and above reproach." The reasons for this turnabout are not entirely clear, but they appeared to stem from a confluence of long-standing grudges and current anxieties. Many Holyokers saw Crafts as an unscrupulous politician who actively sought the saloon vote. Few Holyoke manufacturers were prohibitionists, but they did desire that some checks be placed on local liquor interests. At

a hearing on unlimited licensing the following spring, representatives from the city's twenty largest mills voiced their collective concern that the enactment of such a measure would reduce worker efficiency and lead to higher taxes by causing increased crime and pauperism. Older Republicans also remembered Crafts's lukewarm support of the war effort and recoiled at the thought of supporting such a person as the party's standard bearer. During the campaign, James Ramage, a paper manufacturer and Democrat, played on these fears in his endorsement of Delaney:

> Why should you resort to the extreme measure of putting at the head of your ticket the rankest Democrat of all. Do you fear the Irish vote? Your candidate will out-Irish the most rabid Irishman. Do you fear the rum element? Your candidate has allowed their Sunday business to go on for the last two years with only one or two feeble pretenses to stop it.[19]

Yet, at least some of these men had supported Crafts during the previous two elections. What made the 1883 election different from earlier campaigns? As Ramage indicated, two years of Crafts's rule had alienated some of his former supporters. Beyond that, though, the election signalled a grudging recognition of the inevitability of Irish rule. Each year more and more Irish were becoming naturalized citizens and adding their names to the voting lists. Before they united behind a labor spokesman like P. J. Moore or an agitator like Jonathan Allen, it seemed best to accept a safe nominee like James Delaney. As a former clerk at the Holyoke Water Power Company and the son of the city's most prominent Irish contractor, Delaney could be counted upon not to rock the boat. His reelection the following year, with continued strong support from Wards 6 and 7, suggests that he did not. By 1885, however, working-class enclavists had formed the Trades and Labor Assembly and were looking for a new candidate.[20]

At a joint meeting of the Trades and Labor Assembly and the Knights of Labor in November 1885, the delegates rejected Delaney in favor of Edward O'Connor, a High Street clothing merchant. When the former brickmason and president of the St. Jerome's Temperance Society chose not to run, the workers turned to Dr. James J. O'Connor, the unsuccessful 1880 candidate. Hoping for a more vigorous enforcement of the liquor laws, the Republicans also endorsed O'Connor, who defeated Delaney, running as the Democratic nominee. The following year the city's labor organizations again endorsed O'Connor

by "an almost unanimous vote." The two elections clearly demonstrated the cultural divisions among Holyoke workers. Whatever Delaney's initial intentions, he soon became dependent on support from the saloon interest, which in 1885 organized as the Holyoke Retail Licensed Liquor-Dealers Protective Union. As it pooled its funds to reelect Delaney, rank-and-file saloonists spread the word that should O'Connor be elected "we shall not be able to get anything to drink Sunday morning." Enclave respectables were no less ardent in their support of O'Connor. Speaking on behalf of the Trades and Labor Assembly, P. J. Moore depicted the 1886 election as a contest between the forces of righteousness and rapacity:

> Common report has it that a supreme effort will be made at the coming city election to change the [liquor] policy of the present administration by removing the present executive officers. . . . It is deemed not only prudent but expedient that steps should be taken at once to organize the friends of law and order into a working body, so that we may be able to resist the encroachments of men who are banded together, not for the public good, but for private interest.[21]

In 1887, the Knights of Labor and the Trades and Labor Assembly, now organized as the Holyoke Political Labor Club, briefly considered fielding its own mayoral nominee. Instead, it asked its endorsee to pledge his support of a municipal program requiring the establishment of a city hospital, municipal bathhouse, and public reading room; initiation of a measure before the General Court placing the police under civil service rules; and passage of ordinances granting city workers a nine-hour workday and compelling the city to furnish them work tools. When Mayor O'Connor failed to stand for reelection, the club initially endorsed James Delaney, who accepted its support but refused to commit himself on the group's program. At this, the club instructed its members to vote for whichever candidate they wished. Delaney's reply was a forceful reminder of labor's continuing dependence on middle-class representatives.[22]

Why these workers chose not to form an independent labor party is a question that merits further attention, because to address it requires a close examination of class relations during these years. In part, the answer lies in their relatively narrow organizational base. By 1890, French Canadians comprised nearly 20 percent of the city's total population. Few of these workers belonged to either the Knights of Labor or

the Trades and Labor Assembly. Underrepresented politically as well, they viewed politics through a narrow ethnic prism. An 1889 meeting at the French-speaking carpenters' union, attended by "nearly every French citizen in Holyoke," decided that French Canadians should give their "undivided support" to any of their countrymen running for office. Nor did all Irish workers belong to labor organizations, as even a cursory glance at the line of march in one of the period's Labor Day parades revealed. The main body of these processions comprised metal and building craftsmen, joined by lesser delegations of cigarmakers, printers, clerks, and barbers. The only unskilled workers to participate were from the laborers' union and they were closely allied with the Democratic machine, which saw to it that municipal laborers received a wage rate well above the regional scale. Skilled tour workers and mule spinners alone represented the majority of the local work force who labored in paper and textile mills.[23]

Furthermore, the political interventions of Holyoke workers were not entirely fruitless. From 1885 to 1888, they sent Jeremiah J. Keane to represent the lower wards in the state legislature. A member of the St. Jerome's Temperance Society, Keane doubled as a bricklayer and bookkeeper at the Lynch Brothers construction business. In securing the 1885 Democratic nomination, he defeated "Captain" John Wright, a favorite among the saloon crowd, who had parlayed his role as commanding officer of local forces during the Fenian expedition into a successful political career. In the legislature, Keane worked tirelessly for his working-class supporters, pushing through an 1888 measure that prohibited fines for imperfect weaving and introducing a tour-workers' bill that, had it been approved, would have required shorter hours. Equally important, after 1886 Massachusetts Democrats acquired a reputation as the state's "labor party" by enacting laws to create a State Board of Arbitration and Conciliation, require weekly wage payments, prohibit yellow-dog contracts, and strengthen the state's child-labor statute, in addition to other measures designed to aid Bay State wage earners.[24]

The general tone of class relations within the city also worked against efforts to launch an independent labor party. The aversion to class struggle among enclave respectables, coupled with their flexible definition of class interest, made class development contingent on upper-class behavior to a larger degree than might elsewhere have been the case. On more than one occasion the Holyoke upper class averted potential conflict by demonstrating a shrewd awareness of

class relations. We have already seen how it sought to direct the developing political power of the Irish into safe channels through its intervention in the 1883 election. It also remained circumspect in its social activities.

In 1883, a group of the city's younger men of wealth formed the Arlington Club to bring together Holyoke's "first families." The group's badge of membership was a "small gold pin with the monogram 'A.C.' " Over the next few years the club sponsored a series of lavish entertainments for its select membership. The main event of the 1885 season was a reception at city hall for Governor Robinson, which the club hoped would be a "representative gathering of the best people in the state, political, professional, manufacturing, and mercantile." In the days preceding the reception, area notables badgered club members for tickets and local newspaper coverage was, to say the least, effusive. A few days after the event, however, the *Transcript* had second thoughts and asked just who were the "very best people" and what made them so. Although the rich "are positively, yes, comparatively good," the editor continued, they did suffer the temptations of speculation, deception, and display. He concluded that the "superlative excellence in every city of the country can be found more often among the middle class than in wealth or poverty." The unspoken, but even less subtle response of the city's Irish middle-class politicians came in the form of a city-hall rental fee far in excess of that charged less notable organizations. When club president J. G. MacKintosh protested the bill's unfairness and refused to pay, city solicitor Terence B. O'Donnell filed suit against the club. In passages laden with sarcasm, he later explained his action in his annual report: " 'With malice toward none and charity toward all,' it is obviously the duty of all officers charged with the collection of claims due the city to at least try to collect them from all classes of supposed debtors, and to try to collect them by suit if necessary." The upshot of it all was that the club paid the bill, and the Holyoke upper class did not stage a social event comparable to the governor's reception for another eleven years; and that was a charity ball. The middle class thus not only functioned as a buffer between the upper class and Holyoke workers, but also reminded the local bourgeoisie when it was getting out of line.[25]

A final factor inhibiting the formation of an independent labor party was the close ties between Irish workers and the immigrant middle class. The two groups went to the same churches, belonged to

the same clubs, shared similar backgrounds and experiences, and together gave expression to this common heritage through their support of Irish nationalism. Where conflict arose between them, an enclave consciousness that emphasized the harmony of interests among a loosely defined amalgam of producers mitigated its intensity.

By the late eighties, however, there were signs that the bond was beginning to dissolve. The mere fact that some workers were sufficiently dissatisfied with middle-class political leadership to suggest the formation of an independent labor party indicated that all was not well. Increasing conflict between local construction workers and two of the city's leading Irish contractors, Daniel O'Connell and Maurice Lynch, revealed further tensions between the two groups. Where a decade earlier Lynch had led a cross-class coalition of enclave respectables in their struggle with Father Harkins, he was now pitted against some of these same men in a series of strikes. At the same time, other Catholic workers were beginning to voice a new militancy. One such spokesman was the special labor correspondent of the Boston *Pilot*, New England's most prestigious Irish Catholic weekly.[26]

The *Pilot* in many ways epitomized enclave respectability. News from the old country appeared regularly in its pages, articles promoting temperance advanced the cause of Irish self-improvement, and its editor, John Boyle O'Reilly, ranked high on anyone's list of prominent Irish nationalists. Although O'Reilly endorsed a number of strikes during the mid-eighties and set forth a savage indictment of industrial concentration that contained radical implications, his approach to class relations more often fell safely within the bounds of Catholic teaching. Following the lead of social commentators like the *Catholic World*'s Father John Talbot Smith, many of whose articles he approvingly reviewed, O'Reilly urged workers to better their lot through arbitration and legislative reform. But whatever his own beliefs, O'Reilly proved willing to open the *Pilot*'s columns to more militant voices.[27]

The *Pilot*'s special labor correspondent was a New Haven–based reporter who used the pseudonym "Phineas" and whose articles demonstrated a close familiarity with the national labor movement. At first glance, "Phineas" appeared to advocate a conservative "bread and butter" trade unionism. While advising rank and filers to select responsible leaders, he reminded labor organizers that most workers "do not see far into the future" and demand "immediate results." Moreover, such moderate counsel was periodically linked to attacks

on socialism and those "so-called labor leaders" who were "threatening to array the labor movement against the Catholic Church." Socialism, he stated, discouraged workers from making the fullest use of
their talents and was at odds with "the American sentiment that to
the individual must be given the greatest possible freedom consistent
with the welfare of the community." Citizens who opposed labor,
warned "Phineas," only strengthened the "hands of the Socialists"
and invited anarchy:

> If organized capital succeeds in crushing the labor organizations, what will
> it have accomplished? The unorganized masses, with no regular methods,
> without recognized leaders, often arbitrary and unreasonable, yielding
> obedience to no organization and sometimes recognizing no law higher
> than mob rule, will they be less exacting than is organized labor?[28]

"Phineas" clearly did not believe so, but neither did he believe that
organization alone would usher in an era of worker affluence and
class harmony. For it was here that "Phineas"—by demonstrating an
acute sense of class consciousness and accepting the fact of class
struggle—parted company with Ford, O'Reilly, and other champions
of enclave respectability. Workers, he wrote, "must remember that
their interests and the interests of the capitalistic class are antagonistic." The tepid approach to industrial conflict exhibited by labor leaders like Terence Powderly indicated that not everyone understood
this. But if recent events held any lesson for labor, it was that workers
could only protect their rights through unremitting struggle:

> While the workmen were aggressive, no employer questioned the right of
> labor unions to exist, and no judge would have decided that boycotting
> was a crime. But when the workmen became conservative, combined capi-
> tal swept savagely down upon the labor unions, and several judges were
> ready to convict for the 'crime' of boycotting.[29]

"Phineas" had no romantic illusions about industrial conflict.
"Strikes are injurious to the workmen in the same sense that war is
injurious to a nation," he grimly commented. "But under present
conditions workmen must strike, or fall easy victim to the insatiable
greed of Dollarism." As labor's most effective weapons, strikes and
boycotts simply could not be abandoned, for workers "have found
them more powerful than the legislature, more considerate than the
executive, more just than the judiciary, [and] more loyal than the

press." Although the statement suggests that "Phineas" subordinated political action to economic struggle, he by no means ignored politics. On one occasion, in fact, he urged labor to form a third party because wage earners "can never expect consideration at the hands of party managers until they demonstrate their ability to bolt in large numbers." Such counsel underscored the extent to which "Phineas" stood apart from the enclave and rejected the hegemonic role that the middle class played in that world.[30]

"Phineas" still hoped to retain the middle class as an ally, but he recognized that to do so on favorable terms without submitting to its leadership would require an impressive demonstration of worker solidarity. "A sentiment friendly to labor, and hostile to its foes," he remarked, "cannot be maintained unless the labor unions are strong enough to exert considerable influence upon the community." The "well-fed citizen" would support organized labor once he realized that "no other force can ensure him peace and security to an equal degree during the fight between capital and labor"; that it "will restrain the violence of the workmen better than the law; it will protect property better than the police; and it will prove a just and powerful arbitrator between entrenched selfishness and helpless humanity."[31]

In April 1888, Holyoke brickmasons announced that they would strike on May 1, if they were not granted an increase in wages. Speaking for the city's master masons, Maurice Lynch refused the demand, stating that apart from economic considerations he was particularly annoyed by the "arbitrary spirit of the men." By urging Irish workers to assert their interests as a class, labor spokesmen like "Phineas" helped promote that "arbitrary spirit" Lynch found so offensive. For "Phineas" was not alone in his search for new ways to meet labor's needs. Contemporary developments in Holyoke indicated that growing numbers of local workers shared his dissatisfaction with existing patterns of social relations.[32]

THE EARLY NINETIES witnessed an unprecedented surge of militancy among Holyoke wage earners. In the city's largely unorganized and traditionally quiescent textile industry, wage-and-hour disputes idled machinery at the Farr Alpaca Company, Lyman Mills, and Merrick Thread Company. Elsewhere, threatened strikes were narrowly averted at the Skinner Silk Mill and Hadley Thread Company. Even

more indicative of the changing temper of local workers was an 1891 molders' strike at the Holyoke Hydrant and Iron Works. In June, after the company had refused to discharge nonunion employees and recognize the union's one-to-eight apprentice ratio, eighteen molders walked out. As the strike continued into August and the company hired a force of strikebreakers, broad elements of the working-class community moved into the streets to support the molders. In one incident, over one thousand strikers and sympathizers converged on the company and verbally assaulted the strikebreakers, some of whom found themselves "being used as footballs by the infuriated crowd." Policemen sent to restore order performed their task without enthusiasm; one reportedly stated that "I would not arrest a striker if I saw him hit a scab." Although few strikebreakers subsequently chose to brave the crowd, Holyoke Hydrant held out and defeated the molders. Yet this extraordinary outpouring of support for a small group of skilled workers demonstrated a new, more acute awareness of class interest on the part of Holyoke wage earners and their families. At that year's Labor Day parade, ironmolders carried placards reading, WHAT A TRAITOR IS TO HER COUNTRY A SCAB IS TO LABOR, and invoking the ethic of the Knights of Labor, AN INJURY TO ONE IS THE CONCERN OF ALL.[33]

The most militant workers in the Gilded Age labor force were the carpenters, masons, and other building tradesmen responsible for the physical transformation of late nineteenth-century urban America. Between 1880 and 1905, construction workers engaged in nearly three times as many strikes as wage earners in any other industry. Holyoke was no exception to this general trend. As the ground thawed out each spring and construction began, contractors and workers faced off against each other in what by 1890 had become an annual ritual. The workers set forth their demands and required a response by May 1, a carefully selected deadline that allowed them time to accumulate savings in the event of a strike. In late April, each side declared its resolve to stand firm, and local newspapers carried the gloomy forecasts of realtors who invariably predicted a poor building season if the workers did not relent.[34]

In 1892, the carpenters sought $2.25 for a nine-hour day and a closed shop. One builder acceded to their demands after a brief December strike, but the city's remaining contractors proved considerably less compliant that May. When James Fowles's carpenters protested against working with nonunionists, he flew into a rage and narrowly escaped a beating after throwing their tools into the street. Other

contractors reacted more calmly and formed a building association, whose constitution prohibited members from granting a closed shop. The organization also obtained assurances from local businesspeople that if a general strike ensued its members would not be held responsible for unmet contracts.[35]

In response, the carpenters warned local businesspeople that they should first consult their own interests before entering the dispute. Merchants especially, declared ex-alderman Michael Manning, should assess the respective numerical strength of the two sides and ask whether they received more from a "score of Shylocks" or the city's 2,000 trade unionists. It was no idle threat. The Central Labor Union (CLU) promptly extended its support to the carpenters, and a host of individual unions later expressed their solidarity: The painters refused to work on buildings with nonunion carpenters; the molders sought permission from their international to refuse to make castings for builders employing nonunion carpenters; the bricklayers petitioned their international for authority to decline to work beside nonunion carpenters; the printers levied a weekly assessment for the strikers' support; and in late May the brickmasons, mason tenders, and plumbers threatened a walkout if the strike was not soon settled. These expressions of solidarity doubtlessly influenced a compromise settlement reached a month later in which the builders acceded to the carpenters' wage-and-hour demands, but refused to grant a closed shop.[36]

Job actions like the 1892 carpenters' strike are of particular interest because, as David Montgomery has written, the building trades provided an arena for the interaction of two major developments in Irish American history:

> One is the much celebrated rise of some immigrants from rags to riches. The other is the much ignored forging of a working-class ethical code, which exalted mutuality over acquisitive individualism and promoted the group welfare in preference to individual success.

Although there are no extant records for Holyoke building trades' unions of the period, the minutes of a Springfield carpenters' local with a substantial Irish membership do exist and reveal elements of that ethical code. One was craft protection. At the union hall, an admissions committee carefully examined the qualifications of prospective members, while on job sites a walking delegate ensured that

93

local contractors observed an evolving body of work rules. Apart from trade concerns, the union also exhibited a strong sense of class solidarity by providing aid to striking wage earners in a variety of industries: Boston brewery workers, Lynn leather workers, Pennsylvania coal miners, and building tradesmen from various locales all received financial support from the local.[37]

Equally important, the Springfield union absorbed a number of the traditional functions of ethnic organizations by serving as a benevolent society and social center. Besides establishing a death assessment and sick-benefit fund, it periodically appointed committees to investigate the needs of ailing members and their families, taking up special collections whenever necessary. In other areas, a dance committee attended to the leisure concerns of members, while speakers at union-sponsored public meetings provided instruction in trade-union principles. As they moved from enclave to trade union, the carpenters remained preoccupied with group respectability and adopted measures to protect their new corporate identity. Prior to participating in the 1889 Labor Day parade, they resolved not to smoke during the march. The following year they went a step further and voted to "carry canes [and] wear white gloves and badges."[38]

This is not to suggest that ethnicity no longer mattered. The experience of the Springfield carpenters' local examined above demonstrates that such was hardly the case. As growing numbers of French Canadians joined the union, tensions arose and in 1892 it divided into French- and English-speaking locals. Like other Franco-Americans of the period, these carpenters were deeply committed to preserving the language and customs of French Canada and were unwilling to abide the cultural chauvinism of more Americanized coworkers. Nor did workers uniformly develop new views of class relations. During the 1892 carpenters' strike at Holyoke, one union official stated that the strikers had no desire "to injure any contractor for they realize how necessary capital is to labor"; and union organizer William Shields applauded the formation of the building association, declaring that there should be a "mutual understanding" between builders and carpenters: "The master builders should organize for their protection, not to attempt to put down labor unions but for the protection of contracts."[39]

Although the strikers' ranks held firm throughout the dispute, these views were not shared by all carpenters. A letter to the *Transcript* from NOT A MEMBER OF ANY UNION decrying the closed shop

because it deprived workers of their freedom brought this response from one striker:

> We all know we are not getting all the profit there is in the business, but you wait until we get every carpenter into the union, and see if we don't, or make the contractor sick. . . . We should also like to know by what particular right or privilege the contractor presumes to buy lumber that is not chopped by union choppers, drawn by union teamsters, sawed by union sawyers, planed by union planers, and approved by our walking delegate whom we pay to do nothing but go around and find out what they can about the contractor's business and report to us so we can regulate the things. We would like to know what right Ranger [a local contractor] or any other man has to raise the price for planing without giving us the extra he charges. We should like to know what right your correspondent had to claim American freedom unless he belongs to our union anyways.

In addition to the writer's ringing defense of trade unionism, his emphasis on a labor theory of value is also worth noting: Where local union leaders wished to formalize existing patterns of class relations under the safe rubric of business unionism, this striker expressed sentiments that struck at the very existence of the profit system. The statement also indicates that the proselytizing efforts of Peter J. McGuire, founder of the carpenters' union, had not been in vain. For McGuire, trade unions were not ends in themselves, but way stations to a cooperative commonwealth in which workers would receive the full value of their labor. In a local address during the strike, McGuire joined Shields in accepting the existence of the contractors' association, but at the same time he urged carpenters to "go forth and meet the builders on their own ground by seeking for contracts themselves on the cooperative plan."[40]

Differing approaches to class relations also surfaced within the Central Labor Union. Formed in 1891 to coordinate local union activity, the CLU comprised three delegates from each union with at least ten members and by the spring of 1892 represented 1,600 workers from seventeen unions. Although the *Republican* characterized its leaders as "conservative men, who believe that arbitration is the best way to secure the benefits for which the laboring men are asking," there were indications that some rank and filers viewed the world differently. One faction, the *Transcript* observed, considered CLU president John F. Sheehan too conservative and preferred "someone who will throw the labor classes into conflict with the corporations." When

STRIKER implied that Sheehan had betrayed local molders during the Holyoke Hydrant and Iron Works dispute, ex-alderman Manning called him a "cowardly cur," who only attacked Sheehan because he was a Republican. Manning may have been right, but the appearance of similar differences among local carpenters suggests that other workers shared STRIKER's frustration.[41]

Whatever their approach to class relations, CLU leaders did not hesitate to employ political leverage to advance labor's cause. When in 1891 Daniel O'Connell replaced twenty-three French Canadian laborers with lower-paid Italian help, the CLU voted to withhold support from any party nominating O'Connell for office that fall. O'Connell did not seek reelection to his Ward 5 council seat, but his son did. Accordingly, the CLU threatened to oppose the entire Democratic ticket, which frightened enough party members that O'Connell was defeated at the nominating caucus. This was by no means the extent of CLU political intervention. During the molders' strike, it induced the water commissioner to delay ordering new hydrants from the Holyoke Hydrant and Iron Works; when the Street Railway Company refused to grant its laborers a closed shop and pay a "fair rate of wages," the CLU instructed its delegates to contact their aldermen and urge them to oppose any extension of the company's privileges; and Frank Rivers lost a sewer contract when alderman Jeremiah Callanan accused him of underpaying his workers. Although an attempt to prevent a nonunion contractor from receiving the bid on two schoolhouses failed, this did not diminish the CLU's accomplishments. As the *Transcript* observed, such "aggressive action" attracted workers and was a major reason for the organization's growth during the early nineties.[42]

Another spur to organization was the late summer observance of Labor Day after 1890. The day began with a parade that by 1892 counted more than 1,500 workers in its line of march, followed by a series of field events and baseball games, and concluded with a picnic, at which the cultural divisions separating Holyoke wage earners momentarily dissolved in a sea of beer and whiskey. When police raided the 1891 celebration, some later suggested that it cost Mayor Griffin his bid for reelection. After 1890, local entrepreneurs did their part to make the day a success. At the CLU's urging, merchants decorated their stores in 1891 and by the following year most mills shut down for the occasion, allowing textile and paper workers to enjoy the day's festivities. For the 1893 celebration, the CLU issued an

eight-page program filled with advertisements from local merchants, and the *Transcript* announced that it would not publish that day.[43]

Yet, petty-entrepreneur support of Labor Day was a deceptive mirror of relations between workers and the middle class during the early nineties. In addition to mounting conflict between contractors and building tradesmen, the increasing use of boycotts forced small businesspeople to reconsider where there interests lay. Some sided with labor. During the carpenters' dispute, a number of Irish and French Canadian merchants contributed to the strike fund. Others vacillated and maintained a prudent silence. But whichever side one chose, the fact that there was increasing pressue to choose at all indicated that the enclave's ethno-religious definition of communal organization was giving way to new concepts of group interest. Where a decade earlier, immigrant entrepreneurs could demonstrate communal loyalty by going to church, contributing to the parish building fund, and supporting the Land League or St. Jerome's Temperance Society, they were now being forced take a stand in local contests between capital and labor—contests in which capital was no longer a vaguely defined money power, but a concrete entity with real power.[44]

While boycotts strained relations between labor and the middle class, they fostered a spirit of cooperation among workers. In addition to its embargo of the Holyoke Hydrant and Iron Works's castings, the CLU placed a local outlet of Forbes and Wallace on the unfair list when the parent concern employed nonunion painters on a new department store in Springfield. It threatened similar action against any store that did not accede to the Friday-night closing demand of the clerks' union. At the same time, it instructed its members to confine their purchases to union-made goods. During the early nineties, cigarmakers inspected saloons to insure that they stocked union-made cigars, United Garment Workers officials checked clothes in stores for the union label,and the CLU enforced a national boycott of Ehret's beer. As Norman Ware observed more than a half-century ago, prior to the consumer revolution of the 1920s there were a wide range of identifiable working-class commodities. Boycotts thus fused consumer consciousness to class consciousness, reinforcing and developing the latter in the process. In so doing, they also gave expression to the molders' Labor Day placard: AN INJURY TO ONE IS THE CONCERN OF ALL.[45]

There were, to be sure, limits to the practical application of this sentiment. In paper mills, continued owner resistance to tour-worker demands for shorter hours led the latter to obtain a charter from the

American Federation of Labor and form Local No. 1 of the International Brotherhood of Paper Makers. But membership was restricted to skilled engine and machine room personnel as craft exclusivity remained an integral feature of local paper unionism. Textile unionism followed a similar course of development. Although mule spinners, loom fixers, and wool sorters maintained strong organizations, no effort was made to bring the majority of textile operatives within the union fold, despite signs of growing unrest among weavers and other semiskilled workers during the early nineties.[46]

Nevertheless, Holyoke workers were more organized and more cohesive than ever under the aegis of the Central Labor Union. As an enclave consciousness slowly gave way to a more militant trade unionism, even CLU moderates who sought a compromise with capital did not hesitate to move into the streets when their demands met resistance. In the political arena, local wage earners ignored "Phineas" 's counsel to form an independent labor party, but their efforts to use government as an instrument of economic struggle suggested that the politics of the enclave, with its cultural and reformist emphases, was no longer adequate. Meanwhile, CLU-sponsored boycotts, Labor Day celebrations, and massive strike demonstrations touched the lives of all workers. Catholic commentators also noticed the difference. Although *The Messenger* still counseled patience and warned that strikes "should not be undertaken lightly," it conceded that until "the masters mend their ways it seems cruelty itself to argue against the stand taken by men who cry out for more bread to eat or more leisure to rest from the chains of toil." "Strikes are a very dangerous evil," declared another editorial, which concluded with the admonition: "But when you do strike—win." They did not know it then, but Holyoke workers would celebrate few victories during the next five years as the city entered the worst depression of the nineteenth century.[47]

5

DEPRESSION AND UPHEAVAL, 1893–1905

THE DECADE and a half after 1890 was a period of tremendous ideological flux among Holyoke's Irish workers. In their efforts to forge a new worldview that moved beyond and yet retained still-cherished features of the previous era's enclave consciousness, workers gave serious attention to a range of competing philosophies. Although they would in time submerge their differences in a shared culture of Catholic trade unionist respectability, the road to this new consensus contained a number of twists and turns. One major obstacle was the depression of the 1890s. As unemployment mounted, trade unions disbanded and growing numbers of wage earners retreated to the safe confines of the enclave, where they could draw upon kin and neighborhood resources in their search for subsistence. During these dark years bold assertions of class interest gave way to more elemental concerns as workers struggled just to stay alive.

At Holyoke, a general tightening of credit during the summer of 1893 marked the onset of hard times, though it soon became apparent that the economy faced problems considerably more serious than a liquidity crunch. "Every day one learns something new about the closing of mills and very little about any of them starting up again," the *Republican* reported in mid-August, a month that saw local paper mills curtail production by more than half. Those making fine writing paper were especially hard hit, as businesses reduced clerical departments and shifted to cheaper lines of stationery. The response of the American Paper Makers' Association gave little hope of an upturn: In September it announced an indefinite postponement of its next convention when it became clear that few members could or would attend

99

the fall gathering. If capital was demoralized, labor was approaching destitution. Half-production meant smaller paychecks, and even those workers employed at mills that returned to full output during the winter had to tighten their belts as employers sharply cut wages. In January, the Nonotuck Paper Company offered its employees a choice between half-time or five-days pay for six days labor: the hard-pressed workers accepted the latter option.[1]

The city's textile manufacturers wasted even less time lightening pay envelopes. Early August found Lyman Mills agent Ernest Lovering hard at work on a plan to slash wages without precipitating a strike. If the company closed down for two to four days and posted notices "to the effect that work would be resumed at a 10% reduction," he suggested in a letter to treasurer Theophilus Parsons, "I think this reduction would come *more easily*[,] . . . giving the help a chance to size up the situation." Lovering also thought it best to wait for Lawrence and Fall River to act first, "as then, we should not be *considered as promoters.*" The Hadley and Merrick Thread mills, he added, seemed willing to cooperate. A month later Lovering proudly reported that the workers had accepted the pay cuts with "no complaints," and in mid-September the Hadley Mills announced a similar cut after an extended shutdown, contending that wage decreases in eastern textile centers had "enabled those corporations to underbid the Hadley Company." Other mills followed in subsequent months. After a two-week shutdown in October, the Farr Alpaca Company resumed operation on a four-day schedule and with a 10 percent reduction in wages.[2]

Before it ended the depression would exact a staggering toll in human misery. The costs began mounting early. Increased deprivation soon overwhelmed the resources of the municipal relief department, and in October local Protestant churches organized a relief association, comprising the pastor and two delegates from each congregation. Conjoining organizational rigor and cold calculation to Christian compassion, the group established an executive committee, divided the city into districts, and appointed visitors to weed out "professional paupers" as they determined the "worthiness" of relief applicants. In January, a group of Catholic women met at former mayor Sullivan's home to plan a fund-raising fair for the St. Vincent DePaul Society. The following month, they formalized their activities by establishing the Catholic Aid Association.[3]

As the depression deepened during the winter months, not everyone became discouraged. At a union Thanksgiving service, Presbyte-

rian minister G. A. Wilson admitted it "may appear inconsistent that people gather to thank God for benefits, when all around are sufferings and wants." But, he added, "God has provided enough." Less intemperance and fewer strikes, explained Wilson, would reduce waste, further human brotherhood, and lead the way to better times. In his annual address, Mayor Farr assured Holyokers that the city had experienced less distress "than has been the case *in almost any other city of like* size and character." Yet in December the *Transcript* felt compelled to issue a plea for greater charity, because of reports it had received of the "most pitiful poverty." The following spring, a passerby found the body of an infant in the second-level canal. "The lungs showed that the child had breathed," reported the *Republican*, and it "was either suffocated and thrown into the canal, or was wrapped up while alive and drowned." Depression-engendered destitution was by no means the only explanation for the tragedy. It might have been the act of a young woman destroying an illegitimate child. But after the awful depression winter of 1893 no one could be sure—despite the assurances of Mayor Farr and the Reverend Wilson that all was well.[4]

During 1894, there were few signs of improvement. In February, Holyoke paper workers suffered their first general wage reduction in a decade. With the exception of a brief strike at the Dickinson Paper Company, where the cut went especially deep, workers grudgingly accepted the decrease. Among the owners, the August meeting of the American Paper Makers' Association lacked bodies, ideas, and enthusiasm. In textiles, the situation was much the same. Apart from German workers at the Germania Woolen Mills, who walked out for three weeks in September, only the more skilled operatives tried to defend themselves against employer exactions. Some even demanded improved wages. The mule spinners at the Lyman Mills, for example, sought a 10 percent increase. Agent Lovering noted that their treasury was still "well supplied with funds," but feared other departments would insist on a comparable raise if he acceded. He also believed New Bedford and Fall River would soon slash wages and thus decided to reject the demand. A short while later he could report that all was "quiet" among the mule spinners: "The men I wanted to get rid of are gone, and will not get a chance to come back."[5]

Although business revived during 1895, the depression had not yet run its course. After showing signs of improvement throughout much of the year, the economy again went belly-up the following spring. Numerous mills reduced hours or shut down for weeks at a time;

CHAPTER FIVE

others ceased production altogether as bankruptcies mounted. The most notable failure, the Albion Paper Company, elicited a mixed reaction from the Holyoke business community. Local millowners, who usually empathized with one another in the crunch, showed little sympathy on this occasion. The company's owner, E. C. Taft, had expended his wealth in a most extravagant manner, and the local upper class deemed such violations of its more staid sumptuary norms bad class relations as well as bad business. Thus, while it offered no cause for cheer, the Albion failure did provide local manufacturers grim reassurance of their own rectitude. Millowners also parlayed hard times into political advantage. In the 1896 election, normally Democratic Holyoke went overwhelmingly for McKinley in part because manufacturers told workers that a vote for Bryan was a vote for unemployment.[6]

For most workers continued hard times meant unmitigated misery. Many gladly accepted part-time work at the almshouse farm, and at year's end the Overseers of the Poor reported that aid applications exceeded those of any previous year in the city's history. Children could be found doing their part to aid ailing families in the city's back alleys, rummaging through garbage boxes and trash bins, hunting for potato parings and rags. Some workers took to the road, hoping that better times awaited them elsewhere. Where many German and Polish textile operatives returned to Europe, the police station noted a marked increase in the number of "tramps," many of whom were ordinarily secure "artisans or mechanics." A few gave up altogether. Kate Sullivan left home one August morning presumably to attend mass at St. Jerome's. She never reached the church and later that day a passerby found her body in the river. Although no one knew for sure whether she had committed suicide or drowned while bathing, relatives remarked that she had been deeply despondent since losing her job at the Farr Alpaca Company some months earlier.[7]

During the first half of 1897 most mills still ran part-time with intermittent shutdowns. By September, though, a few textile mills had returned to full production, and William Whiting observed that a growing demand for better grades of paper foreshadowed the arrival of "better times": "People who have been using cheap paper buy better as times improve and they can afford it." Yet as the year closed the Overseers of the Poor stated that relief applications had reached an all-time high and wearily concluded that the "causes which have made it necessary for so many able-bodied men and

102

women to apply for assistance are well known to all, and need not be explained by us."[8]

The crisis did abate finally, though workers would not soon forget it. Nor did they forget the vigorous labor movement that for them was one of the depression's more conspicuous casualties. And as they began once again to work regularly they also recalled the many concessions forced upon them during the previous few years. These recollections would inform their actions during the immediate post-depression period.

IN THE CLOSING years of the century, a flood of mergers transformed the nation's industrial structure, eliminating or absorbing countless smaller firms and replacing them with huge, multiunit corporate entities. At Holyoke, the Deane Steam Pump Company became part of the International Steam Pump Company, the Hadley and Merrick Thread companies entered the American Thread Company, and the Holyoke Envelope Company joined a combine in that field. The most striking indication that a new era had arrived came in 1899 when sixteen paper manufacturers sold out to the American Writing Paper Company.[9]

The merger movement was not the only postdepression phenomenon to affect Holyoke. The period from 1899 to 1903 also saw an unprecedented number of strikes. As the economy gradually revived, workers throughout the nation began to repair moribund unions and demand the restoration of wage cuts and other concessions made during the depression. Holyoke wage earners recovered slowly from hard times. As late as July 1898, the *Republican* observed that relief applications were still abnormally high, and the following month an American Federation of Labor (AFL) convention at Springfield reported that Holyoke trade unionism was in a "demoralized condition." That same month, though, a small band of weavers at the Connor Brothers Woolen Mill walked out in protest against the seventy-to-eighty-hour work week they had to endure. The strike failed, but the following spring and summer other textile operatives obtained greater success.[10]

In May, 400 weavers walked out at the Farr Alpaca Company, demanding a 10 percent wage increase and abolition of the fines system for poor cloth. Because business had just returned to predepression

levels, Farr wished to avoid an extended struggle. The strikers, most of whom were French Canadian women, quickly accepted a company offer to revise the fines system and increase wages by 5 percent, but not before they had formed a union. Within a few weeks, Polish and French Canadian weavers at the Lyman Mills also established separate unions and joined operatives from other departments in seeking to restore the 1896 wage schedule. The strike began on June 8 when the yard laborers laid down their tools; a week later the doffer boys and ring spinners deserted their respective frames. Anticipating a general walkout, and with an excess of cloth on hand, the company locked out the remaining workers before they too left of their own accord. The mills remained closed until early July, at which time all but the doffers and ring spinners returned to work. When they sought help from the CLU, it declared that they belonged to no union and refused to aid them. The strike was effectively over.[11]

Company agent Ernest Lovering attributed the strike to "outside agitators," as he assured his superiors that their efforts had proved fruitless:

> The most active strikers did not apply for work July 5th. Their places are now filled. There is no union of Lyman employees. H. S. Mills has recently left Holyoke, probably to try similar tactics in another town. . . . Have your Association [the Arkwright Club] look out for him.

That December, however, the doffer boys again walked out, demanding a 15 percent wage increase. In all likelihood they were dispatched by the mule spinners for whom they worked, and their departure warned of wider grievances. This time the workers chose to act during a period of heavy demand, and the company promptly came to terms by granting a general wage increase ranging from 5 to 10 percent. It was also apparent that the "outside agitators" whom Lovering believed he had vanquished in July were more persistent than he had imagined. By June, Holyoke boasted six textile unions with more than one thousand members, the majority of whom were women. But textile unionism was not destined to prosper locally. An examination of the last major textile strike of the period discloses some of the reasons for its decline.[12]

The dispute involved the mule spinners at the Lyman Mills. In April 1902, a committee representing the spinners and their helpers demanded a 10 percent wage increase to match that recently obtained

by New Bedford spinners. Agent Lovering first attempted to put them off by arguing that the work performed by the mule spinners at the Lyman Company and thus their scale of remuneration bore a closer resemblance to mills in Lawrence, Lowell, and Manchester than those in New Bedford. The argument was to no avail and when the spinners threatened to walk out if the company did not accede, treasurer Parsons informed Lovering that business was so poor that a shutdown would be to the mill's advantage. Accordingly, on May 5 the mills closed, locking out 1,400 workers. Still hoping to placate the spinners, Lovering sent one of the hands to Lowell to investigate wages there—after he had insured that they were indeed no higher than those paid at the Lyman Company. The ploy failed and when after two weeks all but the mule spinners returned to work, both sides settled in for a long struggle.[13]

The company's initial strategy was simple: replace the mules with ring spindles and the mule spinners with semiskilled ring spinners. It soon found, however, that ring-spun yarn did not meet product specifications, and it had to begin purchasing filling from other mills. Despite the failure of this tack, the company publicly maintained that the installation of ring frames had rendered the mule spinners superfluous. In addition to planting articles to that effect in the local press, it went ahead and ordered new frames, asking one supplier to ship "*any part* of our work at an *early* date" in order "to convince the mule spinners that we have new frames coming to in part take care of mule spun yarn." But the mule spinners were less easily duped than the fourth estate. With the national union's backing, they prevented the employment of strikebreakers and threatened to boycott any mill supplying yarn to the company, thus forcing the Lyman management to take elaborate precautions to disguise the identity of its suppliers.[14]

Because it added to the cost of manufacturing, buying yarn from outside sources could be no more than a temporary expedient. Yet, the company believed that if it too readily acceded to the mule spinners' demands, it would embolden other operatives to seek comparable wage increases. As it was, recent gains by the weavers had already added significantly to production costs. After comparing cost-of-manufacturing data for the third quarter of 1902 with the previous year, treasurer Parsons wrote Lovering that a "good saving is made in wages of Carding, Spinning, and Dressing to offset [the] cost of yarn bought, but Weaving has gone up out of sight." With labor militancy on the rise, however, Lovering worried that if the strike continued

into the spring it might spill over into other departments. In a letter to Parsons, he summarized the company's dilemma:

> Should a compromise or entire surrender to spinners be made, I figure that with present going conditions, labor agitation will be on the increase next spring and summer and there will be further effort to unionize all our help.
> The better way to control labor troubles is when help are at work and not when they are loafing, owing to the high perfection of the labor leader of today as the kingpin in a dispute.[15]

By November, Lovering recognized that he had to come to terms with the spinners. To prevent local strike leaders from taking credit for the conflict's outcome, he chose to deal exclusively with Samuel Ross, president of the National Mule Spinners Association. Although the spinners obtained their demands, the strike did more to retard than foster textile unionism at Holyoke. The fact that they went it alone for nine months reinforced the craft exclusiveness of mule spinners. Where earlier they had coupled their demands with those of less-skilled operatives and appeared to be spearheading a campaign to organize all textile workers, the spinners subsequently made their own deals with the bosses. A few years later when they notified Lovering of a recent increase at New Bedford, he advanced their wages 5 percent "to hush up the matter." "By this method," he explained, "there was to be no publicity and upset to the other departments." This resurgence of craft exclusiveness, which involved loom fixers as well as mule spinners, would inhibit textile organization for decades to come.[16]

The turn of the century also witnessed a marked rise in activity among paper workers. During the depression a succession of wage cuts and the reinstitution of the seventy-two-hour week for tour workers insured the reemergence of Eagle Lodge, the machine tenders and beater engineers union, at the first sign of better times. The formation of the American Writing Paper Company further encouraged organization. Shortly after the company's establishment, C. S. Hemingway of West Springfield's Mittineague Paper Company told a Holyoke audience that trusts would provide prosperity for workers as well as manufacturers. By eliminating competition and maintaining high prices, he explained, the combine would be able to raise wages. In fact, Hemingway argued, higher wages enforced by workers' organizations were essential to the trust's success, as independents could only meet its

wage scale if they followed the existing price line; and this they would
be forced to do if workers avoided the employ of any company not
paying combine wages. It was a marvelous vision, but the industry
did not work that way. Few manufacturers shared Hemingway's
equanimous view of trade unions. Nor did the workers themselves
assume that trust formation augured a new affluence; one of their
number conceded that the combine's greater efficiency might reduce
hours, but contended that it would also mean less pay and fewer jobs.
Paper workers did recognize the necessity of organization, though,
and by 1900 Eagle Lodge claimed nearly 1,500 members.[17]

A 1901 strike by the city's stationary firemen provided the occasion
for the most notable job action by Holyoke paper workers before 1903.
Because state law required mills using steam boilers to employ licensed firemen, the firemen's threat to leave their posts on June 1 if
they were not granted an eight-hour day was in effect a threat to shut
down all of the city's mills. Upon hearing of the impending action,
Eagle Lodge prepared demands of its own. As the strike deadline
neared, the Holyoke Businessmen's Association dispatched a special
committee to dissuade the firemen from walking out and the *Republican* urged the unions to give management more time to consider the
matter. But the owners needed no aditional time. With the exception
of the Whiting Paper Company and three other mills, they had mutu-
ally resolved to stand firm, and on the morning of June 1 production
halted at twenty-five mills.[18]

They did not resume operation for two weeks. Nor could the owners use the shutdown to undertake repairs, as the bricklayers resolved
to do no work on mill buildings and the teamsters refused to handle
their products and supplies. Among the strikers no one broke ranks.
The women "seemed especially happy," observed the *Transcript.*
"There was a feeling of satisfaction manifest among them and nearly
all expressed the greatest confidence in the results." The manufacturers were less cheerful, largely because William Whiting, owner of the
city's largest independent mill, had chosen to go his own way despite
their appeals for class solidarity. The news that a mass meeting of
strikers repeatedly applauded the mere mention of Whiting's name
did little to lift their spirits. In mid-June, following the intervention of
the State Board of Arbitration, the owners capitulated on a wide range
of demands: firemen obtained an eight-hour day, tour workers received a sixty-five-hour week, and semiskilled paper workers won a
wage increase.[19]

Apart from the immediate benefits secured by its members, the strike proved a particular boon to Eagle Lodge. During its first week the union formed a division of women paper workers that rapidly grew to more than one thousand members as total membership soared past the four thousand mark. By late June, it felt sufficiently powerful to request a closed shop. The owners stoutly resisted, one declaring that he would shut down "until eternity first," and when William Whiting joined them the union decided to defer the demand until a later date. Nonetheless, Eagle Lodge had traveled a considerable distance from its beginnings seventeen years earlier, when it comprised an intensely craft-conscious band of machine tenders and beater engineers unwilling even to organize their helpers. The two groups still possessed an influence within the union that far exceeded their numbers, but they now realized that the organization of all workers improved their bargaining position and enhanced their power. Like the manufacturers for whom they worked, they too had adjusted to the changed social and economic environment of the new era of corporate capitalism.[20]

By reason of their militance and numbers, paper workers spearheaded the resurgence of Holyoke labor. Yet, they were by no means alone. Between 1899 and 1901, strikes by local cabinetmakers, brick-masons, painters, plumbers, laborers, brewery workers, pressmen, and stage employees met with varying degrees of success. Meanwhile, the Central Labor Union coordinated local activity and extended moral and financial support to strikers in neighboring communities. Still brandishing the boycott as its most effective weapon, the CLU placed bans on saloons refusing to employ union bartenders, enforced national boycotts of Ballantine Ale and American Tobacco Company products, and urged workers to patronize merchants who employed union clerks. Such, apparently, was Holyoke's reputation for ale consumption that Herbert Ballantine himself appeared before the CLU in an effort to relax the boycott on his product.[21]

The most notable boycott of the period was prompted by the union-busting practices of the Street Railway Company. In June 1901, company president W. S. Loomis ordered the disbandment of the motormen and conductors union because, he argued, "if his men belonged to a labor organization they would become so independent that they would become negligent." The CLU retaliated by placing a boycott on Mountain Park, a local amusement area in the northernmost corner of the city, which most residents could only reach by

trolley. The *Transcript* immediately declared the injunction of "dangerous significance, since it strikes at the root of the liberty the Constitution affords every man," while complacently adding that few merchants would observe it anyway. The CLU anticipated such a response and appointed a committee to take down the names of all businessmen and their families who patronized the park. As union members threatened businessmen seen riding the cars with economic reprisal, relations between workers and the middle class became increasingly tense. One merchant angrily declared, "I don't propose to have the Holyoke unions tell me what clothes I shall buy, what I shall eat, or where I shall go for pleasure."[22]

Despite, or perhaps because of the acrimony engendered by the boycott, the CLU sought to repair its links with the middle class. In January, a committee appeared before the Holyoke Businessmen's Association and agreed to do its utmost to promote local trade. CLU president James M. Kennedy also suggested that the businessmen form an arbitration committee to settle any future disputes. But it was an uneasy truce at best. The following month the CLU instructed workers to "trade only in such establishments as employ union clerks" and warned that a "close watch will be maintained."[23]

The Mountain Park boycott ended in August after the motormen and conductors voted not to unionize. CLU secretary Edward F. Dowd declared the vote fraudulent, but still lifted the ban, disingenuously observing that, with a major steel strike looming, "the unions would doubtless soon be called to aid them and they did not desire to continue fights on minor matters." However disappointing the boycott's conclusion, the Holyoke labor movement could take pride in the progress it had made in recent years. During 1901, the CLU added more than a dozen newly formed unions to its ranks and total membership doubled to more than 7,500 workers. That September nearly 25,000 people lined the city's main thoroughfares to watch 6,000 workers—ranging from "the humble bootblack to the skilled laborer"—parade through the streets of Holyoke.[24]

As the new year dawned, building tradesmen and metalworkers girded for imminent struggles with their respective employers. On March 1, 400 carpenters left their jobs demanding recognition of the Building Trades Council and $2.50 for an eight-hour day. Construction soon came to a standstill, and when the strike continued into April contractor solidarity began to collapse. The settlement accorded the carpenters their wage-and-hour demands and provided for the

establishment of a six-person arbitration committee comprised of three builders and three members of the Building Trades Council. In a quest for shorter hours, the machinists eschewed a general strike in favor of a strategy that entailed picking off one shop at a time. By late June they too had largely succeeded.[25]

Yet, as 1902 closed there were indications that the postdepression tide of labor militancy had crested. At the CLU, James M. Kennedy defeated Edward F. Dowd in a bitter contest for business agent. A brickmason and member of the St. Jerome's Temperance Society, Kennedy represented a faction that embraced an older, enclavist approach to class relations and saw a mutuality of interest among social classes. Believing that "tact and courtesy" should be the governing characteristics of labor's relations with capital, Kennedy strongly opposed strikes and asserted that most labor disputes could be resolved through "frank dealing and mutual concessions." Labor unions, he told a meeting of the men's league at the Second Baptist Church, did not seek to "antagonize employers or wring unjust concessions [from them], but to increase the wages of the men and lessen the hours of labor to such a point that men could give their families more of their time and afford to give their children a better chance in life."[26]

Dowd's followers were no less committed than the Kennedy faction to higher wages, shorter hours, and a richer family life, but they did not share Kennedy's faith in the beneficence and goodwill of capital. Instead they cast class relations in a more confrontational framework and favored "taking up a grievance hammer and tongs fashion." At the January meeting between the CLU and the Businessman's Association, Kennedy had recommended forming an arbitration committee, where Dowd had warned that in any agreement between the groups the businessmen must "come half way" and cease discriminating against union members in their hiring practices. Although Dowd engineered his reelection as business agent the following spring, mounting tensions between the two factions did not augur well for the future.[27]

Just as signs of discord appeared in labor's ranks, the Skinner Silk Company decided to test the power and influence of the CLU. Because the company would not grant its stationary firemen an eight-hour day, it had been on the CLU's unfair list since 1901, and local building tradesmen refused to do any work for the concern. In 1903, the company planned to expand its operations, but rather than settle with its handful of firemen, it chose instead to confront the CLU by

announcing that it would build outside Holyoke. "No mill man would come here and build a mill," said William Skinner, Jr., as he made the decision public. "You are not allowed to run your own business." The Holyoke Businessmen's Association reacted immediately to the announcement. In addition to appointing a committee to meet with the firemen, association president Marcienne Whitcomb released a letter from a manufacturer who had considered locating in the city, but feared that "Holyoke is a pretty tough place if the Skinner episode is any example." The firemen's union quickly gave way, deciding that "it was a case in which the good of the city as a whole and themselves as individuals would be better conserved by a change in their position." And a week later the CLU removed the Skinner Mills from its unfair list. Yet the company still refused to build that year because, Joseph Skinner stated, the "union labor market is in too dangerous a condition now." Meanwhile, by raising the specter of capital flight, the Skinners had prompted the middle class to abandon any pretense of neutrality and identify its interests with those of local millowners; they also deepened the rift within the CLU by strengthening the hand of those who believed in the interdependence of capital and labor.[28]

Despite its troubles, the CLU continued to grow. In May 1903, the forty-five unions affiliated with it had 8,000 members. By a considerable margin the largest was Eagle Lodge, which had added to its ranks during the previous year by supporting two successful job actions for shorter hours and stepping up its campaign to enlist women paper workers. In the spring of 1903, it demanded a closed shop and wage increases ranging from 20 to 30 percent for different categories of workers. The American Writing Paper Company assumed the role of spokesperson for local manufacturers and refused to discuss wages until the union dropped its demand for a closed shop. When a strike vote in late May showed that a majority of paper workers would not walk out on the unionization issue alone, Eagle Lodge appointed a committee to secure a new wage schedule. Negotiations quickly broke down. Because many owners believed the union's increasing boldness made a test of strength inevitable, American Writing submitted a wage package sufficiently at odds with the workers' request to prompt a second strike vote. Again, the majority opted to stay on the job. The following day, however, 300 cutter women took matters into their own hands and left their machines.[29]

The walkout surprised union leaders, who initially ordered the women to return to work. They not only refused, but demanded

support; one observer hinted that the women questioned the manhood of male workers who declined to join them. Within a few days, another 1,200 paper workers had also walked out, closing seven mills and forcing Eagle Lodge to conduct yet another strike vote. This ballot showed a large majority supported the strike and, with the exception of five exempted plants, the Holyoke paper industry ground to a halt as 3,500 workers deserted the mills. In the following weeks the millwrights refused to do repair work, the stationary firemen voted not to furnish steam for paper machines, the CLU placed the mills on its unfair list, and in the streets striking workers did what they could to make life miserable for a small band of strikebreakers. As the strike dragged into July, though, signs of sagging morale began to surface. It was then that American Writing Paper, sensing an imminent victory, reanimated striker spirits by arrogantly refusing to make any conciliatory gestures, despite the pleas of local businesspeople and the State Board of Arbitration that it deal with the workers. On July 19, the strikers overwhelmingly supported a motion to remain out until the trust submitted to arbitration.[30]

The company refused to budge. An ultimatum declaring that only those who returned to work by August 6 would be granted the wage increase proffered at the strike's outset represented its sole concession. Most workers by now at least sensed that the trust not only wanted a favorable settlement, but to crush the union as well. Yet, as strike funds and worker savings diminished, it became clear that they could not hold out indefinitely. In mid-August, a committee of machine tenders met with Mayor Chapin and expressed a desire to return to work. In the next few days a handful of mills recommenced operation. Recognizing that it was all over, the strikers voted on August 18 to terminate the sixty-five-day-old struggle. The vote also signaled the temporary decline of Eagle Lodge. Financially exhausted and stripped of its leadership by a company blacklist, the union quickly passed into a state of desuetude. Its demise in turn crippled the CLU, though not before the carpenters assembled for one last hurrah during the spring of 1904.[31]

On May 1, more than four hundred carpenters packed up their tools and joined fellow tradesmen from Chicopee and Springfield in a valley-wide strike. The struggle continued for more than two months and before it was over involved major elements of the middle class. Emboldened by the Skinner episode of the previous spring and the recent defeat of the paper workers, the petit bourgeoisie

scented the blood of a dying labor movement and moved against the carpenters with an uncharacteristic decisiveness. At Springfield in mid-May, sixty-five businesspeople banded together to "correct abuses resulting from organized labor," while Holyoke merchants refused credit to strikers and local lumber dealers assured the Master Builders' Association that they would not sell to striking carpenters seeking to contract on their own. At the police court, Judge E. W. Chapin, the mayor's father, did his part by sentencing to six months in jail two carpenters convicted of assaulting a strikebreaker. By mid-August the strike had collapsed and carpenters throughout the valley began returning to work. In its wake, James Kennedy's followers moved to the fore and established a new structural-trades alliance that required an affirmative vote from each member local before a strike could be called.[32]

By 1905, then, the Holyoke labor movement consisted of a quiescent and largely unorganized textile work force, a badly demoralized and nearly moribund paper union, and a Building Trades Council led by conservative unionists reluctant to confront capital. But factionalism, craft exclusiveness, and an inability to match capital's material resources only partially explain its rapid descent. An equally noteworthy failure in the political arena both preceded and foreshadowed its defeat on the economic front. Unlike the upsurge of the early 1890s, labor marched into the postdepression years with few friends at city hall.

LABOR'S POLITICAL influence did not collapse overnight. During an 1894 printers' strike at the *Transcript*, the City Council approved an ordinance requiring that all city printing be done in union shops and amid charges of "class legislation" overrode Mayor Whitcomb's veto of the order. Nor was this the only occasion on which Democratic city councillors intervened on labor's behalf during the year. In January, they overrode another Whitcomb veto of a measure to maintain municipal laborers' wages at $2 per day, despite the mayor's contention that "Holyoke should [not] pay more than the market price for any commodity, labor included." Later, a March order required the city to employ union carpenters, and in June a demonstration by the laborers' protective union demanding increased expenditures for public works prompted a $20,000 appropriation by the council.[33]

Yet, even at this point there were indications of future trouble. Although united on labor measures, local Democrats remained divided along cultural lines. During the early nineties, Patrick W. Shea joined Jeremiah Callanan as the principal representative of Irish respectables. Born at Dingle, Ireland, in 1865, Shea was a onetime textile operative who trained as a pipe fitter and later opened a shoe store. Posing as the "democratic labor nominee" and a steadfast opponent of the liquor interest, Shea first secured an aldermanic seat in 1891 by defeating T. J. Dillon, a Ward 4 liquor dealer, in a raucous and slanderous contest that left neither candidate's reputation untainted. During the campaign, a statement by WARD FOUR WORKMAN criticizing the liquor dealers who currently sat on the City Council expressed the sentiments of Shea's supporters:

> Do they think we workingmen are going to be led astray in two ways, just to drink their stuff and not have them legislate for us? I hope the laboring men of ward four will rise in arms and say it is about time that the monopolists and liquor dealers of ward four shall not dictate to them by electing as their standard bearers P. W. O'Shea for alderman, Thomas J. Sears, Michael J. Casey, and Frank Blanchette as their councilmen.[34]

The party's saloon faction was headed by Michael Connors, a Ward 3 cigar manufacturer known to friend and foe alike as "Mikeleen." During the mid-eighties he had unsuccessfully run for alderman as a candidate of the Trades and Labor Assembly. After a brief sojourn in California, where he participated in Dennis Kearney's anti-Chinese movement, Connors returned to Holyoke and secured the Ward 3 aldermanic seat. He was the consummate ward politician. Generous to a fault—even when it meant digging into his own pocket—Connors could, it was said, "sell cigars where no one else could give them away." Within Ward 3 his ties to the saloon interest did not impair his standing with the German community, and he was just as comfortable addressing a Socialist Labor Party gathering on the shorter-hours question as he was on the street, where he mobilized a neighborhood youth gang to serve as the "Connors Guards."[35]

Connors's relations with working-class respectables were often less amicable. Appearing before a group of French Canadians during the 1894 mayoral contest, which pitted James J. Curran, a Connors henchman, against Henry A. Chase, Mikeleen charged the Republicans with buying votes. But rather than decry the practice, he alienated

respectables in the crowd by urging them to accept the bribes. As one of his auditors remarked:

> He came right up and told us to sell our votes to them and take the money and not vote for them afterwards, but to keep the money. We could have it to buy beer or to "rush the growler." Now does Mikeleen Connors think that we are a lot of bums. . . . We are democrats and we believe in the [liquor] license commission, as it is, and we would not have Mikeleen run it, and we were waiting to see if Mr. Curran was in favor of it. As he is not, we know who is the right man for mayor, and that is Mr. Chase.[36]

Cultural issues bulked large in citywide elections because Democratic mayoral candidates generally avoided direct class appeals in order to broaden their base of support. In ward-based City Council contests, on the other hand, Republicans could not defeat nominees pledged to support labor, despite the bitterness that marked some Democratic caucuses. By 1894, the political power exercised by labor spokesmen from the lower wards had engendered a sharp reaction among the established classes. "In the past year," declared the *Transcript*, "the union labor men have dominated city politics and domineered over the city fathers." But that fall the election of state senator Marcienne Whitcomb, who as mayor had consistently vetoed the "class legislation" of the "Labor Lords," led the *Transcript* to rejoice that the "Union Labor nightmare" was at an end. Whitcomb did not disappoint his well-wishers. As a first step toward reuniting political authority with economic power, he introduced a bill that would empower the governor to appoint a police commission for the city and that included a provision allowing local authorities to appoint an indefinite number of special policemen upon "apprehension of riot, tumult, mob, insurrection, etc."[37]

Whitcomb and his local partisans justified the measure as a necessary antidote to police complicity in the liquor traffic and departmental involvement in city politics. Under the current "rum controlled regime," Whitcomb argued, patrolmen ignored liquor ordinances and police tenure often depended more on how many votes an officer controlled than how he performed his duties. Unmentioned, but no less important, reasons for restraining police activity included the department's conspicuously lax oversight of picket lines, which had outraged the *Transcript* during the printers' strike, as it had other employers during previous disputes. Some patrolmen also evinced a

flagrant lack of deference toward their social betters. Agent Ernest Lovering of the Lyman Mills had his skull creased by a police billy the following winter for disobeying an officer's orders, and the *Transcript* complained that other patrolmen lacked a due "regard for superior power." All this had contributed to a local resurgence of nativism, as a chapter of the anti-Catholic, anti-immigrant American Protective Association (APA) briefly flourished during the mid-nineties. Not all the bill's supporters belonged to the APA, but its obvious appeal to the organization may explain why a petition urging its passage contained no Catholic signatures, even though French Canadians had more reason than anyone to resent the sometimes overbearing behavior of a largely Irish police force.[38]

Nor did all of Holyoke's upper class support the police commission bill. Governor Greenhalge vetoed the measure primarily because its opponents included William Whiting and William Skinner, the city's two wealthiest millowners. Whiting's stated reason for opposing the bill was that it would defame the city of Holyoke, while Skinner, an old Democrat, objected to state intervention in local affairs. These explanations may not fully encompass the reasons why Whiting and Skinner chose to break with their class on the measure, but they do possess the ring of truth. As a former congressman, Whiting seemed to feel that his name was in some way synonymous with that of the city and that any slight to Holyoke's reputation diminished his own; and no one ever questioned Skinner's attachment to the principle of local autonomy.[39]

At that year's municipal elections the split among the established classes, coupled with the effects of APA activity, allowed the Connors machine to place James J. Curran in the mayor's chair. Divisions within the city's monied classes proved short-lived, however, and the following spring they formed a cohesive phalanx in an effort to obtain a new city charter that would strip ward-based labor spokesmen of their political power. This time William Whiting, who always appreciated the difference between half-way measures and innovations that involved a real transfer of power, stood among the movement's leaders, declaring that "local government ought to be run on the same plan as a mill, by a Board of Directors presided over by a President." The reformers chose an opportune time to act. The nearly moribund state of the CLU prevented local unions from giving deliberate and organized consideration to the charter's long-term impact on Holyoke labor. This was all the more unfortunate in that by depicting the new charter as a

reform measure designed to clean up city politics, its supporters disarmed potential opposition among working-class respectables. As it turned out, ward politicians could only muster support from the saloon-linked protective laborers' union in their unsuccessful campaign to prevent the charter's passage.[40]

The new charter provided for a unicameral City Council with twenty-one aldermen, fourteen of whom would be elected by the city at large. It also augmented the mayor's appointive authority in an effort to curtail machine patronage, especially its control of the Board of License Commissioners. In its first year of operation the charter worked better than its most sanguine promoters could have hoped. The new Board of Aldermen contained eleven Republicans, ten of whom occupied at-large seats, and a Republican won the mayoral contest. In 1897, Michael Connors secured the mayor's seat by donning the robes of respectability and running as a "reform" candidate, but the era of Democratic control had ended.[41]

The unstable coalition that propelled Connors into the mayor's chair quickly unraveled during the course of his administration. Besides his giving free reign to the saloon interest, a major scandal irreparably damaged Connors's credibility with working-class respectables. In August, tax collector James C. Keough, a long-time Connors crony, resigned under fire. A subsequent audit of his books showed numerous instances of tax payments made, credited, and then erased; it also revealed a $15,000 shortage. As Keough prepared to enter the county jail, opposition Democrats joined with Republicans to heap abuse upon Connors' "business government," and at St. Jerome's Father Harkins asked his parishioners to turn the "knaves" out by forming a "citizen's movement in which representative men from both parties could join hands and nominate a strong, clear, responsible candidate for mayor."[42]

Although Connors still retained sufficient strength within the party to obtain the mayoral nomination for John Sheehan, a former state representative and one-time president of the CLU, Sheehan lost the election to Arthur B. Chapin. The contest marked the ascendancy of a Republican machine, headed by Chapin's brother-in-law William F. Whiting, that would dominate Holyoke politics for the next fifteen years. Through a shrewd, ethnically balanced, non-partisan dispensation of patronage, Whiting quickly established a formidable organization; at the same time, M. J. Bowler, a former Democrat and Whiting appointee to the license commission, kept the saloon vote in line,

though press and pulpit generally took little notice of the "reform" government's lax enforcement of liquor laws. As the *Republican*'s Sunday correspondent observed in 1901, "with the exception of that sturdy old opponent of evil, Rev. P. J. Harkins," what shocked the "pious folks" during the Connors years now occasioned little concern. Lastly, workers still influenced by enclave notions of class relations viewed the Whitings as the embodiment of a cherished mutuality of interest between capital and labor. Some of the same men who cheered the mention of William Whiting's name during the 1901 strike also cast ballots for his son's mayoral choices.[43]

The Whiting machine was especially solicitous of corporate interests. After local residents had voted to purchase the Holyoke Water Power Company's lighting plant, upper-class fears of higher taxation and the company's reluctance to sell prompted Chapin to arrange a second referendum. Despite his intervention, Holyoke voters again opted for public ownership, but in a tax case involving the Lyman Mills that evoked widespread interest among manufacturers sensing rebates, Chapin kept company officials closely informed of the city's position, thus helping them to obtain a favorable settlement. Caution was the primary characteristic of Chapin's approach to labor. He avoided any overt attacks, but at the same time did little to aid it, and in 1902 Edward F. Dowd decided to challenge the "capitalistic barons" who had assumed control of local politics.[44]

Dowd depicted the election as a struggle between capital and labor. It was actually a contest between opposing CLU factions. As Dowd's operatives worked to sabotage the aldermanic campaign of James M. Kennedy, the latter's supporters publicly criticized Dowd, A LABOR MAN writing that he did not "represent the trade union movement in its true sense—and as a representative of labor unionism in Holyoke he has been tried and thrown into the discards." On Election Day, they carried their animus against Dowd into local voting booths and helped reelect Chapin by a decisive margin.[45]

CLU factionalism was not the only reason for labor's failure during the period. Capital's superior resources would have severely tested the best-organized movement. The split nevertheless remains noteworthy for what it reveals about the measure of ideological flux labor experienced as it moved from enclave to trade union. On one hand, the two decades following 1890 witnessed a transformation of the social bases of the enclave. After 1894, upwardly mobile Irish flocked into the Knights of Columbus and deserted older, multi-class Catho-

lic lay organizations like the St. Jerome's Temperance Society, which by 1910 and for many years thereafter was headed by CLU president Urban Fleming. At the same time, Irish businessmen and professionals broadened their range of contacts with the Yankee middle class. Although it failed to penetrate the city's most prestigious social organization, the Bay State Club, the Irish middle class did mix freely with its Yankee counterparts at meetings of the Holyoke Club and Businessmen's Association. It also played a prominent part in establishing the Holyoke Country Club, a matter that did not escape worker notice. When authorities invoked state blue laws to halt Sunday afternoon baseball games in 1919, worker protests forced the closing of local golf courses as well. Lastly, the founding of Holy Cross Parish in 1905 allowed Catholics who had left older, ethnic neighborhoods for the more exclusive Highlands to worship alone with their social peers. In Mary Doyle Curran's novel about Holyoke, an elderly Irishman wistfully recalled a time when the city's Irish "were all the same" and lived peacefully together in the lower wards. "You will never see those days again," he lamented, "for they are gone . . . and it's the Hill that did it, the Hill with its pot of gold and Irishman fighting Irishman to get at it." By 1910, that earlier time had largely passed.[46]

These developments, together with the postdepression merger movement, hastened acceptance of the belief that wage earners constituted a separate class with distinct interests. But this was an uneven process. Some workers continued to embrace enclave principles and viewed the world as a loose amalgam of producers with convergent interests. It is hardly surprising that CLU factionalism occurred largely within the building trades, where small-scale enterprise still flourished and where workers could still hope to establish businesses of their own. Of more enduring importance, the nearly total defeat of Holyoke labor during these years insured that some features of the previous era's enclave consciousness would inform the culture of Catholic trade unionist respectability that emerged after 1905.

THE PRECIPITATE DECLINE of the local socialist movement at the turn of the century also slowed the wheels of ideological change and removed a strong voice that had played an important role in shaping the post-enclave consciousness of local wage earners. After initiating

the Trades and Labor Assembly in the mid-eighties, the Socialist Labor Party (SLP) remained an integral part of Holyoke trade unionism. With its large German membership, the party's base of operations was the Turnverein Vorwaerts, which after seceding from the middle-class-dominated Turnverein in 1890, became the focal point of a well-rounded socialist culture in Ward 3. In addition to fielding one of the best gymnastic teams in the region, Holyoke's socialist Turners also distributed poor relief, staged socialist Christmas plays, and held periodic balls as they sought to best their middle-class rivals socially as well as ideologically. At times their influence within the German community reached hegemonic proportions. When Lutheran pastor August Bruhn announced plans to establish a parochial school, he quickly retreated after the Turners objected that the project would undermine the public-school system and the "republican form of government" that it buttressed.[47]

In 1893, the SLP formed an English-speaking section in an attempt to broaden its base of influence. At the same time, it stepped up its activities within the local labor movement. In 1894, the CLU created a political club at SLP urging and that October voted by a narrow margin to endorse Plank 10 of the AFL political program, which called for "the collective ownership by the people of all means of production and distribution." The following year John H. Connors, Mikeleen's younger brother and a party member, became president of the CLU. And at that September's Labor Day festivities, party leader Moritz Ruther was one of the featured speakers.[48]

It even seemed for a time that the SLP might become a political equal of the two major parties. In 1898, as the Whiting machine toppled the Connors administration, Ward 3 voters placed Moritz Ruther on the Board of Aldermen, and the party's congressional candidate obtained 17 percent of the vote. SLP electoral support had gradually increased during each of the four previous elections and predictions that it would soon become a serious force in local politics did not seem farfetched. But this was not to be. Ruther lost his aldermanic seat the following year, and in July 1900 party factionalism at the national level touched the local branch, prompting a group led by E. A. Buckland, a Yankee machinist and former Prohibitionist, to form a chapter of the Social Democratic Party (SDP). In succeeding months, as Buckland and Ruther questioned each other's political aptitude and revolutionary commitment, both parties faded from view. Again, though, we need to look beyond the evident harm caused by factionalism to ob-

tain an adequate assessment of the problems that the movement faced.[49]

A signal failure was the deterioration of SLP—trade-union relations on the eve of the most militant strike wave in the city's history. During the nineties, Moritz Ruther had regularly addressed gatherings of trade unionists on "Unionism and its Benefits." After 1899, however, the amicable relationship between Ruther and the CLU visibly soured. Increasingly, he spoke of the "labor union idolatry" of the "pure and simplers" and characterized local labor leaders as "labor skates." Never having fully accepted the late summer observance of Labor Day, Ruther remarked that under such leadership "St. labor day" would soon become the "annual funeral day" of the working class. Thus isolated from the labor movement, he could only applaud from the sidelines as ever greater numbers of workers took their case into the streets.[50]

Ruther's changing conduct was in part a reaction to anti-socialist attacks from local trade unionists. In March 1900, he complained of "erstwhile labor leaders who are strutting about the streets of Holyoke with a billy in their hands as 'protectors of peace and order'[,] . . . denouncing the socialists because they 'broke up the unions.' " Despite such opposition from trade unionists who probably resented and feared SLP influence with wage earners as much as they disagreed with the party's ideological stance, Ruther continued to appear before labor audiences for some months afterwards. Later that year, however, the national body enacted measures restricting the union activities of party members.[51]

In 1895, socialist trade unionists formed the Socialist Trade and Labor Alliance (STLA) to propagate a class-conscious unionism. Although the STLA was deliberately created as a rival to the AFL, party leader Daniel DeLeon allowed members considerable discretion in their trade-union activities and did not demand that they desert existing organizations. This liberal policy may well have been a response to the counsel of local leaders like Moritz Ruther. "At this stage of the movement," he wrote DeLeon in 1895, "we have to exercise a great deal of tolerance. . . . We ought to take advantage of every sympathetic feeling towards us rather than repulse it because it may not be exactly up to date." But all this changed after 1898 when the growing independence of STLA locals caused DeLeon to circumscribe trade-union activity with stringent regulations that sacrificed organizational development to ideological purity.[52]

The Social Democratic Party was no less isolated from the local labor movement than the SLP. Although E. A. Buckland avoided attacking local labor leaders and chided Ruther for doing so, his conviction that labor could achieve "the final abolition of the entire wage system" only through politics left him disdainful of economic action. Strikes and boycotts, Buckland contended, are "wholly ineffectual in a genuine test of strength between capital and labor and are the wornout methods of pure and simple trade unionism." He considered compulsory arbitration an improvement upon these archaic weapons because "it does away with strikes and its attending interruption of business and shifts the conflict to the more orderly and less costly means of legislation." The postdepression strike wave thus found Buckland too on the sidelines.[53]

Broader institutional problems compounded these difficulties and partly explain why Holyoke socialists failed to maintain their influence with the labor movement. Speaking wherever workers gathered, Ruther and others worked tirelessly to spread the socialist gospel. But the slender resources at their command limited such efforts, and the disappearance of workers' debating clubs and literary societies during the depression deprived the movement of potential staging areas for a more effective advance. As a result, the SLP never replicated the socialist culture that sustained it within the German community outside Ward 3.

Lastly, Holyoke socialists faced opposition from a Catholic church that remained influential with local workers. Postdepression labor insurgency hardly gladdened Catholic observers. A *Messenger* editorial, promoting organization, counseled workers to better their lot through education, "legislation, the moulding of public opinion, . . . the establishment of various agencies for mutual aid, and strengthening arbitration"; only when these methods had failed should labor resort to strikes and boycotts. Even though wage earners often acted on a reverse set of tactical priorities during the period, Catholic spokesmen refused to condemn them. "The capitalists may feel that they are crowded and bullied by labor," Father J. J. McCoy told a gathering of the Holyoke Businessmen's Association, "and when labor is badly officered we can readily believe this instance to be true, but labor any day is not far from hunger, and hunger will drive men mad." And while a 1901 *Messenger* editorial on the recent rash of strikes continued to urge prudence and restraint, it also observed that "labor unions have grown out of a fact, learned by hard experience,

namely, that the individual laborer in the face of the trust and other forms of lawless capital is utterly helpless."[54]

Such tepid support of strike actions scarcely explains why priests retained a hold on Catholic workers. More important was an acute awareness of their parishioners' most basic hopes and fears, and an ability to articulate those concerns. At Holyoke, Father Harkins probably never better demonstrated that awareness than in a 1901 sermon condemning high-school social events at a local hotel:

> Naturally the pride of every student is aroused, the poor man's son and daughter endeavoring to appear as well dressed as the children of those financially stronger, but no better otherwise. The danger to these children is to view life from the . . . ballroom, rather than from the practical schoolroom and more useful store, shop, or trade. I do not wish to decry the professionals, but I desire to speak for the majority, whose future life will deal mostly with the weekly wage and the direct care of children. The education of today is not only useless and outrageous in the burden it imposes on the people and the false ideas of life it is more than apt to teach the pupils of public schools, but it has the extremely dangerous quality of giving wrong impressions regarding the hereafter.
>
> I must refer . . . to a certain class of young girls who can be seen nightly in hallways on High Street, and on streetcorners hobnobbing with things dressed in trousers, a wide expanse of shirtfront, a necktie and a hat. These girls do not form the acquaintance of these things in the parochial schools. . . . Suffice it for me to say I regret most painfully that these girls value the acquaintance of these things more highly than they do the manly young men who wear overalls when at work and who are attentive to all the duties imposed by church, family, and state.

The passage speaks volumes as to the reasons why the Catholic church was, during a period of ideological transformation when it had in a sense lost control of its working-class constituents, still able to exercise some measure of influence over them. Unable to dictate the means labor used to advance its interests during these years, the church still had much to say about the ends that workers sought. In sermons like the above, pastors helped define those ends by linking the dignity and self-worth of working people to the most basic—indeed visceral—questions of sexuality and family.[55]

That the church retained its capacity to address the deeper needs of workers was of more than passing importance. During the course of the depression, SLP declarations that emphasized the irrationality of

the capitalist system and irreconcilable antagonism between capital and labor sounded increasingly more compelling, while the subsequent merger movement made the party appear positively clairvoyant. In the late nineties, a number of Irish candidates stood for local office on the SLP ticket, and in an extraordinary departure from customary practice Worcester's Irish Catholic weekly, *The Messenger*, let Dennis Doyle use its pages to explain "Why I Am a Socialist." This was, in short, a time of questioning when workers were in the process of redefining themselves and when traditional injunctions against socialism lacked their usual force. That further defections did not occur was due in no small part to the pastoral work of shrewd parish priests like Father P. J. Harkins.[56]

Although the church would never reestablish the degree of control it had exercised in earlier decades, it would after 1905 again play an influential role in shaping worker consciousness. Father Harkins suggested the nature of that influence in his appeal to family concerns; as did an 1898 *Messenger* editorial that accorded special significance to labor's struggle for a "living wage, upon which the existence of home, its wifehood, and childhood depend." In the decades after 1900, the family–living-wage doctrine would become the core element in a mature culture of Catholic trade-unionist respectability.[57]

6

CATHOLIC TRADE-UNION
RESPECTABILITY, 1905–1920

FOLLOWING the turn-of-the-century strike wave, Holyoke trade unionists slowly regrouped and began to take stock of their situation. They had been beaten, and beaten badly. This they knew and would not soon forget. Aware of the limits that class power placed on what was possible, their thoughts increasingly centered on one demand: that workers be paid a family wage. This chapter examines the culture that grew up around this demand. It also looks at how the family-wage doctrine shaped worker views on politics and relations with other social groups, both manufacturers and workers. Among the latter, French Canadian textile operatives, whose cultural orientation and economic status differed markedly from that of Irish trade-union respectables, receive special attention. We begin with a brief look at the men who headed the Holyoke labor movement after 1905.

Across from Hampden Park on Maple Street next to the Central Fire Station stood a three-story structure that housed the Alden Press. Its proprietor, Edward Alden, employed the first two floors for his business, which in the dozen years after 1908 included publishing the local labor weekly, *The Artisan*. But it was what transpired on the building's third floor that often determined what appeared in the paper. There each Saturday evening one could find Holyoke's leading trade unionists, engaged in heated discussion of the principal local and national issues of the day. Dubbed the Dynamiters Club by some members, others called it the Holyoke Labor College because speakers from area colleges often began an evening's proceedings with a lecture.

Although Edward Alden was a Yankee printer, the club largely

attracted Irish Catholic trade unionists like Urban Fleming, a mule spinner who served as president of the CLU for more than three decades, and Thomas Rohan, another mule spinner who maintained a keen interest in labor matters long after he left the mills to pursue a varied career as a merchant, insurance agent, and probation officer. Other members included George Lane, business agent of the carpenters' union, John Bresnahan, president of the operating engineers' union, and Francis M. Curran, a stationary fireman who was later appointed to the State Industrial Relations Board. Local paper workers were represented at club gatherings by Michael McLain, a native of Pennsylvania where he had been an organizer for the United Mine Workers before coming to Holyoke in 1905. With the exception of a few younger members, the club's most active participants had been born in the 1870s and 1880s and had reached maturity during the labor struggles of the early twentieth century. The philosophy of labor that evolved from their debates and later appeared in the columns of the *Artisan* reflected this formative experience. It was also shaped by the overwhelmingly Irish Catholic composition of the club's membership.[1]

The basic principles of Catholic trade unionism included values shared by all unionists. One was independence. "Throw off your shackles, ye wage slaves," declared the *Artisan*, "Remove the hoodwink and see the light of better things through the trade union movement." Unlike Yankee artisans, for whom an escape from wage slavery usually meant some form of independent production, trade unionists saw wage slaves as those who refused to stand in solidarity with their fellow workers. Simply joining a trade union, though, was not enough. The dutiful trade unionist needed to develop a number of "good habits":

> Get into the habit of attending meetings and paying your dues. Get into the habit of wearing the button of your organization on the lapel of your coat. Get into the habit of speaking a good word for a fellow workman. The above habits thoroughly mastered will give you that feeling of satisfaction that comes to the man who does his duty.[2]

The reference to the "man who does his duty" was no unconscious lapse. A loosely defined manliness formed another of the basic values of local unionists. Despite the large number of women in the work force, appeals to manhood pervaded the language of Holyoke trade unionism. In publishing a list of strikebreakers, *The Artisan* declared

that these were "men who have forsaken honor and a right to a place in the haunts of men." And an editorial attacking dual unionism stated, "the duty of the true blue, sensible, thinking union man is to fight for unionism within its ranks and not in the ranks of any opposing scheme of organized labor which seeks but to destroy the recognized organization which labor has."[3]

As they struggled to preserve some semblance of independence, trade-union respectables displayed an intense commitment to learning, not only for themselves but for all working people. The Dynamiters regularly badgered the state legislature to appropriate funds for university extension classes, and individual members like John Bresnahan, Thomas Rohan, and George Fitzgerald periodically organized adult-education programs for local wage earners. Even more important than these efforts was the meaning that trade-union respectables attached to education. In their quest for knowledge they were not seeking to emulate or impress the local bourgeoisie. Rather, they saw learning as a valuable resource that could be used to engage life's problems. The Dynamiters thus maintained a file of the *Congressional Record* and other reference sources that members consulted to frame legislative petitions, contest the actions of local authorities, and challenge the assertions of visiting academics who, as the *Springfield Republican*'s Sunday correspondent observed, "came [to Dynamiters Hall] hotfoot for argument and got it good and plenty."[4]

An aversion to drink also remained a distinguishing characteristic of trade-union respectables. Their position on temperance not only combined the themes of manliness and independence, but added a concern for family welfare. Locally, the leading proponent of temperance was Urban Fleming, who for many years doubled as president of the CLU and the St. Jerome's Temperance Society. Largely because of Fleming's influence, the CLU consistently refused to endorse licensing, despite the urgings of the bartenders' union that it support the measure. At one 1917 debate on the license question, Fleming linked child labor to paternal drunkenness and argued that saloonkeepers were no friends of labor. On more than one occasion when the unions had attempted to defeat an administration inimical to labor, he asserted, "every saloonkeeper in the city gave money into a slush fund to defeat the unions." A 1909 *Artisan* editorial also complained that bar owners frequently hired nonunion men to undertake repair work. The same article expressed shock at finding that many women were "habitual users of intoxicating liquors" and called for laws forbidding

women from entering saloons and prohibiting waitresses from serving liquor.[5]

Some unionists believed that saloons threatened the very survival of trade unionism. A letter to *The Artisan* from A SCOT outlined the manner in which intemperance impoverished the family and sapped the worker's manhood as it undermined unions. "Every drunkard's wife can tell you the struggle she has to keep his working card clear, to enable him to get the standard rate of wages, and because she is ashamed to let his fellow workmen understand the character of her husband at home." But only so much can be done, he continued, and "as things get worse she is compelled to let it fall back a month, then two, and so on, until the stage is reached" at which the intemperate worker "has to break the bonds of brotherhood, the result being that he falls into the ranks of scab labor." Most workers probably did not see the problem in such ominous terms. Even *The Artisan* opposed prohibition, labeling it an attack on individual rights that signalled a "New Paternalism." Few trade-union respectables wished to replace the tyranny of drink with a broader oppression. Indeed, the real significance of the saloon lay in the fact that it served as a negative referent. For respectables, saloon culture bore the mark and threat of servility: to millowners, to political bosses, and to the demon rum itself.[6]

The respectables' attitude toward the family best disclosed the masculine ethos that underlay Holyoke trade unionism. The trade union, declared one 1908 *Artisan* editorial, was the "defender of the Home." No other institution so steadfastly demanded a "living wage" that would allow the worker to "maintain a creditable home, to bring up his children, and educate them into honest, moral men and women and useful citizens of the commonwealth." A dozen years later the message remained unchanged: "In the old theory of an American standard of living, it was considered that the father or the head of the family should be the breadwinner, and that his wages should be adequate to properly support the family." Any other arrangement, the editorial bluntly stated, was "wrong, fundamentally, economically, and vitally wrong."[7]

By the twentieth century, worker demands for a living wage were scarcely new. Similar concerns had influenced the protests of early nineteenth-century artisans' associations, and as Christine Stansell has shown, the National Trades' Union of the 1830s made the family-wage ideal an integral component of its worldview. As capitalist development eroded their social position, artisan efforts to maintain some

degree of independence centered increasingly around the family. Although the NTU disappeared during the depression of the 1830s, its commitment to a family wage proved more enduring. "Throughout the nineteenth century," Stansell adds, "union men tended to think of themselves in the paternalist terms the NTU first defined, as breadwinners for women at home or, at best, as supporters of women at work, lending aid from a more authoritative position."[8]

Yet for all its appeal, many nineteenth-century working people viewed the family wage ideal with a certain ambivalence. This was particularly so among those who refused to accept the permanence of the wage system. The family wage thus had no place in the formal ideology of organizations like the Knights of Labor, which sought to abolish wage labor and erect new societies based on cooperative production. By the early twentieth century, however, the depression of the 1890s and the merger movement that it inspired had not only reshaped the structure of American industry, but had also transformed the way people looked at society. As Martin Sklar has observed, the crisis of the nineties was a "combined cyclical and secular crisis" that set it apart from earlier economic contractions:

> In essence, previous cyclical crises spontaneously interrupted and reactivated existing market relations. The combined crisis of the nineties, however, entailed an alteration of market structure and property ownership that reverberated in the alteration of the nation's party politics, legal order, social thought, government policies, and foreign relations.[9]

With these developments, doubts about the permanence of the wage system faded, along with worker visions of a cooperative commonwealth. As they did, the family-wage ideal attained an unprecedented salience among worker demands. It also drew increased support from individuals and organizations outside labor's ranks. The numerous family-budget studies that began to appear after 1890 at least implicitly assumed employer payment of a male-earned family wage, as did the Social Creed of the Federal Council of Churches in America in its call for "a living wage as a minimum in every industry." The AFL made its position clear in a 1910 statement, which asserted: "We believe the man should be provided with a fair wage in order to keep his female relatives from going to work. The man is the provider and should receive enough for his labor to give his family a respectable living."[10]

The family-wage ideal was particularly popular among Irish workers. A number of studies of nineteenth-century working-class communities have found that Irish wives consistently had the lowest employment rates among the different ethnic groups examined. Although these women performed a multitude of household tasks, some of which produced income, they rarely engaged in paid labor outside the home. "Unless there was no other possible breadwinner," Constance Green has written of Holyoke, "the mother of an Irish family did not work in the mills, as was frequently true of other nationalities." Former Dynamiter George Fitzgerald seconded Green's observation, declaring that it was "almost unheard of for women to work after marriage." Irish views on the matter stemmed from a variety of factors that included labor-market considerations as well as traditional notions of manhood and family. According to Ellen Horgan Biddle, the Irish believed "that a working wife diminishes the status of her husband, that women should stay home and rear children, and that jobs in a marginal economy should go to others."[11]

The belief that married women should not work outside the home, Biddle adds, was also a "church view." That it surely was. Indeed, the family-wage ideal fit well with the socioreligious outlook of a broad range of Catholic spokesmen, from traditionalist hierarchs who believed family disintegration was the root cause of all social disorder to progressive priests who viewed the family wage as a necessary basis for a more just society. At St. Jerome's in Holyoke, Father J. J. Broderick expressed a popular Catholic viewpoint when he declared the working mother one of the "most serious evils of our industrial system." The family wage, he added, was thus "founded on the principle . . . that God has declared special work for women; has ordained the mother His helpmate in caring for the youthful soul and implanting there, as none other can, the everlasting truths of religion."[12]

The foremost Catholic exponent of the family living wage was Father John A. Ryan, who popularized the demand in countless books, articles, and addresses. During the 1920s he coauthored a syndicated column for the National Catholic Welfare Conference, "Expert Catholic Discussion of Capital and Labor," which appeared in Springfield's *Catholic Mirror* and many other church publications. Despite their wide dissemination, the degree to which Ryan's writings directly influenced Catholic workers is open to debate. Less arguable was his ability to identify and appeal to the innermost aspirations of Catholic wage earners. Ryan wrote with a profound understanding of his audi-

ence, and because his exposition of the family–living-wage doctrine possessed this descriptive as well as prescriptive character, it merits more than passing attention.

Ryan located authority for the family wage in man's natural right to full personal development. Because celibacy was unnatural in lay society, he argued, "the majority of men cannot reach a proper degree of self-development outside of the conjugal state." From this Ryan concluded that the " 'minimum of the material conditions of decent and reasonable living' comprises, for the adult male, the means of supporting a family." The right to a living wage applied to single as well as married workers. For if employers could pay single wage earners less, "they would strive to engage these exclusively," thus placing a premium "upon a very undesirable kind of celibacy." The argument illustrates recurring patterns in Ryan's thought and indicates why his writings were so compelling. He not only grounded his abstractions in an earthy shrewdness that addressed the deepest longings of Catholic male workers, but he could move with breathtaking swiftness from the metaphysical world of natural rights to the hard reality of contemporary labor markets.[13]

As one might suspect, Ryan's views of marriage and women were militantly conventional. "The welfare of the whole family, and that of society likewise," Ryan declared in language similar to that used by Father Broderick, "renders it imperative that the wife and mother should not engage in any labor except that of the household." There her chief duty was to bear and raise children. In condemning birth control, Ryan characteristically framed his attack in class terms: "The birth control advocates hope to see a situation in which the poorer classes would deliberately keep their families small while the comfortable and rich classes would have fairly large families." In reality, though, the "comfortable classes" were too selfish and "too deeply sunk in a quagmire of egotism" to raise large families. Only those who found birth control morally objectionable would continue to procreate freely: "In other words, they will be mainly the Catholic element of the population. Thus the fittest will survive; that is, the fittest morally."[14]

Despite the limited role that he prescribed for women, Ryan fully realized that many were compelled to enter the work force. Rather than ignore what for him was an unpleasant reality, he not only declared that women should be paid the same wages as men for comparable work, but also urged that steps be taken to organize them into unions. As with his insistence that single as well as married

CHAPTER SIX

workers be paid a living wage, the demand stemmed from an unsenti-
mental analysis of the labor market. The more women received in
wages, the less employable they would be: "Unless we hold that an
increase in the proportion of women workers is desirable," Ryan contended, "we must admit that social welfare would be advanced by the
payment of uniform wages to both sexes for equally efficient labor."
Ryan also spoke from a conviction that all workers needed the protection afforded by organization, and that no worker would be secure
until all belonged to labor unions. He found it a cruel irony that
unskilled wage earners, who most needed protection, were among
the least organized. An examination of Holyoke trade unionism after
1900 shows that Ryan's views on women workers and organized labor
bore some resemblance to current reality.[15]

Holyoke trade unionists brooked no expansion of women's work
that infringed upon traditional preserves. When in July 1911, the
Deane Steam Pump Company hired a group of women to work in its
coremaking department, sixty molders and coremakers immediately
walked out, claiming that once a job became defined as women's
work, women's wages would soon follow. They also insisted that
propriety debarred women from such work, an argument that received broad public support. That fall the dispute became an issue in
the gubernatorial campaign when it was learned that Governor Foss
employed women at his foundry. John Sheehan, a former head of the
molders' union and ardent Foss supporter, who had condemned the
practice at the Deane Steam Pump Company, tried to explain that
Foss's foundry was managed in a "model manner." But as the *Republican* observed: "In this he got himself rather in the mire." In the end,
the company refused to submit and the molders' union appointed a
committee to lobby for a bill forbidding the employment of women in
foundries.[16]

By contrast, in industries where women had traditionally constituted a large proportion of the work force, Holyoke trade unionists
encouraged their organization. In 1897, Eagle Lodge petitioned the
AFL for permission to organize all local paper workers, women as
well as men. As it turned out, women paper workers often needed
less prompting than male unionists believed. In fact, the post-1910
history of paper unionism can scarcely be recounted without recognizing the integral role played by women workers. After the 1903 strike,
American Writing Paper blacklisted union leaders and in subsequent
years continued to dismiss anyone suspected of union activity. Al-

though Eagle Lodge reappeared in 1907, it led a shadow existence during the next few years. Besides fear of dismissal, craft exclusiveness also inhibited union development. A BACK TENDER wrote that if machine tenders had any "backbone" the trust would be forced to deal more justly with its workers:

> There isn't a machine tender working for the American Writing Paper "combine" that dares to say a word about the union and I know that because I am working in the mill. They are moral cowards and wage slaves. The company owns them. They are not men—they are tools, that's all.

This was the state of paper unionism when the American Federation of Labor targeted the trust for organization in 1911.[17]

The AFL organizing campaign staggered along for the better part of a year until the following January when a strike by the plater women at the Holyoke and Riverside divisions of American Writing Paper pumped fresh blood into the anemic effort. Unable to effect any significant changes in the organization of work in the engine and machine rooms, the trust had turned its efficiency experts loose in the finishing department. It proved to be a serious mistake. As *The Artisan* later observed of the women affected:

> They had several grievances, but the principal trouble was the "efficiency" expert with his little stop watch. He, this "efficiency" expert, got the economy bug in his head, some say it was introduced into his head by a little learning, and he had made the officials believe that with his "hoss-race" watch he could get as much work out of two girls as they were getting from three.
>
> He tried it and to the discredit of his stop watch be it said the girls refused to be driven like so many cattle. They struck, and what's more they stayed struck for four weeks.[18]

The first meeting of the strikers attracted J. T. Carey, president of the Brotherhood of Paper Makers, but few paper workers. A week later, another gathering drew a larger crowd, and numerous men signed applications before departing. Additional young male workers doubtlessly took out their pens after attending the benefit dances staged by the striking women at Temperance Hall, and *The Artisan* bluntly reminded others of their duty in words that embodied the most fundamental tenets of trade union respectability: THROW OFF THE YOKE, YOU

MEN, AND ENROLL UNDER FREEDOM'S BANNER—the BROTHERHOOD OF PAPER MAKERS. The trust sensed the mounting solidarity generated by the strike and in late February acceded to the women's demands. But by then it was too late. The Brotherhood of Paper Makers had already enrolled most of the city's plater women and loftmen, and a short while later the beater engineers and machine tenders moved in to gather the spoils from a victory to which they had contributed precious little. Paper unionism had returned to Holyoke.[19]

As was earlier the case, subsequent efforts to extend the organization of women in local paper factories would depend largely on the initiative of women workers themselves. In January 1915, rag-room workers at the Valley Paper Company walked out, declaring that a recent pay reduction had deprived them of a living wage. Although the women belonged to no union, other paper workers immediately proffered their support. Large crowds joined the women on picket lines, and only the intervention of the State Board of Arbitration prevented Eagle Lodge from calling a sympathetic strike. One reason for the outpouring of aid was suggested by an *Artisan* editorial attacking company president George Fowler, which underscored the religious basis of the living wage demand:

> It is easy to go to Church on Sunday and, with a smirk, raise a head toward heaven and pray the good Lord to watch and protect him and his, peace on earth, good will toward men. Sanctimonious hypocrisy. How easy it is for the individual with a stomach full of good, nourishing food to pray for others and be a good Christian—until it hits his business. Until living his Christian professions means paying a living wage, it is easy to be a Christian.

The strike failed, but it did result in the formation of a new rag-workers' union. Henceforth, even Holyoke's least skilled paper workers could draw on the protection offered through organization.[20]

Holyoke paper workers after 1912 thus achieved a formidable degree of organization. The same cannot be said of local textile workers. In contrast to textile centers in eastern Massachusetts, quiescence reigned among Holyoke operatives following the turn of the century burst of strike activity. In 1912, the Lyman Mills granted a wage increase as soon as the news arrived that Lawrence strikers had secured a favorable settlement. Considering it "bad policy" to wait, treasurer Theophilus Parsons instructed the company agent to announce a raise

immediately, before the workers banded together to issue demands. The Lyman Mills also maintained a blacklist of known organizers and consulted with other mills on wage matters in order to anticipate worker discontent.[21]

Persisting craft exclusiveness also inhibited organization, as the Lyman Mills continued to cut special deals with its mule spinners and loom fixers. "I am in hopes," treasurer Ernest Lovering wrote company agent James A. Burke of one wage increase, "that you can quietly swing whatever additional adjustments become necessary without using a percentage figure for public purposes, and at the same time keep in favor with the desirable class of help." The company discontinued the practice after 1917 when an acute shortage of semiskilled workers made it too risky, but prior to that time the preferential treatment accorded mule spinners and loom fixers gave them little reason to make common cause with their less skilled and less fortunate fellow workers.[22]

Mule spinners and loom fixers were not the only textile workers to prosper during the period. Technological innovation reduced the number of weavers, but increased the wages of those who remained. When the Lyman Mills began replacing its plain looms with automatic Draper looms in 1914, it caused a noteworthy restructuring of the work force in a typical weave room, reducing the number of weavers needed to tend 300 looms from 52 to 20, and thus forcing them to tend 15 Draper looms instead of 6 to 8 plain looms. The company hoped an accompanying 25 percent wage increase would not only reduce dissent, but make the work attractive. Apparently it did.[23]

The foregoing indicates some reasons why textile workers were not more active, but it is hardly sufficient. Paper workers received higher wages than textile operatives, machine tenders and beater engineers were no less aloof than mule spinners and loom fixers, and while no correspondence exists to document the practice, one can safely assume that paper manufacturers also stayed abreast of regional wage movements. Why, then, did paper workers prove so much more willing to organize than textile operatives? We need first to recall that the paper and textile industries comprised two separate, if overlapping, labor markets for the Irish and French Canadians; and that by 1900, French Canadian predominance in textiles extended to all departments and skill levels. To determine whether the pattern endured, a study was made of geographical and job mobility among French Canadian textile operatives and Irish paper workers between the years

1905 and 1915. It showed that, even though French Canadian textile operatives earned less, their persistence rate nearly equalled that of Irish paper workers. Also, French Canadian paper workers were more likely to move or change their line of work than were French Canadian textile operatives. Finally, where, 14 of 170 French Canadian paper workers later sought employment in textile mills, only 4 of 313 textile operatives left for paper factories. Yet this is only the beginning of the story. The divisions between Irish trade unionists and French Canadian textile operatives involved cultural as well as economic matters. To obtain a fuller understanding of these differences and see how they inhibited the expansion of textile unionism, we must first take a closer look at the development of Holyoke's Franco-American enclave and the ways in which French Canadians adapted to their roles as industrial workers.[24]

GROUPS OF French Canadians first entered Holyoke factories during the spring of 1859 when a shortage of workers prompted the Lyman and Hampden mills to dispatch several labor recruiters to Canada. The enclave that they established grew slowly over the next two decades. Then, during the late seventies, Quebec's deepening economic crisis, coupled with a revival of production in depression-battered New England mill towns, caused a massive increase in French Canadian immigration. In 1880, nearly one of every four Holyokers hailed from French Canada. Most lived in South Holyoke near the mills in which they worked.[25]

South Holyoke was also the site of Precious Blood Church, the city's first French Canadian parish. Much has been written about the ways in which the church shaped and ordered the lives of Franco-Americans. Because some of this literature overstates the submissiveness of French Canadian Catholics, a few caveats are in order before proceeding with this line of analysis. In New England, priests who claimed the kind of authority they had exercised in rural Quebec, where the curé oversaw both the administrative and spiritual concerns of a parish through his domination of local boards of wardens, often encountered real problems. One such cleric was Holyoke's first French Canadian pastor, Father Dufresne. In the decade prior to his death in 1887, Dufresne engaged in a series of battles with leading parishioners that was every bit as acrimonious as Father Harkins's

conflict with the St. Jerome's Temperance Society. Through his with-holding of the sacraments, threats of excommunication, and personal attacks from the pulpit, Dufresne sought to establish a paternalistic regime at Precious Blood similar to that found in the parishes of rural Canada. In so doing, he alienated a substantial proportion of the laity. Father Dufresne learned the hard way, if indeed he ever learned at all, a lesson that later pastors intuitively understood: The parish relations of rural Quebec could not be arbitrarily imposed on the Franco-American enclaves of New England. As one American-born French Canadian priest told Holyoke's Jacques Ducharme, pastors may be asked to serve as mediators, advisors, or sources of material aid. "On the other hand, the Franco-American looks upon his pastor as a man, also, and reserves a right to criticize him personally."[26]

Keeping these reservations in mind, it can still be said that the church profoundly influenced French Canadian immigrants. As it had been in Canada, the parish quickly became the focus of social life in French Canadian enclaves. At church-sponsored card parties and beano games, French Canadians obtained a much-needed respite from their more arduous daily activities, exchanged neighborhood and family news, and sometimes met future spouses. There were also minstrel shows, musical presentations, and plays. During the early decades of the twentieth century, all three of Holyoke's French Cana-dian churches had theater clubs. In addition to offering a variety of entertainments, these organizations provided a forum for the develop-ment of individual talents. Madeleine Biehler recalled how member-ship in the Precious Blood orchestra served as an important outlet for her musical interests.[27]

The church also remained the primary driving force behind *la survivance*, the struggle to preserve the language and customs of French Canada in a hostile Anglo world. In their role as spiritual advisors, French Canadian priests often equated maintenance of the French language with the preservation of religion itself. According to Jacques Ducharme, "they reasoned that loss of the French language meant loss of faith, and loss of faith meant loss of identity." Parents were thus urged to enroll their children in French-language parochial schools. At Holyoke, these injunctions elicited a positive response from local Quebecois. By the 1890s, more than half of the city's school-aged French Canadian youths attended such institutions.[28]

In its efforts to preserve the language, customs, and faith of French Canada, the church enlisted the aid of immigrant professionals and

business leaders. Middle-class organizations like the Société de St. Jean Baptiste limited membership to regular churchgoers and became vociferous exponents of *survivance*. The church also influenced what appeared in the French-language press, which was the main source of news for most newcomers. At one time or another between 1874 and 1963, Holyoke was the home of sixteen French Canadian newspapers. In his study of Franco-American journalism in the Paper City, Ernest Guillet found that editors rarely challenged the assertions of local priests. "If they did," he explains, "a word from the pulpit could result in the newspaper's extinction." In most cases, though, coercion was unnecessary. The typical Franco-American journalist had received an extensive education in French culture and was by training and instinct an ardent advocate of *survivance*.[29]

In his novel on Franco-American Holyoke, Jacques Ducharme wrote that Jean Baptiste Delusson had been in the city only a short while before he felt that he had known it a long time. "In fact, apart from the place itself, there was little real difference [from Canada], as all the people with whom he mingled were French Canadians." As the great-grandson of Nicholas Proulx, a founding member of the city's French Canadian community, Ducharme knew his subject well. By the 1880s, local French Canadians had established a self-contained enclave that was in large measure culturally isolated from the rest of Holyoke. It was a world in which people spoke French both at home and on the street, read French-language newspapers, sent their children to French-language parochial schools, and sought relaxation and companionship in a host of social activities sponsored by French Canadian churches.[30]

Despite certain cultural and institutional similarities, Holyoke's French Canadian enclave and the consciousness it engendered differed in important ways from its Irish counterpart. It was a difference one can sense reading the local correspondence columns of the *Irish World*—in the assertive pride, often bordering on boastfulness, with which writers described institutional developments in Irish enclaves. It was a difference Constance Green observed when she noted that the Holyoke Irish built churches not only to worship God, but also to secure "recognition of their great organization from a Protestant public depicted as yielding them only grudging admiration." And it was a difference that Fall River Franco-Americans felt acutely when, during their struggle to obtain a French Canadian pastor for Notre Dame de Lourdes Church in the mid-eighties, they complained of a Catholic

hierarchy intent on "making us Irish in the shortest amount of time." It was, in effect, the difference between cultural preservation and cultural imperialism. "To the Irish," Paul Kleppner has written, "French Canadians were 'foreigners' who were clannish and slow to accept American (i.e., Irish) ways."[31]

Among Irish and French Canadian workers, these cultural differences were exacerbated by equally intractable economic tensions. Irish wage earners viewed increased immigration from French Canada during the late nineteenth century with genuine alarm, believing the influx would destabilize regional labor markets and undermine existing work and wage standards. The French Canadian practice of sending children into the mills at an early age, coupled with their reluctance to participate in strikes and join unions, added to these fears and gave rise to ethnic stereotypes that branded Franco-Americans as congenital scabs. These caricatures soon acquired a life of their own and began to appear in the studies of state labor agencies and various journalistic accounts. In his 1881 report for the Massachusetts Bureau of Labor Statistics, Carrol Wright characterized French Canadians as the "Chinese of the Eastern States." "These people have one good trait," Wright observed. "They are indefatigable workers, and they are docile. All they ask is to be set to work, and they care little who rules them or how they are ruled."[32]

French Canadian community leaders protested and condemned these stereotypes. In so doing, though, they gladly admitted the tendency of French Canadians to avoid strikes, which they ascribed to a reverence for law and order. However self-serving these statements may have been, they reflected more than the class interests of an ethnic elite in search of respectability. Franco-American workers also conceded that French Canadians were less likely than other groups to become involved in union affairs. "The French would always go work somewhere else during a walkout," recalled Adelard Janelle, a former textile worker from Lewiston, Maine. "The Irish were the organizers but the French would work." Yet, there were occasions when French Canadian textile workers did strike and did join unions. During the early 1880s, it happened in Cohoes, New York, where French Canadian textile operatives were not only the primary participants in several walkouts, but also formed an assembly of the Knights of Labor. And it happened a decade later in Fall River, the main center of textile militancy in New England during the period.[33]

How do we sort all this out? We can begin by looking at a few

pieces of evidence uncovered by Holyoke's Jacques Ducharme in his research on French Canadians. The first is a letter from an early immigrant to a relative in Canada:

> The pay is good, Basile. We work from sunrise to sunset, but on Sundays the mills are closed, and it is like a Church holyday. The work is not hard. I am in the cotton mill. Some of the children are working . . . and we make more money than we can spend. Let me know what you decide and if you want to come, I will speak to the foreman.

What we can see here is the early formation of the family networks that became a distinctive feature of the way in which French Canadians adapted to their role as industrial workers. In her study of Manchester's French Canadians, Tamara Hareven showed how they fortified their position within the textile work force by creating shop-floor kin networks that placed and assisted newcomers, protected group members from mistreatment by management, and generally eased one through the workday. Similar networks appeared in Holyoke, where it was not uncommon, Louis Gendron recalled, to find three generations of a single family working in the same plant.[34]

To the above, we can add the following set of figures that Ducharme found on a scrap of paper:

Wages—1.00 per day

Five working in family

5 × 6 equals 30.00 week and 120.00 month

Tenement 15.00 month

Food 20.00

Other items 10.00 month

Amount saved 75.00 month

These calculations illustrate another important feature of the way in which French Canadians adapted to industrial work: by operating family economies that required the paid labor of several members. They also suggest that the family economy was, initially at least, part of a strategy to accumulate savings, capital that would be used to purchase a farm or perhaps start a small business. For all too many immigrants, though, these hopes were soon dashed. Because of sea-

sonal and cyclical unemployment, and the low wages associated with textile work, what began as a saving strategy quickly became a survival strategy. In some cases, working mothers provided necessary additional income. More commonly, these families depended on the labor of children. According to contemporary studies, "family circumstances" was the most frequently expressed reason for child labor. Interviewed decades later, Holyoke workers who had left school for factory employment at an early age stated the matter even more simply: "It was necessary."[35]

Nevertheless, people capable of making such calculations as the foregoing were scarcely the congenitally submissive wage earners of Francophobic lore. A final piece of evidence, an interview with an early immigrant to Maine conducted by the Federal Writers' Project in the 1930s, both supports the point and adds the last few brush strokes to this condensed portrait of Franco-American textile workers. Before coming to New England, Ovide Morin had been a farm laborer in Canada, where he was often fortunate to earn five dollars a month. "One man offered me 25 cents a day if I worked for him," Morin recalled. "We worked from four o'clock in the morning until six o'clock at night, and then the farmer put us down cellar storing potatoes until twelve o'clock at night." This was not Morin's idea of a day's work and he told the farmer so: "I told him I'd work for 25 cents a day, but I wouldn't do two days' work in one. I told him he hired me for 25 cents a day, and if he wanted me to do two days' work in one he'd have to pay me 50 cents." After straightening the matter out, Morin continued at this and similar jobs for another five years before deciding he had had enough. "When I was nineteen I told my father I was going to Maine. I wasn't going to work all my life for nothing, and I knew I could get a dollar a day in Maine."[36]

Ovide Morin's recollections provide vivid evidence of the lower work and wage standards of French Canada that so alarmed Irish wage earners in New England. But Morin's story also indicates that having lower standards is a far different matter than having no standards at all. One can be sure that he was not the only Franco-American who vowed not to work a lifetime for nothing. Morin's account further suggests that French Canadian workers had their own inner calculus of exploitation, a point beyond which they could not be pushed. And when employers violated that boundary, as happened in Cohoes during the 1880s and in Fall River a decade later, they became eminently organizable.

A similar break point was reached in Holyoke at the turn of the century. When employers refused to restore wage cuts exacted from textile workers during the depression, French Canadian operatives participated in a series of strikes and enrolled in a number of newly formed unions. As we saw in the last chapter, these efforts soon ceased after several unsuccsssful job actions and a resurgence of craft exclusiveness. But the story does not end here. There is evidence—in the changing ethnic composition of the overseer force—that after 1900 local millowners began taking special precautions to prevent a recurrence of worker militancy.

New England textile manufacturers were slow to elevate French Canadians to positions of authority within their mills. Manchester's Amoskeag Mills did not appoint a Franco-American overseer until 1901. The record of Holyoke millowners was somewhat better, but not appreciably so. An examination of the 1900 manuscript population schedules of the federal census shows that only nine of sixty-one textile overseers were French Canadians. These figures become even less impressive when it is noted that four of the nine were employed by one small blanket mill, and of another nineteen individuals who identified themselves as overseers, without specifying the industry in which they worked, only one was from French Canada. By 1910, however, the number of Franco-American overseers in local textile mills had increased markedly: 27 of 113 (24 percent) floor bosses were either born in Quebec or of French Canadian descent.[37]

It can be argued that this near doubling of the proportion of French Canadians in the overseer force was the result of ethnic succession: as Poles and other newer immigrant groups moved in, French Canadians moved up. There are several reasons to question the sufficiency of this explanation. As late as the mid-nineties, many New England textile bosses believed French Canadians were inherently incapable of assuming managerial duties. In an 1898 article, William MacDonald observed that, according to regional mill agents, "comparatively few [French Canadians] become competent foremen or overseers, and [they] are likely to work best under the supervision of some one not of their own race." When it is further noted that the use of French Canadian organizers was an important factor in the success of the 1900 unionization drive, it seems even less likely that the increased appointment of French Canadian overseers was a simple case of ethnic succession. What the changes do indicate is that local textile manufacturers began to view Franco-Americans differently after the turn of

the century. A little militancy can be a wonderful dissolvant of ethnic stereotypes.[38]

These developments were important for two reasons. One was the attitude that French Canadian overseers brought to the job. Compared with their Yankee, English, and Irish counterparts, they were likely to be more understanding of the needs of textile operatives. This is evident in the observations of Philippe Lemay, the first French Canadian overseer at Manchester's Amoskeag Mills. Although he had little use for unions or "strike agitators," Lemay sympathized with the demands of Amoskeag operatives during the 1922 walkout. As an overseer, he recalled, "I couldn't join their ranks in the labor union nor help them in any way, but neither could I be against them."

> I had worked long hours for anything but high wages. I knew what it meant to be poor, what sacrifices must be made if you want to lay something aside for a rainy day. . . . Even as a second hand and an overseer, I never forgot my humble beginnings and always considered myself a textile worker. These strikers were textile workers, too, and I was sorry for them.

Lemay's comments are all the more remarkable in that overseer inflexibility was a major cause of the 1922 Amoskeag strike, and there is every reason to believe that such attitudes were appreciated by Franco-American operatives especially. When one of their number received a promotion in local mills, Jacques Ducharme observed in his novel on Holyoke, there was "little jealousy" among French Canadians, "for they realized that their strength lay in their remaining together."[39]

They also recognized that overseers played a vital role in the successful operation of shop-floor kin networks. Within textile mills, overseers hired and fired workers, gave them their orders, and often decided on their requests for improved working conditions, job transfers, and the like. This dependence on managerial cooperation not only reduced the attractiveness of unionization for French Canadian textile workers; it also increased trade-unionist suspicions about their suitability as union members. Most Dynamiters, George Fitzgerald observed, believed the majority of both paper and textile workers were unorganizable. Although local labor leaders wanted to bring these workers within the union fold, they needed prompting. The militancy of women paper workers, which often exceeded that of their self-styled male benefactors, provided ample cause for action. Textile operatives, on the other hand, appeared both quiescent and

uninterested. The truth is that they may not have been interested. As Hareven persuasively contends, the shop-floor kin networks constructed by French Canadian textile workers functioned as surrogates for labor unions. Moreover, in Holyoke these networks were increasingly controlled by French Canadians themselves rather than by Irish labor leaders.[40]

Lastly, these differences were reinforced by the inability of most textile workers to meet the socioeconomic standards embodied in the family-wage ideal. However necessary child labor may have been for textile families, trade-union respectables viewed the practice with uncomprehending disapproval. It not only mocked their commitment to worker education. Child labor also threatened existing work and wage standards, and led them to support laws to restrict immigration. A 1917 *Artisan* editorial endorsing legislation that would require immigrants to take literacy tests thus declared:

> While we would be the last to try to exclude all who wish to come to this country, we are sick and tired of seeing poor, ignorant aliens brought to this country in droves for the sole purpose of bringing down labor conditions existing here, and preventing betterments. We must Americanize those we have before we can afford any more wholesale importations.

Given the devotion of this generation of French Canadians to *survivance*, it is easy to imagine how these attitudes on the part of trade union respectables gave way to the worst forms of ethnic stereotyping. What must be understood is that such intra-class discord did not stem from ethnic differences alone. Sustained material deprivation had led French Canadian textile workers down a different sociocultural track than that of their Irish coreligionists: one based on the family economy rather than the family living wage. As we shall see, the misunderstandings that resulted from these differences would continue to divide Holyoke workers into the 1930s.[41]

IN ADDITION to influencing trade-union development and intra-class relations, the family–living-wage doctrine also shaped the political views and actions of Catholic trade unionists. Father Ryan felt that one should not look to employer benevolence for a living wage: "Only visionaries put any faith in this method." He invested greater confi-

dence in unions, but did not consider them adequate to the task either, because so few unskilled workers were organized. Ryan thus saw government as the institution most apt to insure that all workers received a living wage and advised labor unions to take an active part in politics. Such participation was all the more essential because of a regrettable tendency in American politics to ignore the existence of class interests. The legislative process, Ryan argued, disregarded "the fact that for the great majority of individuals their class interests were their primary interests: that where they have one interest in common with all other citizens of the country they have ten that are vital only to their particular class." The Constitution seemed to assume, he added, "that laws will be framed which will be equally favorable to all individuals, while, as a matter of fact, the balance of effect of almost every legal enactment is to benefit one class at the expense of another." Catholic trade unionists acted on similar assumptions.[42]

At Holyoke, *The Artisan* eschewed AFL voluntarism and applauded legislative proposals ranging from the old-age pension bill of Victor Berger, the Milwaukee socialist, to demands for a living wage by the American Federation of Catholic Societies. Prior to World War I, though, local trade unionists rejected calls to form a labor party. In 1916, *The Artisan* labeled one such proposal premature and argued that current AFL policy, which enjoined trade unionists to vote for the candidate, "no matter of what party, that will give the most to labor, is the best plan for some time to come." Three years later it would be more receptive.[43]

Although *The Artisan* endorsed the war effort, its support was lukewarm. Editorials criticized the draft as unnecessary and decried the Espionage Law as a "violation of the liberty for which we are supposed to be fighting." When wages failed to keep pace with spiraling prices, it lashed out at "greedy employers" who used wartime calls for austerity to deny the just grievances of workers and "raised the cry of IWW" whenever they sought adequate wages. At the same time, it linked its most zealous declarations of "patriotic duty" to labor's legislative demands. One editorial urging workers to buy war bonds stated:

> As trade unionists we have asked from State and Union the enactment of laws and the establishment of policies calculated to improve the condition of wage earners. Now the nation is calling upon us for support and it is for us to denote by the support we give at this time, that we are entitled now

and in the future to extra consideration at the hands of the law makers of State and Nation.

The government's postwar retreat on the labor front caused a rare criticism of AFL policy for failing to secure laws "concerning the eight hour day, the minimum wage, and the recognition of unions." Noting that "We have the power," *The Artisan* asked, "Why not use it?" In November 1919, it congratulated the Boston CLU for sending a delegate to a Chicago conference considering the formation of an independent labor party. By the following March it had drawn back from the venture. But the same issue that announced its capitulation to the AFL line on labor parties also carried an editorial on the family warning that "any economic system which impairs this institution is wrong and will work to the detriment of the whole structure of American ideals."[44]

In the local arena, the formation of a wage-earners' club in 1906 that sought to divorce the saloon from politics and generally improve the "condition of all workers" signaled the political resurgence of Holyoke trade unionists. Among the issues exciting the interest of local workers was the playground movement. In urging support of a 1908 referendum requiring cities with populations exceeding 10,000 to build playgrounds, *The Artisan* declared that the "great aim of the trade union movement, if it has one aim that is greater than another is for the emancipation of the child; the freedom of the child from the slavery of toil at too early an age." It later demanded that labor be accorded equal representation on the municipal playground commission because it "is labor's children, principally, who are the one's to be benefited." The CLU also took a keen interest in the industrial-education movement to insure that local programs did not become hatcheries of scab labor and to guarantee that such courses provided a broad, well-rounded education, rather than one that "caters only to machine operatives."[45]

The CLU's chief nemesis in local politics was the political machine of Republican boss William F. Whiting, whose principal spokesman after 1910 was Mayor John White. White's refusal in 1913 to explain his municipal labor policies before the CLU led Edward Alden and Urban Fleming to try their hand at political versification:

Oh, Lord Mayor, listen to us, Thou who does up all things well,
Hearken to our supplication ere we hit the padded cell.

Since you frowned upon our efforts we are feeling mighty blue,
Condescend, your Royal Highness; come and run the CLU.

Certain aldermen, they tell us, when you speak, are stricken dumb,
Board of Public Works and License, you have got beneath your thumb.
When you speak the cops all shiver—when you cuss they see the Boss.
Save the CLU Your Honor; in other words, please come across.

Treat our supplications kindly; do not try to get our goat.
Fall is coming and remember that we both have got a vote.
Keep your bonnet tied on tightly and your ire to somewhat curb.
We'll be with you just as ever

Yours truly,
ED & URB

In response, White first lost his temper and threatened to sue *The Artisan*. That winter he also lost his bid for reelection, an event that Alden and Fleming memorialized with another piece of doggerel:

Well, Jacko, we reached out and got cha; we derricked you out of the chair.
When we called your bluff you hadn't the stuff, to wit, Jacko, you wasn't there.
For in spite of your stale, smutty stories, your bushwa and blatherskite scoff,
Your stay in Room One won't be long, Father John, for right here is where you get off.

You were some snobbish gink while you had it, but that mayor for life stuff don't work,
For you sure hit the mud with a dull, sickening thud; yes, Jacko, you sure got a jerk.[46]

As gratified as Alden and Fleming were by White's defeat, it did little to aid the local labor movement. Even *The Artisan* admitted that his successor, John H. Woods, had never shown "any conspicuous act of friendship for organized labor." After Woods served two lackluster terms, White regained the mayor's chair for a few years before again being defeated in 1917. Although a postelection *Artisan* editorial claimed the victor, John D. Ryan, as one of labor's own, a headline urging Ryan's reelection the following year evinced declining enthusiasm: VOTE TO ELECT JOHN RYAN. MAYBE MIGHT HAVE DONE BETTER BY LABOR BUT COULDN'T BE AS BAD AS MCKAY. In 1919,

147

mayor-elect John F. Cronin, a former trade unionist, bluntly informed the CLU that labor would not dominate his administration. The membership applauded the address anyway; he could be no worse than Woods or Ryan.[47]

Because of its unwillingness to chart an independent political course, Holyoke labor remained dependent on the Democratic party and Irish middle-class leadership. It is easy to criticize the CLU for accepting an arrangement in which it was treated as a junior partner, often forced to endorse marginally appealing candidates, and rarely able to obtain all that it wanted. Yet, it was by no means a one-sided relationship. Running on the Democratic ticket, several CLU members won political office and performed yeoman service on behalf of their class. As an outspoken member of the city's Fair Price Committee, Eagle Lodge's Michael Griffin led aldermanic efforts to keep a lid on the rising cost of living during the immediate postwar years. Holyoke labor also sent David Sullivan, another papermaker, to the Massachusetts House of Representatives, where he joined other Democratic lawmakers in efforts to augment the commonwealth's already sizable body of social and labor legislation. During the 1910s, the General Court enacted measures to reform employer liability laws, create a workmen's compensation system, and establish a minimum-wage commission for women and minors.[48]

Furthermore, there was always some advantage to be gained from supporting party choices in municipal elections, however disappointing the nominee may have been. Democratic mayors not only solicited labor votes, but listened to trade-union views on political appointments and consulted with CLU leaders before making decisions that affected labor's interests. There was also the vital matter of jobs. According to Fred Garvin, a retired papermaker interviewed in 1979, the main sources of employment in Holyoke during his youth were paper, textiles, and the Board of Public Works. Of the three, the last-named became even more important after 1920 as the city's two major industries entered a long period of decline. By lining up behind Democratic candidates, the CLU insured that unemployed members would have access to these jobs.[49]

In addition to these more tangible benefits, the loose political coalition that developed between trade unionists and the Irish elite affected the local disposition of class forces in ways that would help protect labor during the dark years of the twenties. Although the Irish middle class could not be characterized as a friend of labor, it did play

a moderating role within the councils of the Holyoke bourgeoisie. In 1916, for example, when the Chamber of Commerce condemned a federal measure that would grant railroad workers an eight-hour day, Dr. D. F. Donoghue informed the *Springfield Republican* that the vote was not unanimous. He and other Democrats supported both President Wilson and the legislation in question. The existence of such sentiments within the chamber was at least in part responsible for the forging of a unique postwar accord between that organization and the CLU. In 1920, the two bodies approved a declaration of principles that recognized "representative negotiation," which was defined as talks "between an employer and duly accredited representatives of his employees, regarding hours, wages, and all other matters affecting their relationship." The agreement also established machinery for the arbitration of labor disputes.[50]

As it turned out, the pact did not last long. A lengthy carpenters' strike the following year led the CLU to withdraw from the arrangement. The accord was nevertheless notable, particularly in view of what was then happening in other areas of the country. After 1920 in many industrial centers, capital mobilized under the aegis of the American Plan to restore the open shop. Rather than developing means of conciliating organized labor, these offensives were designed to destroy it. In many places they succeeded. That capital did not pursue a similar course of action in Holyoke was due in no small measure to the class alignments of local politics. Without solid middle-class support, employers lacked the social base for such an assault. And with an Irish Democratic mayor in Room One, they were even less likely to secure whatever political backing may have been necessary for success.[51]

The foregoing analysis also sheds light on the relative ineffectiveness of French Canadians in Bay State politics. Compared with the Irish, Massachusetts Franco-Americans were consistent political underachievers. At Holyoke, Peter Haebler observed, enclave leaders "were continually frustrated in their efforts to organize an effective voting bloc." One reason these initiatives were not more successful was the group's reluctance to identify itself with either of the two major parties. With the exception of some elements of the middle class, Franco-Americans were never comfortable among Republicans because of the party's nativist heritage. At the same time, however, the cultural chauvinism of Irish Democrats, coupled with their tendency to shortchange French Canadians in the distribution of

patronage, cooled whatever ardor the latter may have felt for the party of Jackson.[52]

This ambivalence often resulted in irregular voting patterns. Between 1898 and 1910, voters in Holyoke's Ward 2, the heart of the city's Franco-American enclave, regularly supported the mayoral candidates put forward by William Whiting's Republican machine, while returning a Democratic majority in gubernatorial races. One need not dig too deep to uncover an explanation for the above: The Whiting machine's patronage policy, which provided an equitable distribution of jobs among the city's different ethnic groups, was a welcome departure from Democratic practice; and the unwillingness of French Canadians to pull the Republican lever in statewide races during the age of Henry Cabot Lodge is equally understandable. But voter behavior in several other races is less easy to explain. In 1899 and again in 1906, Ward 2 residents failed to get behind the candidacies of French Canadians who were running for the State Senate on the Republican ticket. Moreover, Franco-American abstentions decisively influenced the outcome of at least one of these contests. Peter Haebler estimates that if 500 Ward 2 voters had not sat out the 1899 election, Daniel Proulx might have bested his Irish Democratic opponent. These findings are particularly noteworthy because this was not the only occasion on which French Canadians stayed at home. According to Paul Kleppner's calculations, approximately 40 percent of Massachusetts Franco-Americans voted in statewide elections between 1900 and 1928. By contrast, Irish turnout for these same elections approached the 75 percent mark.[53]

A variety of reasons have been advanced to explain Franco-American political behavior. They include intra-group jealousy, personal feuds, "an over-abundance of individuality," and an inability to "stick together." Apart from their vagueness, these explanations suffer from another shortcoming: Although they suggest why French Canadians sometimes refused to support other Quebecois, they do not tell us why Franco-American voter turnout was so much lower than that of the Irish. In their common focus on intra-group social tensions, however, these observations do provide a starting point for a fuller treatment of the problem by indicating where we might find a more adequate answer: in an examination of the social relations of the enclave. A good place to begin such a query is Franco-American associational life.[54]

The two main Franco-American community organizations in Hol-

yoke during the late nineteenth century were the Société de St. Jean Baptiste and Union Canadienne, which in 1898 merged to form L'Union St. Jean Baptiste. Although French Canadians from all walks of life bought insurance from L'Union and its predecessor societies, there is strong reason to believe that the social gatherings sponsored by these groups catered to a much more exclusive element. In the mid-eighties, for example, when the Société and Union Canadienne pooled their resources to construct a social hall, the site chosen for the building was located in Ward 6, a solidly middle-class area well removed from the center of the city's French Canadian enclave. The selection of this site was no accidental occurrence. An occupational analysis of the officers of these associations led Peter Haebler to conclude that "social activity was largely confined to the middle and upper classes." All this is in striking contrast to the operation of the St. Jerome's Temperance Society, which as late as the 1890s had an active cross-class membership that drew its leaders from a wide range of occupations. And the foregoing suggests that, compared with the Irish, social differentiation among French Canadians both began earlier and cut deeper.[55]

This impression is reinforced by Jacques Ducharme's observations in his novel on Franco-American Holyoke. Two of the work's principal characters are Nicholas Dulhut, an intensely status-conscious early immigrant, and Jean Baptiste Delusson, a later arrival who despite growing material success retains a more modest view of his place in society. In one exchange, Delusson remarks that the world of Yankee Holyoke "is different from ours. Let us be content with our own race." But Dulhut is not so easily satisfied. He complains that "we are becoming Americans, and yet they refuse to recognize us." Dulhut thus joins an early group of "monied people" who flee Ward 2 to relocate "on the hill, as tho mounting the hill were a tangible proof that they were climbing the social ladder."[56]

In time, even Delusson joins the exodus, largely for the sake of his offspring. "All the good families are moving away," one had remarked. And his older children, particularly, "were glad that they were moving to The Hill, for it was an upward step socially, and they were of an age when they liked to say they lived on The Hill and not in the 'Flats.' " Throughout, Delusson remains the same unpretentious person he has always been and does his best to prevent his children from contracting "the snobbishness then rampant in Holyoke." Yet class lines were being drawn, lines that marked significant

social distinctions among Franco-Americans. "The most important thing, in the view of the French Canadians," Ducharme later observes, "was to marry within one's class. The worst that could be said of a candidate for marriage was the remark: '*Il n'est pas de notre monde*'—'He is not of our world.' "[57]

This brief account of social differentiation among French Canadians provides the context for a closer look at the group's political conduct. In relating class differences to voter choices, though, we need to be very careful. For a much longer time than was the case in Irish Holyoke, French Canadians pursued an enclave existence in which group interests were defined in ethnic rather than class terms. Moreover, many enclavists subscribed to a petty bourgeois ethic that made a virtue of independent entrepreneurship. Social advancement per se was not resented. What people did resent were the social pretensions that sometimes accompanied material success. And they were most likely to identify French Canadian Republicans with such behavior. In joining the GOP, Franco-Americans were both expressing a political choice and making a social statement, the same kind of statement that upwardly mobile, status-conscious Methodists made when they shifted their religious allegiance to Episcopalianism. Voters drew the connection and acted accordingly. This not only accounts for the defeats of Daniel Proulx and John Goddu, the Republican senatorial candidates rejected by Ward 2 voters. It also explains why, during the same years that they were backing William Whiting's mayoral nominees, these voters consistently elected Democratic aldermen.[58]

In short, those members of the Franco-American elite who joined the GOP—and by all accounts there were many—carried a special political burden. To a far greater extent than was required of French Canadian Democrats, they had to convince voters that they represented the entire enclave, and not simply "the good families." The senatorial candidacies of Daniel Proulx and John Goddu demonstrate that they were not always successful. Given these divisions, both within the elite and the broader enclave itself, it is scarcely surprising that French Canadian community leaders failed to organize an effective voting bloc.

At this point one might well ask, "Didn't similar social differences exist in Irish Holyoke?" They certainly did. As we saw in chapter 5, increased residential segregation and changes in associational life at the turn of the century sharpened class divisions and undermined the

social bases of the city's Irish enclave. Equally important, these developments did not go unobserved. When it came to deflating lace-curtain pretensions, no one could be more savage than the Irish themselves. In Mary Doyle Curran's Holyoke novel, status-conscious members of the Irish elite were depicted in terms that were, to say the least, unflattering:

> Aunt Josie more and more cultivated the middle-class Yankees who lived near her, though when she was with us she had not a good word to say for them. The side of them my mother and I liked she never saw. Both she and her husband picked up their worst traits, their stinginess, their hard-headed business methods, the ways of the Yankees that had made them owners of the mills in Irish Parish and family-proud with nothing but a shopkeeper's ancestry behind it.

The question thus arises, how did the Irish bridge these social differences and maintain a united political front?[59]

The answer can be found in the political activities of the city's Irish-dominated trade unions. Although trade unions embodied and exacerbated class divisions in Irish Holyoke, they did not create them. These divisions and the social friction they engendered existed independently of trade unionism, among French Canadians as well as the Irish. But where the social tensions that festered beneath the surface of enclave life in Franco-American Holyoke were never given concrete expression, trade unions brought these tensions to the fore and made them the subject of political bargaining: in the hard coin of labor legislation, jobs, and political protection against employer assaults. In so doing, they helped mobilize voters. Here we might recall *The Artisan*'s 1918 election eve headline: VOTE TO ELECT JOHN RYAN. MIGHT HAVE DONE BETTER BY LABOR BUT COULDN'T BE AS BAD AS MCKAY. On one hand, the headline acknowledged that labor was not getting, or likely to get, all that it wanted. At the same time, though, it expressed an important attitude toward politics: one that said politics counts, better to obtain half, or even a tenth, of a loaf than nothing at all. Given the existence of these attitudes, it is not surprising that, during a period of declining voter turnout nationally, nearly three of every four Irish voters in Massachusetts continued to show up at the polls. It is even less surprising that Irish middle-class politicians found it expedient to deal with organized labor. Though had they not, it would have still been difficult to ignore a group of trade unionists that

spent its leisure hours poring over the *Congressional Record* and debating professors from local colleges.[60]

JUST AS IT shaped their approach to trade unionism and politics, the family–living-wage doctrine influenced the manner in which Catholic workers viewed class relations. When working for capitalists who paid a living wage and required reasonable hours, *The Artisan* stated, workers should not only take pride in their work, but also show an interest in their employer's business: "Make the employer feel that you have a material interest in his welfare, as well as you can, and you will force him to respect the union card." Local manufacturers reputed to pay high wages received effusive obituaries. At their deaths, *The Artisan* praised William Whiting's philanthropy and remarked that Joseph Metcalf of the Farr Alpaca Company had "set a high mark in fair dealing with his employes, for he paid the best wages in his line."[61]

Yet, not all manufacturers enjoyed the commanding positions in their respective markets that allowed Whiting Paper and Farr Alpaca to be so openhanded with their workers. Trade-union relations with these firms were often more adversarial. "The antagonism existing between the great forces in our industrial life," declared *The Artisan*, "exists because the workers seek by organization to bargain for a living wage with an employer whose dominant ambition in life is to get wealthy—not comfortably rich, but wealthy—at whatever cost to humanity." By treating their workers as "so many beasts of burden," such employers invited class war. "One has only to read the signs to perceive an approaching crisis," warned a 1909 editorial. "The struggle *may* be bloodless, but it will be none the less severe."[62]

The prospect of such struggles in turn conditioned worker—middle-class relations. On one hand, Holyoke trade unionists actively sought support from local merchants and petty entrepreneurs. A two-column *Artisan* editorial addressed "To the Merchants of Holyoke" announced, "We shall continue to print papers; we shall continue to ask your patronage. We want it; we need it; we believe we (especially) deserve it; we believe we are fighting your battles for a steady wage and working conditions that mean contentment and prosperity to the workers." The latter assertion—that labor's struggles benefited the middle class as well as wage earners—was a recurring theme of *Arti-*

san editorials: "If the merchant only studied the matter more thoroughly he would find that it is the union man he can rely on also to put up the fight for the elimination of unfair combinations that are now bearing down so hard upon the merchant by decreasing the profits of his business."[63]

Not all local businesspeople agreed. Some, *The Artisan* noted, "have been buncoed into believing that the manufacturers' interests were the merchants' interests." This was a serious miscalculation. For they could be no more prosperous than the workers who constituted the overwhelming majority of their customers. *The Artisan* thus urged wage earners to support local merchants and petty entrepreneurs, but only those who engaged in fair-labor practices, stocked union-label goods, refused to handle boycotted commodities, and generally aided the labor movement. In an effort to maintain a safe logistical base from which to conduct relations with recalcitrant manufacturers, trade unions carefully observed the actions of local businesspeople during labor disputes. At the conclusion of the plater women's strike, *The Artisan* declared, "Those who have made known open hostility to the demands of the strikers will not be forgotten; those who demonstrated a friendly spirit to the girls will be remembered." However much it irked them, most small-business people at least tacitly accepted the trade-union definition of worker–middle-class relations. When Fred Burnham, proprietor of a coal and grain company, attempted to organize a merchant boycott of *The Artisan* after being placed on the unfair list, he found few supporters and had to come to terms with the CLU.[64]

In sum, although worker–middle-class relations were not strife ridden, they remained uneasy. The men who assumed control of the Holyoke labor movement after 1905 had come of age during a period when local workers were beginning to define themselves in class-specific terms; these years also saw the dissolution of the social bases of the enclave. Holyoke trade unionists had thus developed a hard-eyed, instrumental approach to worker–middle-class relations that sometimes made *Artisan* declarations of mutual interest seem less sincere than disingenuous. The social relations of the enclave could not be reconstituted in a world of boycotts, unfair lists, and increasing social exclusivity.

Nevertheless, there were real continuities with the previous era. Despite brief interest in forming an independent labor party, Holyoke workers continued to accept—or at least could pose no alternative

155

to—middle-class political leadership, and the anti-voluntarist, reformist emphases of Catholic trade unionist politics clearly drew on enclave precedents. The period after 1905 also saw a markedly reduced
level of industrial strife. Holyoke trade-union leaders had imbibed the
class consciousness so prevalent during their formative years, but it
was a nonrevolutionary consciousness. Moreover, those years of insurgency had ended in crushing defeat along a broad front. This they
also remembered and on the basis of that experience sought to protect
class interests through means—legislation, community pressure, and
arbitration when necessary—that did not require their moving into
the streets. Many of these same men would dominate Holyoke trade
unionism into the 1930s, and it is to those decades that we now turn.

7

THE CHURCH AND LABOR, 1920–1945

IN 1919, as Allied leaders gathered at Versailles to determine the shape of the postwar world, unprecedented numbers of American workers took to the streets in an effort to realize their own peacetime agenda. Depicted as the work of communist radicals, influenced by the Russian Revolution, the strikes were swiftly crushed by the combined forces of capital and government. Their most enduring legacy was a general climate of conservatism that kept labor activists and social reformers on the defensive into the 1930s. In Washington during the period, the national mood was sustained by a series of Republican administrations that unabashedly identified corporate interests with the national interest. For at least one GOP standard bearer, the actions of capital were part of a broader providential design. "The man who builds a factory builds a temple," Calvin Coolidge reverently intoned, and "the man who works there worships there."[1]

Despite Republican boasts that the nation had entered a golden age of prosperity, the 1920s had a bleak underside and for many working people these were, in Irving Bernstein's apt phrase, the "Lean Years." In few places was this more so than in Massachusetts. Where prior to 1925 the state economy had followed national trends, it afterwards contracted sharply. Bay State industries lost 80,000 jobs between 1926 and 1928 alone, and conditions were so grim by the latter year that Republicans did not place the famous "Chicken in Every Pot" advertisement in Massachusetts newspapers. At Holyoke, many firms never fully recovered from the 1921 recession; by 1928, local industries not only employed 18 percent fewer workers than they had in

1920, but were also paying them less, as wage disbursements declined 27 percent during the period.[2]

Although the 1920s would be a cheerless decade for both trade unionists and social activists, the period opened on an optimistic note. In 1919, Father John Ryan penned a sweeping statement on contemporary social problems that was subsequently adopted by the National Catholic War Council. Popularly known as the Bishops' Program on Social Reconstruction, it called for minimum wage legislation, unemployment and old-age insurance, public housing for workers, and the abolition of child labor. The document also urged organized labor to look beyond its own immediate interests and assume a more active legislative role. Although their proposals were in many respects similar to a statement recently issued by the AFL's Reconstruction Committee, the bishops chided labor leaders for leaving such vital matters as a living wage and eight-hour day to union voluntarism, an approach that failed "to give sufficient consideration to the case of the weaker sections of the working class, those for whom trade union action is not practically adequate."[3]

A persisting commitment to voluntarism was not the only feature of the AFL declaration that the bishops found wanting. They also faulted labor leaders for an unwillingness to develop means by which workers might "become owners as well as users of the instruments of production" and recommended that steps be taken to provide labor participation in management through copartnership agreements and producer cooperatives. Intended as a moderate alternative to the British Labor Party's postwar social reconstruction agenda, the bishops cast their proposals in a framework of reciprocal rights and duties that would preserve the interests of labor, capital, and society at large. The laborer, they concluded,

> must come to realize that he owes his employer an honest day's work in return for a fair wage, and that conditions cannot be substantially improved until he roots out the desire to get a maximum of return through a minimum of service. The capitalist must likewise get a new viewpoint. He needs to learn the long-forgotten truth that wealth is stewardship, that profit-making is not the basic justification of business enterprise, that there are such things as fair profits, fair interest, and fair prices.[4]

Despite its conservative features, the bishops' program was not what American corporate leaders had in mind when they enthusiastically endorsed Warren Harding's call for a "return to normalcy."

The statement looked much further down the road of industrial reform than capital was willing to travel, and the National Civic Federation (NCF), acting on behalf of the nation's largest businesses, mounted a counteroffesnsive. The NCF gathered "expert testimony" from anonymous Catholics who collectively affirmed that the bishops had exceeded their authority by issuing so wrong-headed and radical a declaration. Their program, a 1921 NCF report asserted, tended to undermine public confidence "in the government and institutions of this country," and was apparently the work of a small band of radical priests sympathetic to Marxism.[5]

However self-serving, NCF contentions that the bishops did not speak for all Catholics were only too accurate. During the early 1920s, conservative hierarchs opposed to the social-justice orientation of the recently formed National Catholic Welfare Conference persuaded Pope Benedict XV to lift his approval of the organization. Although Benedict's successor, Pius XI, resanctioned the council, episcopal opposition would continue to hinder its activities, particularly efforts to implement the bishops' program. As Father John Ryan, head of the council's Social Action Department, observed: "The first obstacle confronting the department is the fact that neither the bishops, the priests, nor the laity are convinced that our industrial system should be reorganized in this radical fashion." If anything, Ryan understated the difficulties facing Catholic progressives. For as the decade unfolded, traditionalist churchmen, seeking to restore a threatened hegemony, would mount one final campaign to impose their paternalistic nostrums on American Catholics. This chapter examines the degree to which they succeeded.[6]

Before proceding, a few words of explanation are in order concerning the structure of this and the next chapter. Because certain developments like the contraction of paper employment and emergence of the CIO form important parts of both chapters, I initially tried to present this information in an integrated, chronological fashion. I found, however, that such an approach prevented me from giving sufficient force to the arguments developed in these chapters. As a result, I opted for a thematic treatment of this material despite the resulting chronological overlap this imposes on the narrative.

DURING THE FIRST week of September 1923, Holyokers briefly set aside more mundane cares and staged an elaborate celebration to

commemorate the city's semicentennial. Among the week's many speakers was Father John J. Griffin who, after an obligatory tip of the hat to local business and social leaders, chose to emphasize the contributions made by "those who realized that, having exhausted their native resources in the struggle were content to accept whatever measure of success Divine Providence meted out to their honest efforts." Taught by the church that "perfect happiness is not fully attainable," these people achieved personal fulfillment through a devotion to "home and country and to God." In the process, Griffin added, the entire city benefited:

> If we have had a peaceful community all these years it is due in great measure to the fact that our common citizenship has not been infected with the insidious germ of a false Utopia of bolshevistic destruction and individualistic dreams flowering into fierce jealousies and antagonisms. On the contrary, the individual seeing at times apparent injustices in our industrial and governmental relations, seeing the apparent uneven distribution of the fruits of labor, fortified by Christian forbearance and charity, encouraged by the American ideal of freedom of opportunity and submerging their own individual comfort to the common good, this ennobled and ennobling citizenship labored and sacrificed and were content withal. Happy and content in their childlike confidence in Him who marks the individual sparrow's fall.[7]

This was not a message addressed to the Irish Catholic trade unionists who dominated the Holyoke labor movement. Its oppressively fatalistic overtones effectively wrote them out of the city's history and denied much that they stood for. But it did reflect the thinking of many Catholic churchmen, perhaps none more so than Boston's traditionalist archbishop, William Henry Cardinal O'Connell. The son of immigrant working-class parents, O'Connell was elevated to the see of Boston in 1907 and for the next thirty-seven years ruled the archdiocese with an iron hand, rigidly centralizing a heretofore loose administrative structure. According to Donna Merwick, his authority over subordinates became so pervasive as to constitute "thought control." Although Merwick may have overstated her case, rank-and-file priests generally recognized that dissenting from the archbishop placed one's current comforts and career prospects in real peril. O'Connell's views on intra-church power relations were unambiguous and easily understood: "When I ask you to do something, trust me and do it."[8]

O'Connell's social views, stated in numerous addresses and pastoral letters, were more contradictory. Although suspicious of trade unions, he acknowledged labor's right to organize and even strike, particularly when "greedy capitalists" refused to pay a living wage that would permit workers to provide for their families. Invariably, however, these concessions appeared in a constrictive framework of reciprocal rights and duties that looked to a world in which workers dutifully submitted to the dictates of benevolent employers and paternalistic pastors. Priests, he declared in a 1912 pastoral letter on industrial relations, should "announce fearlessly to the rich the duties of their station and the responsibility of their stewardship." Workers, on the other hand, should avoid giving "themselves over too much to the pleasures of life," as such behavior "leads people to live beyond their incomes and is the fruitful source of family troubles and discontent with one's station in life." Priests entrusted with the care of working-class souls should regularly remind "the workman that the consolations which religion holds out to him are the only real and lasting foundations of true happiness below; and that the envy, the jealousy, and hatred of class only render more and more bitter the contest which, even were it victorious, would end only in the ashes of disillusionment."[9]

O'Connell further believed that employer paternalism should not cease at the factory gate, but extend to all of life's relations. Where rich and poor lived in close proximity to each other, he stated in a 1923 address before the Guild of the Infant Saviour, "the social problems of the wage earners are consistently in the eye of the upper classes and the solution of these problems comes about more expeditiously, from the spirit of understanding which exists between the classes and the masses." As he knew and regretted, residential segregation along class lines was an irreversible fact of American social life, no less so among Catholics than other religious groups. Yet if upwardly mobile Catholics were more concerned with a home in the suburbs than overseeing the behavior of working-class coreligionists, there were other ways they could do their part to preserve social order and further the church's institutional interests. No organization proved more energetic in these matters than the Knights of Columbus, a fraternal order founded in the 1880s to fuse the social aspirations of middle-class Catholics with their religious concerns.[10]

One activity warmly appreciated by Cardinal O'Connell was the Knights's unremitting warfare against socialist influences in American life, an ongoing campaign that acquired renewed intensity during

periods of labor militancy. When, for example, workers took to the streets in unprecedented numbers after World War I, Massachusetts Knights flooded manufacturing centers with a host of "experts in industrial relations" like David Goldstein, coauthor of *Socialism: The Nation of Fatherless Children*—a raggedly arranged compilation of socialist declarations criticizing the traditional family that served as a veritable seed catalogue for lecturers tilling the rich fields of Catholic antiradicalism. The K of C could also be counted upon to assist church efforts to extirpate political radicalism in other countries. During the mid-twenties, it sponsored a nationwide movement to publicize religious persecution in Mexico, where, it claimed, a revolutionary government was seeking to "introduce sovietism into the hemisphere."[11]

In addition to its antiradicalism, the K of C rendered considerable aid to church authorities on the legislative front. Lobbyists helped defeat a bill that would have legalized the dissemination of birth-control information and organized resistance to state and federal measures intended to improve public education. The hierarchy acknowledged these efforts and encouraged the Knights to keep up the good work. In 1920, Bishop Beaven of Springfield purchased the *K-C Mirror* and made it the diocesan organ after it had proved its worth during a campaign to turn back educational legislation that he deemed detrimental to Catholic schools. Speaking before local Knights a few years later, Beaven's successor, Bishop Thomas M. O'Leary labeled "the modern drive against an irreligious press and non-Catholic schools for Catholics, a crusade in which the Knights of Columbus should enroll with the fervent zeal of the crusaders of old." It was an aptly phrased call to arms, for in many ways the Knights functioned as modern-day equivalents of the "crusaders of old": an elite band of holy warriors doing battle to protect the Church against the machinations of birth controllers, educational reformers, domestic radicals, and agents of the great red conspiracy emanating from Moscow.[12]

With the possible exception of Father Peter Dietz's Militia of Christ, which had few local adherents, no organization comparable to the Knights existed among Catholic wage earners. There is nevertheless evidence that during the 1920s many Holyoke workers were, to adopt traditionalist phraseology, content with their "station in life." Interviewed years later, retired textile operatives remembered this as a period of "no unions [and] no strikes," characterized by an easygoing relationship with the bosses. This was by no means an experience shared by all New England textile workers. In 1922, a strike by opera-

tives in the Pawtucket Valley of Rhode Island seeking a restoration of earlier wage reductions spread to Massachusetts and New Hampshire and ultimately involved between sixty and eighty thousand workers. Other regional job actions included a 1925 walkout by 2,500 workers at American Thread's Willimantic, Connecticut, plants and a 1928 strike by New Bedford operatives that lasted five months before a compromise settlement was reached. To understand why Holyoke workers differed from more militant operatives in other areas of New England, the devices local manufacturers employed to maintain quiescence within their mills need to be examined.[13]

As was the case in many locales during the twenties, welfare capitalism had an important influence on labor relations within the Holyoke textile industry. Among local mills engaged in various forms of welfarism, none instituted so comprehensive a system as that operated by the Farr Alpaca Company. Its program included health and recreation services, a pension scheme, and profit-sharing plan. Founded in the wake of the 1912 Lawrence strike and designed to reduce labor turnover, the profit-sharing plan contained a vaguely defined "satisfactory service" clause. Company directors arbitrarily determined what constituted "satisfactory service," and there were no provisions for employee appeals. The clause was thus intended to deter even modest expressions of worker self-assertion and, as Frances Cornwell Hutner observed, underscored "the paternalistic, company-dominated character of the Farr scheme."[14]

Despite its heavy-handed features, Farr's profit-sharing plan was popular with employees. It therefore had citywide significance. Farr Alpaca, which employed nearly four thousand workers in the mid-twenties, occupied a strategic position in the local labor market, and its employment policies were watched closely by other manufacturers. In 1918, for example, Lyman Mills agent James A. Burke provided his superiors with an assessment of the company's profit-sharing program, noting that it "does help to make the working people more contented, and does prevent a great many people from moving about." Yet, Burke added, such schemes were no substitute for high wages, and in this area Farr Alpaca had no local peers:

> [T]heir loom fixers receive about 17% more than ours, and their weavers will probably average about 20% more. . . . The average degree of the skill of their employees in these two lines is doubtless higher than ours, for as a result they draw only the best of our help.

These are telling observations. They suggest that Farr Alpaca functioned as a safety valve within the local labor market. Dissatisfied textile operatives at low-wage concerns saw little need to strike or form unions when they could improve their lot by simply transferring to the Farr.[15]

Although most welfare programs were intended to pacify the general work force, some were directed at specific groups of workers. One such scheme employed by several local mills involved holding mortgages on the homes of a carefully selected loyal cadre: When hard times struck after 1925 it was these operatives who retained their jobs. Other programs served to coopt a company's more energetic and active employees by providing them an outlet for their ambitions. In 1920, for example, Farr Alpaca established a cooperative store to help its operatives combat the high cost of living. After financing the project, management insisted that it be employee operated, and company operatives elected a seven-member board of directors—comprising one clerk and two production workers from each of the firm's three mills—to manage the venture. The employee-managers subsequently became so absorbed in their duties that they developed a proprietary interest in the store. And when the Falco Athletic Association, another employee-directed company organization, began selling candy and dry goods around the mills, the cooperative association's board of directors strenuously objected, informing the Falco managers that as "we were brought into being for the purpose of selling candy, etc., to the employees of the Farr Alpaca Company, we consider that you are encroaching upon our territory."[16]

Within the mills some workers voiced complaints about working conditions. More typical was the attitude of Nora Labrecque. Plant conditions were all right, she remembered, but "I didn't care so long as I was getting my money." Most jobs outside the picker and carding rooms were compensated according to an incentive system so complex that many operatives did not know what coworkers in the same department were making. Besides undermining concerted action on the all-important wage front, the system substantially augmented the authority of shop-floor supervisory personnel. At a time when the "foreman's empire" was collapsing in other industries, textile overseers retained real power in their departments. Anna Sullivan, who began working in the mid-twenties and later became a prominent CIO official, recalled that weavers who sought good wages "had to be in with the boss" if they were to be regularly supplied with good warps:

as the saying went in weave rooms, "no warp, no work." Overseers controlled access to these and other materials as they continued to play a vital role in the day-to-day operation of textile mills. When coupled with local variants of welfare capitalism, the mode of remuneration in Holyoke textile mills effectively divided the work force and helped induce worker submissiveness.[17]

Welfare capitalism was also a noteworthy—albeit less significant—feature of labor relations in the Holyoke paper industry. In December 1920, the Crocker-McElwaine Company adopted a policy requiring all its employees to sign individual contracts. Designed to reduce labor turnover as well as combat unionism, the agreements contained seniority provisions that superimposed "service differentials" on existing wage scales and guaranteed workers with at least five-years service "continuous employment as long as contractual relations existed between the company and employee." The company also took steps to reinforce managerial authority on the shop floor by instituting productivity bonuses and making service differentials contingent on the recommendations of foremen and department managers. Although company president R. F. McElwaine insisted that the contracts were not compulsory, he added that "those who sign are going to be protected in dull times to the advantage of those who refuse."[18]

In attempting to impose the contracts on his employees, McElwaine made no secret of the fact that their "main feature [was] the principle of the open shop." If McElwaine was trying to provoke local trade unionists, he succeeded. Eagle Lodge urged workers not to sign the pacts and, when McElwaine refused to back down, began picketing his two local mills. As paper production declined during the course of 1921, however, McElwaine's not very subtle threat that those who accepted the contracts would "be protected in dull times to the advantage of those who refuse" took on added meaning. By early spring, all company employees had signed and Eagle Lodge had withdrawn its pickets. "It is better to go back to work at this time than to fight a losing fight," International Brotherhood of Paper Makers (IBPM) president J. T. Carey explained. "Conditions will be better in the future to fight this proposition."[19]

Carey was much too optimistic. Not only did the individual contracts continue to govern labor relations at Crocker-McElwaine into the mid-thirties, but many workers came to accept and even praise them. Raymond Beaudry, who began working at Crocker-McElwaine's sister concern, the Chemical Paper Company, in 1952, recalled that old timers

spoke well of the benefits provided by the agreements. This raises a question that cries out for explanation. Why would such traditionally independent minded workers endorse what were in effect "yellow dog" contracts? To answer that question we need to take a closer look at the Holyoke labor market during the period.[20]

The history of the Holyoke paper industry after 1900 is largely an account of the American Writing Paper Company (AWP). Formed in 1899, AWP was originally a thirty-three-plant trust intended by its promoters to dominate the manufacture of fine writing paper. With sixteen mills at Holyoke, it was both the major source of paper employment and local wage leader. Despite the enormous power that it exerted locally, AWP was from its founding a stricken giant that, for several reasons, would never meet the expectations of its stockholders. One shortcoming was its failure to integrate backwards and control its source of raw materials. As a result, AWP not only had to pay more for wood pulp than its integrated competitors, but was occasionally forced to curtail production when this vital resource was in short supply. An even more serious problem was AWP's rickety financial structure. Burdened with a heavy funded debt throughout much of its existence, it was also overcapitalized and had to rely on current earnings to update aging equipment. As one company executive remarked, AWP's record "of not having paid a single cent on stock in the form of dividends for many years makes the raising of capital exclusively from investors a difficult procedure." Although expressed in 1946, this colossal understatement could have been uttered at any of numerous junctures in American Writing Paper history. Not surprisingly, AWP usually lagged behind its competitors in replacing obsolete machinery.[21]

Like Crocker-McElwaine, AWP also tried its hand at welfare capitalism. In 1918, it adopted a group insurance plan and instituted an "Old Guard" program that accorded special recognition to senior employees: Workers with more than twenty-years service received gold buttons "as an ensignia of their rank of service"; and those with between ten and twenty years were given silver buttons. The same year it began publishing an employees' monthly, *Eagle "A" Unity*, designed to foster worker identification with company interests. Besides profiling "Old Guard" members, *Eagle "A" Unity* reported on the activities of company athletic teams and as a regular feature contained a section, "Between Ourselves," which welcomed newcomers, dispensed shop gossip, commented on the special talents and interests of indi-

vidual workers, and applauded especially industrious employees. Special editions recounted in detail the fun that was had by all at company-sponsored outings.[22]

In 1920, American Writing Paper established an industrial relations department, headed by Adam Wilkinson. As a former United Mine Workers' official and friend of Samuel Gompers, Wilkinson was a shrewd choice for the post. Among other duties, it was Wilkinson's job to investigate worker grievances, advise on employee transfers, and prepare comparative studies on industrial wages and working conditions. He was also expected to develop a "spirit of cooperation and mutual understanding" between management and labor. The available evidence indicates that, with the exception of a 1923 strike, Wilkinson carried out this last task with notable success. In 1927, for example, Eagle Lodge endorsed the international's call for a five day week and 5 percent wage increase, but announced that it would "take no action on the proposed wage increase here for some time, due to adverse business conditions"; the following year it abandoned attempts to secure a five-day week because it "would be an imposition on the Holyoke manufacturers at this time," given the dearth of organization elsewhere; and during the early thirties, it assented to a series of wage reductions. With this record, Wilkinson had ample reason to praise Holyoke union leaders, as he did in a 1935 address, for "their intelligent understanding of conditions" in the paper industry. At his death three years later, Eagle Lodge reciprocated by voting to purchase a floral piece for his casket and send a delegation to the funeral.[23]

Yet Wilkinson's achievements were not solely attributable to a winning personality and profound knowledge of trade unionism. There were more important reasons why Holyoke paper workers acted as they did. One was the threat of capital flight. The 1923 strike ended shortly after AWP president S. L. Willson declared that he would transfer local production to company plants outside Holyoke "if the papermakers do not desire to operate the mills here." Another was AWP's visibly shaky financial condition: In 1923, it filed a bankruptcy petition and went into receivership for four years. An Eagle Lodge correspondent captured the general mood of local paper workers during these years in a 1928 letter to the *Paper Makers Journal*:

I am not able to give you much good news from Holyoke. Every once in a while a mill is shut down and the employees are told to get out—your

services are no longer required. The Paper Makers are guessing now which will be the next one to go down. We'll perhaps be able to tell you next month which mill has shut down.

Well, now I close, hoping that all our members are getting their share of the prosperity we hear so much about. Of course we have to be told we are prosperous.[24]

To return to Crocker-McElwaine, this was the context in which worker support for the individual contracts took hold. When it is recalled that the agreements contained seniority provisions, it is easy to understand why some workers would later speak well of them. In a locale where job security became increasingly tenuous after 1921, such safeguards had a special allure for wage earners. The pacts further offered workers what was in effect a guaranteed annual wage: senior employees continued to be paid during shutdown periods. These were matters of no small importance to Catholic respectables, given the culture's job and wage emphases, and the program's apparent success suggests the susceptibility of even these assertively independent workers to an adequately financed employer welfarism.[25]

The degree to which welfare capitalism actually shaped the actions and attitudes of Holyoke wage earners is difficult to assess. Welfarism does not always result in paternalism. Workers are quite capable of appreciating the benefits provided by profit-sharing plans and other welfare schemes without internalizing corporate goals. Even at Manchester's Amoskeag Mills, where Tamara Hareven found substantial worker identification with company aims, "[m]ost interviewees perceived the Amoskeag's welfare programs not as a substitute for the higher wages to which they were entitled but as a supplement." At Holyoke, where no single concern exerted the kind of local dominance that Amoskeag did in Manchester, workers were less likely to develop a sense of corporate identity. In fact, some had no illusions whatsoever about employer beneficence. Anna Sullivan recalled that whenever the Skinners—perhaps the most self-consciously paternalistic local millowners—made a contribution to a favored philanthropy, operatives knew a wage cut was impending.[26]

Nevertheless, welfarism had its impact. To many workers, "the Skinners were nice people," as were other local millowners. One of the characters in Mary Doyle Curran's novel on Irish Holyoke was a wool sorter whose unswerving belief in his employer's good intentions led him to oppose any form of collective action on the part of

wage earners: "Joe Hayden has always treated me all right and I'll stick no knife in his back. If the men want a raise, all they have to do is go up to Joe Hayden's office and he'll treat them right." It is against the backdrop of sentiments such as these, and the welfare measures that prompted them, that the impact of Catholic traditionalism must be judged. For in Holyoke as elsewhere during the 1920s, those notions of Christian stewardship and employer benevolence so cherished by Catholic traditionalists appeared, to some at least, to have become social reality. Indeed, it can well be argued that during the course of the twenties traditionalism and welfarism became symbiotically bound together: that each stimulated, reinforced, and gave credibility to the other.[27]

DURING THE TWENTIES, at least one group of local wage earners made no pretense of its aversion to Catholic traditionalism. Continuing an approach to life begun a half-century earlier at the St. Jerome's Temperance Society, Holyoke's Irish Catholic trade-union respectables looked not to paternalistic pastors for political guidance, but drew instead on their own resources, developing and refining their social views in active dialogue with each other at regular meetings in Dynamiters Hall. They also sponsored more formal programs. A course on "Labor Problems in Modern Society" conducted by Paul Douglas, then a professor at Amherst College, covered such topics as wealth and income distribution, recent wage movements, family-allowance systems, unemployment insurance, and the history of organized labor. During discussion periods, participants debated whether centralized labor markets reduced unemployment, why welfare capitalists so often opposed worker organization, and what impact technological innovation had on trade unionism, among other questions.[28]

Although the Dynamiters tried to avoid overt conflict with the church, it was almost inevitable that some differences would arise. It is not likely, for example that a lecture by Granville Hicks on "Religion in the Light of Science" would have elicited approval from Cardinal O'Connell, who still considered Darwinism suspect and declared Einstein's theory of relativity a passing "fad." It is even less likely that he would have appreciated an address by Paul Douglas condemning U.S. imperialism in Latin America, a talk which so impressed his auditors that they drafted resolutions urging a Senate investigation of

U.S. activities south of the border—this at a time when Catholic spokesmen were charging that Mexico, backed by the Soviet Union, was fomenting revolution throughout Central America.[29]

No issue better illustrated the distance between trade union respectables and a paternalistically inclined hierarchy than child labor. In 1924, when Massachusetts voters were asked to decide upon the merits of an amendment to the U.S. Constitution banning child labor, Cardinal O'Connell made it clear that no Catholic should support the bill. At masses throughout the commonwealth, priests followed the archdiocesan lead and instructed their parishioners to vote down the measure. Bay State trade unionists proved considerably less accommodating, and at Holyoke the CLU, led by Urban Fleming, a former president of the St. Jerome's Temperance Society, appointed a committee to marshal support for the initiative. What ensued was a struggle for the allegiance of Massachusetts wage earners that pitted the sociocultural interests of Catholic trade-union respectables against the institutional authority and hegemonic claims of traditionalist churchmen.[30]

In making their case against the amendment, church spokesmen and their middle-class allies portrayed a power-mad federal government seeking its own self-aggrandizement at the expense of parochial schools and the patriarchal family. "The measure has been shown to be Socialistic in its origin and purport," stated a typical editorial in *The Pilot*, house organ of the Boston archdiocese. "It contravenes the fundamental principle that parents, not Congress, shall have control of children, it paves the way for further encroachments upon the education and training of the youth, it subjects parents to a meddlesome centralized bureaucracy, it threatens to eat up the people's subsistence by taxes to support a new horde of officeholders, and it gives Congress the power to pass legislation hitherto unconstitutional, affecting the most sacred rights of parents, children, education, home, and family life." At Holyoke, attorney M. J. O'Connor reiterated many of the same charges in a letter to the *Transcript* warning that passage of the amendment would enable Congress to "close any and all private schools of every denomination, including parochial schools, for persons under 18 years of age."[31]

These arguments were scarcely new. In Massachusetts—as a battalion of educational reformers could wearily attest—they had long been standard rhetorical weapons in Cardinal O'Connell's polemical arsenal. What is sometimes overlooked and deserves emphasis is that traditionalist antistatism looked well beyond customary concerns

with family and school. Thus, in the 1912 pastoral letter urging employer benevolence as a remedy for industrial conflict, Cardinal O'Connell had also declared that class antagonism was largely immune to legislative amelioration. Such laws, he asserted, reinforced current tendencies "to exalt unduly the state, and to regard it as the creator of all rights and privileges which we enjoy, and to look to it for the solution of all our problems." Seven years later, speaking before the Catholic Education Association, O'Connell elaborated on these views by specifying some ways in which "paternalistic legislation" had invaded individual rights:

> In the industrial field it tends to weaken excessively individual management and enterprise by immoderate governmental regulation. The work of charity and reform it is gradually controlling or taking over from private concern; it has legislated religion from its schools; and over the schools themselves, public and private, its power is day by day developing into a monopoly.

In short, O'Connell's opposition to the amendment stemmed from fears that expanding state authority imperilled a broad range of traditional church functions. It not only threatened its educational activities, but also diminished its role as social mediator and dispenser of alms.[32]

In keeping with this larger design, traditionalists placed the family at the center of a privatistic, inward-looking approach to life in which the home functioned as a "haven in a heartless world." As one *Pilot* editorial instructed, Catholics should look to the Holy Family for behavioral models: to Christ the model child, who was "obedient and reverent always"; to Mary the model mother, who led a life of "sublime, unselfish, joyous sacrifice"; and to St. Joseph the model father, who spent his days in "constant toil in behalf of those whom God had entrusted to his care." Believing that all social problems "can be traced to the family," traditionalists deemed it absolutely necessary that nothing be allowed to impede their capacity to dictate family behavior.[33]

Some Catholic trade unionists accepted this familial paradigm and, echoing Cardinal O'Connell, expressed their opposition to "any measure that gave the government the right to invade the sanctity of the home." But many others did not. Despite their commitment to the patriarchal family, they knew that home life was not the source of all social problems, just as they knew that employer benevolence was no

wellspring of social justice. As Father Ryan had so aptly put it, "Only visionaries put any faith in this method." More important, dissenting trade unionists viewed the social functions of family life from a fundamentally different perspective. Where traditionalist churchmen based their cultural hegemony on an ability to influence and mold family development, trade-union respectables saw the family as the foundation of social personality: as a vital element in a carefully elaborated cultural world comprised of independent, self-assertive wage earners. To them, family responsibilities offered no excuse to withdraw from society; rather, such duties served as a spur to an active defense of class interests and provided them reason to become involved in and change the world in which they existed.[34]

What must be recognized is that in their efforts to secure a family living wage, Catholic trade-union respectables were not only seeking to preserve traditional notions of manhood. They were also, as their strong commitment to worker education indicated, concerned about their own reproduction as a reputable social group. In 1937, for example, a CLU committee headed by Dynamiters John J. Bresnahan and Francis M. Curran expressed alarm that local trade-school students seemed to possess an "inferiority complex." To correct the situation, the committee urged that steps be taken to integrate the educational activities of these youths with those of the broader student body. However trivial they may at first glance seem, such incidents tell us much about what these workers deemed important. In the world of Catholic trade-union respectability, there was no place for anyone with an "inferiority complex."[35]

Progressive clergymen encouraged trade unionists to act out these convictions. In a 1926 address before a New York labor audience, Father John Ryan warned that workers should not be misled by "the shallow and false theory that the interests of labor and capital are identical." For once wage earners ceased struggling to better their condition, they risked becoming victims of a "benevolent serfdom" that engendered a "slave mind" in its vassals. Ryan's remarks help to clarify important distinctions between progressive and traditionalist thought. Although both groups often addressed class relations within a framework of reciprocal rights and duties, progressives rejected the frank inegalitarianism undergirding Catholic traditionalism. This is not to suggest that they were social levelers with visions of a classless society. But they did seek a world in which wage earners possessed real power to influence the conditions determining their work and

lives; they further recognized that workers themselves would have to create this world.[36]

Not surprisingly, there was little agreement between progressive priests and traditionalist churchmen on the child-labor amendment. When Father John Ryan publicly endorsed the measure in a monthly newsletter that he wrote for the National Catholic Welfare Conference, a *Pilot* editorial, applauding those "distinguished Prelates" who had fearlessly exposed the amendment's "disastrous effects upon state and family," reminded its readers that the NCWC did not speak for the hierarchy; and a letter from "J. L. L.," which the *Pilot* prominently featured on its editorial page, not only condemned Ryan for having "favored a movement widely regarded as radical and socialistic," but expressed hope that Catholic University, where Ryan was a faculty member, would "not suffer from the disillusionment." "J. L. L." need not have worried. At that very moment, Cardinal O'Connell was working behind the scenes to have Ryan dismissed from his teaching post. As it turned out, O'Connell could not obtain his removal, but he did keep Ryan out of Massachusetts by making it known that neither he nor his progressive colleagues from the NCWC were welcome within the archdiocese.[37]

Election Day finally arrived, and as the returns rolled in, it was clear early which side had triumphed: statewide, voters repudiated the amendment by a substantial three-to-one margin; at Holyoke, the result was even more lopsided, 10,555–2,254. In making its case, the church was able to exploit persisting economic and cultural divisions among local wage earners. On one hand, assertions that the amendment would outlaw the labor of all children under eighteen years of age undoubtedly influenced workers still enmeshed in family economies. Unlike trade-union respectables, for whom child labor was an unacceptable abridgement of those cultural aspirations embodied in the family–living-wage doctrine, many French Canadian and Polish textile families relied upon the earnings of several members. These workers still viewed the family as a productive unit and could ill afford to support a measure that threatened to deprive them of the added income provided by child workers.[38]

Arguments that the amendment would undermine Catholic education also had their effect. Many Polish and French Canadian workers were still living out an enclave experience in which ethnic concerns overshadowed class interests. The parish schools that they helped construct with their labor and hard-earned savings served as repositories

of ethnic culture as well as disseminators of religious instruction. Any measure that threatened the autonomy of these institutions could expect to encounter stiff resistance. Equally important, trade-union respectables were in no position to allay such fears, given their own generally favorable view of Americanization programs.[39]

Apart from these and other reasons that might be adduced to explain the vote, one fact manifestly stood out: For Holyoke's trade-union respectables, it was a stunning setback that indicated just how little influence they possessed during the heyday of welfare capitalism. The contest also highlighted the strengths and weaknesses of a worker culture based on the family–living-wage doctrine: its capacity for independent political action as well as its insensitivity to the economic problems and cultural concerns of less-favored groups of wage earners. Yet whatever their shortcomings, these workers did keep the spirit of trade unionism alive during a decidedly inhospitable era. This was a real achievement. And in so doing, they made it easier for those who would follow them.

WHERE THE Great Depression dazed and discredited a multitude of prosperity-era visionaries, reducing their prophecies of an approaching secular millennium to ashes, it dealt no less harshly with the neo-feudal assumptions of Catholic traditionalism. After 1930, this centuries-old social philosophy, which had weathered the Enlightenment and belatedly made its peace with capitalism, lost what authority it had acquired to order social relations. Like welfare capitalism, which had briefly given it new life during the 1920s, it was ill equipped for survival in a world of mass unionism and the welfare state. As we shall see, Catholic traditionalists did not simply fade away. Their fears of social upheaval and worker self-activity would, by the late thirties, be incorporated in a resurgent antiradicalism designed to moderate social change in a world that, to them at least, seemed to be spinning out of control. In the meantime, other counsel, from voices too long muted, could again be heard.

Although Catholic progressives suffered a loss of visibility during the twenties, it was not because they had embraced a self-imposed monasticism. Their main problem was that few people were listening to what they had to say. Instead of paying tribute to the decade's much publicized material successes, commentators like John Ryan

believed they rested on a false bottom; and that prosperity could not be indefinitely sustained because wages were not keeping pace with either profits or advances in industrial productivity. Mounting exports, coupled with increasing foreign investment by American capitalists, Ryan warned in a typical article, indicated "there is something wrong with the domestic market . . . —an inequitable distribution of the national income." Nor was this the only problem caused by recent surges in industrial productivity. The technological innovations propelling these developments, Springfield's *Catholic Mirror* observed in a 1927 editorial, had given "those in control greater strength" and made it "all the more necessary that labor unions, cooperative societies, and government do what is required to bend the new industrial revolution to the welfare of those who work in it and those who buy its products."[40]

These and similar statements foreshadowed Catholic analyses of the depression. With few exceptions, Catholic commentators adopted an underconsumptionist interpretation that attributed economic distress to a maldistribution of wealth and prescribed higher wages and shorter hours as a cure for hard times. In 1931, these views received authoritative support from Pius XI's encyclical, *Quadragesimo Anno*, which explicitly sanctioned the family-living-wage doctrine; urged that wage contracts be modified to allow workers to share "in the ownership, or the management, or the profits"; and recommended the establishment of "vocational groups," organizations that would bring capital and labor together in a given industry. The *Catholic Mirror* responded enthusiastically to the encyclical, reiterating its call for greater worker participation in management and reminding employers, "It is the natural right of man to marry and establish a home." "The industrial system which does not provide for such homes," one editorial admonished, "sins against the God-given rights of the laborers and cries to heaven for vengeance."[41]

The *Catholic Mirror* also noted that "Pope Pius, like Pope Leo XIII, has little sympathy for any 'hands-off' policy on the part of the state." It thus eagerly endorsed early New Deal initiatives, likening the NRA's industrial codes to the occupational groups recommended in *Quadragesimo Anno*. It was not alone in its enthusiasm. In September 1933, a convention of diocesan lay societies not only pledged to support the NRA, but resolved that "no one should deal with any concern which refuses to lend a helping hand." "The absence of the NRA card," the declaration continued, "is *prima facie* evidence of a sweat

shop . . . [and] it is our moral duty to refuse patronage to any sweat shop, even though we have to pay higher prices to patronize men who pay living wages to their help." By 1934, however, initial support for Roosevelt's programs had begun to wane. At the first signs of stabilization, traditionalist churchmen began subjecting the New Deal to increasingly severe criticism.[42]

The most strident attacks came from Cardinal O'Connell, who after first welcoming New Deal reforms was by the summer of 1934 equating such measures with "autocracy" and socialism in addresses denouncing the "drab uniformity of collectivism." Locally, there were growing indications that Catholic authorities had also lost their initial ardor for New Deal initiatives. During the winter of 1933, diocesan high schoolers were asked to debate whether, "without considering current emergency legislation, federal encroachment on states' rights had reached alarming proportions;" and a year later, the *Catholic Mirror* began to question rising federal expenditures in editorials criticizing the belief that government "owes every man a living rather than a chance to work for a living." For the most part, however, the *Mirror* refrained from directly attacking the New Deal and adopted a neutral stance that was as uncritical as it was unsupportive.[43]

Where local churchmen paid occasional lip service to Cardinal O'Connell's anti–New Deal tirades, most workers ignored them altogether. Although Holyoke was Al Smith country and many residents attributed his defeat to "religious bigotry," the city gave Roosevelt the same 67 percent of the vote Smith had received. Local wage earners were not disappointed. The CLU eagerly embraced the NRA, placing two of its members on the local recovery committee and periodically dispatching investigative teams about the city to ensure that businesses displaying the Blue Eagle did not violate code-sanctioned labor standards. As it cheered this and other New Deal measures, the CLU sought to move the government to even further activity by endorsing Dr. Townsend's old-age-pension plan—a reform made necessary by technological unemployment and "the displacement in industry of older and often capable men by younger men." Enthusiasm for the new administration was not confined to local labor chieftains. The general sentiment of Holyoke workers was perhaps best expressed by Nora Quinn, who remembered Roosevelt as a "beautiful man": "He was good to the poor [and] he was a good man to the working people."[44]

The declining influence of traditionalist antistatism was accom-

panied—and in part caused—by the dissolution of welfare capitalism. At Holyoke, the demise of welfarism began during the late twenties when unanticipated style changes destroyed the alpaca- and mohair-lining market that the Farr Alpaca Company had long monopolized. By the early thirties, this one-time bastion of welfarism had not only ceased distributing wage dividends on its profit-sharing plan; it had stopped paying stockholder dividends as well. In an effort to revive its fortunes, Farr Alpaca diversified its product line and, forced to enter highly competitive markets, hired efficiency experts to increase work loads and intensify the pace of production. The resulting changes had a particularly jarring impact on employees habituated to the paternalistic relations of production characteristic of the previous era. The Irish wool sorter described by Mary Doyle Curran was one such worker who, accustomed to the "quiet, slow pace of the old mill," could not adapt to the new regime. Nor could he pose any alternative to it. Having become too set in his ways and having placed too much trust in his employer's benevolent intentions, this worker drifted into a state of sullen passivity. Most of his fellow workers would respond in a much different fashion.[45]

In June 1933—one month after the passage of the National Industrial Recovery Act, section 7 (a) of which guaranteed wage earners the right to organize and bargain collectively through their chosen representatives—Holyoke operatives sent a letter to the CLU asking that it organize the city's textile industry. Local labor leaders were only too eager to oblige, and the ensuing campaign was headed by two of the city's leading Catholic trade union respectables, Urban Fleming and Thomas Rohan. Both former mule spinners, they were founding members of the Dynamiters Club and officers of the St. Jerome's Temperance Society. Organizing efforts fortuitously coincided with a slight upturn in textile production, and if local operatives were still uncertain that the moment had arrived to address accumulating grievances, successful wage actions by workers at the Germania Woolen Mills and Mabson Silk Company washed away any lingering doubts. By late summer, textile workers were streaming into a galaxy of different unions: organized along craft and product lines, separate units represented loom fixers, mule spinners, ring spinners, woolen weavers, and silk and rayon workers. Despite craft segregation, a growing sense of solidarity was palpable and the following summer when the United Textile Workers' leadership broached the idea of a general strike, Holyoke operatives voted by a two-thirds margin to

support any action that the executive board deemed necessary to advance labor's cause.[46]

Worker grievances focused on the inequitable enforcement of NRA codes. Signed by President Roosevelt in June 1933, the basic textile code included minimum-wage and child-labor provisions, in addition to the full text of section 7 (a). In the months that followed, however, the board appointed to administer the code made no effort to enforce section 7 (a). By the summer of 1934, textile workers had decided it was time to take matters into their own hands. The strike began on September 1. It would last three weeks and involve more than four hundred thousand wage earners in states extending from Maine to Georgia; over four thousand Holyoke workers participated. In stark contrast to the violence that erupted in Rhode Island and many areas of the South, tranquility reigned at Holyoke, where Mayor Toepfert placed the city hall auditorium at the union's disposal. Local quiescence hardly betokened an absence of enthusiasm among strikers, nearly four thousand of whom attended one mass demonstration addressed by Fleming, Rohan, and AFL organizer Thomas Burns; a benefit dance drew another one thousand two hundred supporters. But enthusiasm alone proved insufficient. The UTW could obtain little aid from the AFL and, by mid-September, employer resistance, often backed by military force, had effectively smashed picket lines in many areas. Moreover, the UTW had taken its people out at the wrong time. Prior to the walkout one Holyoke manufacturer had declared that a general strike "would be the best thing that could happen at his plant." Another explained why this was so: "Markets are sluggish and there is stock ahead for some time." Before the strike collapsed altogether, UTW leaders declared victory and accepted a settlement that left conditions unchanged.[47]

At Holyoke, as elsewhere, the strike's outcome had a chilling effect on textile unionism. Old timers able to recall the brief and abortive outbreak of militancy following the depression of the 1890s must have experienced sensations of déjà vu. But much had happened since then. Stretchouts, speedups, wage reductions, and the elimination of numerous welfare programs had, by the mid-thirties, undermined whatever faith workers once had in their employers' good intentions. It is thus not surprising that renewed activity among textile operatives occurred at the Farr Alpaca Company, where in February 1936, 600 spinners, complaining of a stretchout, deserted their frames and moved into the streets. The strike was short-lived and brought no

concessions from the company, but another walkout two months later involved 2,300 workers and lasted six weeks. At its conclusion, Farr Alpaca signed the first written trade agreement ever secured by Holyoke textile workers. And when CIO organizers began filtering into town that winter they found a work force that was both willing and able to rehoist the union colors.[48]

The CIO drive to organize the textile industry began in April 1937, a month after the nearly moribund UTW had merged with the Textile Workers' Organizing Committee (TWOC), and a few days after the Supreme Court had affirmed the constitutionality of the National Labor Relations Act. At Holyoke, CLU leaders did not assume an active role in the effort. Nor did they stand in the way. According to one TWOC organizer, their general attitude was, "If you can get the textile workers to organize—fine. We can't." Compared with labor veterans like Urban Fleming, most TWOC leaders were a generation younger, in their early- to mid-thirties. But apart from age, they were not a homogeneous group. Former UTW members Edward Vanasse and Lionel Jubinville continued to believe that workers should be organized on a craft rather than industrial basis. Thomas F. Burns and his sister, Anna Sullivan, on the other hand, viewed the campaign from a much different perspective. Burns was a vice president of the United Rubber Workers-CIO and member of the national TWOC board; Sullivan would later become director of the Holyoke joint board of the Textile Workers' Union of America. Although they had received their first lessons in trade unionism from their father—an old-line craft unionist and founder of the Holyoke Loom Fixers Union—both were committed industrial unionists.[49]

Despite differences among TWOC leaders, success came swiftly and with little resistance. Holyoke, with its twelve mills and 5,500 operatives, was the focus of regional efforts and within fifteen months the city's foremost producers had signed contracts with the new organization. The high point of the campaign came in February 1938 when Farr Alpaca, with its 3,000 workers, recognized TWOC as sole bargaining agent. CIO leaders would, however, have little time to celebrate. By May, internal dissension had ripped the fledgling union apart, as 600 workers, led by Edward Vanasse, departed to form a competing AFL local. In the heated interchanges that followed, the dissidents reproached TWOC for its "dictatorial policies," while CIO officials labeled Vanasse and his associates "traitors to the working people." Although the division stemmed largely from

thwarted ambition—Vanasse deserted TWOC after a reorganization designed to reduce expenses had resulted in his dismissal as business agent—there is evidence that more was at issue.[50]

During the late thirties, as it continued efforts to diversify its product line and expand output, Farr Alpaca recruited a number of new executives who, in their hiring practices, demonstrated a marked preference for young workers and dismissed some of the company's older, more experienced operatives. It was these latter workers whom Vanasse represented. In an August 1938 letter to the Farr board of directors, he complained that superintendent George McCarthy had allowed CIO officials "to choose the workers who were brought into work regardless of their seniority or their qualifications." He also questioned McCarthy's competence, suggesting that he lacked sufficient "practical knowledge of weaving and loom fixing" to determine which workers should be held accountable for faulty production. "It has been Mr. McCarthy's contention the weavers are responsible for the seconds that are made," Vanasse observed, "but if he would make it his business to investigate and check upon the other departments that prepare yarn for the weave shed he would find that" weave room personnel were blameless. In closing, Vanasse stated that he only wanted "to see justice done for the old employees that have been faithful to the Farr Alpaca Company and always proud to hold a job and produce fine quality and ample quantity." Despite this appeal to company tradition, the letter had no discernible impact on the Farr directors. McCarthy remained on the job and TWOC continued to grow. The following January, when McCarthy resigned, CIO leaders issued a statement praising his "wise and honest treatment of labor."[51]

In the meantime, relations between labor and local churchmen, though free of conflict, could scarcely be characterized as cordial. Holyoke priests did nothing to obstruct textile organizers, but they did equally little to aid them. Local union leaders believed the one exception, a curate from Holy Rosary Church who had conducted labor education classes for textile workers, had been transferred to a remote rural parish because of his activities. More typical was the Willimansett priest who advised his parishioners "to think twice before calling a strike"—one of numerous occasions, according to the *Catholic Mirror*, "where vigilant pastors warned their people against the possible and probable dangers of hastily considered actions in industrial relations."[52]

The cautious and admonitory nature of diocesan labor policy was in large measure a reflection of the antiradical obsessions of Springfield's traditionalist hierarch, Thomas M. O'Leary. In a 1921 address, delivered shortly after he took charge at Springfield, Bishop O'Leary warned that "plans were in preparation to disrupt the social order." But, he added, there was no cause for alarm, as he was confident that all "right-thinking men and women of other beliefs would recognize that the 'old Catholic Church' was the great conservative bulwark." O'Leary's views changed little in later years. Speaking on the current crisis before the Knights of Columbus in March 1933—at the very nadir of the depression—he emphasized the need to prevent diplomatic recognition of the Soviet Union, "a diabolical movement for the destruction of our present civilization." As labor militancy escalated nationally after 1933, the antiradicalism of local churchmen became more virulent. In 1934, the *Mirror* attributed recent industrial conflict to "foreign agitators" and asked, "Has the Department of Labor gone communist? How do these agitators get in?" This was only the beginning. Subsequent editorials regularly warned against Communist influences in the labor movement; applauded the red-hunting activities of J. Edgar Hoover and the Dies Committee; and congratulated a state legislative committee for its "laborious examination of alien isms within the commonwealth."[53]

These preoccupations explain why CIO efforts received so little support from local churchmen. Even when defending the CIO against charges of Communist domination, the *Catholic Mirror* expressed hope that Catholic trade unionists would "peacefully penetrate [CIO] units and make a beginning of a safe and sane leadership." It also objected to CIO tactics, declaring the sit-down "essentially unjust" and "made to order for the communist, who everywhere has only one purpose: to make a bad situation hopeless." Despite these reservations and a clear preference for the AFL—its leadership had never "shown any of the noticeable Moscow complexion with which the face of the CIO glows"—the *Mirror* stopped short of advising workers to desert CIO unions. Instead, it encouraged the two organizations to join forces in the hope that labor unity would serve to dispel Communist influence among workers. "What labor must have," stated a 1938 editorial urging AFL-CIO cooperation, "is more leaders with a love for the 'Red, White, and Blue' and less leaders with a fanatical tendency toward the Red banner of radicalism."[54]

Perhaps the most pernicious byproduct of Catholic antiradicalism

181

was the fear it engendered of any form of worker self-activity. In voicing these concerns, the *Mirror* sought, without notable success, to mask their authoritarian implications by drawing a spurious distinction between intent and practice. For example, when Holyoke trade unionists organized a Workers' Forum in 1939, the *Mirror* observed that, though the project had "much to commend it in theory," it involved equally great dangers: "It will be of no advantage to workmen, often unskilled and unlettered, to be exposed to the theorizing of speakers who may offer them principles currently popular in certain schools of social and economic thought—principles which disclose their fallacy only when put to practice, as in that great experiment, the soviet dictatorship." Similarly, the *Mirror* acknowledged that formation of a labor party could bring workers real benefits— were it not that Communists believed "such a development would bring progress in their direction." Catholic red-baiting later forced the local directors of CIO-PAC to defend their electoral efforts in large newspaper advertisements.[55]

One should not conclude from all this that the *Catholic Mirror* was a forum for distempered reactionaries. Such was not the case. Over the years it had freely opened its columns to both progressives and traditionalists and, as Kenneth Underwood observed, it often adopted positions on labor matters well in advance of those expounded by local churchmen. This brings us to the real significance of Catholic antiradicalism—its impact on moderates and progressives. For what happened to the *Catholic Mirror* happened to others as well: to individuals like Father Charles Owen Rice, who during the forties went from union organizing to union purging; and to organizations like the Association of Catholic Trade Unionists, which during the same period largely replaced its broad social agenda with a single-minded concentration on red-hunting. These developments in turn transformed the Church itself: at a time when it might have become a forceful proponent of the social democratic visions of progressive priests like John Ryan, it instead became a vehicle for the neo-traditionalism of Francis Cardinal Spellman. This was no small loss.[56]

8

UNIONS, LABOR MARKETS, AND DEINDUSTRIALIZATION

AS THE UNIONS moved in, the mills moved out. This is a common explanation of deindustrialization that can still be heard in many former New England industrial centers. The reasons for its appeal are not hard to understand. Such an interpretation can easily be adapted to fit the ideological predispositions of a broad range of people, from trade unionists who consider corporate irresponsibility the primary cause of social distress to a wide assortment of capitalists who believe the same of organized labor. Like all popular beliefs, this explanation contains an element of truth. Yet it also hides a much more complex reality. Some unions adopted special measures to aid ailing concerns; and some corporations, recognizing the benefits to be derived from relations with unions, showed little interest in terminating them. The International Brotherhood of Paper Makers was one of those unions, and Holyoke's American Writing Paper Company was one of those concerns. The first section of this chapter examines industrial relations at AWP during its final decades of operation.

In textiles, the story was even more complex. For one thing, not all manufacturers acted on the same assumptions. Some displayed a genuine commitment to maintaining production in New England plants, and at the same time demonstrated a willingness to deal with organized labor; others were only waiting for the right opportunity to close down. Equally significant, the process of deindustrialization influenced and was influenced by important changes in the textile labor force. With each mill closing, it became increasingly difficult to persuade young workers to follow their parents into regional factories. The ways in which these developments interacted to shape the course

183

of deindustrialization in the New England textile industry constitute the main focus of the final sections of the chapter.

ALTHOUGH a greater proportion of its working people labored in textile plants than paper mills, Holyoke achieved national renown as the "Paper City." This reputation was based less on the quantity than the quality of the paper produced in local factories. As a manufacturer of fine writing paper, Holyoke possessed several locational advantages. One was its canal system, which not only served as a power source, but also provided paper producers with ample quantities of chemically pure water. To make fine writing paper, rags needed to be bleached and washed before being sent to the beater room. In the process, each pound of fiber was inundated with hundreds of gallons of water, and even small traces of chemical impurities could impair the stock's character. Another advantage derived from the fact that the city was also a textile center. This assured papermakers easy access to adequate supplies of rags, the most important raw material used in the production of high-grade paper.[1]

By the 1920s, however, changes in the paper market had negated these advantages. The introduction of the pulp-sulphite process enabled manufacturers to produce ragless writing paper that approached rag-content bond in appearance, but cost less to make. Mounting demand for these lower-cost papers undermined the market for high-grade products and forced local mills to expand production of lower-content rag papers. This shift in grades required the use of increased quantities of wood pulp, a raw material that was in short supply locally. Although wood-pulp production had flourished briefly in the neighboring Berkshires during the 1870s, the industry had largely disappeared a decade later, leaving in its wake broad stretches of despoiled forest lands. The absence of any alternative sources of supply in the immediate region placed Holyoke manufacturers at a competitive disadvantage with producers in geographically favored areas like Wisconsin and northern Maine, whose vast woodlands facilitated the creation of integrated concerns that did not need to rely on market pulp.[2]

Local papermakers were also unable to take advantage of recent advances in plant construction. By the turn of the century, most new factories were being built as a series of interrelated buildings. This

design gave manufacturers greater flexibility in routing the flow of work among departments than was possible in large single structures. The physical layout of Holyoke's manufacturing district prevented millowners from adopting such innovations. Bordered on both sides by water, most paper producers had little or no space for expansion and were stuck in less efficiently designed multistoried structures. The city's canal system, which had made Holyoke an ideal site for producing high-grade paper, now hindered the industry's future development.[3]

In addition to these problems, paper producers were part of an industry that prior to World War II was plagued by chronic overproduction. Between 1919 and 1939, the average level of operation was only 75 percent of capacity. It was an intensely competitive environment in which few firms prospered. Simply surviving was difficult enough. This was particularly so for troubled concerns like Holyoke's American Writing Paper Company. Formed in 1899 to monopolize the production of fine writing paper, AWP proved unable to maintain its position even in that shrinking market. Between its founding and 1910, the company's share of total fine-paper output dropped from 80 percent to 40 percent. With its rickety financial structure and aging machinery, it faced an increasingly uncertain future. By the late thirties, AWP operated only seven of its original sixteen Holyoke plants.[4]

Local paper workers watched these developments with deep foreboding and lived in constant dread of total liquidation. During the twenties, they were particularly ill prepared to confront such problems. By 1925, the Paper Trade Council, which at one time had comprised nine unions and a membership ranging from rag sorters to machine tenders, had been reduced to a few craft outposts. Its demise was largely a result of internal dissension. In 1920, a walkout by 600 unskilled workers collapsed after machine and engine-room personnel helped AWP to maintain production by working overtime. The disillusionment and bitterness engendered by this incident was in turn exacerbated by an unsuccessful 1923 strike, which left most workers payless for seven weeks without any subsequent gains. A final blow to the already crippled council came in 1925 when a resurgence of craft exclusiveness within the international elevated W. R. Smith to the International Brotherhood of Paper Makers (IBPM) presidency on a platform restricting membership to skilled machine and beater-room workers.[5]

Throughout the late twenties there was much talk around Eagle

Lodge about reviving the council, but it generated little action before 1933 when section 7 (a) of the NIRA finally prompted Holyoke paper unionists to start organizing. In the next few years, rag- and finishing-department workers flocked into a host of newly created unions. Afterward, as the dust settled and a new organizational structure emerged, it became clear that craft divisiveness would remain a hallmark of local paper unionism. Eagle Lodge continued to represent skilled engine and machine-room workers, while semiskilled operatives established Local 226 to protect their interests. Nor was there any likelihood that the two locals would soon merge. As one Eagle Lodge official observed, such a development might allow the more numerous membership of 226 to dictate the terms of wage settlements for all paper unionists; and this simply was not acceptable, he bluntly explained, because machine tenders and beater engineers are the "key men": "If we don't make the paper, they don't work."[6]

Despite persisting divisions among different groups of workers, American Writing Paper can scarcely be said to have welcomed this revival of unionism. If nothing else, the organization of rag- and finishing-room employees promised unsettling wage pressure from a numerically substantial and poorly compensated segment of its work force. Yet in many respects AWP was better prepared than most employers to deal with the emergence of mass-production unionism, and as events unfolded its response constituted little more than a formalization of existing relationships with both the IBPM and other area manufacturers. In June 1937, Adam Wilkinson, labor relations director at AWP, signed a contract recognizing the IBPM as bargaining agent and providing for a general wage increase. The agreement, which covered 4,100 workers from more than a dozen concerns, in effect regularized an informal, multiplant bargaining arrangement that had existed since 1916 among regional producers of rag-content, fine-grade paper. Although Wilkinson's death in 1938 temporarily disrupted the system, it was quickly restored by his successor, Harold Martin, and would govern industrial relations at AWP for the remainder of its existence.[7]

Union leaders responded warmly to these developments, stating that local employers are "to be congratulated and thanked for their part of the negotiations." This initial enthusiasm soon waned, however, as manufacturers secured wage decreases ranging from five to nine cents per hour in the 1938 contract. One faction in Eagle Lodge especially resented the reductions and used them to mount a cam-

paign against the union's current leadership. To protect their position, the embattled officials first tried to justify the cuts. "When the expected improvement in business comes to pass," one declared, "we shall be much further ahead by the experience gained now, and we shall be in an immeasurably better position to demand our just desserts." They also sought support from management. The union's "officers have stated to me many times that they have suffered abuse and criticism as a result of the wage cut," AWP executive W. J. Norton reported in a December 1938 memorandum, "and apparently the disappointed and radical element . . . have now come into power." These growing differences within the union came to a head during the 1940 contract talks.[8]

As much as any series of events, the 1940 round of negotiations shaped the course of industrial relations in Holyoke's paper industry during AWP's final decades of operation. The talks began when Harold Martin, acting on behalf of the manufacturers' group, issued a statement listing a familiar litany of troubles: Poor profit performance in recent years coupled with aging machinery and an inability to produce its own wood pulp imperiled AWP's capacity to maintain production. Moreover, because "wage rates are now higher in Holyoke than they are in competing companies," local paper workers lacked any justification for demanding an increase. Eagle Lodge did not agree. It wanted a 5 percent wage hike to compensate for a recent reduction in hours, and when the manufacturers refused, it began preparations for a strike.[9]

In the meantime, Local 226 came to terms with Martin, agreeing to a three-cent hourly increase. In so doing, its representative declared they could not accept a percentage-based wage hike because their lower paid membership had gotten the "short end of it" in previous such agreements. At the same time, the international also turned on Eagle Lodge. Acting behind the scenes, IBPM president Arthur Huggins informed Harold Martin that if Eagle Lodge did not accept the three-cent hourly increase he would not only refuse to sanction a strike, but actively oppose a walkout by "tak[ing] into Local 226 the members of Eagle Lodge who wished to work." With this assurance, the manufacturers held their ground; and Eagle Lodge, effectively isolated, assented to the pact. As it turned out, not all Eagle Lodge officials were disappointed. Huggins's intervention was in part designed to bolster the shaky position of union moderates. In a letter to the *Paper Makers Journal*, an Eagle Lodge correspondent afterwards

dismissed the 5 percent demand as the work of "a group of antique left wingers."[10]

There are several reasons why the international acted as it did. On one hand, competition from CIO unions during the late thirties had forced it to pay greater attention to the interests of semiskilled workers, and it became IBPM policy during these years to support cents-per-hour wage increases. It thus had no more sympathy than Local 226 did with Eagle Lodge's insistence on a percentage-based pay hike. Even more important in the long run, it was also IBPM policy to urge local unions dealing with troubled firms to make regular concessions in order to keep them in operation. This bargaining tack particularly affected workers in New England mills producing high-quality rag-content papers, many of which were, like American Writing Paper, inefficient operations with obsolete machinery and poor long-term profit expectations. Consequently, where in 1940 AWP's wage scale was marginally higher than that of its principal Great Lakes competitors, a decade later most groups of Holyoke paper workers were earning slightly less than their counterparts in Wisconsin rag-bond mills; and where in 1940 Harold Martin had relied on comparative wage data to open negotiations, he subsequently placed greater emphasis on AWP's "gloomy" future. Local union leaders grew weary of hearing these woeful prognostications, but given IBPM policy—not to mention whatever fears they themselves might have had concerning AWP's future—there was little they could do.[11]

In sum, American Writing Paper learned relatively early that it could not only live with independent trade unions, but could also use them as a stabilizing force. As its fortunes declined over the years, AWP managed, sometimes with active assistance from the IBPM, to secure a wage-cost advantage over competitors who had traditionally paid their workers less. One should not conclude that Holyoke paper workers passively accepted these developments. There was a brief strike in 1942 that the international characteristically refused to sanction; and Harold Martin's memos on contract negotiations at times reflected real frustration and annoyance—he found such labor epithets as "chiselers," "crooks," and "the opposition" particularly upsetting. Yet for the most part, AWP had little reason to regret its relationship with the IBPM. When the CIO tried to organize paper workers during the 1940s, it had little success. Local wage earners, one Eagle Lodge member later recalled, felt the CIO was "too domineering" and wanted to hold "a club over the head" of management.

Though the observation may have overstated the conservatism of Holyoke paper workers, it did contain more than an element of truth. As an AWP executive remarked in a 1946 memorandum, the company could expect little support from rank and filers, but "local and general leaders of the unions understand the problems and are willing to cooperate to any reasonable extent."[12]

NEW ENGLAND textile manufacturers first ventured into the South during the depression of the 1890s. These initial probes were tentative and with returning prosperity ceased altogether. Most northern producers then believed, as one English observer related, that "the 'mountain whites' were already fully employed, that the negro would never become an efficient machine-minder, and that whenever the South should come into competition with the North for immigrant mill labour the South will have to pay more than the North to get it." They were wrong of course. Southern labor supplies proved more than adequate, and the region would never compete with the North for immigrant workers. During later crises, additional branch plants would be built in the South, plants that would become the bases of vast interregional empires. These corporations would play a major role in the deindustrialization of the New England textile industry, though they were by no means alone. Other capitalists, absentee owners who recognized that the days of super profits had passed and who had no commitment to the communities affected by their investments, withdrew completely from the industry. The flight began in earnest during the 1920s.[13]

Just as textiles had spearheaded the Industrial Revolution in Great Britain and the United States, the industry's relatively modest capital requirements and labor-intensive character made it a favored starting point for newly industrializing regions from the American South to the Far East. By the mid-twenties it was a "sick giant," crippled by intense competition and massive overproduction. As inventories accumulated and prices plummeted, Bay State manufacturers seeking respite from their woes could look to a series of industrial studies whose findings were trumpeted throughout the commonwealth by a legion of Rotary Club speakers. The reports all focused on southern competition and the proposed solutions are easily summarized: reduce wages, increase hours, and abolish state labor laws. Although

organized labor resisted successive assaults on the legislative front, including a vigorous campaign to rescind a statute limiting working hours for women operatives, textile manufacturers did successfully reduce wages. Holyoke workers suffered major pay slashes in 1921 and 1925, while statewide, cotton-mill wages fell 26 percent between 1920 and 1928. Meanwhile, where some millowners cut costs and curtailed production, others chose to shut down altogether. A 1933 survey reported that western Massachusetts had lost twenty-five mills in the previous twenty-five years. At Holyoke, the first major concern to close its gates was the Lyman Mills.[14]

In March 1926, Lyman treasurer Ernest Lovering asked agent James A. Burke to prepare comparative cost data on a product line made and distributed by an Alabama competitor. Burke's findings quickly dispelled any thoughts Lovering might have had about entering the market. There was, Burke calculated, a "40% net differential" in labor costs alone between the two mills: "compared with Lyman wages of (say) $18 weekly—for 48 hours product—the Alabama relative might be $13.50 for 60 hours." Although Lovering knew that southern production costs were lower than those in the North, he was still surprised by Burke's findings, which he characterized as "instructive and interesting," adding that "we never before realized that there was such a spread in wages." Northern manufacturers, he concluded, "would seem to have no chance against such competition."[15]

Burke and Lovering nevertheless remained committed to production at Holyoke. They recognized that the mill's coarse-goods division could no longer meet southern competition, but they believed that by expanding its output of fine goods the company could still make a profit. To do so, however, would require a half-million dollars in new machinery, and the Boston bankers who held a majority position on the board of directors had little desire to forego a few dividends just to maintain operations in a field that was daily becoming more competitive. As word spread that major stockholders, led by Boston's Old Colony Trust Company, were pressing for liquidation, Holyoke's Chamber of Commerce marshaled evidence demonstrating ways in which the company could "be operated profitably if there is a will to do it." There was not, and on 14 September 1927 Lyman stockholders voted, by a 10,125–4,021 margin, to liquidate.[16]

Some observers afterwards claimed that the "reckless way in which city officials of Holyoke play with the taxes" was a major factor behind the decision to shut down. But most people knew that this was at best

a secondary consideration. When Ernest Lovering had suggested the need for lower taxes in his correspondence with Chamber of Commerce officials, the organization obtained assurances that the city would grant a "liberal reduction in valuations." Moreover, spokesmen for the Old Colony Trust Company were ruthlessly candid about their motivation, publicly stating that the "amount to be received per share through liquidation conservatively invested would seem to afford better possibilities of return than an investment in the Lyman Mills." Long accustomed to receiving substantial dividends on a regular basis, these investors, as the *Holyoke Transcript* observed, had become "too tired, too terribly prosperous [and] too sure of investments elsewhere to get busy and keep New England industry alive." Yet, while most Holyokers understood why the Lyman Mills had shut down, proposals to prevent other manufacturers from following suit were conspicuously absent in local postmortems. Indeed, a *Transcript* editorial analyzing "New Problems in Industrialization" could do no better than state that, where community and stockholder interests collided, communities lacked any means to protect themselves. "We are," the editorial concluded, "in the grip of a phase of our new industrialization which we have not yet learned to master."[17]

As the *Transcript* feared, the Lyman Mills shutdown was no anomaly. Throughout the 1930s a number of smaller enterprises pulled up stakes, and in his 1937 inaugural address Mayor William P. Yoerg reported that Holyoke had lost $42 million in taxable properties during the previous decade. To make matters worse, there were growing indications that Farr Alpaca, the city's largest textile concern, might soon be putting its spindles and looms on a southbound train. With its nearly four thousand employees and extensive welfare program, the company had for many years occupied a strategic position in the local labor market. During the late 1920s, however, the dissolution of a mohair- and alpaca-lining market that it had long monopolized led Farr to cut back on employee benefits and initiate steps to intensify the pace of production within its mills. Concomitant efforts to develop new product lines appeared to have succeeded when a sharp recession, beginning in late 1937, caught Farr executives by surprise and left the company with a warehouse full of unsold goods and a hefty packet of unpaid loans; it also resulted in 2,000 layoffs.[18]

In November 1938, Farr Alpaca president A. B. Chapin issued a public statement directed at Mayor Yoerg and local union leaders. "Other communities today are endeavoring to have the Farr Alpaca

Company move to their localities under very attractive offers such as reduced labor cost and even an abatement of taxes for ten years," warned Chapin. If the company was to remain at Holyoke, it "must have local assistance." Mayor Yoerg favored aiding the company, but expressed concern over rumors that it planned to retain a reduced work force at local mills. Until he received assurance that Farr Alpaca would maintain a "full schedule of operations," Yoerg replied, he could not consent to the desired tax relief. Yoerg was, if anything, more resistant to Farr demands than local unionists, who by that point must have wondered what more they could do. In February, the Textile Workers Organizing Committee (TWOC) had assented to a 12.5 percent wage reduction in exchange for company recognition, even though rank and filers had rejected the cut by a 1338 to 6 vote; and that summer CIO leaders had initiated a community program "to arouse bankers, businessmen, merchants, and clergy" to support the ailing concern.[19]

What labor leaders and city officials did not know was that Farr Alpaca's future depended less on their concessions than the outcome of an intra-corporate struggle between two factions of owners. One group, comprised largely of local stockholders and led by company treasurer Donald Green, supported a reorganization plan that promised to put the company back on its feet. Arguing that a return to full production would best serve both stockholder and community interests, Green asserted that Farr had "acquired a recognized standing" in the cut-rayon market and could "profitably manufacture fabrics in adequate volume to justify building our operations up to something approaching last year's peak." Before the company could resume full production, however, it needed to restore its working capital, which Green estimated would require borrowing at least $2.5 million.[20]

This was, given Farr's current financial woes, a formidable barrier to recovery. For pitted against Green and his supporters was another stockholder faction, led by Boston investment counselor Elmer Carr, that believed the company had seen its best days. This faction not only objected to further investment in the enterprise; it also considered Green part of the problem. In an October 1938 interview with company president Chapin, Carr complained that Farr assets were "not being conserved as well as they might be" and declared that Green and the current board of directors seemed "more concerned about prosperity for the city of Holyoke—the banks, merchants, and residents, than that the stockholders should have their rights." Be-

cause Farr had made its last dividend payment six years earlier, Carr added, any plan that required deferring stockholder returns to an even later date was out of the question: "the assets must be realized upon or be a total loss." That December, Farr stockholders gave the board of directors authority to appoint a liquidation committee.[21]

Community leaders accepted the decision with surprising equanimity. The *Transcript* noted that Farr Alpaca had lost nearly $13 million since 1930 and, calling liquidation "no great tragedy," observed that "such action as was taken yesterday may be the means of bringing new capital to the mills." Subsequent events dealt harshly with this simple faith in the redemptive powers of capital mobility. When initial bids on the entire mill proved disappointingly low, Donald Green submitted another, albeit more modest, reorganization scheme that would preserve upwards of two thousand jobs. But like earlier plans, it never left the drawing board. Meanwhile, panicky stockholders, afraid of losing everything, sold out to Carr and his group of Boston investors, who—carrying out Carr's dictum that "the assets must be realized upon"—began selling mill machinery to southern manufacturers. Although a group of dissenting stockholders obtained an injunction that November to halt the sales, it was all too clear that Farr Alpaca's days at Holyoke were numbered. In March 1940, the company severed what few remaining ties it had with the city.[22]

The Lyman Mills and Farr Alpaca shutdowns had much in common. Despite Farr's troubled past, neither company ceased production because of an inability to make a profit. Rather, faced with the need to modernize existing operations, a majority of stockholders believed that the distribution of assets following liquidation would generate proceeds substantially in excess of the current value of company stock. They thus decided it was time to seek safer and potentially more profitable outlets for investment. The Lyman and Farr shutdowns also demonstrate that—as a 1939 study of mill closings undertaken by the Massachusetts legislature suggested—the distinction between liquidation and migration was in many cases meaningless. Although both Holyoke companies formally liquidated, each sold major portions of its mill machinery to southern manufacturers. Moreover, the Lyman Mills closing may have been part of a broader migration effort: In the late twenties, Lyman's sister concern, Chicopee's Dwight Manufacturing Company boarded up its local mills to concentrate production in Alabama, where it had maintained a plant since 1894.[23]

The Lyman and Farr closings were part of what might be called the first phase of deindustrialization in the New England textile industry. Between 1920 and the outbreak of World War II, Massachusetts lost nearly 45 percent of its textile production jobs. But after 1940, a large infusion of military contracts, promising unprecedented profits, stabilized the regional industry and even led some manufacturers to reopen deserted plants. As late as 1948, Bay State textile factories still employed 140,000 workers; and at Holyoke in 1950, the Textile Workers Union of America (TWUA) claimed more than two thousand members in city mills. Although a far cry from the mid-twenties when Farr Alpaca alone listed 4,000 operatives on its payroll, this was by no means a negligible showing. A decade later, however, most of these position would also be gone as a second wave of liquidations and migrations stripped state textile mills of another 95,000 jobs.[24]

For several reasons, the notion of two distinct phases of deindustrialization offers a convenient means of periodizing the dissolution of the New England textile industry. The interwar period was largely a nonunion era in which organized labor lacked both the power and resources to mount a concerted campaign against capital flight; and where cotton-mill liquidations led the first wave of shutdowns, woolen and worsted closings predominated during the 1950s. Yet one must be careful, for in other ways the distinction is artificial and misleading—a number of important concerns were equally involved in both phases.[25]

One such corporation was Holyoke's American Thread Company. Formed in 1898, American Thread was, together with J. P. Coats and Company, part of an English-owned trust that monopolized both the domestic and manufacturers' thread markets until 1914 when a federal court ordered the two concerns to dissolve their relationship. The ruling had no immediate effect on Holyoke—after enlarging their capacity in 1916, the company's two local plants employed upwards of two thousand workers—but later developments had a much more serious impact. As the textile crisis deepened during the twenties, American Thread's local work force declined to 700 operatives; and as labor mobilized after 1930, the company began to reassess its long-term plans for Holyoke.[26]

In mid-March 1933, following notification of another in what must by then have seemed an endless series of wage reductions, more than two hundred American Thread operatives walked out. They quickly returned after agent William Clark threatened to "close the mills or fill

their places," but in subsequent months the discontent lingered and spread. A year and a half later, the entire work force enthusiastically supported the 1934 general strike, this time citing company efforts to impose a stretchout as their main grievance. At this point, American Thread was only waiting for the right moment to shut down. During the early thirties, William Clark told an acquaintance that the company had already decided to abandon its Holyoke works. "Labor conditions are said to be more favorable in other states," a reporter explained, "and many corporations having plants in such states make their enlargements there." With plants in Georgia, Tennessee, and other parts of New England, American Thread was well prepared to pursue such a strategy, and in January 1938—at the high point of TWOC's local campaign—it transferred most of its local operations elsewhere.[27]

As it turned out, the removal was short-lived. By year's end, American Thread had restored most of the jobs it had recently terminated. It would be cheering to attribute this unexpected turnabout on the part of company owners to a belated sense of community responsibility and dawning recognition of labor's right to organize. But such was not the case. In the fall of 1938, a hurricane destroyed a plant at Pawcatuck, Connecticut, and rather than rebuild there—where a recent strike had forced the company to recognize TWOC as bargaining agent—American Thread decided it was time to move on, despite an offer from town officials to finance the building of a million-dollar factory. Thus, in one of those cruel ironies so characteristic of the dissolution of New England's textile industry, Holyoke became for a time a beneficiary of capital flight.[28]

Once back in Holyoke, American Thread resisted unionization until the summer of 1942 when a regionwide campaign by the Textile Workers Union of America resulted in the organization of company plants at Fall River and Willimantic as well as Holyoke. With these successes there was brief hope that the union banner might soon be flying over the entire American Thread empire. Although plants at Milo, Maine, Bristol, Tennessee, and Tallapoosa, Georgia, remained unorganized, workers at another mill at Dalton, Georgia, had achieved collective-bargaining rights in 1937 and subsequently preserved them in the face of company-provoked strikes, a grand jury investigation, persistent race baiting, and the hiring of armed Pinkertons as mill guards. As it turned out, the TWUA was never able to expand this southern beachhead. With the failure of repeated organizational efforts in Tallapoosa

and Bristol, American Thread was free to carry out a long-term strategy of abandoning its unionized New England properties to concentrate operations in unorganized southern plants. In 1948, it began shipping spindles from Fall River to Tallapoosa; and during the early fifties, it finally terminated production at Holyoke.[29]

Thus it happened that during the postwar years American Thread joined other national chains like Pacific Mills, Pepperell, and Textron in reestablishing an industrial policy that approximated the open-shop conditions of an earlier era. With branch plants already located in unorganized, antiunion southern communities, these corporations were well positioned to shift production to locales where they would not have to deal with the TWUA. In the end American Thread did not liquidate all of its northern mills. Nor did it have to. Once the company had concentrated the greater part of its operations in the South, it was able to join with other interregional producers to keep a lid on northern wages by exploiting worker fears of additional plant closings.[30]

ALTHOUGH national chains like American Thread played a major role in the destruction of the New England textile industry, their actions do not constitute the whole story. A number of smaller firms lacked sufficient resources to follow the lead of the large inter-regional producers. Other companies investigated relocation offers from southern communities and decided to stay in New England. One such concern was the Crown Manufacturing Company of Pawtucket, Rhode Island. In a 1948 interview with the *Boston Globe*, Joseph H. Axelrod, Crown's president stated that, compared with the South, New England had more capital and skilled labor, was closer to major product markets, and possessed better research and training facilities. A further advantage, he maintained, was the region's "more mature labor movement": New England "had weathered the problems created by unionization, where the South still had to face them."[31]

It will come as no surprise to learn that most regional millowners took a less-charitable view of organized labor. Indeed, what is surprising is that Crown's president was not alone, and that other factory bosses also considered the rise of textile unionism an asset rather than an liability. But a survey of thirty-seven Massachusetts

textile manufacturers conducted by the Federal Reserve Bank of Boston during the late forties showed that one-sixth of the respondents thought that "relations with labor" gave them a competitive advantage over southern producers, while another 30 percent believed it of little importance.[32]

How do we explain these beliefs? Before concluding that Crown's president and those who shared his opinion of textile unionism were either insincere or temporarily deranged, it should be noted that there were several reasons why New England millowners could at this moment assume a relatively sanguine view of organized labor. The wartime demand for textile products had carried over into the immediate postwar years, and in 1947 manufacturers North and South posted record profits. More important, even though 65 percent of those surveyed in the Federal Reserve study believed that existing wage scales placed them at a competitive disadvantage with southern producers, regional differentials had declined markedly in recent years. Where the wage costs of New England mills were more than 50 percent higher than those of southern manufacturers during the mid-twenties, adoption of the NRA textile codes in 1933 had reduced the spread to less than 20 percent. The differential widened again after the NRA was declared unconstitutional. But the subsequent passage of the Fair Labor Standards Act of 1938, with its minimum-wage provisions, raised the pay of 44 percent of southern textile workers, while affecting only 6 percent of those in northern factories. And during the war years, several National War Labor Board decisions, coupled with unprecedented competition for labor supplies between southern textile mills and the numerous war industries that located in the region, exerted further upward pressure on southern wage scales. By the late 1940s, the regional wage differential was less than 10 percent.[33]

Lastly, there was some prospect that southern textile workers would soon be dues-paying members of the TWUA. Begun with much fanfare by the CIO in the spring of 1946, Operation Dixie promised to achieve in the South what the great organizational drives of the 1930s had accomplished in northern industries. From the outset, organizing textiles was the first priority of Operation Dixie. TWUA official George Baldanzi was assistant director of the drive, and the union's financial contributions to the early campaign totalled $95,000 a month, which was more than the total amount donated by all other CIO internationals. It was with these developments in mind that

Crown's president declared it "hard to conceive of any section of the country ringing about itself an iron curtain for the purposes of shutting out organized labor."[34]

As it turned out, this moment of hope for the New England textile industry passed quickly, so quickly in fact that many people later forgot it had ever existed. On one hand, demand for textile products began to contract during the late forties. Between 1947 and 1957, as total industrial production shot up 45 percent, the textile industry registered a 2 percent decline. During the period annual consumer purchases of textile goods fell from 44.5 to 36.2 pounds per person. Although a substantial increase in population offset reductions in per capita consumption, a corresponding drop in industrial purchases proved considerably more problematic. At the same time, there were ominous signs of future trouble on the foreign-trade front. Where textile imports totalled 6 percent of exports in 1947, this figure had risen to 22 percent a decade later.[35]

Of even greater importance, CIO hopes for a unionized South were not to be. The inspiring accounts of recent organizational victories and optimistic predictions of greater successes in the near future, which appeared regularly in union papers like *Textile Labor* and the *CIO News* during the late forties, masked a much grimmer reality. As Barbara S. Griffith has persuasively demonstrated in her fine study of Operation Dixie, the campaign was by this time dead in the water—and had been since the fall of 1946. During their first six months in the field, organizers made little headway at the region's leading textile concerns. Then at its 1946 convention, the CIO sharply reduced funding for the operation, which necessitated drastic cuts in an organizational staff that was already spread too thin. From that point on everything went downhill, until the CIO formally dissolved the campaign in 1953.[36]

Because southern workers received wage increases that roughly approximated those obtained by their northern counterparts during the late forties, CIO officials were able to maintain a bold public front. Within their own councils, however, they had no illusions about the magnitude of their defeat. As TWUA research director Solomon Barkin later recalled:

From 1945 to 1950 the [southern] mills were devoted to the job of mergers and concentrations. The men building the large corporate enterprises decided on wage policy. They could determine the wage pattern in the South.

No one in our ranks fooled himself into thinking that we made the wage increases. Nevertheless, the wage increases between 1945 and 1950 followed the pattern of the wage increases of the rest of the country. That was the extraordinary thing.

In one sense, Barkin was being too modest. The mere presence of CIO organizers outside the gates of southern textile plants had a salutary influence on regional wage policy. Yet his broader point was well taken: The TWUA manifestly lacked the power to equalize continuing interregional differences in wages and labor conditions.[37]

The full implications of this shortcoming, as Barkin's remarks suggest, did not become apparent until the early fifties. When the Korean War began during the summer of 1950, government orders poured in and the New England textile industry experienced a temporary boom. Taking advantage of the situation, the TWUA demanded and received a wage hike for its northern members. In the South, however, both union and nonunion mills refused to match the increase, and the regional wage differential shot up from an historic low of between 7 and 8 percent to 18 percent. To correct the problem, the union called out 40,000 members in six southern states for a five-week strike the following spring. Forced to contend with "gunplay, police violence, mass arrests, and the inevitable court injunctions," the walkout failed and conditions remained unchanged.[38]

The outcome of the strike had a devastating impact on the TWUA. As *Textile Labor* afterwards conceded in a remarkably frank editorial, the strike demonstrated that "the tail can't wag the dog if the dog really plants his feet and resists." Forty thousand union members "just aren't enough in a southern industry employing more than 400,000." "Down in our hearts we've known it all along," the editorial added, "but up to this year we were lucky." The TWUA's luck had indeed run out. Between 1951 and 1958, it would lose more than one hundred sixty thousand members. Most of these losses occurred in northern mills. Although a major arbitration decision in 1952 pushed wages back to the 1950 level, the events of the early fifties, reinforced by a shrinking product market, touched off a massive wave of mill closings. In Massachusetts between 1950 and 1958, textile employment declined from 113,000 to 46,000 workers. The New England textile industry had entered its final days as a major employer of regional labor.[39]

Were we to stop at this point we might well conclude that those

199

who attribute the demise of the New England textile industry to the actions of organized labor are essentially correct. Such a conclusion would be premature, a fact that becomes abundantly clear if we take a closer look at the circumstances surrounding the 1950 northern wage hike. The increase in government orders following the outbreak of war in Korea created jobs and tightened labor markets throughout New England. This development had a particularly severe impact on low-wage industries like textiles. At Holyoke, the situation enabled union negotiators to couple strike threats with assertions that a pay increase was necessary to keep workers in the industry. Without a wage hike, one union official declared, "our people will [be forced] to leave the textile industry for more money in war work." Nor was Holyoke alone in this regard. In neighboring Ludlow, a textile company that for many years had employed a "major portion" of local workers experienced similar problems. Most Ludlow males now commuted to higher-paying jobs in area plants like Westinghouse and Chapman Valve. To maintain an adequate labor force, the company was compelled in late 1950 to launch a special campaign to entice local women into the mill.[40]

The importance of these developments can scarcely be overstated. For what happened in western Massachusetts occurred in other textile centers as well: As an area's economy expanded, it became increasingly difficult for textile producers to meet their labor needs. In essence, what we have here is an industry that could not stand prosperity. To understand the forces that created these conditions, and at the same time obtain a fuller appreciation of the TWUA's role in the deindustrialization of the New England textile industry, we must first go back to an earlier era and examine the changing nature of the textile work force.[41]

AS NOTED in the preceding two chapters, the low wages associated with textile employment forced many worker families to adopt survival strategies that required the paid labor of several members. These family economies were particularly dependent on the earnings of children, many of whom entered the mills shortly after their fourteenth birthday. It was a system that fit well with the labor needs of textile employers. As the economy expanded, fourteen- and fifteen-year-old children left school for local factories; and when the economy con-

tracted, they returned to their classrooms. During World War I in Holyoke, for example, there was a notable decline in school attendance. "Labor is now at a premium and wages are high in practically all kinds of employment," the superintendent of schools explained in his 1916 report. "Employers who would not engage persons between 14 and 16 years of age because it necessitated arranging a 48 hour per week working schedule . . . are now glad to hire." Later, during the postwar recession, mounting unemployment caused a "remarkable increase" in school enrollments.[42]

By 1950, all this had changed. The enactment of more stringent child-labor laws was in part responsible. The Fair Labor Standards Act of 1938 prohibited the employment of children under sixteen years of age. But something else had happened as well. As early as the 1920s, there were indications that the social and ideological bases of French Canadian enclaves were beginning to erode. External forces like the media revolution of that decade stirred ambitions and interests that both transcended the opportunity structure of the enclave and challenged the relevance of *survivance*. The depression slowed these changes, but did not reverse them. "The younger generation is turning away from tradition," Jacques Ducharme lamented in the early forties, "and finds the American way more interesting than the life of their fathers. It is a question of milieu, circumstances, and ambition. There is no future in the maintenance of survival."[43]

As this new outlook slowly took hold, those children who had entered the mills in the 1910s and 1920s married, had children of their own, and wanted something better for their offspring. Madeleine Biehler's mother, who had begun work at a Holyoke textile plant at age fourteen, urged both of her children to take advantage of whatever cultural and educational opportunities might be available. Cecile Barthello gave her children similar counsel, as did Claire Lefebvre's mother. How many other parents exhibited a similar zest for education is difficult to determine. In all likelihood many displayed the ambivalence of an Alabama mill parent, interviewed in the late twenties for a study on child labor by Katharine DuPre Lumpkin and Dorothy Wolff Douglas: "It is a great help to parents with a lot of children to be able to get a little help from them, but on the other hand the children cannot do much of anything but work in a cotton mill unless they have an education."[44]

In the end, what attitudes toward education might have been at any given point in time was less important than the fact that they

were changing. And as they changed, children were staying in school longer. The crucial decade was the 1930s. As Marc Miller has written of Lowell during the depression, "a natural partner to high unemployment was exemplary school attendance." By the early forties in Holyoke, Claire Lefebvre observed, attaining a high-school education had become a common goal among French Canadian families. It was, to be sure, a goal that not everyone achieved. As late as 1950 in Holyoke, median school years completed was still only 9.9. But this was an increase of nearly a full school year since 1940, and there was every indication that this and related measures would continue to rise in the future.[45]

Increased educational achievement both reflected and was influenced by changing worker aspirations for their children. In some cases, parental advice regarding work was quite specific. Jerome Lefebvre's father, who was an overseer at Farr Alpaca, urged him to "stay out of the mills." Similarly, Louis Gendron and his wife recalled with pride how they had kept their children out of local factories: "That's what we worked for." And in Adams during the 1930s, school authorities shelved several requests for the institution of programs to train textile workers because most parents hoped their children would have access to better employment opportunities than those offered by local textile plants.[46]

More often, though, parental counsel regarding employment was less directive. A number of parents simply stated that they wanted their children to be happy, to be able to do what they wished. However vaguely phrased, these statements tell us much about the meaning of social mobility in working-class America. What these parents most wanted for their children was that they have choices, choices that they as children did not have; and in the end, what their children chose to do was less important than that they be able to choose at all. As Madeleine Biehler said of her mother, "It was always do what I didn't do."[47]

When the next generation began making these choices, textile employment ranked low on its list of career alternatives. "Mills were for older people," Doris Kos observed, the children "didn't want that." This was the case not only in Holyoke, but throughout much of New England as well. From Adams, Massachusetts, Wauregan, Connecticut, West Warwick, Rhode Island, and Biddeford, Maine, came similar reports after World War II, all stating that young people were consciously avoiding textile work. The reasons for their decisions

were perhaps best summarized in a 1950 study of the state textile industry by the Massachusetts House of Representatives:

> It was represented to the Commission that because of beliefs such as that mill work entailed lack of opportunity, unpleasant surroundings, absence of progressive personnel and industrial relations policies, relatively low wages, and the uncertainty of regular employment, a stigma is attached to employment in the industry in the Northern States. These beliefs repel younger persons and children of textile workers, the normal labor replacement, and results in their turning to other forms of employment.

Holyoke TWUA official Anna Sullivan put it more bluntly: textiles was "at the bottom of the heap."[48]

Some youths were able to find suitable employment in other local industries. One was Raymond Beaudry, who started work at the Chemical Paper Company in the early fifties and later became president of Eagle Lodge. Despite the troubled condition of Holyoke mills, the 1950s was a propitious time for French Canadians to enter the industry. An older generation of Irish and German machine tenders was passing from the scene, and their children were no longer there to replace them. This created fresh opportunities for talented and ambitious young men from other ethnic groups. Eager to take advantage of such openings, Beaudry bent his energies to learning the mysteries of the fourdrinier. In the process, he also learned that for machine tenders making paper was not simply a job but a way of life. When senior members of his crew saw him leaving the mill in work clothes, they let him know that this was inappropriate behavior by hosing him down after work the next day. Afterward, Beaudry both understood and appreciated the meaning of this initiation rite: work clothes were fine during working hours; on the street, machine tenders dressed in a manner that reflected the respectability of their craft.[49]

In time, new job-related interests weakened Beaudry's attachment to the enclave without obliterating it altogether. He had grown up amid a dense network of kin relations in a Ward 2 tenement called the "Beaudry Block," and he continued to live in the old neighborhood for more than a decade after beginning work at Chemical Paper. Yet not everything was the same. His duties as a union officer forced him to adopt a social and economic perspective that extended well beyond the boundaries of French Canadian Holyoke. Meanwhile, the enclave

itself was changing. As people advanced occupationally, Beaudry explained, they moved up in the community as well, which meant departing Ward 2 for "the hill" or suburbs. And when he finally obtained his own machine, he left too, purchasing a home in the ponds area of West Holyoke. Thus, while he still resided in Holyoke and retained the strong commitment to family that was part of his French Canadian heritage, Beaudry now lived in a different world than that of his youth: one based on craft and unionism rather than neighborhood and ethnicity.

When young people could not find alternative employment in the old textile centers, they increasingly chose to move elsewhere. In Fall River between 1940 and 1950, Bruce Saxon found that the number of people aged fifteen to twenty-four declined 30 percent, while total population fell only 3.7 percent. A similar development took place in Holyoke during the period: Although total population rose slightly, the number of people aged fifteen to twenty-four dropped 27 percent. Not surprisingly, the age structure of the textile work force by the 1950s was, according to a U.S. Senate study, higher than that of most manufacturing industries. In many New England mills that closed during the period, the average age of workers was forty-five years or higher.[50]

These were matters of vital concern to textile manufacturers. Although few jobs in textile plants required long periods of training, experience counted in many departments. Moreover, southern competition had forced New England producers to concentrate on the manufacture of high-quality goods, which increased the need for capable and experienced workers. Millowners who could not recruit young people with a commitment to textile production faced serious long-term problems. As the current generation of veteran operatives retired, manufacturers could not expect to maintain acceptable levels of productivity or product quality with a labor force comprised largely of casual workers.[51]

One way that millowners hoped to resolve the problem was by reducing labor needs through increased work assignments and the installation of new machinery. Between 1947 and 1957, a decade when average annual increase in output per man-hour was 3.2 percent for manufacturing industry as a whole, the corresponding figure for textiles was 4.9 percent. A 1959 Senate study labeled technological change the "principal cause" of declining employment in the industry: "Productivity has gone up sharply, and the domestic textile indus-

try today is able to turn out almost as much cloth as it did ten years ago with substantially lower manpower requirements." New England manufacturers asserted, however, that southern producers benefited most from these developments, and that regional productivity and workload differentials further undermined their competitive position. The main stumbling block, they argued, was the New England textile operative.[52]

To keep their jobs, New England operatives will have to recognize "the fact that workers in the North must be as productive as workers in the South." So declared Robert C. Sprague, president of Associated Industries of Massachusetts, in a 1952 statement. Coming from the head of a business-lobbying group, such counsel was scarcely novel and would ordinarily excite little notice except that similar sentiments were then being expressed by many others as well: by Republican congressmen, by state and regional committees investigating capital flight, and even by academics otherwise sympathetic to labor interests. At the same time, some migrating manufacturers insisted that they were moving South mainly because of work-load differentials. Textron president Royal Little went so far as to assert that boarding up the company's Nashua, New Hampshire, mills might have a salutary effect on the regional industry if it forced New England workers to "realize that they can no longer demand and receive a premium over other areas for their services unless their productivity and skill justify it."[53]

Other manufacturers complained that resistance to work-load increases had attained the sanction of tradition among New England wage earners. "The northern textile operative," Seabury Stanton, a New Bedford millowner, stated in 1951, "through habit and through the teachings of the old craft unions and his father before him, has become accustomed to thinking of his work assignments in terms of the number of machines which he is required to operate, rather than in terms of the actual time and effort required." Southern operatives were, by contrast, "less bound by custom, habit, and prejudice." These assertions did not go uncontested. In testimony before a congressional committee, TWUA research director Solomon Barkin declared Stanton had done no more than echo "the mouthings of his southern employer confreres that the 'southern textile worker is more flexible.' " The most cursory review of southern labor struggles, Barkin added, would quickly dispel that simplistic notion. Furthermore, to the extent that southern operatives accepted larger work

assignments than their northern counterparts, it was less a result of worker custom "than the submission of the repressed: . . . the silence of the man who has no freedom to question; [and] no freedom to combine and secure the bargain which will reduce the human cost of change."[54]

In its dealings with New England textile manufacturers, the TWUA tried to balance "the human costs of change" with the need to modernize aging plants. Aware that underinvestment often presaged liquidation, TWUA officials supported technological innovation and signed contracts permitting millowners to install new machinery without prior union consent. At the same time, however, they insisted that displaced workers be granted separation bonuses, preferential hiring rights, and training for new employment, whenever practicable. To prevent surreptitious stretchouts, they also demanded that union representatives be allowed "to appraise the level of work effort before and after the change": for, as Solomon Barkin declared, any alteration in work assignments that required operatives to expend greater energy "should be compensated directly in proportion." In short, the TWUA sought to influence the flow of textile capital by linking productivity increases to investment policy.[55]

In theory, TWUA bargaining policy on work loads and technological change represented a shrewd response to the dilemmas posed by capital flight. But in practice it encountered major problems. As manufacturers charged, New England textile workers were instinctively resistant to increases in work assignments, regardless of whether they were accompanied by the introduction of new machinery. TWUA officials knew this as well. They also knew that earlier instances of union-management cooperation had sometimes had disastrous consequences: At Salem's Pequot Mills, for example, UTW efforts during the early thirties to help management increase productivity had ended in a rank-and-file rebellion against union leaders. On the other hand, TWUA insistence on overseeing the implementation of technological innovation and work assignment changes was even less acceptable to millowners, who viewed it as an unwarranted infringement on their right to manage. "We have no common base," one union spokesperson acknowledged, "because every management in New England treats the problem as an area of conflict."[56]

Despite the problems involved, new job-eliminating machinery was introduced in New England textile plants. And faced with a choice between vacant mills or increased work assignments, regional

operatives went along with the changes—up to a point. That point was reached in 1952 when northern manufacturers secured an arbitration award that overturned the 1950 wage hike. As Solomon Barkin then observed:

> employees have cooperated with management in the effectuation of economies with the result that their manhour productivity has risen. . . . Their past reward was loss of jobs for some and higher earnings for those who remained. Now even the latter solace has been removed. . . . "What price cooperation?" we now ask ourselves.

Barkin's use of the first person plural was more than a rhetorical device. Many wage earners afterwards asked the same question: "What price cooperation?" In some places like Maine and parts of the South, workers would continue to help manufacturers to increase productivity. But in most northern areas they concluded that the price was too high. A veteran Fall River operative spoke for many of his fellow workers when he declared:

> Here is what they tell us folks who work in the mills. You've got to come down to the southern level so we can run, then when we get there they'll want us to come down to the Puerto Rican level, and after we get there, they'll want us to come down to the coolie level. I have spent 45 years in the mills north and south. When a worker is under pressure, when he is told day in and day out that his job can't last. and is thereby always in fear of that job disappearing, he finally comes to these conclusions, close up and be done with it! My nerves can take no more.

As such attitudes spread, it became increasingly difficult for union officials to enlist rank-and-file support for efforts to boost productivity. "You go to a mill in Massachusetts, Connecticut, Rhode Island, or Philadelphia," Barkin later told the TWUA executive board, "and you talk about problems of that management and you get booted out."[57]

   In 1957, when Barkin made this observation, it was already late in the day. By then, the second phase of deindustrialization in New England textiles was nearly complete, and there was little more that the TWUA or anyone else could do to save the industry. In many respects, it had died a decade earlier, in the streets and police courts of Tallapoosa, Georgia, Kannapolis, North Carolina, and a hundred other southern mill towns. When the southern textile strike of 1951 fully exposed the failure of CIO organizing efforts in the

region, the contradiction between a changing New England labor market and persisting regional wage and work-load differentials became insurmountable.

One should not conclude from the foregoing that deindustrialization in the New England textile industry involved nothing more than a simple readjustment of the regional labor market. Such was hardly the case. The entire process was shot through with personal tragedy. In 1951, an unemployed Lawrence textile worker, no longer able to feed his family, jumped to his death from a local bridge. Less dramatic, but of greater consequence was the plight of older workers who were left jobless when a mill closed. Many were too old to secure employment in other occupations, yet not old enough to qualify for social security benefits. Those who did find work invariably suffered reductions in income.[58]

One should also bear in mind that deindustrialization during the period was not confined to low-wage industries like textiles. As a result, many young workers faced increasingly uncertain futures as well. In western Massachusetts during the mid-fifties, American Bosch, a Springfield-based electrical goods producer, sent 500 jobs to Mississippi, while the Springfield division of Westinghouse threatened similar moves. At Holyoke beginning in 1963, a wave of mill closings decimated much of the local paper industry. These and other job losses in turn undermined the area labor movement. Between 1958 and 1961 alone, the president of the Greater Springfield Central Labor Council reported in the latter year, council membership declined from 20,000 to 12,000 workers. In short, this was not a happy time for anyone who had to work for a wage.[59]

BY THE CLOSE of World War II, organized labor had become, in the words of one Chamber of Commerce official, "a power in our land." In the immediate postwar decades, unions negotiated contracts that markedly improved the living standards of industrial workers. Collective-bargaining agreements provided union members with substantial increases in real wages, paid vacations, and a host of security provisions such as pension plans and health and insurance benefits. When the UAW established an employer-funded system of supplemental unemployment benefits in its 1955 talks with Ford, labor appeared to be on the verge of achieving its long desired

goal of a guaranteed annual wage. And when Walter Reuther later declared that the labor movement was "developing a whole new middle class," there were countless wage earners who would have agreed.[60]

Although these advances were accompanied by the creation of a rigidly legalistic system of industrial relations that, as David Brody observed, put "a permanent brake on the self-activity of American workers," the benefits obtained were real. So was the impact of mass-production unionism on the consciousness of wage earners in the nation's ethnic enclaves. Once initial fears had been dispelled, Slavic workers in Michigan auto centers and Pennsylvania steel towns became staunch unionists. In the process, they came to view the world and their place within it in new and ever more expansive ways. What began as a quest for economic security was often transformed into a struggle to overturn decades of inequitable treatment in the community as well as the workplace. In Steelton, Pennsylvania, for example, eastern European workers not only signed union cards, but also became eager participants in a CIO-sponsored voter-registration drive. Later, as Slavic workers joined with other recent immigrant groups to establish a new political order, Steelton's traditional WASP elite withdrew from community affairs.[61]

Like the Slavic enclavists of Michigan and Pennsylvania, French Canadian textile workers grew up in a culture that valued hard, physical labor. They recall their days on the shop floor with pride. "We are workers," declared one former Holyoke operative. "We worked hard to raise our families." And like Slavic enclavists, they were also union members. But of this they remember little. Unlike the auto centers and steel towns of the North Central region, where mass-production unionism became associated with worker empowerment and improved living standards, it was more often linked to unemployment and community decline in the decaying industrial centers of New England. During the peak years of the American Century, as mill closings annulled the benefits of unionization, the most valuable export of these towns would be their talented young people. For the New England labor movement, these events left behind a terrible legacy, one that continues to undermine organizational drives in the region's newer industries. But this is not a history that should be feared. As this final chapter has atttempted to show, deindustrialization occurred despite, not because of, the actions of organized labor.[62]

CONCLUSION

"THE STRIKE has been a hindrance and an incubus upon the power of labor organizations at all times," Patrick Ford wrote in an 1888 editorial. All true friends of labor "should refrain from giving encouragement to class antagonisms and the use of offensive language calculated to estrange rather than conciliate." The message was not new. Ford had repeated it on numerous occasions during the previous decade. By the late eighties, though, such declarations had begun to evince a special urgency. Within labor circles, the Knights of Labor and its vision of an economic world based on the cooperative endeavors of a broad amalgam of producers was in eclipse. So was its leader, Terence Powderly, whose various reform efforts and moderate approach to economic conflict had unfailingly elicited warm applause from Ford. A new generation of labor leaders, people who viewed the world in more explicitly class-conscious terms, was coming to the fore. Ford saw what was happening and acted accordingly. "As the Knights of Labor declined," Ford biographer James Rodechko observed, "the [Irish] World showed no inclination to support the emerging American Federation of Labor."[1]

Ford's declining enthusiasm for organized labor mirrored and was influenced by important changes in Irish America. By the 1890s, there were several indications that the social bases of an enclave consciousness that wove ethnic and class interests together in a seamless web was beginning to erode. One was the growing residential and associational exclusivity of Irish American social life. Another can be found in the observations of post-famine immigrants who, according to Kerby Miller, "complained less of harsh treatment from native Americans, from whom indifference or exploitation was perhaps expected, than from fellow countrymen." There was also a sharp rise in the level and intensity of industrial conflict, which increasingly pitted Irish wage earners against Irish employers and challenged enclave notions

of a mutuality of interests among a loosely defined community of producers.[2]

With these developments, enclave activists like Ford, who sought social justice without class struggle, faced hard choices. Ford opted to go with his class. During the 1890s, his primary polemical targets gradually shifted from greedy monopolists to radical labor leaders as he urged Irish workers to abandon the "Red flag of socialism" for the "Green flag of St. Patrick." At the same time, he began to espouse a middle-class brand of respectability that idealized hard work, individual initiative, and a host of other bourgeois values necessary for material success. This was not the same person whose writings had once inspired a Holyoke nationalist to wish "the *Irish World* the prosperity and success it deserves as the fearless champion of the persecuted and oppressed of all lands."[3]

Ford was not the only one who had changed. Among Irish workers, the labor struggles of the late nineteenth and early twentieth centuries gave rise to a trade-union consciousness that subordinated ethnic concerns to class interests. This is not to say the ethnicity no longer mattered. The Irish trade unionists who gathered at Holyoke's Dynamiters Club continued to celebrate St. Patrick's Day and occasionally debated recent developments in Ireland. But these activities were overshadowed by efforts to secure a family living wage, a goal whose attainment formed the basis of a fully rounded culture of Catholic trade-unionist respectability that celebrated the independence and self-worth of working people. Similarly, although trade unionists continued to support Irish middle-class politicians, they did so less to advance their claims as Irish Americans than to protect their class interests.[4]

Labor rarely obtained all that it wanted in the political arena. Yet, it did demand recognition and could make life unpleasant for Democrats who resolutely ignored its wishes. In 1935, for example, the CLU appointed a committee to confer with state senator Frank Hurley of Holyoke concerning several labor measures then before the legislature. Hurley apparently did not tell CLU leaders what they wanted to hear, and the following year local trade unionists organized to deny his bid for reelection. Although Hurley managed to mobilize sufficient support from Springfield and Chicopee Democrats to secure the party nomination, he was defeated in November by a Polish Republican from Chicopee. At Holyoke, trade unionists

expressed "satisfaction" with the outcome, observing that the election of a Republican "is not likely to be permanent."[5]

Nevertheless, however strained worker–middle-class relations may have become in Irish communities, they never broke down altogether. A number of factors acted to mitigate whatever tensions existed at a given point in time. One was family. Kinship ties not only created and sustained emotional bonds that cut across class lines but also influenced worker consciousness in more tangible ways. More than one Irish wage earner obtained employment through the intercession of a well-placed uncle or cousin. The social significance of such aid was doubtlessly great, given the job and wage emphases of the culture of Catholic trade-unionist respectability. The latter, coupled with Irish–middle-class attitudes toward government, also magnified the consensual implications of Democratic politics. As late as the 1950s, the Holyoke Taxpayers' Association had little success enlisting Irish support for its efforts to curb municipal expenditures. According to Kenneth Underwood, association leaders attributed this resistance to "Irish identification of the government as an Irish-dominated institution." Not surprisingly, Irish workers benefited disproportionately from the practical application of this belief. In 1947, Underwood calculated, 78 percent of Holyoke police officers were Irish, as were 74 percent of the city's fire fighters.[6]

The much-discussed social fluidity of Irish America also reduced worker–middle-class tensions by reshaping elite perspectives. As the children of trade-union respectables attained positions of influence, many continued to embrace the cultural and political values of their parents. A case in point is Thomas P. "Tip" O'Neill, Jr. O'Neill's father was a one-time bricklayer who remained staunchly committed to trade-union principles long after he had left the building site to become superintendent of sewers in Cambridge. "Nobody in our house," O'Neill recalled, "was allowed to wear anything that didn't have a union label." O'Neill did not forget these principles during the course of his long political career. In his first campaign for a seat in the Massachusetts legislature, he ran on a platform based on his own version of the family–living-wage doctrine. "I stood for what I called the O'Neill Family Plan," he later observed, "by which I meant that the breadwinner ought to be able to support his family with enough food, clothing, and shelter—and have a little extra to set aside for a rainy day." Such political initiatives indicate that class development in Irish America was not one long, unbroken process of embourgeoisment. The culture

of Catholic trade-union respectability both influenced and was influenced by the Irish middle class.[7]

The allegiance of trade-union respectables to the Catholic church placed further limits on their militancy. They did not, to be sure, submit unconditionally to the dictates of church officials. Hierarchical positions that violated their cultural convictions engendered vigorous resistance. Thus, when Cardinal O'Connell continued to oppose a child-labor amendment, Francis Fenton denounced the archbishop before the 1936 state AFL convention and asserted that "I and other Catholics have a right to have a voice in questions relating to industry and the economic conditions under which we live." The following year John Nolan of the Progressive Shoe Workers declared that, although a Catholic, "nobody representing the Church to which I belong is going to tell me or thousands of the same Church what they are going to do about the welfare of their children." At the same time, Catholic trade unionists pointed to the arguments of progressive priests like John Ryan, whose deep commitment to social justice served as an important counterweight to the reactionary pronouncements of church traditionalists.[8]

Yet it was the traditionalists who triumphed in the end. Although the emergence of mass-production unionism and the welfare state forced tradtionalists to retreat from some of their most archaic notions, they were able to use a resurgent antiradicalism to slow the wheels of social change. Long before the formal outbreak of the Cold War, Catholic spokespersons had begun to equate the slightest deviation from political orthodoxy with communist subversion. The increased acceptance of these views not only helped check worker militancy, but also deepened divisions within the labor movement. During the late thirties, state AFL bosses focused on the alleged communist beliefs of CIO leaders in their efforts to discourage cooperation between the two labor federations. And a decade later, similar tactics ended in the 1949 purge of left-wing unions within the CIO. At the time, a letter to the *Catholic Mirror* from the recording secretary of UE Local 278 at Chapman Valve urged the church to "officially take a more active part in the labor movement in order that the control of Unions does not fall into the hands of communists." It was certainly the right place to look for such assistance.[9]

By mid-century, most of the men who had founded the Dynamiters Club and helped forge a culture of Catholic trade-unionist respectability among Holyoke wage earners had had their day. Throughout, they

had tried their best to make it a good one, not only for themselves but for all working people. Although sociocultural divisions within the local work force limited the scope of their efforts, they did not diminish their unswerving commitment to the dignity of labor. These observations bring us to a central theme of this work. Class differentiation and a consciousness of such differences provided the context for many of the events described in the foregoing pages. As their communities matured, class interests assumed increasingly greater significance in the minds of Irish Americans. Monsignor John Ryan understood this when he wrote that where individuals "have one interest in common with all other citizens they have ten that are vital only to their particular class"; Patrick Ford learned it during the 1890s when he faced a labor movement that was increasingly unreceptive to his counsel; as did Frank Hurley four decades later when the Holyoke CLU helped remove him from office.[10]

Despite these developments, ethnicity still counted. This was especially so with regard to intra-class relations. At Holyoke, the enclave experience of Irish and French Canadians differed in important ways. John Bodnar has written that enclaves fostered "a kind of loyalty based on the knowledge that limitations existed on what was obtainable from the larger society." This is a meaningful observation that underscores the essentially defensive nature of ethnic enclaves. As enclavists reached beyond those limitations, intra-group differences deepened and it became ever more difficult to subordinate class (and individual) interests to ethnic concerns. This is what happened in Irish Holyoke during the late nineteenth century. For Irish workers, it was especially significant that enclave dissolution coincided with and was hastened by the rise of a labor movement in which they would play a leading role. This made it easier for them to transfer their loyalties from ethnic to class institutions than would be the case for newer immigrant groups.[11]

For a much longer time than the Irish, French Canadians from a variety of social backgrounds viewed the world through a narrow ethnic prism. Living in self-contained enclaves that observers aptly described as "Little Canadas," they struggled to protect their cultural heritage from the Americanizing influences of the larger society. Among Irish and French Canadian workers, cultural dissimilarities were exacerbated by occupational differences. Outside the building trades, the one workplace in which French Canadians established a comfortable niche was the low wage textile industry, where to survive

they were forced to operate family economies that depended on the paid labor of several family members. The result was two distinct sociocultural worlds: one peopled by Irish workers who espoused a trade-union version of Americanism based on the family-wage ideal; and another by Franco-American factory operatives who were often reliant on child labor and intent on preserving the language and customs of French Canada in a hostile Anglo society. Bridging these divisions was no easy task. Few tried.

At this point, it is worth considering how different things might have been had the 1900 campaign to organize textile operatives succeeded. To have remained viable, the union would have had to have accorded French Canadians a leadership role commensurate with their place in the work force. Given their devotion to *survivance*, unionization would have had little immediate impact on the enclave consciousness of these workers. The union would have been used to protect their cultural concerns as French Canadians as well as advance their material claims as industrial wage earners. But it would also have given them a firm institutional base from which to deal with both enclave elites and CLU bosses. This could have reshaped the course of local politics in several ways. On one hand, a French Canadian–dominated textile union would have forced middle-class leaders to pay greater attention to worker interests than was typically their wont. Had they proved sufficiently accomodating and perspicacious, they might have been able to forge a solid ethnic voting bloc that challenged Irish dominance of the Democratic party. Had they not, the existence of such a labor organization would have provided the social base for the formation of a viable labor party, which would have freed both Irish and French Canadian workers from middle-class representation.

As it turned out, none of this happened. When unionization came, it did so at a time when the textile industry was in a state of decline. It was also a time when French Canadian youths were beginning to look beyond those limitations that John Bodnar identified as as integral feature of enclave consciousness. Like their youthful counterparts in the ethnic enclaves of the upper Midwest, some would be able to satisfy rising aspiration as union members in industries that paid better wages and had brighter futures than textiles. Others moved on to more promising locales. Whatever the case, they were young enough that they at least had such choices. Many of their parents were not so fortunate. Their reward for decades of hard, ardous toil in

regional textile mills would be a late adulthood of underemployment and financial insecurity. It was obscenely unfair to them and a tragedy for the New England labor movement, which many people mistakenly blamed for the disaster.

NOTES

Introduction

1 Oscar Handlin, *Boston's Immigrants: A Study in Acculturation, 1790–1880* (1941; reprint, New York: Atheneum, 1976); Robert Sean Willentz, "Industrializing America and the Irish: Towards the New Departure," *Labor History*, 20 (1979): 584–585.

2 David Emmons, "An Artistocracy of Labor: The Irish Miners of Butte, 1880–1914," *Labor History* 28 (1987): 275–306; Emmons, *The Butte Irish: Class and Ethnicity in an American Mining Town, 1875–1925* (Urbana: University of Illinois Press, 1989). Earlier efforts to examine the interplay between class and ethnicity in Irish America include Michael Gordon, "The Labor Boycott in New York City, 1880–1886," *Labor History* 16 (1975): 184–229; and Eric Foner, "Class, Ethnicty, and Radicalism in the Gilded Age: The Land League and Irish America," in *Politics and Ideology in the Age of the Civil War* (New York: Oxford University Press, 1980), 150–200.

3 Robert Q. Gray, *The Labour Aristocracy in Victorian Edinburgh* (London: Oxford University Press, 1976); Geoffrey Crossick, "The Labour Aristocracy and Its Values: A Study of Mid-Victorian Kentish London," *Victorian Studies* 19 (1976): 301–328; Crossick, *An Artisan Elite in Victorian Society: Kentish London, 1840–1880* (London: Croom Helm, 1978). My examination of the cultural worlds of Irish wage earners began as an effort to extend the analyses of antebellum worker cultures contained in Paul G. Faler, "Cultural Aspects of the Industrial Revolution: Lynn, Massachusetts Shoemakers and Industrial Morality, 1826–1860," *Labor History* 15 (1974): 367–394; Alan Dawley and Paul G. Faler, "Working-class Culture and Politics in the Industrial Revolution: Sources of Loyalism and Rebellion," *Journal of Social History*, 9 (1976): 466–480; and Bruce Laurie, *Working People of Philadelphia, 1800–1850* (Philadelphia: Temple University Press, 1980).

CHAPTER ONE: Yankee Holyoke

1 Constance M. Green, *Holyoke, Massachusetts: A Case History of the Industrial Revolution in America* (New Haven: Yale University Press, 1939), 1–2, 10; A

Report of the History and Present Condition of the Hadley Falls Company at Holyoke, Massachusetts (Boston: John Wilson and Son, 1855), 4. A copy of this report can be found at the Holyoke Public Library.

2 Margaret E. Martin, "Merchants and Trade of the Connecticut River Valley, 1750–1820," *Smith College Studies in History* 24, nos. 1–4 (Oct. 1938–July 1939), 9–10, 199–200; Edwin L. Kirtland, "The City of Holyoke," *New England Magazine*, New Series, 17 (1898): 730–731; Green, *Holyoke*, 10–11, 15–16.

3 Edward C. Kirkland, *Men, Cities, and Transportation: A Study in New England History, 1820–1900* (1948; reprint, New York: Russell and Russell, 1968), vol. 1, 135, 284–285; Thelma Kistler, "The Rise of Railroads in the Connecticut River Valley," *Smith College Studies in History* 23, nos. 1–4 (Oct. 1937–July 1938), 70, 102; Alfred M. Copeland, ed., *A History of Hampden County, Massachusetts*, vol 3 (Century Memorial Publishing Company, 1902), 12.

4 Kistler, "Railroads in the Connecticut Valley," 70, 102–103; Kirkland, *Men, Cities, and Transportation*, vol. 1, 334; Vera Shlakman, *Economic History of a Factory Town: A Study of Chicopee, Massachusetts* (1935; reprint, New York: Octagon Books, 1969), 28–47; *Present Condition of the Hadley Falls Company*, 4–6.

5 *Holyoke Transcript* (*HT*), July 17, 1888; Green, *Holyoke*, 19–20; Ralph H. Gabriel, *The Founding of Holyoke, 1848* (Princeton: Princeton University Press, 1936), 14–15; Frank H. Doane, "History of Holyoke, Massachusetts from 1830 to 1873" (Unpublished ms., Holyoke Public Library), 11–12; Holyoke Public Library Scrapbook, 18:34, 3:4; Kistler, "Railroads in the Connecticut Valley," 118–119.

6 Green, *Holyoke*, 27–28; Gabriel, *Founding of Holyoke*, 17; Doane, "History of Holyoke," 15; *Paper World* (*PW*) 5 (Nov. 1882): 3.

7 Green, *Holyoke*, 29–31, 34–38.

8 Ibid., 55–62.

9 Alfred Smith to G. W. Lyman, Mar. 6, 1858, vol. AB–7, Lyman Mills Papers, Baker Library, Harvard Business School (LMP); Green, *Holyoke*, 61–65, 91–94.

10 Green, *Holyoke*, 70–87; *Census of Massachusetts, 1860, From the Eighth United States Census*, 203; *Holyoke City Directory* (*HCD*), 1869, 101–105; Green, *Holyoke*, 259; *Census of Massachusetts, 1880, From the Tenth United States Census*, 352–353.

11 *HT*, July 16, 1885; July 20, 1872; Feb. 18, 1871. For the analysis that follows, I have compiled profiles on thirty-five local manufacturers, twenty-seven of whom lived in Holyoke; the remainder resided in Springfield. The men chosen were either the president, vice president, or treasurer of mills employing at least fifty workers in 1880. Two local agents of mills controlled by outside capital were also included. Because these mills employed large numbers of workers, the agents exercised substantial economic power locally. In 1880, the group's average age was nearly fifty and most had been among the city's largest employers for at least a decade. Collectively, they would

continue to wield significant economic power for the remainder of the century. A list of their names, positions, and the sources employed to construct the profiles can be found in William F. Hartford, "Paper City: Class Development in Holyoke, Massachusetts, 1850–1920" (Ph.D. diss., University of Massachusetts at Amherst, 1983), app. 1. In shaping the questions that I subsequently asked of the data, I found the following studies especially useful: John N. Ingham, *The Iron Barons: A Social Analysis of an Urban Elite* (Westport, Conn.: Greenwood Press, 1978); Herbert Gutman, "The Reality of the Rags to Riches 'Myth': The Case of the Paterson, New Jersey, Locomotive, Iron, and Machinery Manufacturers, 1830–1880," in *Work, Culture, and Society in Industrializing America* (New York: Vintage Books, 1977), 211–233; and Ronald Story, *The Forging of an Aristocracy: Harvard and the Boston Upper Class* (Middletown, Conn.: Wesleyan University Press, 1980). Analyses of the development of the free-labor ideology and its influence on postbellum society can be found in Eric Foner, *Free Soil, Free Labor, Free Men: The Ideology of the Republican Party before the Civil War* (New York: Oxford University Press, 1972), ch. 1; Sean Willentz, *Chants Democratic: New York City and the Rise of the American Working Class, 1788–1850* (New York: Oxford University Press, 1984), 271–286; David Montgomery, *Beyond Equality: Labor and the Radical Republicans, 1862–1872* (New York: Vintage Books, 1972), 14–16, 30–32; and Brian Greenberg, *Worker and Community: Response to Industrialization in a Nineteenth-Century American City, Albany, New York, 1850–1884* (Albany: State University of New York Press, 1985). In developing this and the remaining sections of the chapter, Greenberg's work proved particularly helpful.

12 Many other people also used Holyoke as a way station on the road to worldly success. Newspaper items frequently mentioned mill overseers who had secured an agency or begun a small business elsewhere. Membership turnover at the Second Congregational Church, the town's most prestigious congregation, provides some indication of the extent of geographical mobility in mid-century Holyoke. By October 1858, three-quarters of the church's January 1856 membership had departed the town. *Holyoke Mirror* (*HM*), Oct. 30, 1858. The extensive geographical mobility of these years is examined at much greater length in Peter R. Knights, *The Plain People of Boston, 1830–1860: A Study in City Growth* (New York: Oxford University Press, 1971); and Michael Katz, *The People of Hamilton, Canada West: Family and Class in a Mid-Nineteenth Century City* (Cambridge: Harvard University Press, 1975), ch. 3.

13 *Springfield Republican* (*SR*), Mar. 25, 1900; Jan. 17, 1904; Aug. 27, 1905.

14 *SR*, Mar. 25, 1900; Jan. 17, 1904; Aug. 27, 1905.

15 On the deterioration of the family-based mode of craft training during these years and the manner in which one city's churches assumed a role roughly comparable to that of the Hampden Mechanics' Association, see Paul Johnson, *A Shopkeeper's Millennium: Society and Revivals in Rochester, New York, 1815–1837* (New York: Hill and Wang, 1978), 34–48, 121–128.

16 This and the following paragraph are based on materials found in the records of the Hampden Mechanics' Association at the Connecticut Valley Historical Museum.

17 The standard work on ethnic conflict during the antebellum period is Ray Billington, *The Protestant Crusade, 1800–1860: A Study of the Origins of American Nativism* (1938; reprint, New York: Quadrangle Books, 1964).

18 These generalizations are based on biographical profiles that have been compiled for twenty-four members of the Yankee middle class. A list of their names, occupations, and the sources employed to construct the profiles is in Hartford, "Paper City," app. 2. The *Bluebook and Social Directory of Holyoke, Massachusetts, 1889* (Springfield: Index Publishing Company, 1889) can be found at the Holyoke Public Library.

19 *HT*, Jan. 14, 1871; Jan. 11, 1873. No one who could be identified as an Irish Catholic participated in the lyceum's debates during the 1870s.

20 *HT*, Dec. 2, 1871; Dec. 21, 1872.

21 *SR*, June 4, 1878; *HT*, Nov. 12, 1873.

22 *HT*, Mar. 8, 1884.

23 *HM*, Mar. 21, 1857; *HT*, Feb. 27, 1878; Dec. 9, 1871; Dec. 16, 1871. The role of women in the late nineteenth-century temperance movement is examined in Ruth Bordin, *Women and Temperance: The Quest for Power and Liberty, 1873–1900* (Philadelphia: Temple University Press, 1981).

24 *HT*, Nov. 7, 1877; Mar. 2, 1878; Feb. 8, 1873; Apr. 20, 1889.

25 *HT*, Dec. 28, 1881.

26 *HT*, Dec. 31, 1881.

27 *Holyoke Town Records (HTR)*, 1853, 7–8; 1854, 7; 1863, 15; *Holyoke Municipal Register (HMR)*, 1878, 15. A typical editorial on modern machine production asked the reader to "Examine the spinning wheels and looms of our mothers. . . . Look upon the coarse fabric that at length comes from this operation. When you have satisfied your curiosity in that direction, step inside of our Lyman Mills, and behold the wonderful problem that multiplication is daily solving." *HM*, Apr. 26, 1856. Michael Katz provides an excellent analysis of mid-nineteenth-century educational ideology in *The Irony of Early School Reform: Educational Innovation in Mid-Nineteenth Century Massachusetts* (Boston: Beacon Press, 1970).

28 *SR*, Aug. 15, 1878; *HT*, Jan. 14, 1871; Dec. 2, 1871; Sept. 23, 1878. School superintendent Kirtland also addressed the problem in his 1879 report. After tracing the relationship between poverty and truancy, Kirtland recommended the establishment of a permanent benevolent organization to aid children who could not attend school regularly because of family need. The proposal elicited a somewhat more encouraging response than Ewing's, but failed to deal adequately with the problem. *Report of the School Committee*, 1879, 32. All school committee reports can be found in HMR for the year cited.

29 *HTR*, 1853, 4; 1863, 18; 1864, 22–23; *HM*, Mar. 17, 1860; Mar. 24, 1860.

30 *HT*, July 10, 1869; July 17, 1869; Nov. 27, 1869. For a time the YMCA supplemented the work of the high school by attempting to reach the city's young clerks. As part of its lecture series, Horace Greeley delivered his oration on "Self-Made Men." But the institution failed to prosper and in 1871 one member resignedly observed, "How encouraging it is that our blessed Savior does not command us as much to look at the harvest as he does to sow our seed." *HT*, Jan. 4, 1868; Mar. 11, 1871. Allan Horlick examines the organization's presumably more successful efforts with New York City clerks in *Country Boys and Merchant Princes: The Social Control of Young Men in New York* (Lewisburg, Pa.: Bucknell University Press, 1975), ch. 9.

31 *HT*, May 15, 1875; July 3, 1875; May 26, 1875; Mar. 25, 1885. The dominant ethic was by no means the sole cause of these changes, which stemmed more from the bureaucratization of Holyoke's schools and education generally during the period. It did, however, legitimize and encourage such developments. For more on the bureaucratization of schooling during the late nineteenth century, see Michael Katz, *Class, Bureaucracy, and Schools: The Illusion of Educational Change in America* (New York: Praeger Publishers, 1975); and David Tyack, *The One Best System: A History of Urban Education* (Cambridge: Harvard University Press, 1974).

32 *HT*, July 2, 1881.

33 Bruce Laurie and Mark Schmitz, "Manufacture and Productivity: The Making of an Industrial Base, Philadelphia, 1850–1880," in Theodore Hershberg, ed., *Philadelphia: Work, Space, Family, and Group Experience in the Nineteenth Century* (New York: Oxford University Press, 1981).

34 *HM*, Apr. 16, 1859; Aug. 20, 1859; *HT*, Sept. 26, 1863; *Federal Nonpopulation Census Schedules for Massachusetts: Manufacturing, 1850*.

35 Green, *Holyoke*, 46; *SR*, May 9, 1850.

36 *HM*, Oct. 29, 1859; June 12, 1861; Mar. 15, 1856; Feb. 23, 1860; June 23, 1860; July 28, 1860. Antebellum fire companies that functioned as expressions of saloon culture are examined in Bruce Laurie, "Fire Companies and Gangs in Southwark: The 1840s," in *The Peoples of Philadelphia: A History of Ethnic Groups and Lower-Class Life, 1790–1940*, ed. Allen F. Davis and Mark H. Haller (Philadelphia: Temple University Press, 1973).

37 *HT*, May 30, 1863; Greenberg, *Worker and Community*, ch. 5; Richard J. Oestreicher, *Solidarity and Fragmentation: Working People and Class Consciousness in Detroit, 1875–1900* (Urbana: University of Illinois Press, 1986), 40–41.

38 *HM*, June 8, 1861; *HT*, Dec. 19, 1863; Dec. 26, 1863; Dec. 12, 1863; Alan Dawley and Paul G. Faler, "Working-class Culture and Politics in the Industrial Revolution: Sources of Loyalism and Rebellion," *Journal of Social History*, 9 (1976): 476.

39 *Federal Nonpopulation Census Schedules for Massachusetts: Manufacturing, 1880*; *HCD*, 1882, 1884, 1890.

40 *HT*, July 16, 1879; Green, *Holyoke*, 97–98.

41 *HT*, Sept. 11, 1875; Massachusetts Bureau of Statistics of Labor (MBSL), *Sixth Annual Report*, 1875, 460; *Eighth Annual Report*, 1877, 98–99; Norman Ware, *The Labor Movement in the United States, 1860–1890* (1929; reprint, New York: Vintage Books, 1964), 16.

42 MBSL, *Sixth Annual Report*, 1877, 98–112.

43 The statement on the ethnic composition of the Holyoke building trades is based on data compiled from the 1860 and 1880 manuscript population schedules of the federal census. The broader implications of such changes in the Gilded Age work force are explored in Herbert Gutman and Ira Berlin, "Class Composition and Development of the American Working Class, 1840–1880," in Herbert Gutman, *Power and Culture: Essays on the American Working Class*, ed. Ira Berlin (New York: Pantheon Books, 1987), 380–394.

CHAPTER TWO: Social Relations of Production: Textiles and Paper

1 *Holyoke Mirror (HM)*, May 10, 1856.

2 *Census of Massachusetts, 1880, From the Tenth United States Census*, 352–353; Constance M. Green, *Holyoke, Massachusetts: A Case History of the Industrial Revolution in America* (New Haven: Yale University Press, 1939), 47.

3 Anthony Wallace, *Rockdale: The Growth of an American Village in the Early Industrial Revolution* (New York: Alfred A. Knopf, 1978), 136–137; Massachusetts Bureau of Statistics of Labor (MBSL), *Fifth Annual Report*, 1874, 128–149.

4 Wallace, *Rockdale*, 137–138; Tamara K. Hareven, *Family Time and Industrial Time: The Relationship between the Family and Work in a New England Industrial Community* (Cambridge, Eng.: Cambridge University Press, 1982), 398, 402, 406; Melvin T. Copeland, *The Cotton Manufacturing Industry of the United States* (Cambridge: Harvard University Press, 1912), 59–61.

5 Wallace, *Rockdale*, 138–139; Copeland, *Cotton Manufacturing*, 62–64.

6 Wallace, *Rockdale*, 139–143, 193–196; Copeland, *Cotton Manufacturing*, 66–73, 80; Hareven, *Family Time and Industrial Time*, 397–398, 401, 405; MBSL, *Eleventh Annual Report*, 1880, 67. The replacement of mules by ring spindles occurred at an uneven rate, but where the mules were retained, manufacturers increased their speed. In 1889, the Lyman Mills ordered new mules that would operate at 9,500 revolutions per minute rather than the previous 8,000 revolutions. E. Lovering to F. P. Sheldon, Oct. 6, 1889, vol. PG–1, Lyman Mills Papers, Baker Library, Harvard Business School (LMP).

7 Arthur H. Cole, *The American Wool Manufacture* (Cambridge: Harvard University Press, 1926), vol. 1, 361; vol. 2, 88–91; *Springfield Republican (SR)*, May 6, 1881.

8 Thomas Dublin, *Women at Work: The Transformation of Work and Commu-*

nity in Lowell, Massachusetts, 1826–1860 (New York: Columbia University Press, 1979), 64, 67–68; Wallace, *Rockdale*, 143–144; Hareven, *Family Time and Industrial Time*, 398–399, 406–409; Copeland, *Cotton Manufacturing*, 77–78. Ever on the lookout for labor-saving innovations, Lyman Mills treasurer S. L. Bush urged the company agent to look at a slasher adopted by the Indian Orchard Company, which reportedly allowed one boy to do the work of fourteen operatives. The rumor was of course too good to be true, but the installation of slashers did significantly reduce the labor cost of dressing. S. L. Bush to J. S. Davis, Jan. 4, 1870, vol. PB–1, LMP. During the postwar years the development of a wire bobbin holder and improved stop mechanism for warp beamers allowed manufacturers to increase the speed of these machines. Copeland, *Cotton Manufacturing*, 74–76.

9 Wallace, *Rockdale*, 144–147; Copeland, *Cotton Manufacturing*, 80–85, 114. At Holyoke, the Lyman Mills did not assign six looms to a weaver until 1889. The practice of other mills cannot be determined, though an 1887 communication from the Lyman Mills's agent, discussing an increase from four to five looms, suggests that the company was following the lead of other local factories. E. Lovering to T. Parsons, Sept. 1, 1887, vol. PC–6, and E. Lovering to F. P. Sheldon, Oct. 15, 1889, vol. PG–1, both in LMP. During the eighties woolen manufacturers also increased loom speeds. The introduction of the Crompton fancy loom raised loom speeds from forty-five to eighty-five picks per minute; later improvements permitted a loom speed of one hundred five picks per minute. At Holyoke, the Germania Woolen Mills in 1882 reported purchasing twenty new Crompton looms. "As soon as the old wears out," the report added, "new machinery of the most improved American pattern is put in." Cole, *Wool Manufacture*, vol. 2, 91–93; *Holyoke Transcript*, (*HT*), Feb. 11, 1882.

10 *Census of Massachusetts, 1880, From the Tenth United States Census*, 352–353; Lyman Horace Weeks, *History of Paper Manufacturing in the United States* (New York: Lockwood Trade Journal Company, 1916), 145–147; Judith A. McGaw, *Most Wonderful Machine: Mechanization and Social Change in Berkshire Paper Making, 1801–1885* (Princeton: Princeton University Press, 1987), 43–46. McGaw's work is, by a rather considerable margin, the best study available of the nineteenth-century paper industry.

11 Weeks, *Paper Manufacturing*, 172, 190, 270–271; Green, *Holyoke*, 87–88. The average number of employees in each mill was computed from *Federal Nonpopulation Census Schedules for Massachusetts: Manufacturing, 1880*. A lucid, detailed description of the fourdrinier and the various ways in which it was improved during the nineteenth century can be found in McGaw, *Most Wonderful Machine*, 96–108.

12 Alexander Watt, *The Art of Paper-Making: A Practical Handbook of the Manufacture of Paper from Rags, Esparto, Straw, and Other Materials Including the Manufacture of Pulp from Wood Fibre* (New York: D. Van Nostrand Company,

1907), 19–22; McGaw, *Most Wonderful Machine*, 344; *Holyoke Municipal Register* (*HMR*), 1881, 107; 1890, 227. Because Holyoke mills specialized in the finer grades of paper, this discussion concentrates on the treatment of rags. The preparation of wood pulp is described in Watt, *Art of Paper-Making*, 53–79; and C. F. Cross and E. J. Bevan, *A Text-Book of Paper Making* (London: E. and F. N. Spon, 1888), 105–108. The following paragraphs also draw on MBSL, *Forty Fifth Annual Report*, 1914, vii, 75–81; and M. Emory Wright, *The Parsons Paper Mill at Holyoke, Massachusetts: Embracing a Minute Description of the Paper Manufacture* (Springfield, Mass.: Samuel Bowles and Company, 1857).

13 Watt, *Art of Paper-Making*, 22–23; Cross and Bevan, *Paper Making*, 81; *HT*, Dec. 27, 1883; *SR*, July 17, 1883; Jan. 5, 1884; *Paper World* (*PW*), 8 (Jan. 1884): 7; McGaw, *Most Wonderful Machine*, 113, 182. Figures on the proportion of women in the paper work force are taken from *Federal Nonpopulation Census Schedules for Massachusetts: Manufacturing, 1880*; and MBSL, *Forty Fifth Annual Report*, 1914, vii, 14.

14 Watt, *Art of Paper-Making*, 24–29; Cross and Bevan, *Paper Making*, 84.

15 Watt, *Art of Paper-Making*, 34–39, 89–91; Cross and Bevan, *Paper Making*, 88. In some mills, bleaching occurred in the beater engine.

16 Watt, *Art of Paper-Making*, 101–110; Cross and Bevan, *Paper Making*, 143.

17 Watt, *Art of Paper-Making*, 114–127; Cross and Bevan, *Paper Making*, 138; McGaw, *Most Wonderful Machine*, 300. Not all fine writing-paper mills sized their stock in beaters. A number continued to perform this operation on paper machines because, as Judith McGaw explained, "the chemistry of sizing remained poorly understood and size played a crucial role in keeping writing paper from absorbing ink and making it erase well." McGaw, *Most Wonderful Machine*, 183.

18 Watt, *Art of Paper-Making*, 134–137, 142–143, 150–152; *SR*, Sept. 18, 1898.

19 Cross and Bevan, *Paper Making*, 153–157, 176; McGaw, *Most Wonderful Machine*, 105, 180–181, 297–303; Wright, *Parsons Paper Mill*, 20. The quotation is from Wright, *Parsons Paper Mill*, 19.

20 Watt, *Art of Paper-Making*, 154–157; Cross and Bevan, *Paper Making*, 175; *SR*, July 20, 1878; Sept. 24, 1878; McGaw, *Most Wonderful Machine*, 111–112, 340.

21 Donald B. Cole, *Immigrant City: Lawrence, Massachusetts, 1845–1921* (Chapel Hill: University of North Carolina Press, 1963), 210. A convenient summary of Holyoke's ethnic composition can be found in Green, *Holyoke*, 367.

22 Peter Haebler, "Habitants in Holyoke: The Development of the French-Canadian Community in a Massachusetts City, 1865–1910" (Ph.D. diss., University of New Hampshire, 1976), 31–36.

23 *Census of Massachusetts, 1880, From the Tenth United States Census*, 352–353.

24 Rowland Berthoff, *British Immigrants in Industrial America, 1790–1950*

(1953; reprint, New York: Russell and Russell, 1968), 21–28; Green, *Holyoke*, 111–112, 367. For a survey of the conditions prompting nineteenth-century German emigration, see Mack Walker, *Germany and the Emigration, 1816–1885* (Cambridge: Harvard University Press, 1964).

25 Paul McGouldrick, *New England Textiles in the Nineteenth Century: Profits and Investment* (Cambridge: Harvard University Press, 1968), 21–27; Theophilus Parsons notebook, 1873, vol. AD–2a; George A. Hills to T. Parsons, Dec. 8, 1884, vol. PC–4, both LMP.

26 Louis Galambos, *Competition and Cooperation: The Emergence of a National Trade Association* (Baltimore: Johns Hopkins Press, 1966), 20–29.

27 S. L. Bush to J. S. Davis, Dec. 11, 1869, vol. PB–1; George A. Hills to T. Parsons, Dec. 8, 1884, Dec. 10, 1884, vol. PC–4; and E. Lovering to T. Parsons, Dec. 20, 1887, Dec. 23, 1887, vol. PC–6, all in LMP. The generalization on manufacturing costs is based on an examination of the reports in vols. MAE–2, 4, 5, and 7, LMP.

28 Holyoke Public Library Scrapbook, 20: 16–17; *HT*, Dec. 4, 1872; Oct 4., 1879; Mrs. Hugh Bowie to S. Holman, Jan. 19, 1856; Jane Wallace to S. Holman, Sept. 2, 1857; and Catherine McCallum to S. Holman, Oct. 21, 1858, vol. LW–1, all in LMP.

29 Green, *Holyoke*, 48–49, 68–69; Haebler, "Habitants in Holyoke," 53–54; *HM*, Dec. 20, 1856; Dec. 27, 1856; Holyoke Public Library Scrapbook, 4:73.

30 Hareven, *Family Time and Industrial Time*, 50–53, 62, 132–135, 144–145; *HT*, Jan. 25, 1873; Feb. 26, 1876. At Manchester's Amoskeag Mills, Tamara Hareven found that veteran workers resented newly arrived immigrants who behaved too obsequiously before the bosses. *Family Time and Industrial Time*, 135.

31 Green, *Holyoke*, 369–370; *SR*, May 12, 1879; *HT*, Apr. 5, 1879; Nov. 11, 1882.

32 Hareven, *Family Time and Industrial Time*, 396–397; National Loom Fixers Association pamphlet, 1899, in LMP; *HT*, Dec. 20, 1873; Dec. 24, 1873; Feb. 28, 1874.

33 MBSL, *Eleventh Annual Report*, 1880, 59–62.

34 Weeks, *Paper Manufacturing*, 297; *HT*, Feb. 26, 1873; *PW*, 1 (Aug. 1880): 12–13.

35 *HT*, Oct. 25, 1873; Mar. 28, 1874; Nov. 20, 1875; Aug. 19, 1876; Oct. 26, 1878; Feb. 5, 1879; Nov. 20, 1884; *PW*, 1 (Aug. 1880): 12–13.

36 *PW*, 3 (Aug. 1881): 15; 3 (July 1881): 20; 7 (Dec. 1883): 17–18; 16 (Jan. 1888): 7; 19 (Sept. 1889): 2–4; 9 (Aug. 1884): 18; 11 (Oct. 1885): 8; Weeks, *Paper Manufacturing*, 291.

37 *HT*, Jan. 19, 1884; Jan. 26, 1884; Feb. 2, 1884; Feb. 4, 1884; *SR*, Jan. 21, 1884; Jan. 29, 1884.

38 *HT*, May 27, 1882; June 3, 1882; Feb. 4, 1884; Mar. 20, 1886; Jan. 4, 1888; Aug. 11, 1888; Aug. 25, 1892; *PW*, 17 (Aug. 1888): 2.

39 MBSL, *Forty Fifth Annual Report*, 1914, vii, 9; *Tenth Annual Report*, 1879, 153; Green, *Holyoke*, 207–208; Weeks, *Paper Manufacturing*, 293–294; *HT*, July 28, 1886; May 12, 1886; *SR*, Mar. 1, 1887; *PW*, 15 (Aug. 1887): 10–11. Holyoke paper workers had first organized during the mid-seventies as the Paper Makers Protective Union. The union was chiefly a benefit society and collapsed in 1876 amidst an acrimonious dispute over the question of unemployment benefits. *HT*, Jan. 17, 1874; Feb. 18, 1874; Nov. 1, 1876; Dec. 6, 1876.

40 *PW*, 15 (Aug. 1887): 11; *HT*, Apr. 11, 1887; *SR*, May 14, 1887; *PW*, 14 (June 1887): 10; McGaw, *Most Wonderful Machine*, 322–324; *HT*, Aug. 1, 1887; Aug. 10, 1887; Sept. 10, 1887; Green, *Holyoke*, 209–210.

41 *HT*, July 29, 1887; Green, *Holyoke*, 210–213.

CHAPTER THREE: Irish Holyoke

1 John Bodnar, *Workers' World: Kinship, Community, and Protest in an Industrial Society* (Baltimore: Johns Hopkins University Press, 1982), 63. In adapting Bodnar's notion of the enclave to Irish Holyoke, I have benefited greatly from a reading of David Emmons, "An Aristocracy of Labor: The Irish Miners of Butte, 1880–1914," *Labor History* 28 (1987): 275–306.

2 Constance M. Green, *Holyoke, Massachusetts: A Case History of the Industrial Revolution in America* (New Haven: Yale University Press, 1939), 27.

3 Jay Dolan, *The Immigrant Church: New York's Irish and German Catholics, 1815–1865* (Baltimore: Johns Hopkins University Press, 1975), 57; David W. Miller, "Irish Catholicism and the Great Famine," *Journal of Social History* 9 (1975): 61–98; Emmett Larkin, "The Devotional Revolution in Ireland, 1850–75," *American Historical Review* 77 (1972): 625–652; *Holyoke Mirror* (*HM*), Mar. 2, 1861; *Holyoke Transcript* (*HT*), Jan. 24, 1893; Wyatt Harper, *The Story of Holyoke* (Holyoke: N.p., 1973), 81; P. J. Lucey, *History of St. Jerome's Parish, Holyoke, Massachusetts* (N.p., 1931), 29–36, 116–124.

4 *HM*, Dec. 3, 1857; Dec. 16, 1857; Jan. 3, 1858; Jan. 30, 1858; Feb. 27, 1858; Mar. 20, 1858; Mar. 2, 1861; *HT*, Jan. 24, 1893.

5 *HM*, Dec. 22, 1860; Mar. 9, 1861; *HT*, Jan. 24, 1893.

6 Dolan, *Immigrant Church*, 64–65; *Irish World* (*IW*), Mar. 23, 1878. Evidence of the persistence of the traditional Catholic social outlook can be found in S. J. Hecker, "The Duties of the Rich in Christian Society," *Catholic World* (*CW*) 14 (1871–1872): 581; "Who Shall Take Care of the Poor," *CW* 10 (1868–1869): 711–712, 739; George D. Wolff, "Socialistic Communism in the United States," *American Catholic Quarterly Review* (*ACQR*) 3 (1878): 559–561; Dolan, *Immigrant Church*, 122–124; Aaron I. Abell, *American Catholicism and Social Action: A Search for Social Justice* (Notre Dame, Ind.: University of Notre Dame Press, 1963), 53, 72. Some Catholic spokesmen even found cause for cheer in

the world's poverty. Having so little of what makes life pleasant, one writer remarked, the poor "are forced by a happy kind of necessity to find everything in the Church and their religion." "The Duties of the Rich in Christian Society," *CW* 15 (1872): 291.

7 Green, *Holyoke*, 113; *Springfield Republican* (*SR*), July 2, 1900. The practice of faction fighting in nineteenth-century Ireland is described in Samuel Clark, *Social Origins of the Irish Land War* (Princeton: Princeton University Press, 1979), 74–78. Also see Brian C. Mitchell, *The Paddy Camps: The Irish of Lowell, 1821–1861* (Urbana: University of Illinois Press, 1988), 23–24, 45–46, 109–110.

8 This and succeeding paragraphs draw on the work of Alan Dawley, Paul Faler, Bruce Laurie, and Herbert Gutman. The chapter as a whole is in part an effort to chart the later development of the antebellum working-class cultures that they so discerningly examined. See Paul Faler, "Cultural Aspects of the Industrial Revolution: Lynn, Massachusetts Shoemakers and Industrial Morality, 1826–1860," *Labor History* 15 (1974): 367–394; Alan Dawley and Paul Faler, "Workingclass Culture and Politics in the Industrial Revolution: Sources of Loyalism and Rebellion," *Journal of Social History* 9 (1976): 466–480; Bruce Laurie, *Working People of Philadelphia, 1800–1850* (Philadelphia: Temple University Press, 1980); and Herbert Gutman, "Work, Culture, and Society in Industrializing America, 1815–1919," in *Work, Culture, and Society in Industrializing America* (New York: Vintage Books, 1977), 3–78.

9 *HT*, May 21, 1881; Apr. 14, 1897; Green, *Holyoke*, 47. Beyond the barroom, saloon culture had no fixed institutional bases. This complicates the task of securing reliable demographic information on its habitues. To meet this problem, I had hoped to check the Holyoke Police Court records for age and occupational data on those arrested for drunkenness or assault in selected years between 1870 and 1900. I could not, however, obtain access to these records. In lieu of this admittedly imperfect approach, I can only offer the findings of some surveys of different subject populations. An 1881 investigation conducted by the Bureau of Labor Statistics found that, compared to other occupational groups, laborers comprised the largest proportion of those arrested for assault: 434 of a total sample of 1,498. The nearly three hundred people listed as unemployed or who did not give an occupation constituted the only other group that even approached this number. The figures for those arrested for disturbing the peace were strikingly similar. Massachusetts Bureau of Statistics of Labor (MBSL), *Twelfth Annual Report*, 1881, 505–506. Also see Roy Rosenzweig, *Eight Hours for What We Will: Workers and Leisure in an Industrial City, 1880–1920* (Cambridge, Eng.: Cambridge University Press, 1983), 51–52; and Perry R. Duis, *The Saloon: Public Drinking in Chicago and Boston, 1880–1920* (Urbana: University of Illinois Press, 1983), 180–181.

A 1904 MBSL study of absence after payday revealed that textile workers formed one of the most temperate groups, with only one percent of the

sample missing work. The study contained no separate listing for laborers. A similar investigation later that year produced much the same results. One conclusion stressed by both studies was that intemperance was not a serious problem among Massachusetts workers, and that temperance reformers had wildly overstated their case. The studies support my argument along two lines. They indicate that factory operatives were more likely than other workers to avoid the saloon. They also suggest that, as the century progressed, saloon culture assumed an increasingly marginal role in working-class life. MBSL, *Bulletin* 32 (July 1904): 212; 34 (Dec. 1904): 352–355.

10 *HT*, Sept. 13, 1876; Jan. 28, 1884; May 13, 1892; Oct. 16, 1872; Nov. 4, 1876; Nov. 19, 1888. The operation of saloon politics is described in Duis, *The Saloon*, 125–142.

11 *HT*, May 20, 1876; Oct. 21, 1876; Dec. 5, 1877; Apr. 21, 1886. In an essay on the saloon, Jon Kingsdale has also argued the existence of a bachelor subculture among its regulars. His principal evidence is a 1908 Boston study of drunkenness. "The 'Poor Man's Club': Social Functions of the Urban Working-Class Saloon," *American Quarterly* 25 (Oct 1973): 486, 489. Also see Rosenzweig, *Eight Hours for What We Will*, 56–57.

12 *Report of the School Committee*, 1890, 34; *SR*, Mar. 4, 1900; Sept. 14, 1902.

13 *HT*, Mar. 9, 1883; Apr. 7, 1884; Sept. 9, 1889.

14 *HT*, Sept. 19, 1883.

15 *HT*, June 1, 1891; July 11, 1888.

16 *HT*, July 26, 1873; *SR*, Aug. 5, 1879; Aug. 11, 1879; Apr. 21, 1884.

17 *HT*, May 22, 1872; May 13, 1890. Earlier instances in which Yankee policemen invited assault by a too stringent enforcement of the new morality in the city's Irish community can be found in *HM*, June 8, 1861; *HT*, May 1, 1872.

18 *HT*, Dec. 30, 1871; Aug. 11, 1879; *SR*, July 4, 1882.

19 Examples of the many reported cases of nonsupport and domestic violence can be found in *HT*, July 26, 1873; Aug. 3, 1881; July 26, 1883; Oct. 21, 1884; *SR*, Feb. 18, 1878; Mar. 19, 1881; June 13, 1881; Feb. 18, 1892. Roy Rosenzweig offers a similar assessment of saloon culture in *Eight Hours for What We Will*, 63–64, 122–123.

20 Kerby A. Miller, *Emigrants and Exiles: Ireland and the Irish Exodus to North America* (New York: Oxford University Press, 1985), 107–121, 293–300, 325–328.

21 *SR*, Jan. 19, 1890; *HT*, Jan. 1, 1873; Sept. 3, 1883; Stephen Byrne, *Irish Emigration to the United States: What It Has Been and What It Is* (New York: Catholic Publication Society, 1874), 47.

22 John Francis Maguire, *The Irish in America* (1868; reprint, New York: Arno Press, 1969), 21; *IW*, Sept. 23, 1871; Oct. 24, 1874. Also see Timothy Meagher's observations in " 'The Lord Is Not Dead': Cultural and Social Change among the Irish in Worcester, Massachusetts, 1880–1920" (Ph.D. diss., Brown University, 1982), 479–481.

23 *Report of the School Committee*, 1880; 1890, 42.

24 Neil J. McCluskey, S.J., ed., *Catholic Education in America: A Documentary History* (New York: Teachers College, 1964), 71; *SR*, Mar. 13, 1882. The church also sought to use access to the sacraments as a means of controlling the social behavior of Catholics. In 1875, the Roman Congregation for the Propagation of the Faith ruled that the clergy had a duty to refuse absolution to parents who sent their children to public schools without sufficient cause. When a Rhode Island priest invoked the sanction, a writer in the *American Catholic Quarterly Review* defended his action, arguing that the "priest who denies the sacraments to bad Catholics, by no means interferes with family affairs"; for when "parents forget their duties towards members of the family, they commit a sin; and this sin cannot be pardoned without repentance and atonement." At Holyoke, instances of sacramental intimidation appear to have been rare. On one occasion Father Phelan withheld absolution from members of Sacred Heart's temperance gymnastics club because they undertook an outing after he had voiced his disapproval of it. The bishop quickly revoked the sanction. Rev. P. Bayma, "The Liberalistic View of the Public School Question," *ACQR* 2 (1877): 266; *SR*, Aug. 12, 1885; Aug. 14, 1885; Aug. 16, 1885.

25 *HT*, May 7, 1906; Mar. 5, 1900; Dec. 26, 1900.

26 Miller, *Emigrants and Exiles*, 116–117; *IW*, Apr. 13, 1872.

27 McCluskey, *Catholic Education*, 83; Dolan, *Immigrant Church*, 126; "Unification and Education," *CW* 13 (1871): 5–6; George D. Wolff, "Socialistic Communism in the United States," *ACQR* 3 (1878): 531–533; Rev. A. F. Hewitt, "What Shall Our Young Do?" *CW* 38 (1883–1884): 436–439; quotation in "Rapid Increase of the Dangerous Classes in the United States," *ACQR* 4 (1879): 255; "The School Question," *CW* 11 (1870): 103; "Aspects of National Education," *CW* 31 (1880): 398–408.

28 "Immigration," *Massachusetts Teacher* 4 (1851): 290; *Holyoke Town Records* (*HTR*), 1852, 8; 1855, 6–7; *HT*, Jan. 8, 1867; Mar. 22, 1888.

29 *IW*, Oct. 31, 1874.

30 Dolan, *Immigrant Church*, 65; Byrne, *Irish Emigration*, 40–41; Maguire, *Irish in America*, 92–94. Father John O'Hanlon supplied perhaps the most complete list of the values immigrants needed to make their way in America: "Piety, integrity, sincerity, temperance, good temper, cheerfulness, self-respect and respectful consideration for the feelings of others, punctuality, generosity, industry, firmness, fortitude, &c., are the virtues required from religious men; the exercise of these virtues will render him esteemed and respected by his acquaintances." Edward J. Maguire, ed., *Reverend John O'Hanlon's Emigrant's Guide for the United States: A Critical Edition with Introduction and Commentary* (1851; reprint, New York: Arno Press, 1976), 239–240. Also see Jay Dolan's analysis of the intermingling of the gospels of acceptance and success in *Catholic Revivalism: The American Experience, 1830–1900* (Notre

Dame, Ind.: University of Notre Dame Press, 1978), 150–165; and Kerby Miller's observations in *Emigrants and Exiles*, 332–334.

31 Byrne, *Irish Emigration*, 36–37; Paul Messbarger, *Fiction with a Parochial Purpose: Social Uses of American Catholic Literature, 1884–1900* (Boston: Boston University Press, 1971), 137, 142–143; Meagher, " 'The Lord Is Not Dead'," 182–185, 205.

32 Maguire, *Irish in America*, 214–236; Maguire, *O'Hanlon's Emigrant Guide*, 214–215; Byrne, *Irish Emigration*, 4, 26.

33 MBSL, *Sixth Annual Report*, 1875, 369–370, 385–386, 392.

34 Ibid., 429, 436; Byrne, *Irish Emigration*, 36–37.

35 Byrne, *Irish Emigration*, 51; Maguire, *Irish in America*, 281, 287.

36 Maguire, *O'Hanlon's Emigrant Guide*, 271–272; HM, Oct. 10, 1857; HT, Feb. 25, 1870; SR, Sept. 22, 1894. Generalizations on membership are based on an occupational study of the society's officers, using Holyoke city directories.

37 SR, Jan. 18, 1902.

38 Miller, *Emigrants and Exiles*, 88–96, 338–344; Green, *Holyoke*, 114–115. This paragraph is based largely on Thomas N. Brown's observations in *Irish-American Nationalism, 1870–1890* (Philadelphia: J.B. Lippincott, 1966), 19–20, quotation from p. 20.

39 HT, July 27, 1881; Sept. 2, 1881; Oct. 22, 1881; July 9, 1883; Aug. 31, 1883. Studies that link Irish nationalism to a longing for middle-class respectability include Dale B. Light, Jr., "The Role of Irish-American Organizations in Assimilation and Community Formation," in *The Irish in America: Emigration, Assimilation, and Impact*, ed. P.J. Drudy (Cambridge, Eng.: Cambridge University Press, 1985), 113–142; and Brown, *Irish-American Nationalism*, 23–24, 41, 45–46. Victor A. Walsh provides a perceptive critique of Brown's seminal work in "Irish Nationalism and Land Reform: The Role of the Irish in America," in *The Irish in America*, 253–270.

40 HT, July 31, 1875; IW, Nov. 7, 1874; Nov. 28, 1874; Dec. 26, 1874; HT, Sept. 19, 1877; Nov. 12, 1879.

41 Brown, *Irish-American Nationalism*, 69–73; IW, May 18, 1873. Lists of local contributors to the Skirmishing Fund can be found in IW, Jan. 12, 1878; Mar. 23, 1878; June 29, 1878. City directories were used to identify Holyoke Skirmishers.

42 IW, Jan. 12, 1878; June 29, 1878; June 22, 1878.

43 HT, Jan. 31, 1880; SR, Feb. 8, 1881; Feb. 21, 1881; Mar. 15, 1881; Apr. 9, 1881. This section also draws on Dennis Clark, *The Irish in Philadelphia: Ten Generation of Urban Experience* (Philadelphia: Temple University Press, 1973), 132–137; James J. Green, "American Catholics and the Irish Land League, 1879–1882," *Catholic Historical Review* 35 (1949):19–42; and Eric Foner, "Class, Ethnicity, and Radicalism in the Gilded Age: The Land League and Irish America," in *Politics and Ideology in the Age of the Civil War* (New York: Oxford University Press, 1980), 150–200.

44 *HT,* July 9, 1863; *SR,* Mar. 1, 1881; Foner, "Class, Ethnicity, and Radicalism," 161; *IW,* Mar. 23, 1878; July 29, 1878.

45 *IW,* May 6, 1871; May 13, 1871; Dec. 23, 1871; June 8, 1872; Brown, *Irish-American Nationalism,* 57, 109; Richard J. Oestreicher, *Solidarity and Fragmentation: Working People and Class Consciousness in Detroit, 1875–1900* (Urbana: University of Illinois Press, 1986), 59.

46 Brown, *Irish-American Nationalism,* 57; *IW,* May 15, 1880.

47 Brown, *Irish-American Nationalism,* 109; *HT,* Apr. 12, 1884; *IW,* Sept. 29, 1877.

48 *IW,* Sept. 29, 1877.

49 *IW,* July 13, 1878; John McCarthy, "Mr. Mallock and the Labor Movement," *ACQR* 12 (1887): 110; Abell, *American Catholicism and Social Action,* 47; James E. Roohan, *American Catholics and the Social Question* (New York: Arno Press, 1976), 103–118. It should be noted that Catholic traditionalists staunchly opposed church leaders who supported social change. The differences between the two groups are detailed in Robert Cross, *The Emergence of Liberal Catholicism* (1958; reprint, Chicago: Quadrangle Books, 1968).

50 John Talbot Smith, "Workmen Should Not Only Act But Think," *CW* 47 (1888): 843; Rt. Rev. James O'Connor, "Capital and Labor," *ACQR* 8 (1883): 493; John Conway, "America's Workmen," *CW* 56 (1892–1893): 495–496; Abell, *American Catholicism and Social Action,* 82–83, 283; Abell, "American Catholic Reaction to Industrial Conflict: The Arbitral Process, 1885–1900," *Catholic Historical Review* 41 (1956): 385–407. Worcester's Catholic weekly, *The Messenger,* argued that arbitration was the "result of Catholic practice and teaching" in an article that examined disputes ranging from Attila's invasion to the revolutions of 1848 that had been mediated by Popes and other leading Catholics. *Messenger,* Sept. 21, 1889.

51 John Talbot Smith, "Workmen Should Not Only Act But Think," *CW* 47 (1888): 843; "The Homes of the Poor," *CW* 45 (1887): 516–517; "The Land and Labor Question," *CW,* 47 (1888): 58; "The Eight-Hour Law," *CW* 44 (1886–1887): 397–406; Charles F. Wingate, "Moral Side of the Tenement House Problem," *CW* 41 (1885): 164; Abell, *American Catholicism and Social Action,* 75; William B. Stang, *Christianity and Socialism* (New York: Benziger Brothers, 1905), 75; AN AMERICAN WOMAN, "Chiefly Among Women," *CW* 21 (1875): 339–340; "The Woman Question," *CW* 9 (1869): 151–152. John Maguire declared that the "piety and purity" of Irish women provided an important "safeguard against the risk of apostasy and deadlier blight of infidelity." *Irish in America,* 344.

52 *HT,* Apr. 16, 1881; Henry J. Browne, *The Catholic Church and the Knights of Labor* (Washington, D.C.: Catholic University of America Press, 1949); James Cardinal Gibbons, "The Stake of the Church in the Labor Movement," in *American Catholic Thought on Social Questions,* ed. Aaron I. Abell (Indianapolis: Bobbs-Merrill, 1968), 158.

53 Herbert G. Gutman, *Power and Culture: Essays on the American Working Class*, ed. Ira Berlin (New York: Pantheon Books, 1987), 335.

CHAPTER FOUR: Enclave Politics and Worker Organization, 1873–1893

1 *Holyoke Transcript (HT)*, Aug. 11, 1877.
2 Constance M. Green, *Holyoke, Massachusetts: A Case History of the Industrial Revolution in America* (New Haven: Yale University Press, 1939), 138–139; *Springfield Republican (SR)*, Mar. 6, 1877; Mar. 31, 1877; Apr. 4, 1877. Bankruptcy notices can be found in *SR*, Jan. 6, 1877; Jan. 12, 1877; Feb. 5, 1877; Feb. 15, 1877; Feb. 23, 1877; Feb. 24, 1877; Mar. 1, 1877; Mar. 10, 1877; Apr. 2, 1877.
3 *HT*, Aug. 2, 1877; Nov. 5, 1873; Nov. 8, 1873; *Independent Journal*, Nov. 11, 1873; *HT*, May 31, 1876; Dec. 23, 1878.
4 *Holyoke Municipal Register (HMR)*, 1876, 11–12; *HT*, Sept. 11, 1876; Sept. 20, 1876; Feb. 14, 1877. Not all Holyoke Republicans shared Pearsons's views. In his 1879 inaugural address, William Whiting, the city's leading paper manufacturer, declared that "we can look for a decrease of disbursement for the poor not until the business of the country improves to such an extent as to keep employed the surplus labor." *HMR*, 1879, 8.
5 Howard H. Quint, *The Forging of American Socialism: The Origins of the Modern Movement* (1954; reprint, Indianapolis: Bobbs-Merrill, 1964), 13–15; Stuart Kaufman, *Samuel Gompers and the Origins of the American Federation of Labor, 1848–1896* (Westport, Conn.: Greenwood Press, 1973), 56–78; *Labor Standard*, Mar. 24, 1877; Nov. 18, 1877; *SR*, Feb. 15, 1877; Feb. 26, 1877; Mar. 1, 1877; *HT*, Aug. 1, 1877; Oct. 3, 1877. In a letter to the *Labor Standard*, E. F. Sullivan, recording secretary of the English-speaking chapter of the WPUS, wrote that the Holyoke sections fully endorsed its editorial policy. *Labor Standard*, July 14, 1877.
6 *SR*, Aug. 17, 1878; *Irish World (IW)*, Aug. 10, 1878; Aug. 30, 1879; Hans L. Trefousse, *Ben Butler: The South Called Him Beast!* (New York: Twayne Publishers, 1957), 218–221, 239; *SR*, Nov. 6, 1878; Nov. 8, 1882; Nov. 7, 1883; *HT*, Sept. 24, 1884; Oct. 27, 1884.
7 *SR*, Aug. 17, 1878; *Labor Standard*, Nov. 25, 1877; July 7, 1878; Nov. 9, 1878; Eric Foner, "Class, Ethnicity, and Radicalism in the Gilded Age: The Land League and Irish America," in *Politics and Ideology in the Age of the Civil War* (New York: Oxford University Press, 1980), 159; *IW*, Sept. 14, 1878.
8 *SR*, Oct. 14, 1882; Feb. 15, 1885; *People*, Apr. 7, 1888.
9 *HT*, Oct. 29, 1885; *Journal of United Labor*, Feb. 1884, 639; Mar. 25, 1885, 947; Sept. 25, 1885, 1087; *Messenger*, Oct. 6, 1888; Apr. 14, 1888; *IW*, July 22, 1882; May 29, 1886. The Skinner strike, which the weavers ultimately lost, can

be followed in *HT*, Feb. 5, 1886; Feb. 8, 1886; Feb. 9, 1886; *SR*, Feb. 8, 1886; Feb. 9, 1886; *HT*, Feb. 19, 1886; Feb. 20., 1886; Feb. 27, 1886; Mar. 2, 1886; Mar. 4, 1886; Mar. 11, 1886; Mar. 19, 1886; Mar. 20, 1886; Mar. 29, 1886; Apr. 23, 1886. When the Congregation of the Holy Office decided against condemning the Knights of Labor, *The Messenger* exultantly declared, "This action puts a quietus on the statements that the Church looks askance at, if she does not openly discourage, all attempts of the working classes to organize for the amelioration of their condition." *Messenger*, July 14, 1888. I wish to thank Marianne Pedulla for sharing with me material on P. J. Moore that she had gathered during the course of her own research.

10 *Journal of United Labor*, Aug. 10, 1884; *HT*, Oct. 29, 1885. The legislative program of District Assembly 30 also called for a weekly-pay measure, an employers' accident-liability act, and a bill to establish a $300,000 fund that would provide wage earners with low-interest loans for homes. *Journal of United Labor*, Feb. 25, 1885, 921.

11 *HT*, Oct. 15, 1885; *SR*, Nov. 11, 1882; *HT*, Jan. 12, 1886; Feb. 22, 1886; Feb. 23, 1886; Feb. 9, 1887; Mar. 28, 1887; Dec. 18, 1891.

12 *HT*, Oct. 16, 1885.

13 *SR*, Aug. 14, 1877; *HT*, Jan. 11, 1894.

14 *SR*, Oct. 28, 1894; Oct. 25, 1881; *HT*, Feb. 15, 1879. The letter to which this correspondent was responding, "How We Came to Rule the City," was allegedly written by an Irishman and appeared in *Holyoke News*, Feb. 6, 1879.

15 *SR*, Nov. 13, 1880; Nov. 26, 1880; *HT*, July 2, 1877; *HMR*, 1880, 119; Holyoke Public Library Scrapbook, 15:70; *SR*, Dec. 7, 1880.

16 *SR*, Nov. 18, 1880; Nov. 22, 1880; Nov. 11, 1881; Dec. 5, 1881; Dec. 6, 1881; *HT*, Jan. 7, 1882. Commenting on his 1878 mayoral campaign, the *Republican* observed that the "way ex-mayor Crafts went the rounds of the city's liquor shops . . . in search of votes provokes much comment." *SR*, Nov. 29, 1878.

17 *SR*, July 26, 1882; July 27, 1882; July 28, 1882; July 30, 1882.

18 *SR*, Nov. 30, 1882; Dec. 3, 1882; Dec. 5, 1882; *HT*, Dec. 2, 1882.

19 *SR*, Dec. 4, 1883; Dec. 9, 1883; *HT*, Apr. 19, 1884; Nov. 28, 1883. Ramage also voiced the feelings of many of his fellow manufacturers on the temperance question: "I have never pretended to be a prohibitionist, but I shall gladly welcome the day when licenses to sell liquor shall be restricted." Delaney favored higher license fees and a reduction in the number of licenses. *HT*, Dec. 1, 1883; Mar. 21, 1884.

20 A ward-by-ward breakdown of the vote in the three elections can be found in *SR*, Dec. 6, 1882; Dec. 5, 1883; Dec. 3, 1884.

21 *HT*, Nov. 18, 1885; Nov. 30, 1885; Nov. 13, 1886; Nov. 15, 1886; *SR*, Nov. 30, 1885; Dec. 3, 1885; Dec. 6, 1885; Nov. 14, 1886; Nov. 27, 1885; Nov. 10, 1886; Nov. 15, 1886; Dec. 5, 1886; *HT*, Nov. 21, 1885; *SR*, Sept. 19, 1886; *HT*, Nov. 10, 1886. O'Connor's ongoing battle with local saloon interests over the cost and

number of licenses to be issued is covered in *SR*, May 2, 1886; May 1, 1887; June 5, 1887; July 28, 1887; *HT*, July 28, 1887.

22 *SR*, Nov. 27, 1887; Nov. 28, 1887; Dec. 3, 1887; *HT*, Nov. 23, 1887; Nov. 25, 1887; Nov. 28, 1887; Nov. 29, 1887; Dec. 2, 1887.

23 *HT*, Nov. 25, 1889; Sept. 1, 1890; Aug. 31, 1891; Apr. 1, 1892.

24 *HT*, Oct. 22, 1885; Oct. 29, 1885; Sept. 28, 1886; Nov. 7, 1886; Nov. 7, 1887; Feb. 14, 1888; May 4, 1889; Geoffrey Blodgett, *The Gentle Reformers: Massachusetts Democrats in the Cleveland Era* (Cambridge: Harvard University Press, 1966), 128–140. During these years Holyoke sent two representatives to the General Court: one represented Wards 1 through 4; the other was elected by the city's three remaining wards.

25 *SR*, Dec. 28, 1884; June 1, 1885; *HT*, Feb. 11, 1885; *SR*, Feb. 1, 1885; *HT*, Feb. 5, 1885; Feb. 14, 1885; Feb. 17, 1885; Sept. 16, 1885; Sept. 18, 1885; Dec. 17, 1885; *HMR*, 1886, 81–83. The Arlington Club gradually faded out of existence. *HT*, Oct. 12, 1894.

26 Accounts of job actions against Daniel O'Connell and Maurice Lynch can be found in *HT*, Apr. 21, 1887; July 13, 1887; Mar. 30, 1888; Apr. 11, 1888; May 4, 1888; May 8, 1888; June 12, 1888.

27 Arthur Mann, *Yankee Reformers in the Urban Age* (Cambridge: Harvard University Press, 1954), 34–39; *Pilot*, Mar. 31, 1888.

28 Mann, *Yankee Reformers*, 38; *Pilot*, Dec. 25, 1886; June 19, 1886; July 16, 1887; Sept. 10, 1887; June 18, 1887; May 15, 1886.

29 *Pilot*, Oct. 2, 1886; July 17, 1886; Sept. 4, 1886.

30 *Pilot*, Jan. 15, 1889; June 26, 1886; May 8, 1886; Sept. 11, 1886.

31 *Pilot*, Aug. 20, 1887; Sept. 16, 1889.

32 *HT*, Apr. 21, 1888.

33 *HT*, July 1, 1891; July 18, 1892; July 25, 1892; Aug. 1, 1892; Aug. 3, 1892; *SR*, Aug. 3, 1892; Sept. 27, 1892; *HT*, Mar. 14, 1891; Jan. 25, 1892; June 9, 1891; *SR*, Aug. 2, 1891; *HT*, Aug. 6, 1891; Aug. 7, 1891; Aug. 8, 1891; Aug. 10, 1891; *SR*, Aug. 7, 1891; Aug. 8, 1891; *HT*, Sept. 7, 1891. The molders were not the only strikers to elicit such support. That spring when striking laborers marched through the lower wards to close down the building projects of recalcitrant contractors, the *Transcript* reported that "people crowded to the windows and wished them 'good luck,' and showed other expressions of sympathy." *HT*, May 6, 1891; May 7, 1891.

34 David Montgomery, "The Irish and the American Labor Movement," in *America and Ireland, 1776–1976: The American Identity and the Irish Connection*, ed. David Noel Doyle and Owen Dudley Edwards (Westport, Conn.: Greenwood Press, 1980), 211.

35 *HT*, Dec. 24, 1891; Dec. 28, 1891; May 3, 1892; May 5, 1892; May 6, 1892; May 11, 1892; May 14, 1892; May 28, 1892; *SR*, May 11, 1892; May 14, 1892.

36 *HT*, May 11, 1892; May 5, 1892; May 7, 1892; May 27, 1892; May 24, 1892; *SR*, May 25, 1892; May 28, 1892; June 26, 1892.

37 Montgomery, "The Irish and the American Labor Movement," 212; Carpenters, Springfield District Council and Affiliates, Local 96, Minutes, 1885–1892, Archives and Manuscripts, University of Massachusetts at Amherst Library.
38 Ibid.
39 Ibid., Apr. 1, 1892; *HT*, May 5, 1892; May 13, 1892.
40 *HT*, May 19, 1892; June 9, 1892. McGuire's views on the functions of trade unions are examined in Mark Erlich, "Peter J. McGuire's Trade Unionism: Socialism of a Trade Union Kind?" *Labor History* 24 (1983): 165–197; and Robert A. Christie, *Empire in Wood: A History of the Carpenters' Union* (Ithaca, N.Y.: Cornell University Press, 1956), 33–45, 92–93.
41 *HT*, Apr. 27, 1892; Apr. 28, 1892; *SR*, Mar. 15, 1892; *HT*, Nov. 16, 1891; Nov. 17, 1891; May 7, 1892.
42 *HT*, Oct. 23, 1891; Oct. 26, 1891; *SR*, Nov. 15, 1891; *HT*, June 3, 1892; Mar. 13, 1893; July 31, 1893; Aug. 9, 1893; July 3, 1893; Oct. 23, 1893; Mar. 28, 1892.
43 *HT*, Mar. 28, 1892; Aug. 28, 1890; Sept. 1, 1890; Apr. 1, 1890; *SR*, Nov. 15, 1891; Nov. 29, 1891; *HT*, Sept. 5, 1891; *SR*, Sept. 6, 1892; Sept. 2, 1893; *HT*, Sept. 2, 1893. The local Women's Christian Temperance Union journal perhaps best captured the manner in which Labor Day brought a temporary convergence of worker cultures in its depiction of the 1901 event:

Great credit is due to those who planned and carried out this labor day demonstration. It showed man in his best estate; erect, master of himself, in his right mind, the Master piece of creation.
But the black spot on the day's record was the drunkenness at the close.

True Light, 12 (Sept. 1901), 4.
44 *HT*, May 28, 1892.
45 *HT*, May 22, 1893; Apr. 10, 1893; *SR*, July 8, 1892; *HT*, Feb. 29, 1892; Oct. 23, 1893; Aug. 28, 1892; Norman Ware, *The Labor Movement in the United States, 1860–1890* (1929; reprint, New York: Vintage Books, 1964), 334–345. When one store refused to close Friday nights, it did so, the *Transcript* observed, "at a visible weekly loss." *HT*, May 8, 1893.
46 Green, *Holyoke*, 210–216.
47 *Messenger*, Dec. 5, 1891; Mar. 12, 1892; May 14, 1892; May 2, 1891.

CHAPTER FIVE: Depression and Upheaval, 1893–1905

1 *Springfield Republican* (*SR*), Aug. 20, 1893; July 30, 1893; Aug. 29, 1893; *Paper World* (*PW*) 27 (Sept. 1893): 10; *SR*, Jan. 11, 1894.

2 E. Lovering to T. Parsons, Aug. 11, 1893, Sept. 7, 1893, vol. PC-8, Lyman Mills Papers, Baker Library, Harvard Business School (LMP); *SR*, Sept. 8, 1893; Aug. 17, 1893; Sept. 14, 1893; Oct. 6, 1893; Oct. 21, 1893. In November the molders' union reluctantly agreed to a 10 percent cut at the Deane Steam Pump Company, one of the city's largest metal shops. *SR*, Nov. 4, 1893; Nov. 8, 1893.

3 *SR*, Oct. 26, 1893; Oct. 27, 1893; Nov. 20, 1893; Dec. 23, 1893; *Holyoke Transcript (HT)*, Nov. 1, 1893; Nov. 13, 1893; *SR*, Jan. 4, 1894; Feb. 7, 1894. In June, the city's Catholic churches began a subscription list for the unemployed. *Holyoke Labor*, June 23, 1894.

4 *SR*, Dec. 1, 1893; *Holyoke Municipal Register (HMR)*, 1893, 507; *HT*, Dec. 18, 1893; *SR*, Apr. 3, 1894; Apr. 4, 1894.

5 *PW*, 28 (Mar. 1894): 94; *SR*, Mar. 26, 1894; Mar. 28, 1894; *PW*, 29 (Aug. 1894): 47; *SR*, Feb. 2, 1894; *HT*, Sept. 25, 1894; Oct. 2, 1894; Oct. 5, 1894; Oct. 6, 1894; Oct. 8, 1894; Oct. 9, 1894; Oct. 10, 1894; Oct. 26, 1894; *SR*, Sept. 10, 1894; Sept. 11, 1894; E. Lovering to T. Parsons, Apr. 9, 1894, Apr. 16, 1894, Apr. 18, 1894, Apr. 23, 1894, June 1, 1894, vol. PC-8, LMP.

6 *SR*, May 23, 1896; May 24, 1896; Aug. 24, 1896; Sept. 12, 1896; Sept. 15, 1896; Sept. 19, 1896; Mar. 10, 1896; Mar. 11, 1896; Mar. 15, 1896; *HT*, Apr. 18, 1896; *SR*, Sept. 19, 1896; Nov. 30, 1896; Dec. 17, 1896; Jan. 8, 1897; Nov. 1, 1896.

7 *SR*, Aug. 16, 1896; *HMR*, 1896, 477; *True Light*, 7 (May 1896): 13; *HT*, Aug. 21, 1896; Nov. 7, 1896; *SR*, Apr. 4, 1896; Aug. 29, 1896. The Polish had good reason to return to their homeland. As newcomers to Holyoke, they were the last hired, first fired, and had the greatest difficulty obtaining municipal aid. A few years earlier city almoner O'Donnell had told one group of relief applicants that they "should be sent back to Poland as paupers" and would be if they persisted in their demands. *SR*, Feb. 3, 1894. A few days after Kate Sullivan's death another Irish woman attempted to commit suicide by jumping into the second level canal, but was rescued before she drowned. *SR*, Aug. 28, 1896.

8 *SR*, May 21, 1897; May 30, 1897; Sept. 8, 1897; Sept. 12, 1897; *HMR*, 1897, 160.

9 Constance M. Green, *Holyoke, Massachusetts: A Case History of the Industrial Revolution in America* (New Haven: Yale University Press, 1939), 188-193.

10 David Montgomery, *Workers' Control in America: Studies in the History of Work, Technology, and Labor Struggles* (Cambridge, Eng.: Cambridge University Press, 1979), 20; *SR*, July 24, 1898; *HT*, Aug. 3, 1898; Aug. 19, 1898; Aug. 23, 1898.

11 *HT*, May 25, 1899; May 26, 1899; May 31, 1899; *SR*, May 26, 1899; May 27, 1899; May 30, 1899; Massachusetts Bureau of Statistics of Labor (MBSL), *Thirtieth Annual Report*, 1899, 193; *HT*, Jan. 8, 1899; E. Lovering to T. Parsons, June 17, 1899, July 27, 1899, vol. PC-11, LMP; *HT*, June 15, 1899; June 16,

1899; June 19, 1899; June 22, 1899; July 6, 1899; *SR*, June 17, 1899; June 22, 1899; July 7, 1899; July 8, 1899; July 9, 1899; July 10, 1899. A strike by 100 weavers at the Chadwick Plush Mill also failed. *HT*, June 19, 1899; June 20, 1899; June 29, 1899; *SR*, June 30, 1899.

12 E. Lovering to T. Parsons, July 27, 1899, vol. PC–11, LMP; *SR*, July 8, 1899; Dec. 14, 1899; *HT*, Dec. 14, 1899; June 4, 1900. During the latter half of 1899 textile operatives throughout the state obtained at least a partial restoration of depression wage cuts. At Holyoke, the Germania Woolen Mills, Merrick Thread Company, and Skinner Silk Mills also granted pay increases. This in part explains the readiness of the Lyman Mills to meet the demands of the December strikers. *HT*, Dec. 18, 1899.

13 T. Parsons to Horace Wadlin, Chief, Bureau of Labor Statistics, Boston, June 12, 1902, vol. PA–10; C. Merriam to T. Parsons, Apr. 8, 1902, vol. PC–12; C. Merriam to E. Lovering, Apr. 17, 1902, vol. PE–35; T. Parsons to E. Lovering, May 2, 1902; T. Parsons to F. D. Williams, May 3, 1902; T. Parsons to Minot, Hooper, and Company, NYC, May 6, 1902, vol. PA–10; E. Lovering to Agent, Boott Cotton Mills, Lowell, Apr. 25, 1902, May 6, 1902; and C. Merriam to L. A. Auman, Dwight Manufacturing Company, Chicopee, May 13, 1902, vol. PE–35, all in LMP; *SR*, May 3, 1902; May 14, 1902.

14 E. Lovering to Lowell Shuttle Company, May 8, 1902, June 7, 1902; E. Lovering to Whitinsville Spinning Ring Company, June 6, 1902; E. Lovering to Whitin Machine Shop, June 7, 1902; E. Lovering to Mason Machine Works, Taunton, July 17, 1902, vol. PE–35; E. Lovering to T. Parsons, June 9, 1902, July 17, 1902, vol. PC–12, all in LMP; *SR*, May 28, 1902; June 30, 1902; July 25, 1902; E. Lovering to Treasurer, Mason Machine Works, Aug. 13, 1902, vol. PE–35, LMP. In time the *Republican* recognized the company's actual strategy. *SR*, July 6, 1902. The elaborate plans devised by the company to disguise the identity of its yarn suppliers are discussed in E. Lovering to Soule Mills, June 27, 1902, July 2, 1902; E. Lovering to H. K. Lyman, June 27, 1902, July 2, 1902; E. Lovering to Warren Manufacturing Company, July 2 1902, Sept. 25, 1902; E. Lovering to J. M. Pendergast and Company, Boston, Sept. 18, 1902; E. Lovering to Morison and Vaughn, Boston, Sept. 15, 1902, Sept. 25, 1902, vol. PE–35; T. Parsons to James F. Knowles, Sept. 23, 1902, vol. PA–10; E. Lovering to T. Parsons, July 20, 1902, Sept. 18, 1902, vol. PC–12, all in LMP. Unable to find any New England spinners to replace the strikers, Lovering wrote one German overseer seeking work that it "might occur to you to bring over some married mule spinners and their families to this country should you think seriously of coming to America." Lovering also asked a series of questions that reflected a preoccupation with both the strike and textile unionism:

By head spinner, do you have charge of mules as well as spinning frames?
Are you acquainted with Dobson and Barlow (Bolton, England) mules?

What wages per week do your mule spinners make?
How many hours per week?
Are they members of any trade unions?
Are any of the employees in your factories members of trade unions?

E. Lovering to Willy Schubert, Augsburg, Germany, Nov. 12, 1902, vol. PE-36, LMP.

15 T. Parsons to E. Lovering, Oct. 17, 1902, vol. PA-10; E. Lovering to T. Parsons, Oct. 13, 1902, Oct. 14, 1902, vol. PC-12, both in LMP.

16 E. Lovering to Frank Bennett, treasurer, *The American Cotton and Wool Reporter*, Sept. 26, 1902, vol. PE-35; E. Lovering to Samuel Ross, Nov. 20, 1902, vol. PE-36; E. Lovering to T. Parsons, Jan. 30, 1903, vol. PC-12, all in LMP; *SR*, Feb. 2, 1903; *HT*, Feb. 3, 1903; E. Lovering to T. Parsons, July 26, 1906, vol. PD-3, LMP. A few days later the loom fixers also received a 5 percent increase. E. Lovering to T. Parsons, July 30, 1906, vol. PD-3, LMP.

17 *SR*, Mar. 1, 1898; Mar. 28, 1898; *HT*, Oct. 27, 1899; Apr. 12, 1899.

18 *SR*, May 13, 1901; May 20, 1901; *HT*, May 31, 1901; June 14, 1901; *SR*, May 30, 1901; *HT*, June 1, 1901. The few paper strikes before 1901 included successful actions by cutter women at the Dickinson Paper Company and reel boys at the Chemical Paper Company seeking wage increases. *HT*, June 6, 1899; Aug. 2, 1899.

19 *HT*, June 4, 1901; June 5, 1901; June 6, 1901; June 7, 1901; June 8, 1901; June 15, 1901; *SR*, June 15, 1901; *HT*, June 17, 1901; MBSL, *Thirty Second Annual Report*, 1901, 143-144.

20 *HT*, June 5, 1901; *SR*, June 21, 1901; *HT*, June 27, 1901; June 28, 1901; July 6, 1901; July 8, 1901.

21 *HT*, Jan. 20, 1899; Mar. 9, 1900; Apr. 9, 1900; Apr. 14, 1900; Jan. 22, 1900; Aug. 17, 1900; July 3, 1899; Aug. 23, 1899; *SR*, Oct. 13, 1900; *HT*, Aug. 18, 1900; Aug. 20, 1900; June 8, 1900; Apr. 12, 1900; Sept. 5, 1900; MBSL, *Thirty First Annual Report*, 1900, 72; *Thirty Second Annual Report*, 1901, 142-144; *SR*, June 25, 1900; *HT*, Oct. 24, 1898; Jan. 30, 1899; June 12, 1899; July 9, 1900; July 23, 1900; *SR*, July 23, 1900; July 28, 1900; July 29, 1900; Aug. 28, 1900; Aug. 27, 1900; *HT*, Jan. 28, 1901.

22 *HT*, July 3, 1901; June 24, 1901; July 1, 1901; *SR*, July 17, 1901; July 2, 1902. When one teacher told her students to ignore the boycott the CLU urged the school board to reprimand her. *HT*, July 1, 1901.

23 *HT*, Jan. 8, 1902; Feb. 10, 1902.

24 *SR*, July 29, 1901; Aug. 12, 1901; *HT*, July 29, 1901; Aug. 12, 1901; *SR*, June 23, 1901; Nov. 11, 1901; Aug. 11, 1901; Sept. 3, 1901.

25 *SR*, Apr. 7, 1902; Apr. 11, 1902; *HT*, Apr. 11, 1902; Apr. 18, 1902; *SR*, Apr. 18, 1902; June 5, 1902; June 10, 1902; June 19, 1902; June 20, 1902. In another strike that spring, the plumbers and steamfitters obtained a com-

promise settlement of $2.75 for a nine-hour day. *SR*, May 2, 1902; May 21, 1902.

26 *SR*, Sept. 23, 1902; Oct. 5, 1902; Nov. 23, 1902; Mar. 8, 1905. Relieved at Dowd's temporary displacement, one businessman of "high standing" declared that Kennedy "would have a fine chance to make a name for himself . . . and win the confidence of the employer as well as the men." *SR*, Sept. 30, 1902.

27 *SR*, Nov. 23, 1902; *HT*, Jan. 8, 1902; *SR*, Mar. 28, 1903.

28 *SR*, Mar. 12, 1903; Mar. 25, 1903; *HT*, Mar. 23, 1903; Mar. 27, 1903; *SR*, Mar. 27, 1903; Apr. 3, 1903; Apr 5, 1903; Apr. 13, 1903; May 6, 1903.

29 *SR*, May 3, 1902; May 29, 1902; June 10, 1902; *HT*, Sept. 22, 1902; Oct. 7, 1902; Feb. 9, 1903; *SR*, Apr. 10, 1903; Apr. 12, 1903; May 27, 1903; May 30, 1903; May 31, 1903; June 1, 1903; June 8, 1903; June 9, 1903; Matthew Burns, "History of the International Brotherhood of Paper Makers" (unpublished ms., United Paperworkers International Union, Nashville, Tennessee, 1939), 98–113.

30 Burns, "History of the IBPM," 98–113; *SR*, June 9, 1903; June 10, 1903; June 12, 1903; June 13, 1903; June 14, 1903; June 15, 1903; July 2, 1903; July 6, 1903; July 8, 1903; July 19, 1903; July 20, 1903; July 22, 1903; July 23, 1903; July 26, 1903.

31 *SR*, Aug. 1, 1903; Aug. 2, 1903; Aug. 10, 1903; Aug. 11, 1903; Aug. 14, 1903; Aug. 18, 1903; Aug. 19, 1903; Aug. 20, 1903; *HT*, May 25, 1907.

32 *SR*, May 2, 1904; May 14, 1904; June 16, 1904; June 18, 1904; Aug. 8, 1904; Aug. 14, 1904; Aug. 23, 1904.

33 *HT*, Oct. 3, 1894; Oct. 11, 1894; *SR*, Sept. 23, 1894; Oct. 11, 1894; Oct. 13, 1894; *HT*, Jan. 17, 1894; Jan. 25, 1894; Jan. 26, 1894; Mar. 13, 1894; June 7, 1894; *SR*, June 8, 1894; June 21, 1894.

34 *HT*, Nov. 16, 1891; Nov. 19, 1891; Nov. 26, 1891; Nov. 27, 1891; Dec. 2, 1891. In 1892, Shea temporarily resigned his aldermanic seat to protest the manner in which liquor licenses were being distributed. That year he lost a close election to Dillon, but returned to the board in 1893. *HT*, Apr. 3, 1892; Apr. 24, 1892.

35 *SR*, Aug. 23, 1908; *HT*, Dec. 3, 1890; Nov. 23, 1885; Nov. 25, 1885; Feb. 3, 1886; Nov. 3, 1888; Nov. 27, 1892.

36 *HT*, Nov. 27, 1894; Dec. 4, 1894; *SR*, Dec. 9, 1894.

37 *HT*, Nov. 27, 1894; Jan. 25, 1895; *Holyoke Labor*, Mar. 2, 1895. *Holyoke Labor* contended that the bill would give corporations "an almost unprecedented power over their employes during strikes." *Holyoke Labor*, Apr. 27, 1895.

38 *SR*, Feb. 12, 1893; *HT*, Feb. 22, 1893; May 19, 1894; Feb. 15, 1896; Jan. 17, 1895; Mar. 19, 1895. A brief analysis of the American Protective Association can be found in John Higham, *Strangers in the Land: Patterns of American Nativism, 1860–1925* (1955; reprint, New York: Atheneum, 1963), 80–87.

QUEBEC perhaps best expressed French Canadian disenchantment with the police when he proposed a departmental code of ethics that contained the following provisions:

The test of strength of the applicants will be the breath, if strong enough it will take the place of the silver service exam.

Any boy found making fun of a drunken policemen will be hung on the spot.

Any policeman bringing in a drunk must show (a) which is the drunkest, and (b) which got the other drunk.

All policemen must communicate with their first cousin when a raid is to be made so as to keep it still.

Any policeman that has to be dumped into a hack like a dead sow with his feet up on the cushions and his head under the seat and carried home, must pay the hack fare himself.

HT, Jan. 17, 1893.

39 *HT*, Mar. 18, 1895; May 17, 1895; *SR*, Mar. 3, 1895.

40 *SR*, Oct. 20, 1895; Dec. 8, 1895; *HT*, Dec. 4, 1895; *Holyoke Labor*, Feb. 29, 1896; *SR*, Mar. 14, 1896; July 12, 1896; July 20, 1896. The interpretation of municipal reform offered here draws on Samuel P. Hays's seminal article, "The Politics of Reform in Municipal Government in the Progressive Era," *Pacific Northwest Quarterly* 40 (1964): 157–169.

41 *SR*, July 22, 1896; *HT*, Dec. 9, 1896; Nov. 24, 1897; Dec. 8, 1897; Dec. 9, 1897; Dec. 15, 1897.

42 *HT*, Aug. 16, 1898; Oct. 13, 1898; Nov. 22, 1898; Oct. 8, 1898; Oct. 24, 1898.

43 *HT*, Dec. 14, 1898; Peter Haebler, "Habitants in Holyoke: The Development of the French-Canadian Community in a Massachusetts City, 1865–1910" (Ph.D. diss., University of New Hampshire, 1976), 281–284; *SR*, Mar. 29, 1914; Oct. 10, 1901; Oct. 20, 1901; Nov. 30, 1903.

44 E. Lovering to T. Parsons, Mar. 30, 1900, vol. PC–11, LMP; *SR*, May 21, 1899; Mar. 12, 1900; Mar. 14, 1900; July 18, 1900; *HMR*, 1898, 542; E. Lovering to T. Parsons, Dec. 14, 1903; T. Parsons to E. Lovering, Oct. 31, 1904, vol. PD–1, both in LMP; *SR*, Oct. 29, 1904.

45 *HT*, Dec. 4, 1902; Dec. 8, 1902; Dec. 10, 1902; *SR*, Dec. 8, 1902; Dec. 14, 1902.

46 *Holyoke City Directory*, 1895, 1900, 1905, 1910; Kenneth W. Underwood, *Protestant and Catholic: Religious and Social Interaction in an Industrial Community* (1957; reprint, Westport, Conn.: Greenwood Press, 1973), 226, 236; *Dau's Blue Book for Springfield, 1907* (New York: Dau Publishing Company, 1907); *SR*, July 21, 1919; Underwood, *Protestant and Catholic*, 198–201; Mary Doyle Curran, *The Parish and the Hill* (Boston: Houghton Mifflin, 1948), 49. The Knights of

Columbus is today a multi-class organization, but this is a relatively recent development. As late as the 1950s, a Connecticut priest, concerned that Catholic workers belonged to no religious associations, observed that most workers considered the Knights "to be too high and mighty and expensive." Ronald W. Schatz, "Connecticut's Working Class in the 1950s: A Catholic Perspective," *Labor History*, 25 (1984): 97.

47 *SR*, July 30, 1890; Aug. 18, 1890; Dec. 8, 1890; Dec. 26, 1890; June 22, 1891; Feb. 16, 1891; *HT*, Apr. 4, 1890; Apr. 16, 1890; Apr. 22, 1890; July 16, 1890. A fuller description of the social activities sponsored by German American socialists and the important contributions made by women can be found in Mari Jo Buhle, *Women and Socialism, 1870–1920* (Urbana: University of Illinois Press, 1981), 14–17.

48 *SR*, Aug. 20, 1893; *Holyoke Labor*, Apr. 7, 1894; Oct. 20, 1894; *HT*, Dec. 5, 1894; Dec. 4, 1894; Oct. 16, 1894; *SR*, Sept. 2, 1895; Sept. 3, 1895.

49 *HT*, Nov. 9, 1898; Dec. 13, 1899; July 11, 1900; Nov. 15, 1900; Nov. 17, 1900; Nov. 20, 1900; Nov. 21, 1900; Howard H. Quint, *The Forging of American Socialism: Origins of the Modern Movement* (1953; reprint, Indianapolis: Bobbs-Merrill, 1964), 319–349.

50 *SR*, Feb. 16, 1898; Mar. 11, 1898; *HT*, May 11, 1899; Mar. 27, 1899; Sept. 4, 1901; July 3, 1901.

51 *HT*, Mar. 27, 1899.

52 The letter to DeLeon is quoted in Rebecca Brown, "The Socialist Labor Party in Holyoke, Massachusetts, 1893–1900" (senior thesis, Mt. Holyoke College, 1981), 105; L. Glen Seretan, *Daniel DeLeon: The Odyssey of an American Marxist* (Cambridge: Harvard University Press, 1979), 141–171.

53 *HT*, Sept. 5, 1901; May 17, 1901; Sept. 11, 1902; July 5, 1901.

54 *Messenger*, Apr. 2, 1898; *HT*, Feb. 11, 1903; *Messenger*, June 1, 1901. A rambling oration by one Holyoke priest, warning of socialist expansion, is reprinted in *Messenger*, Feb. 4, 1899.

55 *HT*, Apr. 1, 1901.

56 *HT*, Sept. 11, 1899; Sept. 14, 1899; Dec. 7, 1900; *Messenger*, Nov. 17, 1898. Other articles by Doyle on socialism can be found in ibid., Apr. 7, 1898; May 14, 1898.

57 *Messenger*, Apr. 2, 1898.

CHAPTER SIX: Catholic Trade-Union Respectability, 1906–1920

1 Wyatt E. Harper, *The Story of Holyoke* (Holyoke: N.p., 1973), 126–127; *Springfield Republican* (*SR*), May 2, 1922; Wyatt Harper interview, July 1974, American International College Oral History Collection (AICOHC); George Fitzgerald interview, May 14, 1988, from interviews arranged by Christine

Howard Bailey, Holyoke scholar-in-residence, for "SHIFTING GEARS: The Changing Meaning of Work in Massachusetts, 1920–1980," a project of the Massachusetts Foundation for Humanities and Public Policy (SGP); *SR*, Nov. 22, 1929; *Paper Makers Journal (PMJ)*, 41 (Apr. 1942): 2. In his study Harper provides the names of twenty-one of the group's regulars: they include two Yankees, one German, one Alsatian, and seventeen Irish.

2 *Artisan*, July 26, 1910; Apr. 15, 1908.

3 Ibid., May 16, 1913; Apr. 26, 1914.

4 George Fitzgerald interview, May 14, 1988, notes in author's possession; Wyatt Harper interview, AICOHC; *SR*, July 23, 1934; Oct. 16, 1935; Oct. 27, 1935.

5 *Artisan*, Nov. 27, 1914; *SR*, Oct. 7, 1917; *Artisan*, Dec. 1, 1916; *SR*, Dec. 3, 1917; *Artisan*, Feb. 17, 1909. An *Artisan* editorial attacking the Emerald Club sheds further light on the political dimension of the antagonism between trade unions and the saloon interest. Characterizing the club as one of the city's worst "rum holes," the editorial declared, "Here in Holyoke people are getting tired of the manner in which the 'administration' and its license commission perform its 'duties,' and if something is not done to divorce the saloon from politics a change may be sought." *Artisan*, Sept. 9, 1908. For more on this topic, see Francis G. Couvares's fine analysis of Gilded Age labor temperance in *The Remaking of Pittsburgh: Class and Culture in an Industrializing City, 1877–1919* (Albany: State University of New York Press, 1984), ch. 4.

6 *Artisan*, July 28, 1909; July 4, 1919.

7 Ibid., Apr. 15, 1908; Mar. 5, 1920.

8 Christine Stansell, *City of Women: Sex and Class in New York City, 1789–1860* (New York: Alfred A. Knopf, 1986), 138–144; Barbara Kessler-Harris, *Out to Work: A History of Wage-Earning Women in the United States* (New York: Oxford University Press, 1982), 84–86, 153–154. For a stimulating analysis of how nineteenth-century women workers viewed the family-wage ideal, see Mary H. Blewett, *Men, Women, and Work: Class, Gender, and Protest in the New England Shoe Industry, 1780–1910* (Urbana: University of Illinois Press, 1988), 115–141.

9 Martin J. Sklar, *The Corporate Reconstruction of American Capitalism, 1890–1916: The Market, the Law, and Politics* (Cambridge, Eng.: Cambridge University Press, 1988), 44.

10 Martha May, "The 'Good Managers': Married Working Class Women and Family Budget Studies, 1895–1915," *Labor History*, 25 (1984): 354, 369–371; John R. Commons et al, *History of Labor in the United States* (1918–1935; reprint, New York: Augustus M. Kelley, 1966), vol. 3, 63, 77, 88; AFL statement quoted in Julie A. Matthaei, *An Economic History of Women in America: Women's Work, the Sexual Division of Labor, and the Development of Capitalism* (New York: Schocken Books, 1982), 215.

11 Hasia R. Diner, *Erin's Daughters in America: Irish Immigrant Women in the*

Nineteenth Century (Baltimore: Johns Hopkins University Press, 1983), 51–52; Timothy J. Meagher, " 'The Lord Is Not Dead': Cultural and Social Change among the Irish in Worcester, Massachusetts, 1880–1920" (Ph.D. diss., Brown University, 1982), 119, 241–243, 254–257; Constance M. Green, *Holyoke, Massachusetts: A Case History of the Industrial Revolution in America* (New Haven: Yale University Press, 1939), 370; George Fitzgerald interview, May 14, 1988, notes in author's possession; Ellen Horgan Biddle, "The American Catholic Irish Family," in *Ethnic Families in America: Patterns and Variations*, ed. Charles H. Mindel and Robert W. Habenstein (New York: Elsevier, 1976), 95.

12 Biddle, "American Catholic Irish Family," 95; *Artisan*, Feb. 27, 1914.

13 John A. Ryan, *A Living Wage* (1906; reprint, New York: Macmillan, 1920), 85–88.

14 Ibid., 101; John A. Ryan, *The Church and Socialism: and Other Essays* (Washington, D.C.: University Press, 1919), 232–234.

15 Ryan, *A Living Wage*, 76; *Catholic Mirror*, 4 (Oct 1924): 22; Ryan, *Church and Socialism*, 74–75. Trade unions opposed discriminatory pay for the same reasons stated by Ryan. See Kessler-Harris, *Out to Work*, 156.

16 *SR*, July 10, 1911; July 11, 1911; July 14, 1911; Oct. 1, 1911; Oct. 29, 1911; Jan. 15, 1912.

17 Matthew Burns, "History of the International Brotherhood of Paper Makers" (unpublished ms., United Paperworkers International Union, Nashville, Tennessee, 1939), 59; *Holyoke Transcript (HT)*, Feb. 4, 1907; May 25, 1907; *Artisan*, Mar. 17, 1911. Recognizing the degree of fear that the trust had instilled in local paper workers, an *Artisan* editorial assured those who joined the union that, until a comfortable majority had sent in their applications, "No one will know you have joined unless you tell." *Artisan*, Jan. 20, 1911. A BACK TENDER also complained that machine tenders refused to instruct their helpers in the mysteries of the fourdrinier, because they feared they might lose their machines.

18 *SR*, Jan. 12, 1912; *Artisan*, May 3, 1912. Despite the consequences of the strike for capital, local paper manufacturers continued to look to the finishing department for savings. In 1916, fifty plater women at the Chemical Paper Company walked out, complaining that the piece-work system under which they labored "is a driving system and takes it out of the employes in greater measure than they are compensated for." *SR*, Sept. 4, 1914; Feb. 7, 1916; *Artisan*, May 5, 1916; *SR*, Sept. 16, 1916.

19 *SR*, Feb. 5, 1912; Feb. 12, 1912; Feb. 13, 1912; Feb. 15, 1912; Feb. 19, 1912; *Artisan*, Feb. 16, 1912; *SR*, Feb. 21, 1912; *Artisan*, May 3, 1912.

20 *SR*, Jan. 21, 1915; Jan. 28, 1915; Feb. 4, 1915; Feb. 7, 1915; Feb. 13, 1915; Feb. 15, 1915; *Artisan*, Jan. 22, 1915; Jan. 29, 1915; Feb. 5, 1915; Feb. 26, 1915; Mar. 5, 1915; Mar. 12, 1915; Mar. 19, 1915. The *Artisan* editorial lambasting Fowler may also have been directed at the city's Protestant churches. Although the Reverend E. B. Robinson, pastor of Grace Church, a working class

congregation located in the lower wards, supported the demand for a living wage, a more typical attitude was that of Reverend J. B. Lyon at Second Baptist Church: "Too much attention was paid to the subject of wages by the worker," he told his affluent congregation, "and too little to study, the reading of books, and other outside subjects." *SR*, Sept. 4, 1911; May 10, 1909. Unfortunately, local sources provide no evidence as to what criteria the striking women used to define a living wage.

21 *SR*, Mar. 15, 1912; J. A. Burke to T. Parsons, Mar. 12, 1912; T. Parsons to J. A. Burke, Apr. 9, 1912; J. A. Burke to T. Parsons, Dec. 17, 1912, vol. PD-9, J. A. Burke to E. Lovering, May 17, 1916, vol. PD-10; E. Lovering to J. A. Burke, Apr. 10, 1918, vol. PD-12; H. L. Sigourney to J. A. Burke, Dec. 2, 1919, vol. PD-15, all in Lyman Mills Papers, Baker Library, Harvard Business School (LMP). The Farr Alpaca Company also adjusted its wage schedule according to the outcome of labor struggles at Lawrence. Florence Cornwell Hutner, "The Farr Alpaca Company: A Case Study in Business History," *Smith College Studies in History*, 37 (1951): 59-60.

22 E. Lovering to J. A. Burke, Apr. 14, 1916, vol. PD-10, LMP; *SR*, Aug. 9, 1918; J. A. Burke to E. Lovering, June 7, 1918, vol. PD-13, all in LMP.

23 J. A. Burke to T. Parsons, Mar. 31, 1914, vol. PD-11; J. A. Burke to E. Lovering, Aug. 23, 1917, vol. PD-12; J. A. Burke to E. Lovering, June 7, 1918, vol. PD-13, all in LMP. In 1913, Farr Alpaca announced a similar changeover. *SR*, Feb. 8, 1911.

24 The study of geographical and job mobility discussed in the text was based on data taken from the 1905 and 1915 Holyoke city directories. To improve its accuracy, the 1907 and 1910 directories were also consulted.

25 Green, *Holyoke*, 68-70, 201-202, 366.

26 This paragraph is based largely on Peter Haebler, "Habitants in Holyoke: The Development of the French-Canadian Community in a Massachusetts City, 1865-1910" (Ph.D. diss., University of New Hampshire, 1976), 24, 109-127. The quotation is from Jacques Ducharme, *The Shadows of the Trees: The Story of French-Canadians in New England* (New York: Harper and Brothers, 1943), 84. For examples of analyses that overstate the docility of French Canadian Catholics, see Robert C. Dexter, "Fifty-Fifty Americans," *World's Work*, 48 (1924): 366-371; and Calvin E. Amaron's wild-eyed, anti-Catholic screed, *Your Heritage: or New England Threatened* (Springfield, Mass.: French Protestant College, 1891).

27 Christine Howard Bailey, "Precious Blood: Work, Family, and Community in South Holyoke, 1920-1970," unpublished ms., 1988, in author's possession, 17-21; Jeanne Fleury interview, Apr. 28, 1988; Cecile Benoit, Doris Kos, and Juliette Dandelin interview, Apr. 21, 1988; Mary Marconi interview, Apr. 26, 1988; Cecile Barthello interview, Apr. 26, 1988, all in SGP; Ernest Bernard Guillet, "French Ethnic Literature and Culture in an American City: Holyoke, Massachusetts" (Ph.D. diss., University of Massachusetts at Am-

herst, 1978), 150–151, 158–162, 169–171; Madeleine Biehler interview, Apr. 28, 1988, SGP.

28 Haebler, "Habitants," 24–27; Guillet, "French Culture in Holyoke," 19–28; Ducharme, *Shadows*, 92; Guillet, "French Culture in Holyoke," 64–65; Pierre Anctil, "Aspects of Class Ideology in a New England Minority: The Franco-Americans of Woonsocket, Rhode Island (1865–1929)" (Ph.D. diss., New School for Social Research, 1980), 175–178. In Ducharme's novel on French Canadian Holyoke, the decision of a second-generation Franco-American couple to educate their children in a public school provoked the most serious crisis to disturb the family on which the narrative focused. *The Delusson Family* (New York: Funk and Wagnalls, 1939), 280–286.

29 Dyke Hendrickson, *Quiet Presence: Histoires de Franco–Americains en New England* (Portland, Maine: Guy Gannett Publishing Company, 1980), 201, 213; Haebler, "Habitants," 136–139; Gerard J. Brault, *The French-Canadian Heritage in New England* (Hanover, N.H.: University Press of New England, 1986), 76–77; Guillet, "French Culture in Holyoke," 90, 96–97, 115–120.

30 Ducharme, *Delusson Family*, 23; Green, *Holyoke*, 371; Cecile Benoit, Doris Kos, and Juliette Dandelin interview.

31 Green, *Holyoke*, 337; Philip T. Silvia, Jr., "The 'Flint Affair': French-Canadian Struggle for *Survivance*," *Catholic Historical Review* 45 (July 1979): 433; Paul Kleppner, *The Third Electoral System, 1853–1892: Parties, Voters, and Political Cultures* (Chapel Hill: University of North Carolina Press, 1979), 151; Meagher, " 'The Lord Is Not Dead'," 378–384, 479–481, 552–553. Irish irritation at the "foreignness" of French Canadians persisted for many years in Holyoke. Jacques Ducharme recounted the following conversation with an Irish census taker who was annoyed by the number of elderly French Canadians he had interviewed who spoke little or no English:

"Why in hell don't they learn English?"
"Are they breaking any laws?" I asked.
"That isn't the point. The language of the country is English. Why don't they speak it?"
"All right," I replied, "Why don't you people speak Irish?"
"Why should we?"

Ducharme, *Shadows*, 105–106.

32 Haebler, "Habitants," 81; Green, *Holyoke*, 369–370; Philip T. Silvia, Jr., "Neighbors from the North: French-Canadian Immigrants vs. Trade Unionism in Fall River, Massachusetts," in *The Little Canadas of New England*, ed. Claire Quintal (Worcester, Mass.: French Institute/Assumption College, 1983), 52–55; Massachusetts Bureau of Statistics of Labor (MBSL), *Twelth Annual Report*, 1881, 470; William MacDonald, "The French Canadians in New England," *Quarterly Journal of Economics*, 12 (1898): 265, 271–272; Dexter, "Fifty-Fifty

Americans," 366–371. Perhaps the harshest characterization of French Canadians came from Fred Beal, the Lawrence-born Yankee radical, who called them "born slaves." *Proletarian Journey: New England, Gastonia, Moscow* (New York: Hillman-Curl, 1937), 29.

33 MBSL, *Thirteenth Annual Report*, 1882, 18–19, 25–26; Ducharme, *Shadows*, 3; Hendrickson, *Quiet Presence*, 4, 86; Anctil, "Aspects of Class Ideology in a New England Minority," 68–70; Daniel J. Walkowitz, *Worker City, Company Town: Iron and Cotton Worker Protest in Troy and Cohoes, New York, 1855–1884* (Urbana: University of Illinois Press, 1978), 220–229, 249–250; John T. Cumbler, *Working-Class Community in Industrial America: Work, Leisure, and Struggle in Two Industrial Cities, 1880–1930* (Westport, Conn.: Greenwood Press, 1979), 174–194.

34 Ducharme, *Shadows*, 14; Tamara K. Hareven, *Family Time and Industrial Time: The Relationship between the Family and Work in a New England Industrial Community* (Cambridge, Eng.: Cambridge University Press, 1982), 85–119; Louis Gendron interview, May 10, 1988, SGP.

35 Ducharme, *Shadows*, 160; Hareven, *Family Time and Industrial Time*, 189–217; Katharine DuPre Lumpkin and Dorothy Wolff Douglas, *Child Workers in America* (New York: Robert M. McBride and Company, 1937), 141–142; Amy Hewes, "Children Leaving School for Work: Holyoke, Massachusetts, 1920," Apr.–May 1920, in Amy Hewes file, College Archives, Mt. Holyoke College, South Hadley, Massachusetts; Cecile Benoit, Doris Kos, and Juliette Dandelin interview.

36 C. Stewart Doty, *Franco-Americans: New England Life Histories from the Federal Writers' Project, 1938–1939* (Orono: University of Maine at Orono Press, 1985), 60–62.

37 Hareven, *Family Time and Industrial Time*, 20, 263–266, 284; Doty, *Franco-Americans*, 19–20. The discussion of changes in the ethnic composition of the Holyoke overseer force is based on data compiled from the 1900 and 1910 manuscript population schedules of the federal census.

38 *HT*, June 4, 1900; MacDonald, "French Canadians," 265. At Manchester's Amoskeag Mills, where union organizers made little headway before World War I, the proportion of French Canadians in the overseer force was significantly lower than in Holyoke. Hareven, *Family Time and Industrial Time*, 20, 263–266, 284.

39 Doty, *Franco-Americans*, 24–25; Hareven, *Family Time and Industrial Time*, 304–306; Ducharme, *Delusson Family*, 25. "Philippe Lemay" was a pseudonym devised by the Federal Writers' Project employee who conducted the Manchester interviews.

40 Hareven, *Family Time and Industrial Time*, 50–53, 85–119, 132–135; George Fitzgerald interview, May 14, 1988; Hareven, *Family Time and Industrial Time*, 101.

41 Green, *Holyoke*, 370; *Artisan*, Feb. 9, 1917. Further evidence of CLU

Notes to Pages 144–150

support of Americanization efforts can be found in *Artisan*, Nov. 29, 1918; *SR*, Sept. 26, 1921; United Brotherhood of Carpenters and Joiners, Holyoke District Council, Minutes, Dec. 9, 1919, Archives and Manuscripts, University of Massachusetts at Amherst Library (Carps, HDC). Trade-union support of Americanization sometimes caused dissension within the ranks of organized labor itself. In 1918, when the district council passed a resolution requiring carpenters' locals to "transact all business in the English language," the French-speaking membership of Local 390 vigorously protested the action. Ibid., 19 Nov 1918.

42 Ryan, *Church and Socialism*, 74–75, 146–148.

43 *Artisan*, Aug. 18, 1911; Aug. 25, 1916; Apr. 28, 1916; Aug. 4, 1916. Parting company with the CLU, Eagle Lodge endorsed the 1916 proposal to form an independent labor party. Harris Zwerling, "Eagle Lodge, 1914–1922: A Case Study of AF of L Craft Unionism" (unpublished seminar paper, University of Massachusetts at Amherst History Department), 20.

44 *Artisan*, Apr. 13, 1917; May 11, 1917; Mar. 22, 1918; Sept. 14, 1917; Jan. 10, 1919; Nov. 21, 1919; Mar. 5, 1920.

45 *SR*, May 7, 1906; July 23, 1906; *HT*, Nov. 12, 1906; *Artisan*, Nov. 25, 1908; Feb. 4, 1910; May 20, 1908; Apr. 21, 1909; Jan. 22, 1915; *SR*, Apr. 26, 1913; July 14, 1913.

46 *Artisan*, Jan. 27, 1913; July 4, 1913; Aug. 1, 1913; Dec. 5, 1913. While all sources agree that White initially obtained the mayorality through Whiting's sponsorship, there is some question concerning the degree of independence he later carved out for himself. Compare, for example, *SR*, Nov. 20, 1913, with *Artisan*, Feb. 12, 1915.

47 *Artisan*, Nov. 29, 1912; Dec. 7, 1917; Nov. 29, 1918; *SR*, Dec. 15, 1919.

48 Zwerling, "Eagle Lodge," 21; *SR*, June 14, 1920; *PMJ*, 14 (Oct 1915): 33; Richard M. Abrams, *Conservativism in a Progressive Age: Massachusetts Politics, 1900–1912* (Cambridge: Harvard University Press, 1964), 231–234, 257–260.

49 Carps, HDC, Nov. 20, 1917; Apr. 15, 1918; *SR*, Jan. 8, 1918; *HT*, Dec. 17, 1924; Dec. 20, 1924; Fred Garvin interview, Mar. 13, 1979, AICOHC; Kenneth W. Underwood, *Protestant and Catholic: Religious and Social Interaction in an Industrial Community* (1957; reprint, Westport, Conn.: Greenwood Press, 1973), 288; Green, *Holyoke*, 275; George Fitzgerald interview, Apr. 14, 1988, notes in author's possession.

50 *SR*, Sept. 2, 1916; Sept. 4, 1916; Nov. 10, 1919; *Greater Holyoke*, 2 (midsummer 1920): 5, 9–10, 16.

51 *SR*, Apr. 1, 1921; June 17, 1921; Carps, HDC, June 28, 1921; Irving Bernstein, *The Lean Years: A History of the American Worker, 1920–1933* (Baltimore: Penguin Books, 1966), 146–157; Commons, et al, *History of Labor*, vol. 4, 489–514.

52 Haebler, "Habitants," 270; Kleppner, *Third Electoral System*, 151–152, 201, 348–352; Abrams, *Massachusetts Politics*, 50–51; Donald B. Cole, *Immigrant*

City: Lawrence, Massachusetts, 1845–1921 (Chapel Hill: University of North Carolina Press, 1963), 149–151; Ronald A. Petrin, "Culture, Community, and Politics: French-Canadians in Massachusetts, 1885–1915," in *The Little Canadas of New England*, 66–83.

53 Haebler, "Habitants," 257–258, 281–286, 296–300; Paul Kleppner, *Continuity and Change in Electoral Politics, 1893–1928* (Westport, Conn.: Greenwood Press, 1987), 200. Elin Anderson reported similar differences in voter behavior among the Irish and French Canadians of Burlington, Vermont, in her study, *We Americans: A Study of Cleavage in an American City* (1937; reprint, New York: Russell and Russell, 1967), 209–210.

54 Haebler, "Habitants," 296–298; Ducharme, *Delusson Family*, 191; Anderson, *We Americans*, 29, 216–217.

55 Haebler, "Habitants," 240–245. Such social differentiation among French Canadians was not unique to Holyoke. Although they did not elaborate on the point, several New Hampshireites interviewed by Dyke Hendrickson also mentioned a Franco-American elite "that had its own cultural level but provided no conscious assistance for the lower social classes." *Quiet Presence*, 201, 213.

56 Ducharme, *Delusson Family*, 40, 67, 73–74.

57 Ibid., 114–115, 126–128, 139, 168.

58 Haebler, "Habitants," 296–300; Anctil, "Aspects of Class Ideology in a New England Minority." Holyoke's most successful French Canadian politician during this period, city treasurer Pierre Bonvouloir, was also a Democrat.

59 Mary Doyle Curran, *The Parish and the Hill* (Boston: Houghton Mifflin, 1948), 150.

60 *Artisan*, Nov. 29, 1918; Kleppner, *Continuity and Change*.

61 *Artisan*, Mar. 24, 1909; Apr. 22, 1908; Jan. 13, 1911; Nov. 24, 1916; Hutner, "Farr Alpaca Company," 57–72.

62 *Artisan*, Mar. 24, 1909.

63 Ibid., Mar. 15, 1912; Sept. 16, 1910. Other articles and editorials calling for worker–middle-class cooperation can be found in ibid., Apr. 29, 1908; June 10, 1908; Nov. 11, 1908; May 24, 1912.

64 Ibid., Feb. 16, 1912; Feb. 23, 1912; Sept. 5, 1913; Apr. 14, 1909; Nov. 10, 1916; Nov. 24, 1916; Mar. 2, 1917.

CHAPTER SEVEN: The Church and Labor, 1920–1945

1 Robert A. Murray, *Red Scare: A Study in National Hysteria, 1919–1920* (Minneapolis: University of Minnesota Press, 1955); William E. Leuchtenburg, *The Perils of Prosperity, 1914–1932* (Chicago: University of Chicago Press, 1958), 66–103, 188.

2 Irving Bernstein, *The Lean Years: A History of the American Worker, 1920–1933* (Baltimore: Penguin Books, 1966); J. Joseph Huthmacher, *Massachusetts: People and Politics, 1919–1933* (Cambridge: Harvard University Press, 1959), 126, 157–160; Massachusetts Department of Labor and Industries, *Statistics of Manufactures in Massachusetts, 1920–1938*, Public Document No. 36, 24.

3 The Bishops' Program is reprinted in Aaron Abell, ed., *American Catholic Thought on Social Questions* (Indianapolis: Bobbs-Merrill, 1968), 325–348. For a concise summary of what Father Ryan considered the document's principal features, see Neil Betten, *Catholic Activism and the Industrial Worker* (Gainesville: University Presses of Florida, 1976), 37. The most comprehensive analysis of the Bishops' Program is Joseph M. McShane, S.J., *"Sufficiently Radical": Catholicism, Progressivism, and the Bishops' Program of 1919* (Washington, D.C.: Catholic University of America Press, 1986).

4 Abell, *American Catholic Thought on Social Questions*, 330, 348.

5 Aaron I. Abell, *American Catholicism and Social Action: A Search for Social Justice* (Notre Dame, Ind.: University of Notre Dame Press, 1963), 204–205; McShane, *"Sufficiently Radical"*, 209–215.

6 Abell, *American Catholicism and Social Action*, 224; Betten, *Catholic Activism and the Industrial Worker*, 38; McShane, *"Sufficiently Radical"*, 269–270.

7 *Springfield Republican (SR)*, Sept. 3, 1923.

8 Donna Merwick, *Boston's Priests, 1848–1910: A Study of Social and Intellectual Change* (Cambridge: Harvard University Press, 1973), 182–192, 196; Robert O'Leary, "Brahmins and Bully Boys: William Henry O'Connell and Massachusetts Politics," *Historical Journal of Massachusetts* 10 (1982): 3–19; Charles J. V. Murphy, "Pope of New England: A Portrait of Cardinal O'Connell," *Outlook and Independent*, 153 (Oct. 1929): 286.

9 The 1912 pastoral letter was reprinted as William Henry Cardinal O'Connell, *Wage Earners' and Employers' Rights and Duties* (Boston: Boston School of Political Economy, 1913). A later pastoral letter on industrial relations emphasizing many of the same themes can be found in *Pilot*, Nov. 19, 1921.

10 *Pilot*, Feb. 23, 1923.

11 Ibid., Apr. 18, 1919; *SR*, Feb. 4, 1920; July 8, 1922; *Catholic Mirror*, 3 (June 1923): 35; David Goldstein and Martha Moore Avery, *Socialism: The Nation of Fatherless Children* (Boston: Thomas J. Flynn, 1911); *Catholic Mirror*, 7 (Feb. 1927): 28–29.

12 *Catholic Mirror*, 11 (Apr. 1931): 11; James Irene Gallagher, S.S.J., "Analytical Index to the *Catholic Mirror*" (MLS diss., Catholic University of America, 1967), i–ii; *Catholic Mirror*, 7 (June 1927): 10. According to Timothy Meagher, members of the Knights viewed themselves as Catholic "militants." " 'The Lord Is Not Dead': Cultural and Social Change among the Irish in Worcester, Massachusetts, 1880–1920" (Ph.D. diss., Brown University, 1982), 585–586.

NOTES TO PAGES 163-167

13 Dorothy Hamel interview, May 1974; Blanche Manuello interview, May 13, 1974; Oria Ayotte interview, Aug. 22, 1974; Catherine Hart interview, Aug. 1974; William Hart interview, Apr. 13, 1974; Nora Labrecque interview, Aug. 22, 1974, all in American International College Oral History Collection (AICOHC); Robert W. Dunn and Jack Hardy, *Labor and Textiles* (New York: International Publishers, 1931), 220–227; Herbert J. Lahne, *The Cotton Mill Worker* (New York: Farrar and Rinehart, 1944), 208–214.

14 Frances Cornwell Hutner, "The Farr Alpaca Company: A Case Study in Business History," *Smith College Studies in History*, 37 (1951): 62–69.

15 Constance M. Green, *Holyoke, Massachusetts: A Case History of the Industrial Revolution in America* (New Haven: Yale University Press, 1939), 242; J. A. Burke to E. Lovering, Aug. 26, 1918, vol. PD–13, Lyman Mills Papers, Baker Library, Harvard Business School (LMP). Burke provided further evidence of Farr's commanding position in the Holyoke labor market in a 1916 letter informing his superiors that a recent pay increase at the Skinner Mills could be safely ignored unless Farr Alpaca "should fall into line." In which case, "the effect on the other textile mills would be disastrous." J. A. Burke to E. Lovering, May 17, 1916, vol. PD–10, LMP.

16 Anna Sullivan interview, Spring 1974, AICOHC; T. W. Vetterling to Hamilton Watch Company, Lancaster, Pa., May 4, 1920, and W. E. Crosier to Falco Athletic Association, July 6, 1922, both in Employees' Cooperative Association Letterbook, Farr Alpaca Papers, Connecticut Valley Historical Museum (FAP).

17 Nora Labrecque interview; Anna Sullivan interview, both in AICOHC; Daniel Nelson, *Managers and Workers: Origins of the New Factory System in the United States, 1880–1920* (Madison: University of Wisconsin Press, 1975), ch. 4.

18 *SR*, Dec. 14, 1920; Jan. 4, 1921.

19 *SR*, Apr. 12, 1920; Jan. 13, 1921; Carey statement quoted in Harris Zwerling, "Eagle Lodge, 1914–1922: A Case Study of AF of L Craft Unionism" (unpublished seminar paper, University of Massachusetts at Amherst History Department), 51.

20 Raymond Beaudry interview, July 3, 1984, notes in author's possession.

21 Green, *Holyoke*, 188–193, 231–235; Memorandum to the Directors, June 13, 1934, Board of Directors file; Minutes of Joint Conference No. 4, Jan. 17, 1947, both in Master Labor File, American Writing Paper Company Records, Archives and Manuscripts, University of Massachusetts at Amherst Library (AWP Co Rcds); Alfred D. Chandler, Jr., *The Visible Hand: The Managerial Revolution in American Business* (Cambridge: Harvard University Press, 1977), 354; T. H. Blodgett to E. C. Reid, May 21, 1946, Master Labor File, AWP Co Rcds.

22 Minutes of meeting of Executive and Advisory Committees, Nov. 10, 1918, Board of Directors File, AWP Co Rcds; *Eagle "A" Unity*, 1 (Aug. 1918): 1; 2 (Feb. 1920): 1.

23 General Order No. 189, Jan. 8, 1920, Master Labor File, AWP Co Rcds; *SR*, Mar. 21, 1927; Mar. 5, 1928; *Paper Makers Journal (PMJ)*, 27 (Mar.–Apr. 1929): 30; *SR*, Dec. 24, 1931; Nov. 11, 1932; Feb. 15, 1935; Records of Eagle Lodge, Minutes, Aug. 21, 1938, Archives and Manuscripts, University of Massachusetts at Amherst Library.

24 *SR*, Aug. 25, 1923; Aug. 26, 1923; Aug. 28, 1923; Aug. 30, 1923; Green, *Holyoke*, 235, 394; *PMJ*, 27 (Dec. 1928): 27.

25 The best examination of what seniority meant to workers is Ronald Schatz, *The Electrical Workers: A History of Labor at General Electric and Westinghouse, 1923–1960* (Urbana: University of Illinois Press, 1983), ch. 5.

26 Hareven, *Family Time and Industrial Time: The Relationship between the Family and Work in a New England Industrial Community* (Cambridge, Eng.: Cambridge University Press, 1982), 62–66; Anna Sullivan interview, AICOHC. For a more extensive examination of textile paternalism, see Philip Scranton's important article, "Varieties of Paternalism: Industrial Structures and the Social Relations of Production in American Textiles," *American Quarterly* 36 (1984): 235–257.

27 Dorothy Hamel interview, AICOHC; Mary Doyle Curran, *The Parish and the Hill* (Boston: Houghton Mifflin, 1948), 101.

28 Paul H. Douglas and William A. Orton, *Labor Problems in Modern Society* (Holyoke: Alden Press, 1924). I am indebted to George Fitzgerald for making this pamphlet available to me.

29 *SR*, Dec. 6, 1927; Apr. 18, 1927; *Holyoke Transcript (HT)*, Nov. 12, 1939; *Catholic Mirror*, 7 (Jan. 1927): 9.

30 Kate Sargent, "Catholicism in Massachusetts," *The Forum*, 74 (1925): 738–739; *HT*, Oct. 13, 1924; Oct. 27, 1924. Reformers began campaigning for a child-labor amendment after the Supreme Court struck down federal child-labor laws enacted in 1916 and 1919. Katharine DuPre Lumpkin and Dorothy Wolff Douglas, *Child Workers in America* (New York: Robert M. McBride and Company, 1937), 204–205, 265.

31 *Pilot*, Nov. 1, 1924; *HT*, Oct. 30, 1924; Abell, *American Catholicism and Social Action*, 228.

32 O'Connell, *Rights and Duties*, 4–6; *Pilot*, Jan. 28, 1919.

33 *Pilot*, Jan. 10, 1925.

34 *SR*, Jan. 25, 1935. Although this quotation is taken from a discussion of the child-labor amendment at the 1935 state AFL convention, it is reasonably safe to assume that such sentiments were, if anything, even more prevalent a decade earlier. John A. Ryan, *The Church and Socialism: and Other Essays* (Washington, D.C.: University Press, 1919), 74.

35 *SR*, Mar. 4, 1937.

36 Francis L. Broderick, *Right Reverend New Dealer: John A. Ryan* (New York: Macmillan, 1963), 130; McShane, *"Sufficiently Radical"*, 243–244.

37 *Pilot*, Oct. 18, 1924; Nov. 8, 1924; John Deedy, "William Henry O'Connell:

The Prince of Yesterday's Prototypes," *The Critic*, 35 (Summer 1977): 96; McShane, *"Sufficiently Radical,"* 185–186; Charles H. Trout, *Boston, The Great Depression, and the New Deal* (New York: Oxford University Press, 1977), 22, 262; David J. O'Brien, *American Catholics and Social Reform: The New Deal Years* (New York: Oxford University Press, 1964), 44, 131.

38 *HT*, Nov. 5, 1924. In speaking to these workers, the church and its allies focused attention on Section 1 of the proposed amendment, which declared: "The Congress shall have the power to limit, regulate, and prohibit the labor of persons under eighteen years of age." Lumpkin and Douglas, *Child Workers*, vi.

39 Gerard J. Brault, *The French-Canadian Heritage in New England* (Hanover, N.H.: University Press of New England, 1986), 92–97.

40 *Catholic Mirror* 6 (Mar. 1926): 29; 7 (Dec. 1926): 23; 7 (Jan. 1927): 11.

41 O'Brien, *American Catholics and Social Reform*, 104; *Catholic Mirror*, 10 (Aug. 1930): 9; 10 (Dec. 1929): 30; *SR*, Oct. 12, 1931; *Catholic Mirror*, 12 (Nov. 1931): 9; 11 (Jan. 1931): 9. A translation of *Quadraggesimo Anno* is reprinted in Oswald Von-Nell Breuning, S.J., *Reorganization of Social Economy: The Social Encyclicals Developed and Explained* (New York: Bruce Publishing Company, 1936), 395–442. Some Catholic spokesmen continued to view hard times through traditional prisms. Fulton J. Sheen, for example, argued that the depression was "caused by moral rather than economic ills." *Catholic Mirror*, 12 (Nov. 1931): 5–6.

42 *Catholic Mirror*, 11 (July 1931): 5–6; 12 (Sept. 1933): 7, 11–13, 16–17.

43 Trout, *Boston*, 260–262; *Catholic Mirror*, 14 (Dec. 1933): 25; 15 (Jan. 1935): 5, 9.

44 *SR*, Nov. 7, 1928; Nov. 8, 1928; Apr. 27, 1932; Nov. 9, 1932; Aug. 16, 1933; Aug. 28, 1933; Mar. 12, 1934; Jan. 28, 1935; Nov. 26, 1934; Nora Quinn interview, Apr. 8, 1974; Ann Engel interview, Nov. 15, 1974, both in AICOHC.

45 Hutner, "Farr Alpaca Company," 60–65, 71, 75–80, 99–100; Curran, *The Parish and the Hill*, 101–103.

46 *SR*, June 12, 1933; July 14, 1933; Irving Bernstein, *Turbulent Years: A History of the American Worker, 1933–1941* (Boston: Houghton Mifflin, 1967), 301–302; *SR*, July 19, 1933; July 20, 1933; July 21, 1933; Aug. 8, 1933; July 25, 1933; July 26, 1933; July 29, 1933; Dec. 11, 1933; June 30, 1934; Aug. 25, 1934.

47 Bernstein, *Turbulent Years*, 300–315; Lahne, *Cotton Mill Worker*, 224–231; *SR*, Sept. 1, 1934; Sept. 6, 1934; Sept. 8, 1934; Sept. 20, 1934; Aug. 29, 1934; Aug. 31, 1934.

48 *SR*, Feb. 11, 1936; Feb. 13, 1936; Apr. 16, 1936; May 14, 1936; May 24, 1936; May 25, 1936.

49 Bernstein, *Turbulent Years*, 616–619, 641–646; George Fitzgerald interview, May 14, 1988, from interviews arranged by Christine Howard Bailey, Holyoke scholar-in-residence for "SHIFTING GEARS: The Changing Meaning of Work in Massachusetts, 1920–1980," a project of the Massachusetts

Foundation for Humanities and Public Policy (SGP); George Fitzgerald interview, Jan. 19, 1985, notes in author's possession; Anna Sullivan interview, AICOHC; *Textile Labor*, Sept. 2, 1950.

50 *SR*, Apr. 21, 1937; Feb. 19, 1938; Apr. 25, 1938; Apr. 27, 1938; May 2, 1938; May 15, 1938; May 26, 1938.

51 Hutner, "Farr Alpaca Company," 85; George Fitzgerald interview, Jan. 19, 1985; Edward A. Vanasse and Lionel J. Jubinville to Board of Directors, Aug. 5, 1938, Directors File, FAP; *SR*, Jan. 11, 1939.

52 Kenneth W. Underwood, *Protestant and Catholic: Religious and Social Interaction in an Industrial Community* (1957; reprint, Westport, Conn.: Greenwood Press, 1973), 116, 262–263; *Catholic Mirror* 18 (Sept. 1938): 25.

53 *SR*, Sept. 26, 1921; *Catholic Mirror*, 13 (Mar. 1933): 14; 14 (Aug. 1934): 3; 17 (Nov. 1936): 5; 19 (Dec. 1938): 35; 19 (Mar. 1939): 6; 20 (Feb. 1940): 27; 18 (July 1938): 8. The nature of hierarchical authority in the Springfield diocese is examined in Underwood, *Protestant and Catholic*, 114–117.

54 Betten, *Catholic Activism and the Industrial Worker*, chs. 5, 7; *Catholic Mirror*, 17 (July 1937): 17–19; 17 (Feb. 1937): 9–10; 21 (June 1941): 27–28; 18 (Sept. 1938): 7.

55 *Catholic Mirror*, 20 (Nov. 1939): 23; 17 (Nov. 1936): 4–5; Underwood, *Protestant and Catholic*, 358–359.

56 Underwood, *Protestant and Catholic*, 263; Betten, *Catholic Activism and the Industrial Worker*, 77–84, 124–125, 149; O'Brien, *American Catholics and Social Reform*, 81–84, 95–96; Joshua B. Freeman, *In Transit: The Transport Workers Union in New York City, 1933–1966* (New York: Oxford University Press, 1989), 105–106, 148–149; John Cooney, *The American Pope: The Life and Times of Francis Cardinal Spellman* (New York: Times Books, 1984).

CHAPTER EIGHT: Unions, Labor Markets, and Deindustrialization

1 Constance M. Green, *Holyoke, Massachusetts: A Case History of the Industrial Revolution in America* (New Haven: Yale University Press, 1939), 73–74, 87–88; Judith A. McGaw, *Most Wonderful Machine: Mechanization and Social Change in Berkshire Paper Making, 1801–1885* (Princeton: Princeton University Press, 1987), 26; John P. Hickey, "The Holyoke Area Paper Industry, 1899–1951" (M.A. Thesis, University of Massachusetts at Amherst, 1953), 99.

2 Hickey, "Holyoke Paper Industry," 99, 106–107, 112–113; McGaw, *Most Wonderful Machine*, 202–206.

3 Hickey, "Holyoke Paper Industry," 113; Daniel Nelson, *Managers and Workers: Origins of the Factory System in the United States, 1880–1920* (Madison: University of Wisconsin Press, 1975), 17–23.

NOTES TO PAGES 185 – 189

4 Robert M. MacDonald, "Pulp and Paper," in Lloyd G. Reynolds and Cynthia H. Taft, *The Evolution of Wage Structure* (New Haven: Yale University Press, 1956), 101; Hickey, "Holyoke Paper Industry," 5–32, 106. For a convincing and lucid explanation of how combinations like American Writing Paper lost market share, see Naomi Lamoreaux's examination of the International Paper Company in *The Great Merger Movement in American Business, 1895–1904* (Cambridge, Eng.: Cambridge University Press, 1985), 138–141.

5 Minutes of meeting of Executive and Advisory Committees, May 12, 1920, Board of Directors File, American Writing Paper Company Records, Archives and Manuscripts, University of Massachusetts at Amherst Library (AWP Co Rcds); William H. Knowles and Yereth Knowles, "History of the International Brotherhood of Paper Makers" (unpublished ms., United Paperworkers International Union, Nashville, Tennessee, 1948), 95–98.

6 *Springfield Republican* (SR), May 16, 1927; June 24, 1927; Feb. 4, 1929; Mar. 30, 1931; July 17, 1931; July 17, 1933; July 29, 1933; Aug. 9, 1933; Aug. 11, 1933; June 4, 1934; William McFadden interview, Aug. 5, 1974, American International College Oral History Collection (AICOHC). It should be added that rag-and-finishing-department workers had their own reservations about merging with Eagle Lodge. As one machine tender who regretted the separation remarked, "They felt we were always getting the cream of the crop." Paul Chamberlain interview, Mar. 20, 1978, AICOHC.

7 *SR*, June 12, 1937; Official Report of the Proceeding before the National Labor Relations Board, May 7, 1951, CIO Raid Folder, Master Labor File, AWP Co Rcds; Irving Brotslaw, "Trade Unionism in the Pulp and Paper Industry" (Ph.D. diss., University of Wisconsin, 1964), 169–170, 173.

8 *Paper Makers Journal* (PMJ), 36 (Apr. 1937): 36; 37 (Aug. 1938): 28; W. J. Norton to L. M. Yoerg, Dec. 5, 1938, Master Labor File, AWP Co Rcds.

9 H. T. Martin to Manufacturers' Group, June 22, 1940, July 31, 1940; W. J. Norton to T. H. Blodgett, July 6, 1940, Master Labor file, all in AWP Co Rcds.

10 H. T. Martin to Manufacturers' Group, Aug. 5, 1940, Sept. 9, 1940, Oct. 22, 1940, all in Master Labor file, AWP Co Rcds; *PMJ*, 39 (Oct. 1940): 26.

11 Robert M. MacDonald, "Pulp and Paper," 120–123, 132–133, 144–145; H. T. Martin to Manufacturers' Group, June 28, 1940; Comparison of Hourly Wage Rates between Holyoke and Four Wisconsin Mills of Jobs Shown in the A. P. & P. A. Survey, 1948; H. T. Martin to Manufacturers' Group, Mar. 19, 1948, June 13, 1947; Minutes of Firemen's Conference No. 1, May 14, 1948, Master Labor File, all in AWP Co Rcds.

12 H. T. Martin to William H. Davis, chairman, National War Labor Board, June 2, 1942, Master Labor File, AWP Co Rcds; H. T. Martin to Manufacturers' Group, Sept. 25, 1939, memorandum in possession of United Paperworkers International Union, Local No. 1, Holyoke, Massachusetts; William Hunter interview, Mar. 13, 1978, AICOHC; T. H. Blodgett to E. C. Reid, May 21, 1946, Master Labor File, AWP Co Rcds.

13 Gavin Wright, *Old South, New South: Revolutions in the Southern Economy since the Civil War* (New York: Basic Books, 1986), 135–136; Solomon Barkin, "The Regional Significance of the Integration Movement in the Southern Textile Industry," *Southern Economic Journal* 15 (1949): 395–411.

14 Seymour Louis Wolfbein, *The Decline of a Cotton Textile City: A Study of New Bedford* (1948; reprint, New York: AMS Press, 1968), 25, 59; Stanley Vittoz, *New Deal Labor Policy and the American Industrial Economy* (Chapel Hill: University of North Carolina Press, 1987), 21–25; Robert W. Dunn and Jack Hardy, *Labor and Textiles* (New York: International Publishers, 1931), 13, 28–34; Herbert J. Lahne, *The Cotton Mill Worker* (New York: Farrar and Rinehart, 1944), 13–14, 90–92; E. Lovering to H. L. Sigourney, Mar. 26, 1924, vol. PD–22, Lyman Mills Papers, Baker Library, Harvard Business School (LMP); *SR*, Sept. 12, 1933; Mar. 2, 1924; June 9, 1925; Feb. 17, 1933; Nov. 25, 1920; Dec. 22, 1920; Dec. 23, 1920; Dec. 30, 1920; Jan. 18, 1921; Jan. 6, 1925; Aug. 7, 1925; Dunn and Hardy, *Labor and Textiles*, 107; *SR*, Feb. 15, 1933.

15 J. A. Burke to E. Lovering, Mar. 26, 1926, Mar. 29, 1926; E. Lovering to J. A. Burke, Mar. 30, 1926, all in vol. PD–25, LMP.

16 Green, *Holyoke*, 238; Conrad Hemond, secretary, Holyoke Chamber of Commerce, to E. Lovering, Sept. 8, 1927, vol. PD–27, LMP; *Holyoke Transcript* (*HT*), Sept. 7, 1927; Sept. 15, 1927.

17 *HT*, Sept. 17, 1927; E. Lovering to Conrad Hemond, Sept. 9, 1927, vol. PD–27, LMP; *HT*, Sept. 15, 1927; Sept. 12, 1927; Sept. 17, 1927; Sept. 19, 1927.

18 *SR*, Oct. 11, 1932; Mar. 12, 1935; Jan. 7, 1938; Dec. 16, 1938; *Holyoke Municipal Register* (*HMR*), 1937, 8; Florence Cornwell Hutner, "The Farr Alpaca Company: A Case Study in Business History," *Smith College Studies in History* 37 (1951): 84–86.

19 *SR*, Nov. 26, 1938; Dec. 6, 1938; Jan. 25, 1938; Jan. 31, 1938; Feb. 19, 1938; Aug. 28, 1938.

20 D. R. Green to A. L. Green, chairman of the board, Sept. 12, 1938, liquidation file, Farr Alpaca Papers, Connecticut Valley Historical Museum (FAP).

21 Transcript of interview between Elmer Carr and A. B. Chapin, Oct. 22, 1938; President's letter to stockholders, Dec. 21, 1938, liquidation file, both in FAP.

22 *HT*, Dec. 9, 1938; D. R. Green to board of directors, Feb. 18, 1939, liquidation file, FAP; *HT*, Dec. 1, 1939; *SR*, July 9, 1939; *HT*, Nov. 13, 1938; Mar. 8, 1940.

23 Green, *Holyoke*, 238; Hutner, "Farr Alpaca Company," 88; Massachusetts House of Representatives, *Final Report of the Commission on Interstate Cooperation to the General Court, Concerning the Migration of Industrial Establishments from Massachusetts*, Document No. 2495, 1939, 14–15; Vera Shlakman, *Economic History of a Factory Town: A Study of Chicopee, Massachusetts* (1934–1935; reprint, New York: Octagon Books, 1969), 228–229. Ernest Lovering served for many years as treasurer of both the Lyman and Dwight Mills.

24 *Report on the New England Textile Industry by Committee Appointed by the New England Governors*, 1952, 106; Massachusetts House of Representatives, *Report of the Unpaid Special Commission Relative to the Investigation and Study of the Textile Industry and to Prevent Removal Thereof from the Commonwealth*, Document No. 2590, 1952, 6 (pagination based on final draft of document in State Archives); Donald N. Anderson, "The Decline of the Woolen and Worsted Industry of New England, 1947–1958: A Regional Economic History" (Ph.D. diss., New York University, 1971), 227, 239, 251; *Textile Labor*, Sept. 2, 1950.

25 Anderson, "Decline of the Woolen and Worsted Industry."

26 Green, *Holyoke*, 181–182, 236.

27 *SR*, Mar. 17, 1933; Mar. 18, 1933; Sept. 1, 1934; Dec. 30, 1937; Jan. 7, 1938.

28 *HT*, Dec. 20, 1938; U.S. Congress, Senate, Subcommittee on Labor-Management Relations of the Committee on Labor and Public Welfare, *Hearings on Labor-Management Relations in the Southern Textile Manufacturing Industry*, 81st Cong., 2d sess. (Washington: U.S. Government Printing Office, 1950), 10–11.

29 Ibid.; *Textile Labor*, July 7, 1942; Sept. 17, 1949; June 24, 1950.

30 Statement of Executive Board of TWUA: The National Cotton and Rayon Settlement (1965), in New Bedford Joint Board, TWUA, Box 1, John Chupka Correspondence, 1965, Archives and Manuscripts, University of Massachusetts at Amherst Library.

31 *Boston Globe*, Sept. 26, 1948, in U.S. Congress, Senate, Subcommittee of the Committee on Interstate and Foreign Commerce, *Investigation of Closing of Nashua, New Hampshire Mills and Operations of Textron, Inc.*, 80th Cong., 2d sess. (Washington: U.S. Government Printing Office, 1948), part I, 179.

32 The results of the Federal Reserve study can be found in Massachusetts H.R., *Study of the Textile Industry*, Document No. 2590, 1950, 47–48. Of the remaining respondents, 38 percent believed that "relations with labor" placed them at a competitive disadvantage with southern producers, while another 16 percent did not answer the question.

33 Reynolds and Taft, *Evolution of Wage Structure*, 85–86; Wright, *Old South, New South*, 219; Solomon Barkin, "The Significance of Minimum Wages for the Textile Industry," unpublished address, Dec. 4, 1958, in vol. 12, Solomon Barkin Papers, Archives and Manuscripts, University of Massachusetts at Amherst Library (SBP); Solomon Barkin, "Labour Relations in the United States Textile Industry," *International Labour Review*, 75 (1957): 407; Reynolds and Taft, *Evolution of Wage Structure*, 75–78, 87.

34 Barbara S. Griffith, *The Crisis of American Labor: Operation Dixie and the Defeat of the CIO* (Philadelphia: Temple University Press, 1988), 23, 36, 46–48; *Boston Globe*, Sept. 26, 1948, in *Investigation of Textron Operations*, part I, 179.

35 U.S. Congress, Senate, Committee on Interstate and Foreign Commerce, *Report Made by a Special Subcommittee Pursuant to S. Res. 287 on Problems*

of the Domestic Textile Industry, 86th Cong., 1st sess. (Washington: U.S. Government Printing Office, 1959), 7–8, 11.

36 Griffith, *Crisis of American Labor*, 36, 42–43, 161–162.

37 Reynolds and Taft, *Evolution of Wage Structure*, 87; Minutes, Columbia University Seminar on Labor, Dec. 12, 1956, in vol. 10, SBP.

38 Reynolds and Taft, *Evolution of Wage Structure*, 87–88; *CIO News*, Apr. 9, 1951; May 14, 1951; *Textile Labor*, Apr. 21, 1951; May 19, 1951; Nov. 19, 1951.

39 *Textile Labor*, May 19, 1951; Solomon Barkin, *The Decline of the Labor Movement and What Can Be Done about It* (Santa Barbara, Calif.: Center for the Study of Democratic Institutions, 1961), 11; Reynolds and Taft, *Evolution of Wage Structure*, 88; Massachusetts H.R., *Study of the Textile Industry*, Document No. 2590, 1950, 6; Anderson, "Decline of the Woolen and Worsted Industry," 251.

40 *HT*, Sept. 11, 1950; Sept. 12, 1950; *Springfield Daily News*, Dec. 29, 1950.

41 Bruce Saxon, "Fall River and the Decline of the New England Textile Industry, 1949–1954," *Historical Journal of Massachusetts*, 16 (1988): 56, 65. Also see Marc Miller's examination of the impact of World War II on the Lowell labor market in *The Irony of Victory: World War II and Lowell, Massachusetts* (Urbana: University of Illinois Press, 1988), 18–20, 51–56, 116–118.

42 *HMR*, 1916, 125; 1918, 100; 1921, 221, 227.

43 Lahne, *Cotton Mill Worker*, 116; Jacques Ducharme, *The Shadows of the Trees: The Story of French-Canadians in New England* (New York: Harper and Brothers, 1943), 217–219; Dyke Hendrickson, *Quiet Presence: Histoires de Franco-Americains en New England* (Portland, Maine: Guy Gannett Publishing Company, 1980), 71.

44 Madeleine Biehler interview, Apr. 29, 1988; Cecile Barthello interview, Apr. 26, 1988; Claire Lefebvre interview, June 12, 1988, from interviews arranged by Christine Howard Bailey, Holyoke scholar-in-residence for "SHIFTING GEARS: The Changing Meaning of Work in Massachusetts, 1920–1980," a project of the Massachusetts Foundation for Humanities and Public Policy (SGP); Katharine DuPre Lumpkin and Dorothy Wolff Douglas, *Child Workers in America* (New York: Robert M. McBride and Company, 1937), 147.

45 Miller, *Irony of Victory*, 11; Katharine DuPre Lumpkin, "Shutdowns in the Connecticut Valley: A Study of Worker Displacement in the Small Industrial Community," *Smith College Studies in History*, 19, nos. 3–4 (Apr. 1934–July 1934), 220; Claire Lefebvre interview, SGP; *Seventeenth Census of the United States: 1950, Population, I, Characteristics of the Population, Part 21*, 68; *Sixteenth Census of the United States: 1940, Population, II, Characteristics of the Population, Part 3*, 639.

46 Jerome Lefebvre interview, June 12, 1988; Louis Gendron interview, May 10, 1988, both in SGP; W. Stanley Devino, et al., *A Study of Textile Mill Closings in Selected New England Communities* (Orono: University of Maine Press, 1966), 87.

47 Jerome Lefebvre interview; Cecile Benoit, Doris Kos, and Juliette Dandelin interview, Apr. 21, 1988; Madeleine Biehler interview, all in SGP.

48 Doris Kos interview, SGP; Devino, et al., *Textile Closings*, 87, 113, 147; Massachusetts H.R., *Study of the Textile Industry*, Document No. 2590, 1950, 38; Anna Sullivan interview, Spring 1974, AICOHC.

49 This and the following paragraph are based on Christine Howard Bailey, "Precious Blood: Work, Family, and Community in South Holyoke, 1920–1970," unpublished ms., 1988, in author's possession, 35–51; Raymond Beaudry interview, Aug. 7, 1987, Holyoke Heritage State Park; Raymond Beaudry interview, Apr. 29, 1988, SGP.

50 Saxon, "Fall River," 65–66; *Sixteenth Census of the United States: 1940, Population, II, Characteristics of the Population, Part 3*, 648; *Seventeenth Census of the United States: 1950, Population, I, Characteristics of the Population, Part 21*, 61; U.S. Senate, *Report on Problems of the Textile Industry*, 1959, 21; Devino, et al., *Textile Closings*, 12, 65, 126.

51 Miller, *Irony of Victory*, 53; Wright, *Old South, New South*, 134–135; Alice Galenson, *The Migration of the Cotton Textile Industry from New England to the South* (New York: Garland Publishing, 1985), 4–7.

52 U.S. Senate, *Report on the Problems of the Textile Industry*, 1959, 6–7, 20.

53 *Industry*, 17 (Feb. 1952): 5; 17 (Apr. 1952): 58; Massachusetts H.R., *Study of the Textile Industry*, Document No. 2590, 1950, 32–34; *New England Governors' Report*, 1952, 43; Seymour E. Harris, *The Economics of New England: Case Study of an Older Area* (Cambridge: Harvard University Press, 1952), 133, 150–152; *Investigation of Textron Operations*, part I, 14, 18. Other New England textile producers also stated that work-load differentials were a primary consideration in their decision to move South. See, for example, James A. Morris, *Woolen and Worsted Manufacturing in the Southern Piedmont* (Columbia: University of South Carolina Press, 1952), 103–104, 115–117.

54 U.S. Congress, Senate, Subcommittee on Labor-Management Relations of the Committee on Labor and Public Welfare, *Hearings on Labor-Management Relations in the Southern Textile Industry Pursuant to S. Res. 140*, 81st Cong., 2d sess. (Washington: U.S. Government Printing Office, 1951), 38, 66–67.

55 *New England Governors' Report*, 1952, 175; *Hearings on Labor-Management Relations Pursuant to S. Res. 140*, 40, 68–69; Solomon Barkin, "Statement to Massachusetts Special Commission on Textile Industry," Oct. 31, 1949, 19–20, in vol. 3, SBP; Anna Sullivan interview, AICOHC; Solomon Barkin, "Handling Work Assignment Changes," *Harvard Business Review* 25 (1947): 479–482.

56 *New England Governors' Report*, 1952, 44, 175; Richmond C. Nyman, *Union-Management Cooperation in the "Stretch-Out"* (New Haven: Yale University Press, 1934). Some of the problems TWUA officials encountered in their efforts to facilitate and oversee the introduction of new machinery are recounted in Solomon Barkin, "Union's Viewpoint on Human Engineering and

Relations," unpublished address, 1949–1950, in vol. 3, SBP; Minutes, Columbia University Seminar on Labor, Dec. 12, 1956, 7–8, in vol. 10, SBP; *Investigation of Textron Operations*, part I, 41–42, 47, 61–62.

57 Solomon Barkin, "Dissenting Opinion on Bates Manufacturing Decision," unpublished ms., June 1952, in vol. 6, SBP; Fall River textile worker quoted in Saxon, "Fall River," 71; TWUA, transcript of meeting of executive board, June 1957, 74, in vol. 11, SBP.

58 *CIO News*, Oct. 8, 1951; Solomon Barkin, "Testimony on Behalf of TWUA, CIO, before House Committee on Ways and Means on H.R. 2893," Apr. 12, 1948, in vol. 3, SBP; U.S. Senate, *Report on Problems of Textile Industry*, 20–21.

59 IUE Local 206 Records, 1954, Archives and Manuscripts, University of Massachusetts at Amherst Library; Christine Howard Bailey, "Shifting Gears: The Changing Meaning of Work in Holyoke, Massachusetts, 1920–1980," unpublished project proposal, Mar. 1, 1988, 12; Herman Greenberg, president, Greater Springfield CLC to all local unions, Aug. 22, 1961, in IUE Local 206 Records.

60 David Brody, *Workers in Industrial America: Essays on the 20th Century Struggle* (New York: Oxford University Press, 1980), 188–194; Robert H. Zieger, *American Workers, American Unions, 1920–1985* (Baltimore: Johns Hopkins University Press, 1986), 147–158.

61 Brody, *Workers in Industrial America*, 198–211; Peter Friedlander, *The Emergence of a UAW Local, 1936–1939: A Study in Class and Culture* (Pittsburgh: University of Pittsburgh Press, 1975), 4–5, 90–91; John Bodnar, *Workers' World: Kinship, Community, and Protest in Industrial Society* (Baltimore: Johns Hopkins University Press, 1982), 149–152, 156–160; Bodnar, *Immigration and Industrialization: Ethnicity in an American Mill Town, 1870–1940* (Pittsburgh: University of Pittsburgh Press, 1977), 140–149.

62 Hendrickson, *Quiet Presence*, 120, 132; Cecile Benoit, Doris Kos, and Juliette Dandelin interview; Pierre Anctil, "Aspects of Class Ideology in a New England Minority: The Franco-Americans of Woonsocket, Rhode Island (1865–1929)" (Ph.D. diss., New School for Social Research, 1980), 70.

Conclusion

1 *Irish World* (*IW*), Apr. 14, 1888; Aug. 14, 1880; July 22, 1882; May 29, 1886; Richard J. Oestreicher, "Terence V. Powderly, the Knights of Labor, and Artisanal Republicanism," in *Labor Leaders in America*, ed. Melvyn Dubofsky and Warren Van Tine (Urbana: University of Illinois Press, 1987), 30–61; Stuart B. Kaufman, *Samuel Gompers and the Origins of the American Federation of Labor, 1848–1896* (Westport, Conn.: Greenwood Press, 1973), esp. ch. 9; James P.

Rodechko, *Patrick Ford and His Search for America* (New York: Arno Press, 1976), 108–113. One group that did not accept Ford's position on strikes was Holyoke's St. Jerome's Temperance Society. After an 1887 debate, club members rejected the resolution, "Strikes are detrimental to the working classes." *Holyoke Transcript* (*HT*), Jan. 3, 1887.

2 Kerby Miller, "Assimilation and Alienation: Irish Emigrants' Responses to Industrial America, 1871–1921," in *The Irish in America: Emigration, Assimilation, and Impact*, ed. P. J. Drudy (Cambridge, Eng.: Cambridge University Press, 1985), 99. It should be noted that not all Irish enclaves began to dissolve this early, as David M. Emmons demonstrates in his fine study, *The Butte Irish: Class and Ethnicity in an American Mining Town, 1875–1925* (Urbana: University of Illinois Press, 1989).

3 Rodechko, *Ford*, 114–115, 172–174, 214–215, 259–260; *IW*, Jan. 28, 1882.

4 *Springfield Republican* (*SR*), Feb. 20, 1928; Mar. 19, 1928; Mar. 14, 1931.

5 *SR*, Apr. 12, 1935; Aug. 25, 1936; Sept. 30, 1936; Nov. 4, 1936; Nov. 5, 1936.

6 Kenneth W. Underwood, *Protestant and Catholic: Religious and Social Interaction in an Industrial Community* (1957; reprint, Westport, Conn.: Greenwood Press, 1973), 288–289, 460 n. 17, 460–461 n. 29. Also see Emmons, *The Butte Irish*. A major reason that Irish workers in Butte continued to embrace an enclave consciousness beyond the turn of the century was the preferential treatment they received from Irish mine owners and supervisory personnel.

7 Thomas P. O'Neill, Jr., with William Novak, *Man of the House: The Life and Political Memoirs of Speaker Tip O'Neill* (New York: Random House, 1987), 9–11, 39.

8 *SR*, Mar. 5, 1936; Feb. 20, 1937.

9 *SR*, Aug. 6, 1937; Aug. 10, 1937; *Catholic Mirror*, 27 (Aug. 1947): 32.

10 John A. Ryan, *The Church and Socialism: and Other Essays* (Washington: University Press, 1919), 147–148.

11 John Bodnar, *Workers' World: Kinship, Community, and Protest in Industrial Society* (Baltimore: Johns Hopkins University Press, 1982), 63. Again, Butte's Irish miners constitute an exception to the argument stated in this paragraph. See Emmons, *The Butte Irish*.

BIBLIOGRAPHY

Primary Sources

Manuscript and Special Collections

American International College, Springfield, Massachusetts.
    Oral History Collection.
Baker Library, Harvard Business School, Boston, Massachusetts.
    Dwight Mills Papers.
    Lyman Mills Papers.
Connecticut Valley Historical Museum, Springfield, Massachusetts.
    Hampden Mechanics' Association Papers.
    Farr Alpaca Company Papers.
Massachusetts Foundation for Humanities and Public Policy, South Hadley, Massachusetts.
    Interviews arranged by Christine Howard Bailey, Holyoke scholar-in-residence for "SHIFTING GEARS: The Changing Meaning of Work in Massachusetts, 1920–1980," a project of the Massachusetts Foundation for Humanities and Public Policy.
Mt. Holyoke College Archives, South Hadley, Massachusetts.
    Amy Hewes Papers.
U.S. Census Manuscript Industrial Schedules.
    Seventh Census (1850), Hampden County, Massachusetts.
    Tenth Census (1880), Hampden County, Massachusetts.
U.S. Census Manuscript Population Schedules.
    Tenth Census (1880), Hampden County, Massachusetts.
    Twelth Census (1900), Hampden County, Massachusetts.
    Thirteenth Census (1910), Hampden County, Massachusetts.
University of Massachusetts at Amherst Archives and Manuscripts, Library, Amherst, Massachusetts.
    Amalgamated Clothing Workers of America, Local 125, Records.
    American Writing Paper Company Records.
    Solomon Barkin Papers.

International Brotherhood of Paper Makers, Local 1, Eagle Lodge, Records.
International Union of Electrical, Radio, and Machine Workers, Local 206, Records.
Textile Workers Union of America, New Bedford Joint Council, Records.
United Brotherhood of Carpenters and Joiners, Holyoke District Council, Records.
United Brotherhood of Carpenters and Joiners, Springfield District Council and Affiliates, Local 96, Records.

Government Documents

Holyoke, Massachusetts. *Municipal Register.* 1874–1940.
Holyoke, Massachusetts. *Town Report.* 1851–1870.
Massachusetts Bureau of Statistics of Labor. *Annual Report.* Boston, 1870–1915.
———. *Bulletin.* Boston, 1897–1905.
Massachusetts Department of Labor and Industries. *Statistics of Manufactures in Massachusetts, 1920–1938.* Public Document No. 36. Boston, 1938.
Massachusetts House of Representatives. *Final Report of the Commission on Interstate Co-operation to the General Court, Concerning the Migration of Industrial Establishments from Massachusetts.* Public Document No. 2495. Boston, 1939.
———. *Report of the Unpaid Special Commission Relative to the Investigation and Study of the Textile Industry and to Prevent the Removal Thereof from the Commonwealth.* Public Document No. 2590. Boston, 1950.
Report on the New England Textile Industry by Committee Appointed by the New England Governors. n.p., 1952.
U.S. Congress. Senate. Committee on Interstate and Foreign Commerce. *Report by a Special Subcommittee Pursuant to S. Res. 287 (85th Congress) on Problems of the Domestic Textile Industry.* 86th Congress, 1st Session, 1959.
———. Subcommitte on Labor-Management Relations of the Committee on Labor and Public Welfare. *Hearings on Labor-Management Relations in the Southern Textile Manufacturing Industry.* 81st Congress, 2d Session, 1950.
———. *Hearing on Labor-Management Relations in the Southern Textile Industry Pursuant to S. Res. 140.* 81st Congress, 2d Session, 1951.
———. Subcommittee of the Committee on Interstate and Foreign Commerce. *Investigatiion of Closing of Nashua, New Hampshire Mills and Operations of Textron, Inc.* 80th Congress, 2d Session, 1948.
U.S. Department of Commerce, Bureau of the Census. *Sixteenth Census of the United States: 1940, Population, II, Characteristics of the Population, Part 3.* Washington, D.C.: GPO, 1943.

————. *Seventeenth Census of the United States: 1950, I, Characteristics of the Population, Part 21.* Washington, D.C.: GPO, 1952.

U.S. Department of Labor, Bureau of Labor Statistics. *Impact of Technological Change and Automation in the Pulp and Paper Industry.* Bulletin No. 1347. Washington, D.C.: GPO, 1962.

Books and Articles

Biographical Review of the Leading Citizens of Hampden County, Massachusetts. Boston: Biographical Publishing Company, 1895.

Bluebook and Social Directory of Holyoke, Massachusetts, 1889. Springfield: Index Publishing Company, 1889.

Byrne, Stephen. *Irish Emigration to the United States: What It Has Been and What It Is.* New York: The Catholic Publication Society, 1874.

Copeland, Alfred Minot, ed. *A History of Hampden County, Massachusetts.* 3 vols. Springfield: The Century Memorial Publishing Company, 1902.

Cross, C. F., and E. J. Bevan. *A Text-Book of Paper-Making.* London: E. and F. N. Spon, 1888.

Dexter, Robert C. "Fifty-Fifty Americans." *World's Work* 48 (Aug. 1924): 366–371.

Douglas, Paul H., and William A. Orton. *Outline of Labor Problems in Modern Society.* Holyoke: Alden Press, 1924.

Goldstein, David, and Martha Moore Avery. *Socialism: The Nation of Fatherless Children.* Boston: Thomas J. Flynn, 1911.

Hillquit, Morris, and John A. Ryan. *Socialism: Promise or Menace?.* New York: Macmillan, 1917.

Holyoke City Directory. 1874, 1882–1905, 1907, 1910, 1915.

Holyoke Town Directory. 1869.

"Immigration." *Massachusetts Teacher* 4 (1851): 289–291.

MacDonald, William. "The French Canadians in New England." *Quarterly Journal of Economics* 12 (Apr. 1898): 245–279.

McNeill, George E., ed. *The Labor Movement: The Problem of Today.* 1887. Reprint. New York: Augustus M. Kelley Publishers, 1971.

Maguire, Edward J., ed. *Reverend John O'Hanlon's The Irish Emigrant's Guide for the United States: A Critical Edition with Introduction and Commentary.* 1851. Reprint. New York: Arno Press, 1976.

Maguire, John Francis. *The Irish in America.* 1868. Reprint. New York: Arno Press, 1969.

O'Connell, William Henry. *Wage Earners' and Employers' Rights and Duties.* Boston: Boston School of Political Economy, 1913.

A Report on the History and Present Condition of the Hadley Falls Company at Holyoke, Massachusetts. Boston: John Wilson and Son, 1853.

Ryan, John A. *The Church and Socialism: and Other Essays*. Washington, D.C.: The University Press, 1919.
———. *A Living Wage*. 1906. Rev. Ed. New York: Macmillan, 1920.
———. *Social Reconstruction*. New York: Macmillan, 1920.
Sargent, Kate. "Catholicism in Massachusetts." *The Forum* 74 (Nov. 1925): 730–742.
Stang, William. *Socialism and Christianity*. New York: Benziger Brothers, 1905.
Watt, Alexander. *The Art of Paper-Making: A Practical Handbook of the Manufacture of Paper from Rags, Esparto, Straw, and other Fibrous Materials Including the Manufacture of Pulp from Wood Fibre*. New York: D. Van Nostrand Company, 1907.
Wright, M. Emory. *The Parsons Paper Mill at Holyoke, Massachusetts: Embracing a Minute Description of the Paper Manufacture*. Springfield: Samuel Bowles and Company, 1857.

Newspapers and Periodicals

American Catholic Quarterly Review
The Artisan (Holyoke)
Catholic Mirror (Springfield)
Catholic World
CIO News
Eagle "A" Unity (Holyoke)
Greater Holyoke
Holyoke Labor
Holyoke Mirror
Holyoke News
Holyoke Transcript
Independent Journal (Holyoke)
Journal of United Labor
Labor Standard (New York, Boston, Fall River)
The Messenger (Worcester)
Paper Makers Journal
Paper World (Springfield)
The People (Providence)
The Pilot (Boston)
Proletarian (Springfield)
Springfield Daily News
Springfield Republican
Textile Labor
True Light (Holyoke)

Secondary Sources

Books and Articles

Abell, Aaron I. *American Catholicism and Social Action: A Search for Social Justice.* Notre Dame, Ind.: University of Notre Dame Press, 1963.
————, ed. *American Catholic Thought on Social Questions.* Indianapolis, Ind.: Bobbs-Merrill, 1968.
Abrams, Richard M. *Conservatism in a Progressive Age: Massachusetts Politics, 1900–1912.* Cambridge: Harvard University Press, 1964.
Anderson, Elin L. *We Americans: A Study of Cleavage in an American City.* 1937. Reprint. New York: Russell and Russell, 1967.
Bailey, Peter. " 'Will the Real Bill Banks Please Stand Up?' Towards a Role-Analysis of Mid-Victorian Working-Class Respectability." *Journal of Social History* 12 (1979): 336–353.
Baltzell, E. Digby. *Philadelphia Gentlemen: The Making of a National Upper Class.* 1958. Reprint. Philadelphia: University of Pennsylvania Press, 1979.
Barkin, Solomon. *The Decline of the Labor Movement and What Can Be Done about It.* Santa Barbara, Calif.: Center for the Study of Democratic Institutions, 1961.
————. "The Regional Significance of the Integration Movement in the Southern Textile Industry." *Southern Economic Journal* 15 (1949): 395–411.
————. "Handling Work Assignment Changes." *Harvard Business Review* 25 (1947): 473–482.
Beal, Fred E. *Proletarian Journey: New England, Gastonia, Moscow.* New York: Hillman-Curl, Inc., 1937.
Bedford, Henry F. *Socialism and the Workers in Massachusetts, 1886–1912.* Amherst: University of Massachusetts Press, 1966.
Benson, Susan Porter. " 'The Customers Ain't God': The Work Culture of Department-Store Sales Women, 1890–1940." In *Working-Class America: Essays on Labor, Community, and American Society,* edited by Michael H. Frisch and Daniel J. Walkowitz. Urbana: University of Illinois Press, 1983.
Bernstein, Irving. *The Lean Years: A History of the American Worker, 1920–1933.* 1960. Reprint. Baltimore: Penguin Books, 1966.
————. *Turbulent Years: A History of the American Worker, 1933–1941.* Boston: Houghton Mifflin, 1969.
Betten, Neil. *Catholic Activism and the Industrial Worker.* Gainesville: University Presses of Florida, 1976.
Biddle, Ellen Horgan. "The American Catholic Irish Family." In *Ethnic Families in America: Patterns and Variations,* edited by Charles H. Mindel and Robert W. Habenstein. New York: Elsevier, 1976.

Billington, Ray A. *The Protestant Crusade, 1800–1860: A Study of the Origins of American Nativism*. 1938. Reprint. Chicago: Quadrangle Books, 1964.

Blewett, Mary H. *Men, Women, and Work: Class, Gender, and Protest in the New England Shoe Industry, 1780–1910*. Urbana: University of Illinois Press, 1988.

Blodgett, Geoffrey. *The Gentle Reformers: Massachusetts Democrats in the Cleveland Era*. Cambridge: Harvard University Press, 1966.

Bluestone, Barry, and Bennett Harrison. *The Deindustrialization of America: Plant Closings, Community Abandonment, and the Dismantling of Basic Industry*. New York: Basic Books, 1982.

Bode, Carl. *The American Lyceum: Town Meeting of the Mind*. 1956. Reprint. Carbondale: Southern Illinois University Press, 1968.

Bodnar, John. *Immigration and Industrialization: Ethnicity in an American Mill Town, 1870–1940*. Pittsburgh: University of Pittsburgh Press, 1977.

———. *Workers' World: Kinship, Community, and Protest in Industrial Society*. Baltimore: Johns Hopkins University Press, 1982.

———. *The Transplanted: A History of Immigrants in Urban America*. Bloomington: Indiana University Press, 1985.

Bowles, Samuel, and Herbert Gintis. *Schooling in Capitalist America: Educational Reform and the Contradictions of Economic Life*. New York: Basic Books, 1976.

Brandes, Stuart D. *American Welfare Capitalism, 1880–1940*. Chicago: University of Chicago Press, 1976.

Brault, Gerald J. *The French-Canadian Heritage in New England*. Hanover, N.H.: University Press of New England, 1986.

Braverman, Harry. *Labor and Monopoly Capital: The Degradation of Work in the Twentieth Century*. New York: Monthly Review Press, 1974.

Broderick, Francis L. *Right Reverend New Dealer: John A. Ryan*. New York: Macmillan, 1963.

Brody, David. *Workers in Industrial America: Essays on the 20th Century Struggle*. New York: Oxford University Press, 1980.

Brown, Thomas N. *Irish-American Nationalism, 1870–1890*. Philadelphia: J. B. Lippincott, 1966.

Browne, Henry J. *The Catholic Church and the Knights of Labor*. Washington, D.C.: Catholic University of America Press, 1949.

Buhle, Mari Jo. *Women and American Socialism, 1870–1920*. Urbana: University of Illinois Press, 1981.

Buhle, Paul. "The Knights of Labor in Rhode Island." *Radical History Review* 17 (1978): 39–73.

Burchell, R. A. *The San Francisco Irish, 1848–1880*. Berkeley: University of California Press, 1980.

Cawelti, John G. *Apostles of the Self-Made Man: Changing Concepts of Success in America*. Chicago: University of Chicago Press, 1965.

Chandler, Alfred D., Jr. *The Visible Hand: The Managerial Revolution in American Business*. Cambridge: Harvard University Press, 1977.

Christie, Robert A. *Empire in Wood: A History of the Carpenters' Union*. Ithaca, N.Y.: Cornell University Press, 1956.

Clark, Christopher. "The Household Economy, Market Exchange, and the Rise of Capitalism in the Connecticut Valley, 1800–1860." *Journal of Social History* 13 (1979): 169–189.

Clark, Dennis. *The Irish in Philadelphia: Ten Generations of Urban Experience*. Philadelphia: Temple University Press, 1973.

Clark, Samuel. *Social Origins of the Irish Land War*. Princeton: Princeton University Press, 1979.

Clawson, Dan. *Bureaucracy and the Labor Process: The Transformation of U.S. Industry, 1860–1920*. New York: Monthly Review Press, 1980.

Cole, Arthur H. *The American Wool Manufacture*. 2 vols. Cambridge: Harvard University Press, 1926.

Cole, Donald B. *Immigrant City: Lawrence, Massachusetts, 1845–1921*. Chapel Hill: University of North Carolina Press, 1963.

Cooney, John. *The American Pope: The Life and Times of Francis Cardinal Spellman*. New York: Times Books, 1984.

Copeland, Melvin T. *The Cotton Manufacturing Industry of the United States*. Cambridge: Harvard University Press, 1912.

Couvares, Francis G. *The Remaking of Pittsburgh: Class and Culture in an Industrializing City, 1877–1919*. Albany: State University of New York Press, 1984.

Cross, Robert D. *The Emergence of Liberal Catholicism in America*. 1958. Reprint. Chicago: Quadrangle Books, 1968.

Crossick, Geoffrey. *An Artisan Elite in Victorian Society: Kentish London, 1840–1880*. London: Croom Helm, 1978.

———. "The Labour Aristocracy and Its Values: A Study of Mid-Victorian Kentish London." *Victorian Studies* 19 (1976): 301–328.

Cumbler, John T. *Working-Class Community in Industrial America: Work, Leisure, and Struggle in Two Industrial Cities, 1880–1930*. Westport, Conn.: Greenwood Press, 1979.

Curran, Mary Doyle. *The Parish and the Hill*. Boston: Houghton Mifflin, 1948.

Dawley, Alan. *Class and Community: The Industrial Revolution in Lynn*. Cambridge: Harvard University Press, 1976.

———, and Paul Faler. "Working-Class Culture and Politics in the Industrial Revolution: Sources of Loyalism and Rebellion." *Journal of Social History* 9 (1976): 466–480.

Deedy, John. "William Henry O'Connell: The Prince of Yesterday's Prototypes." *The Critic* 35 (Summer 1977): 95–96.

Devino, W. Stanley et al. *A Study of Textile Mill Closings in Selected New England Communities*. Orono: University of Maine Press, 1966.

Diner, Hasia R. *Erin's Daughters in America: Irish Immigrant Women in the Nineteenth Century.* Baltimore: Johns Hopkins University Press, 1983.

Dolan, Jay P. *Catholic Revivalism: The American Experience, 1830–1900.* Notre Dame, Ind.: University of Notre Dame Press, 1978.

———. *The Immigrant Church: New York's Irish and German Catholics, 1815–1865.* Baltimore: Johns Hopkins University Press, 1975.

Doty, C. Stewart. *Franco-Americans: New England Life Histories from the Federal Writers' Project, 1938–1939.* Orono: University of Maine Press, 1985.

Dublin, Thomas. *Women at Work: The Transformation of Work and Community in Lowell, Massachusetts, 1826–1860.* New York: Columbia University Press, 1979.

Dubofsky, Melvyn, and Warren Van Tine, eds. *Labor Leaders in America.* Urbana: University of Illinois Press, 1987.

Ducharme, Jacques. *The Shadows of the Trees: The Story of French-Canadians in New England.* New York: Harper and Brothers, 1943.

———. *The Delusson Family.* New York: Funk and Wagnalls, 1939.

Duis, Perry R. *The Saloon: Public Drinking in Chicago and Boston, 1880–1920.* Urbana: University of Illinois Press, 1983.

Dunn, Robert W., and Jack Hardy. *Labor and Textiles.* New York: International Publishers, 1931.

Emmons, David M. *The Butte Irish: Class and Ethnicity in an American Mining Town, 1875–1925.* Urbana: University of Illinois Press, 1989.

———. "An Aristocracy of Labor: The Irish Miners of Butte, 1880–1914." *Labor History* 28 (1987): 275–306.

Erlich, Mark. "Peter J. McGuire's Trade Unionism: Socialism of a Trade Union Kind?" *Labor History* 24 (1983): 165–197.

Faler, Paul. "Cultural Aspects of the Industrial Revolution: Lynn, Massachusetts Shoemakers and Industrial Morality, 1826–1860." *Labor History* 15 (1974): 367–394.

Fink, Leon. *Workingmen's Democracy: The Knights of Labor and American Politics.* Urbana: University of Illinois Press, 1983.

Foner, Eric. *Free Soil, Free Labor, Free Men: The Ideology of the Republican Party before the Civil War.* New York: Oxford University Press, 1970.

———. *Politics and Ideology in the Age of the Civil War.* New York: Oxford University Press, 1980.

Freeman, Joshua B. *In Transit: The Transport Workers Union in New York City, 1933–1966.* New York: Oxford University Press, 1989.

French, Laurence. "The Franco American Working Class Family." In *Ethnic Families in America: Patterns and Variations,* edited by Charles H. Mindel and Robert W. Habenstein. New York: Elsevier, 1976.

Friedlander, Peter. *The Emergence of a UAW Local, 1936–1939: A Study in Class and Culture.* Pittsburgh: University of Pittsburgh Press, 1975.

Frisch, Michael H. *Town into City: Springfield, Massachusetts and the Meaning of Community, 1840–1880.* Cambridge: Harvard University Press, 1982.

Gabriel, Ralph H. *The Founding of Holyoke, 1848.* Princeton: Princeton University Press, 1936.

Galambos, Louis. *Competition and Cooperation: The Emergence of a National Trade Association.* Baltimore: Johns Hopkins University Press, 1966.

Galenson, Alice. *The Migration of the Cotton Textile Industry from New England to the South.* New York: Garland Publishing, 1985.

Gearty, Patrick W. *The Economic Thought of Monsignor John A. Ryan.* Washington, D.C.: Catholic University of America Press, 1953.

Gilson, Etienne, ed. *The Church Speaks to the Modern World: The Social Teachings of Leo XIII.* New York: Doubleday and Company, 1954.

Gordon, Michael. "The Labor Boycott in New York City, 1880–1886." *Labor History* 16 (1975): 184–229.

Gordon, Richard M. et al. *Segmented Work, Divided Workers: The Historical Transformation of Labor in the United States.* Cambridge, Eng.: Cambridge University Press, 1982.

Gray, Robert Q. *The Labour Aristocracy in Victorian Edinburgh.* London: Oxford University Press, 1976.

Green, Constance McLaughlin. *Holyoke, Massachusetts: A Case History of the Industrial Revolution in America.* New Haven: Yale University Press, 1939.

Green, James J. "American Catholics and the Irish Land League, 1879–1882." *Catholic Historical Review* 35 (1949): 19–42.

Greenburg, Brian. *Worker and Community: Response to Industrialization in a Nineteenth-Century American City, Albany, New York, 1850–1884.* Albany: The State University of New York Press, 1985.

Griffith, Barbara S. *The Crisis of American Labor: Operation Dixie and the Defeat of the CIO.* Philadelphia: Temple University Press, 1988.

Gross, James A. "The Making and Shaping of Unionism in the Pulp and Paper Industry." *Labor History* 5 (1964): 183–208.

Gutman, Herbert G. *Work, Culture, and Society in Industrializing America.* New York: Vintage Books, 1976.

——. *Power and Culture: Essays on the American Working Class,* edited by Ira Berlin. New York: Pantheon Books, 1987.

Handlin, Oscar. *Boston's Immigrants: A Study in Acculturation, 1790–1880.* 1941. Rev. ed. New York: Atheneum, 1968.

Hareven, Tamara K. *Family Time and Industrial Time: The Relationship between the Family and Work in a New England Industrial Community.* Cambridge, Eng.: Cambridge University Press, 1982.

——, and Randolph Langenbach. *Amoskeag: Life and Work in an American Factory City.* New York: Pantheon Books, 1978.

Harper, Wyatt E. *The Story of Holyoke*. N.p., 1973.

Harris, Seymour E. *The Economics of New England: Case Study of an Older Area*. Cambridge: Harvard University Press, 1952.

Hendrickson, Dyke. *Quiet Presence: Histoires de Franco-Americains en New England*. Portland, Maine: Guy Gannett Publishing Company, 1980.

Higham, John. *Strangers in the Land: Patterns of American Nativism, 1860–1925*. 1955. Reprint. New York: Atheneum, 1968.

Hirsch, Susan E. *Roots of the American Working Class: The Industrialization of Crafts in Newark, 1800–1860*. Philadelphia: University of Pennsylvania Press, 1978.

Hobsbawm, E. J. *Labouring Men: Studies in the History of Labour*. New York: Anchor Books, 1967.

Horlick, Allen S. *Country Boys and Merchant Princes: The Social Control of Young Men in New York*. Lewisburg, Pa.: Bucknell University Press, 1975.

Humphries, Jane. "Class Struggle and the Persistence of the Working-Class Family." *Cambridge Journal of Economics* 1 (1977): 241–258.

Huthmacher, J. Joseph. *Massachusetts People and Politics, 1919–1933*. Cambridge: Harvard University Press, 1959.

Hutner, Florence Cornwell. "The Farr Alpaca Company: A Case Study in Business History." *Smith College Studies in History*, Vol. 37. Northampton, Mass.: Smith College, 1950.

Ingham, John N. *The Iron Barons: A Social Analysis of an Urban Elite, 1874–1965*. Westport, Conn.: Greenwood Press, 1978.

Johnson, Paul E. *A Shopkeeper's Millenium: Society and Revivals in Rochester, New York, 1815–1837*. New York: Hill and Wang, 1978.

Karson, Marc. *American Labor Unions and Politics, 1900–1918*. Carbondale: Southern Illinois University Press, 1958.

Katz, Michael. *Class, Bureaucracy, and Schools: The Illusion of Educational Change in America*. New York: Praeger Publishers, 1975.

———. *The Irony of Early School Reform: Educational Innovation in Mid-Nineteenth Century Massachusetts*. Boston: Beacon Press, 1968.

———. *The People of Hamilton, Canada West: Family and Change in a Mid-Nineteenth Century City*. Cambridge: Harvard University Press, 1975.

Kaufman, Stuart B. *Samuel Gompers and the Origins of the American Federation of Labor, 1848–1896*. Westport, Conn.: Greenwood Press, 1973.

Kazin, Michael. *Barons of Labor: The San Francisco Building Trades and Union Power in the Progressive Era*. Urbana: University of Illinois Press, 1987.

Kennedy, Robert E. *The Irish: Emigration, Marriage, and Fertility*. Berkeley: University of California Press, 1973.

Kessler-Harris, Barbara. *Out to Work: A History of Wage-Earning Women in the United States*. New York: Oxford University Press, 1982.

Kett, Joseph F. *Rites of Passage: Adolescence in America from 1790 to the Present*. New York: Basic Books, 1977.

Keyssar, Alexander. *Out of Work: The First Century of Unemployment in Massachusetts.* Cambridge, Eng.: Cambridge University Press, 1986.

Kingsdale, Jon M. "The 'Poor Man's Club': Social Functions of the Urban Working-Class Saloon." *American Quarterly* 25 (1973): 472–489.

Kirkland, Edward C. *Men, Cities, and Transportation: A Study in New England History, 1820–1900.* 2 Vols. 1948. Reprint. New York: Russell and Russell, 1968.

Kistler, Thelma M. "The Rise of Railroads in the Connecticut River Valley." *Smith College Studies in History*, vol. 23. Northampton, Mass.: Smith College, 1938.

Kleppner, Paul E. *The Cross of Culture: A Social Analysis of Midwestern Politics, 1850–1900* New York: Free Press, 1970.

———. *Continuity and Change in Electoral Politics, 1893–1928.* Westport, Conn.: Greenwood Press, 1987.

———. *The Third Electoral System, 1853–1892: Parties, Voters, and Political Cultures.* Chapel Hill: University of North Carolina Press, 1979.

Knights, Peter R. *The Plain People of Boston, 1830–1860: A Study in City Growth.* New York: Oxford University Press, 1971.

Lahne, Herbert J. *The Cotton Mill Worker.* New York: Farrar and Rinehart, 1944.

Lamoreaux, Naomi R. *The Great Merger Movement in American Business, 1895–1904.* Cambridge, Eng.: Cambridge University Press, 1985.

Lamphere, Louise. *From Working Daughters to Working Mothers: Immigrant Women in a New England Industrial Community.* Ithaca, N.Y.: Cornell University Press, 1987.

Larkin, Emmett. "The Devotional Revolution in Ireland, 1850–75." *American Historical Review* 77 (1972): 625–652.

Laslett, John H. M. *Labor and the Left: A Study of Socialist and Radical Influences in the American Labor Movement, 1881–1924.* New York: Basic Books, 1970.

Laurie, Bruce. "Fire Companies and Gangs in Southwark: The 1840s." In *The Peoples of Philadelphia: A History of Ethnic Groups and Lower Class Life, 1790–1940,* edited by Allen F. Davis and Mark H. Haller. Philadephia: Temple University Press, 1973.

———. *Working People of Philadelphia, 1800–1850.* Philadelphia: Temple University Press, 1980.

———. *Artisans into Workers: Labor in Nineteenth-Century America.* New York: Noonday Press, 1989.

———, and Mark Schmitz. "Manufacture and Productivity: The Making of an Industrial Base, 1850–1880." In *Towards an Interdisciplinary History of the City: Work, Space, Family, and Group Experience in Nineteenth-Century Philadelphia,* edited by Theodore Hershberg. New York: Oxford University Press, 1980.

Lazerow, Jama. " 'The Workingman's Hour': The 1886 Labor Uprising in Boston." *Labor History* 21 (1980): 200–220.

Lazerson, Marvin. *Origins of the Urban School: Public Education in Massachusetts, 1870–1915*. Cambridge: Harvard University Press, 1971.

Leuchtenberg, William E. *The Perils of Prosperity, 1914–1932*. Chicago: University of Chicago Press, 1958.

Levine, Susan. *Labor's True Women: Carpet Weavers, Industrialization, and Labor Reform in the Gilded Age*. Philadelphia: Temple University Press, 1984.

Light, Dale B., Jr. "The Role of Organizations in Assimilation and Community Formation." In *The Irish in America: Emigration, Assimilation, and Impact*, edited by P. J. Drudy. Cambridge, Eng.: Cambridge University Press, 1985.

Lucey, P. J. *History of St. Jerome's Parish, Holyoke, Massachusetts*. N.p., 1931.

Lumpkin, Katharine DuPre. "Shutdowns in the Connecticut Valley: A Study of Worker Displacement in the Small Industrial Community." *Smith College Studies in History*, vol. 19. Northampton, Mass.: Smith College, 1934.

——, and Dorothy Wolff Douglas. *Child Workers in America*. New York: Robert M. McBride and Company, 1937.

McAuliffe, Mary Sperling. *Crisis on the Left: Cold War Politics and American Liberals, 1947–1954*. Amherst: University of Massachusetts Press, 1978.

McAvoy, Thomas T., C.S.C. *The Americanist Heresy in Roman Catholicism*. 1957. Reprint. Notre Dame, Ind.: University of Notre Dame Press, 1963.

McCaffrey, Lawrence J. *The Irish Diaspora in America*. Bloomington: Indiana University Press, 1976.

McCluskey, Neil G., S.J., ed. *Catholic Education in America: A Documentary History*. New York: Teachers College, 1964.

McCouldrick, Paul F. *New England Textiles in the Nineteenth Century: Profits and Investment*. Cambridge: Harvard University Press, 1968.

McCoy, John J. *History of the Catholic Church in the Diocese of Springfield*. Boston: Hurd and Everts, 1900.

McGaw, Judith A. *Most Wonderful Machine: Mechanization and Social Change in Berkshire Paper Making, 1801–1885*. Princeton: Princeton University Press, 1987.

McShane, Joseph M., S.J. *"Sufficiently Radical": Catholicism, Progressivism, and the Bishops' Program of 1919*. Washington, D.C.: Catholic University Press of America, 1986.

Mann, Arthur. *Yankee Reformers in the Urban Age*. Cambridge: Harvard University Press, 1954.

Martin, Margaret E. "Merchants and Trade of the Connecticut River Valley, 1750–1820." *Smith College Studies in History*, vol. 24. Northampton, Mass.: Smith College.

Matthaei, Julie A. *An Economic History of Women in America: Women's Work, the Sexual Division of Labor, and the Development of Capitalism*. New York: Schocken Books, 1982.

May, Martha. "The 'Good Managers': Married Working Class Women and Family Budget Studies, 1895–1915." *Labor History* 25 (1984): 351–372.

Mayer, Arno J. "The Lower Middle Class as Historical Problem." *Journal of Modern History* 47 (1975): 409–436.

Meagher, Timothy J., ed. *From Paddy to Studs: Irish-American Communities in the Turn of the Century Era, 1880–1920.* Westport, Conn.: Greenwood Press, 1986.

Merwick, Donna. *Boston Priests, 1848–1910: A Study of Social and Intellectual Change.* Cambridge: Harvard University Press, 1973.

Messbarger, Paul R. *Fiction with a Parochial Purpose: Social Uses of American Catholic Literature, 1884–1900.* Boston: Boston University Press, 1971.

Milkman, Ruth. *Gender at Work: The Dynamics of Job Segregation by Sex during World War II.* Urbana: University of Illinois Press, 1987.

Miller, David W. "Irish Catholicism and the Great Famine." *Journal of Social History* 9 (1975): 81–98.

Miller, Kerby A. *Emigrants and Exiles: Ireland and the Irish Exodus to North America.* New York: Oxford University Press, 1985.

———. "Assimilation and Alienation: Irish Emigrants' Responses to Industrial America, 1871–1921." In *The Irish in America: Emigration, Assimilation, and Impact,* edited by P. J. Drudy. Cambridge, Eng.: Cambridge University Press, 1985.

Miller, Marc S. *The Irony of Victory: World War II and Lowell, Massachusetts.* Urbana: University of Illinois Press, 1988.

Mitchell, Brian C. *The Paddy Camps: The Irish of Lowell, 1821–1861.* Urbana: University of Illinois Press, 1988.

Montgomery, David. *Beyond Equality: Labor and the Radical Republicans, 1862–1872.* 1967. Reprint. New York: Vintage Books, 1972.

———. *Workers' Control in America: Studies in the History of Work, Technology, and Labor Struggles.* Cambridge, Eng.: Cambridge University Press, 1979.

———. *The Fall of the House of Labor: The Workplace, the State, and American Labor Activism, 1865–1925.* Cambridge, Eng.: Cambridge University Press, 1987.

———. "The Irish and the American Labor Movement." In *America and Ireland, 1776–1976: The American Identity and the Irish Connection,* edited by David Noel Doyle and Owen Dudley Edwards. Westport, Conn.: Greenwood Press, 1980.

Morgan, Myfanwy, and Hilda H. Golden. "Immigrant Families in an Industrial City: A Study of Households in Holyoke." *Journal of Family History* 4 (Spring): 59–68.

Morris, James A. *Woolen and Worsted Manufacturing in the Southern Piedmont.* Columbia: University of South Carolina Press, 1952.

Murphy, Charles J. V. "Pope of New England: A Portrait of Cardinal O'Connell." *Outlook and Progressive* 153 (Oct. 23, 1929): 285–288, 318–319.

Murray, Robert A. *Red Scare: A Study in National Hysteria, 1919–1920.* Minneapolis: University of Minnesota Press, 1955.

Nelson, Daniel. *Managers and Workers: Origins of the New Factory System in the United States, 1880–1920.* Madison: University of Wisconsin Press, 1975.

Nyman, Richmond C. *Union-Management Cooperation in the "Stretch Out".* New Haven: Yale University Press, 1934.

O'Brien, David J. *American Catholics and Social Reform: The New Deal Years.* New York: Oxford University Press, 1968.

Oestreicher, Richard Jules. *Solidarity and Fragmentation: Working People and Class Consciousness in Detroit, 1875–1900.* Urbana: University of Illinois Press, 1986.

O'Leary, Robert. "Brahmins and Bully Boys: William Henry Cardinal O'Connell and Massachusetts Politics." *Historical Journal of Massachusetts* 10 (1982): 3–19.

O'Neill, Thomas P., Jr., with William Novak. *Man of the House: The Life and Political Memoirs of Speaker Tip O'Neill.* New York: Random House, 1987.

O'Toole, James M. " 'That Fabulous Churchman': Toward a Biography of Cardinal O'Connell." *Catholic Historical Journal* 70 (1984): 28–44.

Pedulla, Marianne. "Labor in a City of Immigrants: Holyoke, 1882–1888." *Historical Journal of Massachusetts* 13 (1985): 147–161.

Petrin, Ronald A. "Culture, Community, and Politics: French-Canadians in Massachusetts, 1885–1915." In *The Little Canadas of New England,* edited by Claire Quintal. Worcester, Mass.: French Institute/Assumption College, 1983.

Prude, Jonathan. *The Coming of Industrial Order: Town and Factory Life in Rural Masachusetts, 1810–1860.* Cambridge, Eng.: Cambridge University Press, 1983.

Quint, Howard H. *The Forging of American Socialism: Origins of the Modern Movement.* 1953. Reprint. Indianapolis: Bobbs-Merrill, 1964.

Reynolds, Lloyd G., and Cynthia H. Taft. *The Evolution of Wage Structure.* New Haven: Yale University Press, 1956.

Rodechko, James Paul. *Patrick Ford and His Search for America.* New York: Arno Press, 1976.

Roohan, James E. *American Catholics and the Social Question, 1865–1900.* New York: Arno Press, 1976.

Rosenzweig, Roy. *Eight Hours for What We Will: Workers and Leisure in an Industrial City, 1870–1920.* Cambridge, Eng.: Cambridge University Press, 1983.

Saxon, Bruce. "Fall River and the Decline of the New England Textile Industry, 1949–1954." *Historical Journal of Massachusetts* 16 (1988): 54–74.

Schatz, Ronald W. *The Electrical Workers: A History of Labor at General Electric and Westinghouse, 1923–1960.* Urbana: University of Illinois Press, 1983.

————. "Connecticut's Working Class in the 1950s: A Catholic Perspective." *Labor History* 25 (1984): 83–101.

Scranton, Philip. "Varieties of Paternalism: Industrial Structures and the Social Relations of Production in American Textiles." *American Quarterly* 36 (1984): 235–257.

Seretan, Glen L. *Daniel DeLeon: The Odyssey of an American Marxist.* Cambridge: Harvard University Press, 1979.

Shaw, Douglas V. *The Making of an Immigrant City: Ethnic and Cultural Conflict in Jersey City, New Jersey, 1850–1877.* New York: Arno Press, 1976.

Shlakman, Vera. *Economic History of a Factory Town: A Study of Chicopee, Massachusetts.* 1935. Reprint. New York: Octagon Books, 1969.

Silvia, Philip T., Jr. "Neighbors from the North: French-Canadian Immigrants vs. Trade Unionism in Fall River, Massachusetts." In *The Little Canadas of New England*, edited by Claire Quintal. Worcester, Mass.: French Institute/Assumption College, 1983.

————. "The 'Flint Affair': French-Canadian Struggle for *Survivance*." *Catholic Historical Review* 65 (1979): 414–435.

Sklar, Martin J. *The Corporate Reconstruction of American Capitalism, 1890–1916: The Market, the Law, and Politics.* Cambridge, Eng.: Cambridge University Press, 1988.

Stansell, Christine. *City of Women: Sex and Class in New York, 1789–1860.* New York: Alfred A. Knopf, 1986.

Story, Ronald. *The Forging of an Aristocracy: Harvard and the Boston Upper Class, 1800–1870.* Middletown, Conn.: Wesleyan University Press, 1980.

Stricker, Frank. "Affluence for Whom?—Another Look at Prosperity and the Working Classes in the 1920s." *Labor History* 24 (1983): 5–33.

Tager, Jack, and John W. Ifkovic, eds. *Massachusetts in the Gilded Age: Selected Essays.* Amherst: University of Massachusetts Press, 1985.

Thernstrom, Stephan. *Poverty and Progress: Social Mobility in a Nineteenth Century City.* 1964. Reprint. New York: Atheneum, 1975.

Thompson, E. P. *The Making of the English Working Class.* 1963. Reprint. New York: Vintage Books, 1966.

————. *The Poverty of Theory and Other Essays.* New York: Monthly Review Press, 1978.

Trefousse, Hans L. *Ben Butler: The South Called Him Beast!.* New York: Twayne, 1957.

Trout, Charles H. *Boston, the Great Depression, and the New Deal.* New York: Oxford University Press, 1977.

Tyack, David B. *The One Best System: A History of American Urban Education.* Cambridge: Harvard University Press, 1974.

Underwood, Kenneth W. *Protestant and Catholic: Religion and Social Interaction in an Industrial Community.* 1957. Reprint. Westport, Conn.: Greenwood Press, 1973.

Vittoz, Stanley. *New Deal Labor Policy and the American Industrial Economy.* Chapel Hill: The University of North Carolina Press, 1987.

Von-Nell Breuning, Oswald, S.J. *Reorganization of Social Economy: The Social Encyclical Developed and Explained.* New York: Bruce Publishing Company, 1936.

Wade, Mason. "The French Parish and *Survivance* in Nineteenth-Century New England." *Catholic Historical Review* 36 (1950): 163–189.

Wallace, Anthony F. C. *Rockdale: The Growth of an American Village in the Early Industrial Revolution.* New York: Alfred A. Knopf, 1978.

Wallace, Lillian Parker. *Leo XIII and the Rise of Socialism.* Durham, N.C.: Duke University Press, 1963.

Walker, Mack. *Germany and the Emigration, 1816–1885.* Cambridge: Harvard University Press, 1964.

Walkowitz, Daniel J. *Worker City, Company Town: Iron and Cotton Worker Protest in Troy and Cohoes, New York, 1855–84.* Urbana: University of Illinois Press, 1978.

Walsh, Francis. "Lace Curtain Literature: Changing Perceptions of Irish American Success." *Journal of American Culture* 2 (1979): 139–146.

Walsh, Victor A. "Irish Nationalism and Land Reform: The Role of the Irish in America." In *The Irish in America: Emigration, Assimilation, and Impact,* edited by P. J. Drudy. Cambridge, Eng.: Cambridge University Press, 1985.

———. " 'A Fanatic Heart': The Cause of Irish-American Nationalism in Pittsburgh during the Gilded Age." *Journal of Social History* 15 (1981): 187–204.

Weeks, Lyman Horace. *History of Paper Manufacturing in the United States.* New York: Lockwood Trade Journal Company, 1916.

Willentz, Robert Sean. "Industrializing America and the Irish: Towards the New Departure." *Labor History* 20 (1979):579–595.

———. *Chants Democratic: New York City and the Rise of the American Working Class, 1788–1850.* New York: Oxford University Press, 1984.

Wolfbein, Seymour Louis. *The Decline of a Cotton Textile City: A Study of New Bedford.* 1944. Reprint. New York: AMS Press, 1968.

Wolkovich, William. "Cardinal and Cleric: O'Connell and Mullen in Conflict." *Historical Journal of Massachusetts* 13 (1985): 129–139.

Woodham-Smith, Cecil. *The Great Hunger: Ireland, 1845–1849.* New York: Harper and Row, 1962.

Wright, Gavin. *Old South, New South: Revolutions in the Southern Economy since the Civil War.* New York: Basic Books, 1986.

Wylie, Irvin G. *The Self-Made Man in America: The Myth of Rags to Riches.* 1954. Reprint. New York: Free Press, 1966.

Zahavi, Gerald, "Negotiated Loyalty: Welfare Capitalism and the Shoeworkers of Endicott Johnson, 1920–1940." *Journal of American History* 70 (1983): 602–620.

Zieger, Robert H. *Rebuilding the Pulp and Paper Workers' Union, 1933–1941.* Knoxville: University of Tennessee Press, 1984.
———. *American Workers, American Unions, 1920–1985.* Baltimore: Johns Hopkins University Press, 1986.
Zimbalist, Andrew, ed. *Case Studies on the Labor Process.* New York: Monthly Review Press, 1979.

Unpublished

Anctil, Pierre. "Aspects of Class Ideology in a New England Minority: The Franco-Americans of Woonsocket, Rhode Island (1865–1929)." Ph.D. diss., New School for Social Research, 1980.
Anderson, Donald N. "The Decline of the Woolen and Worsted Industry of New England, 1947–1958." Ph.D. diss., New York University, 1971.
Bailey, Christine Howard. "Precious Blood: Work, Family, and Community in South Holyoke, 1920–1970." Unpublished ms., 1988.
Beaudry, Raymond. Author interview, July 3, 1984.
Brotslaw, Iriving. "Trade Unionism in the Pulp and Paper Industry." Ph.D. diss., University of Wisconsin, 1964.
Brown, Rebecca A. "The Socialist Labor Party in Holyoke, Massachusetts, 1893–1900." Senior thesis, Mt. Holyoke College, 1981.
Burns, Matthew. "History of the International Brotherhood of Paper Makers." Unpublished ms., United Paperworkers International Union, Nashville, Tennessee, 1939.
Doane, Frank H. "History of Holyoke, Massachusetts from 1830 to 1870." Unpublished ms, Holyoke Public Library, n.d.
Fitzgerald, George. Author interview, May 14, 1988.
Gallagher, James Irene, S.S.J. "Analytical Index to the *Catholic Mirror.*" M.L.S. diss., Catholic University of America, 1967.
Guillet, Ernest Bernard. "French Ethnic Literature and Culture in an American City: Holyoke, Massachusetts." Ph.D. diss., University of Massachusetts at Amherst, 1978.
Haebler, Peter. "Habitants in Holyoke: The Development of the French-Canadian Community in a Massachusetts City, 1865–1910." Ph.D. diss., University of New Hampshire, 1976.
Hartford, William F. "Paper City: Class Development in Holyoke, Massachusetts, 1850–1920." Ph. D. diss., University of Massachusetts at Amherst, 1983.
Hickey, John P. "The Holyoke Area Paper Industry, 1899–1951." M.A. thesis, University of Massachusetts at Amherst, 1953.
Knowles, William H., and Yereth Knowles. "History of the International

Brotherhood of Paper Makers." Unpublished ms., United Paperworkers International Union, Nashville, Tennessee, 1948.

Meagher, Timothy J. " 'The Lord Is Not Dead': Cultural and Social Change among the Irish in Worcester, Massachusetts, 1880–1920." Ph.D. diss., Brown University, 1982.

Russell, Cliff. "The Path to Holyoke: A Study in Entrepreneurial History." Unpublished ms., Holyoke Public History, n.d.

Schatz, Ronald W. "The Catholic Church, Corporatism, and American Working-Class Consciousness." Unpublished ms., prepared for the Eighteenth International Conference of Historians of the Working-Class Movement (ITH), Linz, Austria, Sept., 1982.

Zwerling, Harris. "Eagle Lodge, 1914–1922: A Case Study of AF of L Craft Unionism." Unpublished seminar paper, University of Massachusetts at Amherst, n.d.

INDEX

Berger, Victor, 145
Bernstein, Irving, 157
Biddle, Ellen Horgan, 130
Biehler, Madeleine, 137, 201, 202
birth control, 131, 162
Bishops' Program on Social Reconstruction, 158–159
blacklisting, 112, 132, 135
blue laws, 119
Bodnar, John, 2, 49, 214, 215
Boston Associates, 6
Boston's Immigrants (Handlin), 1
Bowler, M. J., 117
boxing matches, 55–56
boycotts, 80, 90–91, 97, 105, 108–109, 122, 155
Bresnahan, John, 126, 127
bricklayers, 93, 107, 108
British immigrants, 36, 41–42
Broderick, J. J., 130, 131
Brody, David, 209
Brotherhood of Paper Makers, 133–134
Bruhn, August, 120
Buckland, E. A., 120, 122
Building Trades Council, 109–110, 113
building tradesmen, 25, 64, 87, 92, 93, 94, 97, 109–110, 119
Burke, James A., 135, 163, 190
Burns, Thomas F., 178, 179
Butler, Ben, 78, 79
Butte, Montana, 2
Byrne, Stephen, 58, 63, 64, 65

Callanan, Jeremiah J., 68, 69, 82, 84, 96, 114
canal system, 5, 53, 184, 185
capital flight, 111, 167, 189, 195, 205
capital-labor relations, 3, 14–15, 76, 91, 94; arbitration, 72–73, 80, 89, 109–110, 122, 149; blacklisting, 112, 132, 135; and Catholic church,

72–73, 90, 98, 122–123, 158, 161, 180–182, 213; collective bargaining, 80, 177, 195, 208; employer welfarism, 41, 163–169, 174, 177, 178, 191; failure of shorter hours movement, 47; family living-wage ideal, 128–129; free-labor ideology, 9, 13–14, 18, 19, 21, 23, 25, 26; labor-power capital vs. money-power capital, 71; and middle-class merchants, 93, 97; mutuality of interests, 111, 118; paternalism, 36, 41–43, 161, 163, 168, 177; and Socialist Labor Party, 123–124; worker participation in management, 158, 175
Carey, J. T., 133, 165
Carlton, A. A., 80
carpenters, 92–95, 97, 109–110, 112–113, 126, 149
Carr, Elmer, 192–193
casual laborers, 53–54
Catholic Aid Association, 100
Catholic church: antiradicalism, 122–124, 161–162, 170, 174, 176, 181–182, 213; antistatism, 170–171, 176; Bishops' Program on Social Reconstruction, 158–159; church building, 58–59, 138; church-laity relations, 74, 136–137; and CIO, 181; class relations, 73, 89; conservative hierarchy, 51–52, 75, 159, 162, 213; and enclave consciousness/respectability, 50, 58; and the family, 123, 124, 130, 170, 171; and Great Depression/New Deal, 174–176; labor policy, 49, 72–73, 80, 90, 98, 122–123, 175, 180–182, 213; National Catholic Welfare Council, 158–159; papacy, 70, 74, 159, 175; parochial schools, 58, 59–62, 137, 162, 170, 171, 173–174; paternalistic hegemony, 159,

Emmons, David, 2
employees, nonunion, 92, 97, 127, 134
employer-employee contracts, 87, 165–166, 168
employer-liability laws, 78, 148
employer paternalism, 36, 41–43, 161, 163, 168, 177. *See also* welfare capitalism
employer welfarism. *See* welfare capitalism
employment contraction, 157, 159, 194, 199, 204–205, 208
enclave consciousness: and capital-labor conflict, 97, 110, 210–211; enclave politics and worker organizations, 76–98; enclave respectability, 52, 57, 58–67, 80, 81, 82, 86, 87, 89, 90, 91, 94, 114–115, 117; and free-labor ideology, 74–75; and ideological flux, 75, 99, 118–119, 123, 155, 201, 203–204, 209, 210–211, 214; Irish and French-Canadians compared, 2, 3–4, 49, 50, 89, 138–139, 201, 203–204, 210–211, 214; and social exclusivity, 119, 151, 152, 153
ethnic conflict, 36, 43, 57, 209
ethnic succession, 142, 203
ethnicity and class, 2, 173–174, 211, 214
Ewing, George C., 7, 18–19, 26, 81
Ewing, Henry C., 14

Fair Labor Standards Act (1938), 197, 201
Falco Athletic Association, 164
Faler, Paul, 23
Fall River, Mass., 35, 44, 138–139, 141, 195, 204, 207
family, the, 57, 73, 123, 124, 127, 128, 140, 146, 170, 212

family economies, 35, 64, 140–141, 144, 173, 200, 215
family living-wage ideal, 3, 4, 124, 125, 128–132, 134, 144–145, 154, 173, 174, 175, 211, 212
Farr, Mayor, 101
Farr Alpaca Company, 41, 91, 100, 102, 103–104, 154, 163–164, 177, 178–180, 191–194
Federal Council of Churches in America: Social Creed, 129
Federal Reserve Bank of Boston survey, 196–197
Fenian invasion of Canada, 66, 69, 82, 87
Fenton, M. D., 68, 69
fire companies, 22
firemen, stationary, 107–108, 110–111, 112, 126
Fitzgerald, George, 127, 130, 143
Fleming, Urban, 119, 126, 127, 146–147, 170, 177, 178, 179
Forbes and Wallace, 97
Ford, Patrick, 51, 61, 69–72, 73, 79, 80, 90, 210, 211, 214
foremen. *See* overseers
Foss, Governor, 132
foundry women workers, 132
fourdrinier paper machine, 30, 33, 203
Fowler, George, 134
fraternal orders, 22–23, 92, 93, 161–162
free-labor ideology, 9, 13–14, 18, 19, 21, 23, 25, 26, 74–75
French-Canadian immigrants: associational life, 137, 138, 150–151; enclave consciousness, 3–4, 136–144, 149–152, 201, 203–204, 214–216; ethnicity, 3–4, 94, 139, 144, 173–174; family economy, child labor, and savings strategy, 139, 140–141, 144, 173, 215; generational

Holyoke, Mass.: Board of Aldermen, 117, 120; Board of License Commissioners, 117; Board of Public Works, 148; Chamber of Commerce, 149, 190, 191, 208; city charter, 116–117; City Council, 113, 114, 115, 117; demographics, 9, 35, 36, 204; economic growth, 8–9, 24; The Hill/The Flats, 151; Ireland Parish, 5–7; Mountain Park, 108–109; "Paper City," 184; semicentennial celebration (1923), 159–160
Holyoke Businessmen's Association, 107, 109, 110, 111, 119, 122
Holyoke Club, 119
Holyoke Cooperative Association, 24–25
Holyoke Country Club, 119
Holyoke Envelope Company, 103
Holyoke Hydrant and Iron Works, 92, 96, 97
Holyoke Land League, 67, 69, 71
Holyoke Loom Fixers Union, 179
Holyoke Mirror, 27, 50, 51
Holyoke Paper Company, 8
Holyoke Political Labor Club, 86
Holyoke Retail Licensed Liquor-Dealers Protective Union, 86
Holyoke Taxpayers' Association, 212
Holyoke Transcript, 14, 20, 23, 24, 43, 53, 54, 62, 76, 77, 88, 94–95, 96, 97, 101, 107, 109, 113, 115, 116, 170, 191, 193
Holyoke Water Power Company, 8, 24, 85, 118
home mortgages, employer-held, 164
homeownership, 64
Hoover, J. Edgar, 181
hospitals, 80, 86
housing, 64, 73, 158
Huggins, Arthur, 187
Hurley, Frank, 211, 214
Hutner, Frances Cornwall, 163

ideological flux, 75, 99, 118–119, 123, 155, 201, 203–204, 209, 210–211, 214
immigrant population, 35, 36
immigration laws, 144
incentive systems, 164–165
individualism, 63, 75, 90, 93
industrial codes, 175–176, 178
industrial-education movement, 146
industrial morality, 53, 84–85
industrial reform, 158–159
industrial relations, 161, 167, 186–189, 209
industrial relocation, 189–208
industrial revolution, 52–53, 189; "new," 175
industrial structure, change in, 103, 129
insurance coverage, 151, 163, 166, 208
International Brotherhood of Paper Makers (IBPM), 98, 165, 183, 185, 186, 187–188
International Steam Pump Company, 103
investment policy, 175, 206
Ireland, 1, 35, 49, 66, 69, 70
Ireland Parish, Mass., 5–7. *See also* Holyoke, Mass.
Irish immigrants, 49–75, 210–214; enclave consciousness, 2, 3, 49, 50, 58–67, 83, 118–119; ethnicity, 1–2, 35; family-wage ideal, 130, 131; and French-Canadians, differences between, 3–4, 36, 43, 55, 56, 116, 125, 130, 131, 135–136, 138–139, 141, 144, 149–150, 151, 173, 214, 215; labor force participation rates, 36; labor activism, 49, 56, 81, 87; middle class, 2, 119, 148–149, 153, 211–213; nationalism (Irish), 66–67, 68–70, 78, 82, 83, 89; in police force, 56, 116, 212;

mills: and depression of 1890s, 101–
102; and Great Depression, 157–
158; merger movement, 103;
paper/textile wages compared, 36;
separate paper/textile labor markets, 135–136; welfare capitalism,
163–169. *See also* paper mills; textile mills
minimum-wage laws, 148, 158, 178,
197
Mittineague Paper Company, 106
molders, iron-, 92, 93, 96, 97, 132
money-power capital, 71
Montgomery, David, 93
Moore, P. J., 68, 69, 79–80, 83, 85, 86
Moran, Catherine, 56
motormen and conductors union,
108–109
mule spinners, 28–29, 87, 98, 101,
104–106, 135
mutuality of interests, 74, 75, 93,
110, 118, 210–211

National Catholic Welfare Confer-
ence (NCWC), 130, 158–159, 173
National Catholic War Council, 158
National Civic Federation (NCF), 159
National Industrial Recovery Act
(1933), 177, 178, 186
National Labor Relations Act, 179
National Loom-Fixers Association,
43
National Mule Spinners Association,
106
National Recovery Administration
(NRA), 175–176, 178, 197
National Trades' Union, 128–129
National War Labor Board, 197
nativism, 116, 149
New Deal, 175–176
New England Cotton Manufacturers
Association, 37
New England Industrial League, 22

newspapers, French-Canadian, 138.
*See also Holyoke Mirror; Holyoke
Transcript; Springfield Republican*
Newton, James H., 13, 47
Newton, Moses, 13, 15
Nonotuck Paper Company, 100
nonunion employees, 92, 97, 127,
134

O'Callaghan, Jeremiah, 50–52, 70
O'Connell, Daniel, 89, 96
O'Connell, William Henry Cardinal,
160–161, 169, 170–171, 173, 176,
213
O'Connor, Edward, 68, 85
O'Connor, James J., 83, 85–86
O'Connor, M. J., 170
Odd Fellows, 23
O'Donnell, Terence B., 88
O'Hanlon, John, 63–64
Old Colony Trust Company (Bos-
ton), 190, 191
O'Leary, Bishop Thomas M., 67,
162, 181
O'Neill, Thomas P. ("Tip"), 212
open shop, 149, 165, 196
O'Reilly, John Boyle, 89, 90
overseers, 42, 142–144, 164–165, 202
Overseers of the Poor, 102

painters, 93, 108
Panic of 1857, 8
Paper Makers Journal, 167–168, 187
paper mills: American/Writing Paper
Makers' Association, 44–45; American Writing Paper Company, 185–
189; beater engineers, 30, 32–33,
46–48, 98, 106, 107, 108, 134, 185,
186; craft exclusiveness, 46, 48, 98,
108, 133, 185, 186; cutter women's
strike, 111–112; depression of
1890s, 99–100, 101, 106; employer-
employee contracts, 165–166, 168;

women (*continued*)
35, 73, 130, 131; paper workers,
31, 34, 107, 108, 111–112, 132,
133–134, 143; and saloon culture,
56–57, 127–128; and temperance
movement, 16; textile workers, 27,
29–30, 31, 104; in unions, 104,
108, 111, 131, 132; wages, 29, 131–
132
Woods, John H., 147
work hours, 14, 22, 34, 46–48, 78,
79, 82, 86, 87, 92–93, 97–98, 190
work-load differentials, 204, 205–
207, 208
worker self-activity, 174, 182, 209
working class: ethical code, 93–94;
and middle class, 3, 66, 82, 88–89,
91, 97, 109, 111, 112–113, 148–149,
154–156, 211–212, 215; respectables, 114–115, 117
Workingmen's Party of the United
States (WPUS), 78–79
Wright, Carroll, 139
Wright, "Captain" John, 70, 87
Writing Paper Makers' Association,
44–45

"yellow-dog" contracts, 87, 165–166
Yoerg, William P., 191–192
youth: educational and employment
opportunities, 201–203; gangs, 54–
55, 114; migration of, and percentage decline in population, 204, 209

D15662066